TA Today *Second Edition*

Ian Stewart, PhD, is Co-Director of The Berne Institute, Nottingham, England. He is accredited by the European Association for Transactional Analysis (EATA) and the International Transactional Analysis Association (ITAA) as a Teaching and Supervising Transactional Analyst. He is also a UKCP Registered Psychotherapist and a Master Practitioner and Licensed Training Specialist in Neuro-Linguistic Programming. Ian was the 1998 recipient of the EATA Gold Medal, awarded for "outstanding services to transactional analysis in Europe".

Vann S. Joines, PhD, is a licensed clinical psychologist and a licensed Marriage and Family Therapist. He is President of the Southeast Institute for Group and Family Therapy, Chapel Hill, North Carolina. Accredited by ITAA as a Teaching and Supervising Transactional Analyst, he was the 1994 recipient of the Eric Berne Memorial Award in Transactional Analysis for the Integration of TA with Other Theories and Approaches. He is a Diplomate in Redecision Therapy, an Approved Supervisor of the American Association for Marriage and Family Therapy, a Life Fellow of the American Group Psychotherapy Association and a Certified Teacher in Advanced Integrative Therapy (AI

By the same authors:

*Personality Adaptations: a New Guide to Human Understanding in
Psychotherapy and Counselling*
by Vann Joines and Ian Stewart
(Lifespace Publishing, Nottingham and Chapel Hill, 2002)

Also by Ian Stewart:

Transactional Analysis Counselling in Action
(3rd edition: Sage Publications, London, 2007)

Key Figures in Counselling and Psychotherapy: Eric Berne
(Sage Publications, London, 1992)

Developing Transactional Analysis Counselling
(Sage Publications, London, 1996)

TA Today

A New Introduction to Transactional Analysis

Second Edition

Ian Stewart
Vann Joines

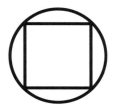

Lifespace Publishing
Melton Mowbray and Chapel Hill

First edition published 1987
Reprinted nineteen times, 1988 – 2011

This second edition published 2012

Lifespace Publishing,
Melton Mowbray LE14 4QG, England
and Chapel Hill, North Carolina 27517, USA
www.lifespacebooks.com

For ORDERING INFORMATION please see back page

Printed and bound in England
by Russell Press Ltd., Nottingham
www.russellpress.com

Body text: Times New Roman 10½/11
Headings and exercise text: Gill Sans MT

Design: Ian Stewart
Indexer: Sue Carlton

British Library Cataloguing in Publication data
A catalogue record of this book is available from the British Library

ISBN 978-1-870244-02-2

MIX
Paper from
responsible sources
FSC® C021423

CONTENTS

Part IV WRITING OUR OWN LIFE-STORY: Life-Scripts

PREFACE

Welcome to this second edition of *TA Today!*

Our aim in this book is to provide you with a clear, concise, easily accessible introduction to the current theory and practice of transactional analysis (TA).

Features

From readers' feedback on our first edition, we were delighted to learn that several features of the book had met with wide acceptance and approval. We are therefore including these same features in this second edition. In brief, they are as follows:

- We have presented the material in a way that will be useful to you whether you are **learning about TA on your own** or taking part in a **taught course.**

- Especially if you are meeting TA for the first time, we hope you will appreciate the book's **informal and conversational style.**

- We have used **examples** liberally to illustrate points of theory.

- **Exercises are incorporated in the text.** We say more about this below.

- If you are reading the book as background to an 'Official TA 101' introductory course in TA, you will find **full coverage of the ' TA 101' syllabus.** After many years in which this syllabus remained unchanged, the international TA associations revised it in 2008. **We have incorporated all the 2008 revisions into this second edition of *TA Today.***

- TA today is international. We hope and expect that the readership of this book will also be international. (The first edition has been translated into fifteen languages). With this in mind, we have chosen **illustrations and examples that will be familiar to people all over the world.**

- To assist in further learning, the book contains comprehensive **endnotes**, a **Glossary** and a **Bibliography.**

The exercises

When we are teaching TA courses, we run frequent exercises along with the taught material. Each block of teaching is followed immediately by a relevant exercise. We find that this is the most effective way of letting students practise and reinforce the theoretical ideas.

In this book we follow the same pattern. Exercises are incorporated in the text. Each exercise comes immediately after the related theory. *To get most benefit from the book, do each exercise as you come to it.*

We signal exercises by a printers' 'blob' and a change to a different typeface.

● When you see this style of print, you are reading an exercise. We recommend that you do it as soon as you come to it. Then go on to the next block of teaching. The end of the exercise is shown by the same sign as you saw at the beginning. ●

We suggest you keep a loose-leaf notebook in which you can compile your responses to the written exercises, together with the other thoughts and ideas you bring to mind while reading the book. This will help you learn TA in the most effective way possible – by using it for yourself.

What this book is and is not

When you have read this book through and completed the exercises, you will certainly know a lot more about yourself than you did when you started. You may also find you can use this knowledge to make some changes in your life which you had been wanting to make. If so, congratulations.

But this book is not intended as a substitute for therapy or counselling. If you have substantial personal problems, you are advised to seek out a reputable therapist or counsellor who can give you the expert personal attention you need.

TA practitioners encourage their clients to learn the ideas of TA. If you decide to enter TA therapy or counselling, or wish to apply TA to your work in education or organizations, you can use this book as a source of that learning.

If your wish is to provide TA therapy or services to others, this book will likewise be useful to you as your first introduction to the basic ideas of TA. Indeed, the book's coverage of TA theory is comprehensive enough to provide you with a solid reference base for use in accredited TA training, up to and including the level of Certified Transactional Analyst. But reading alone does not qualify you to offer professional help. To be accredited as a TA practitioner, you have to complete prescribed hours of advanced study, practical experience in applying TA in work with clients, and supervision. You must pass the examinations set by TA accrediting organizations. We give more details of these in Appendix E.

How the book is laid out

The book employs the same five-part structure as in the first edition. The explanation of theory and practice is built up progressively, and each part assumes knowledge of the parts that have gone before it.

The single-chapter **Part I** is a brief overview of the nature and scope of TA, with 'thumbnail sketches' of the topics that are to follow. **Part II** presents the *ego-state model* of personality structure that is a foundation of TA theory. As in the first edition, the explanation is built 'from the ground up' on Eric Berne's original model of ego-states, rather than starting from some simplified version.

In **Part III** we go on to look at communication. We use the ego-state model to analyse the ways that people communicate, giving us the analysis of *transactions*. We also look at the important topic of *strokes*: how people show recognition of each other. Finally we examine *time structuring*: how people use time when they are communicating in groups or when their time is not structured for them.

Part IV presents the topic of *life-script*: the way in which we 'write a life-story' for ourselves during childhood and tend to live out that story in grown-up life. This concept ranks with the ego-state model as an essential foundation of TA theory. We look at the nature and development of the script, and examine ways in which it may be lived out. This includes a description of *personality adaptations*: six styles of personality each of which represents a 'best option' for dealing with the world.

Part V draws on the area of TA known as Cathexis or Schiffian theory. Practitioners of this approach suggest that whenever people are playing out their life-script, they engage in *passivity:* 'how people don't do things, or don't do them effectively' in order to get others to do it for them. The chapters in Part V present some powerful models for confronting passivity and hence encouraging active problem-solving.

Part VI present's TA's view of a question that has exercised the minds of therapists and philosophers for many years past: why is it that people so often seem to repeat behaviours and emotions that are painful or unproductive for them? In a TA framework these repeating patterns are known as *rackets* and *games*. Both are seen as expressions of the life-script. TA offers an understanding of these patterns, and shows you how to break out of them.

Finally in **Part VII** we take an overview of *TA in practice.* We look at contract-making – a central principle of TA practice – and at TA's view of the aims of change. Two chapters describe the use of TA in therapy and counselling, and in educational and organizational work. The final chapter is a review of how TA has developed, from its origins in the 1950s until the present day.

Changes from the first edition

The 'core' basic theory of TA, described in this book, has remained remarkably stable during the 25 years since our first edition appeared. It isn't that TA theory and practice have stopped developing. Rather, the continuing development has tended to 'move out' from the original core into more specialized areas and applications. (We say more about this in Chapter 30).

The stability of 'core' theory was also illustrated when the syllabus of the 'Official TA 101', round which this book is structured, was revised in 2008. After some very lively and detailed debate among the members of the working party tasked with making the revision (which included one of the present authors), the final revised version covered essentially the same content as the previous version had done. The revisions, which were significant, dealt instead with the process of teaching the course, increasing the flexibility and options available to trainers delivering the '101'.

We (authors) had already decided that our second edition would include all the content specified in the revised '101', including all the optional headings. But it now turned out that all these headings had already been covered in the first edition of *TA Today*. Our initial concern therefore was: were there enough changes in the '101' content to merit a new edition of the book?

So it was with some astonishment that we realized, as we went on drafting the second edition, that we were making changes in almost every chapter. Some of these changes were clarifications in wording, the need for which had been pointed out to us by readers. Others were updates of the 'role-play' illustrations used. For example, social workers who had read the book had made it abundantly clear to us that nobody in social work these days would fall for a game of 'Why Don't You, Yes But'. So we changed the *dramatis personae* in that example to the less touchy scenario of a mother-son exchange.

Still other changes reflect quite subtle but significant shifts in perspective on some features of TA theory. For example, the model of behavioural descriptions (the functional model) has gradually but steadily lost the front-line position that it used to hold in presentations of TA. Also, the prohibition against 'mixing structure and function', for many years a shibboleth in TA training and exams, has been re-thought. While it is still essential to understand the *distinction* between structure and function, the fact remains that Eric Berne himself used the first-order structural diagram to draw all his pictures of transactions.

Another shift in view, this time relating to practice, concerns the merit or otherwise of confronting driver behaviours and process scripts. As we say in Chapter 15, in 1987 most people thought this was therapeutically a good idea; since then, experience has shown that it often isn't, and we have changed our coverage accordingly.

There are some changes that we had decided to make no matter what might happen to the '101' syllabus. The material on the Miniscript has been deleted, since it is now no longer taught by its originator, Taibi Kahler. We have substantially re-cast Chapter 15, which now brings together the (re-thought) material on process scripts and drivers. Chapter 16, an introduction to personality adaptations, is new.

Chapter 28 now contains a section describing the relational approach to TA in addition to the sections on the three 'traditional schools'. Chapter 29, on educational and organizational TA, has been extensively re-written thanks to the input of two highly experienced practitioners in these fields. The history of TA's development in Chapter 30 has been brought up to date (and some past events have been re-evaluated). The factual material in all the Appendices has been updated, as have the Notes and References, Glossary and Bibliography.

Pronouns, genders, names and cases

We, Ian Stewart and Vann Joines, are 'we'. You, the reader, are 'you'. For other people in general, we use 'she' and 'he' at random.

Wherever we give case illustrations, the names used are fictitious. If they bear any relationship to the real name of any person, this is purely by chance.

Thanks and acknowledgements: second edition

We offer our grateful thanks to the following colleagues for their valued input to this second edition:

Julie Hay, FCIPD, MPhil, DMS, and Trudi Newton, BSc, commented extensively and insightfully on the draft of Chapter 29, 'TA in Education and Organizations', enabling it to be re-written in a greatly improved version. They also commented on the Notes on that chapter and suggested a revised and updated listing of 'Key Books on TA' in Appendix B.

We thank Trudi also for the information she gave us about the current operations of the Training and Certification Council, and for permission to use the descriptions of the 'four fields of application of TA' that appear on the T&C Council web site.

Mark Widdowson, MSc, ECP, commented on the description of the relational approach in Chapter 28, as well as giving us a range of other useful suggestions on the coverage and presentation of the book.

Ken Fogleman supplied us with the time-series of ITAA membership figures from 1985 to the present.

And: our especial thanks to the many readers who have made comments and suggestions, whether in writing or by word of mouth, for changes in the book during the lifetime of its first edition. We appreciate every one of these comments, and we hope you'll find we've done them justice in this second edition.

Thanks and acknowledgements: first edition (1987)

Our 'expert reader' for the first edition was Erika Stern, PhD, of the Department of Counselling Studies, University of Utrecht, The Netherlands. She made available to us her acute understanding not only of TA but also of other psychological approaches. And, being multi-lingual, she was able to alert us to uses of language that would have posed problems to readers who are not native speakers of English. In these ways, Erika made a major contribution to this book.

Our 'lay readers' were Andrew Middleton, PhD, and Christine Middleton. They commented on the manuscript from their viewpoint as new learners of TA. They drew our attention to passages where we had assumed that because *we* knew the map, other people would not need signposts. Andy and Christine had a great influence on the final shape of the book.

Richard Erskine, PhD, and Marilyn Zalcman, MSW, ACSW, read the draft chapter on the Racket System and made valuable suggestions for rewording.

Jenni Hine, MAOT, provided data on TA organizations.

Emily Hunter Ruppert, ACSW, suggested the collaboration in authorship of which this book is the result.

We gratefully acknowledge the permission of the following authors to use copyright material originally published in the *Transactional Analysis Journal* or *Transactional Analysis Bulletin*, issues as shown:

John Dusay, MD, for the *Egogram*: *TAJ, 2,* 3, 1972.

Franklin Ernst Jr, MD, for the *OK Corral*: *TAJ, 1,* 4, 1971.

Richard Erskine, PhD, and Marilyn Zalcman, MSW, ACSW, for the *Racket System*: *TAJ, 9,* 1, 1979.

Stephen Karpman, MD, for the *Drama Triangle*: *TAB, 7,* 26, 1968.

Jim McKenna, MSW, for the *Stroking Profile*: *TAJ, 4,* 4, 1974.

Ken Mellor, DipSocStuds., and Eric Sigmund, for the *Discount Matrix*: *TAJ, 5,* 3, 1975.

Your comments, please!

We repeat the invitation we made in the Preface of our first edition: will you please let us have your critique and feedback on this book?

Are there any places where you think we could have been more clear? Anything you'd have liked to see in the book that we do not have in?

Anything we do have in that you'd have liked to see out? Did you find any factual blunders, anachronisms, incongruities? All of them we'd like to hear about.

And if there are features of our book you particularly like, we'd value hearing about those too.

Please contact us in care of Lifespace Publishing, either at Melton Mowbray, England, or Chapel Hill, USA. You can find full contact details on the page of 'ordering information'.

Meantime, we wish you useful and enjoyable reading.

Ian Stewart and Vann Joines

January 2012

Part 1
INTRODUCING TA

Chapter 1
WHAT TA IS

'Transactional analysis is a theory of personality and a systematic psychotherapy for personal growth and personal change'.

That's the definition of TA suggested by the International Transactional Analysis Association.[1] In fact, TA today is all this and much more. Among psychological approaches, transactional analysis is outstanding in the depth of its theory and the wide variety of its applications.

As a *theory of personality,* TA gives us a picture of how people are structured psychologically. To do so it uses a three-part model known as the *ego-state model.* The same model helps us understand how people function – how they express their personality in terms of behaviour.

TA also provides a *theory of communication.* This can be extended to give a method of *analysing systems and relationships,* both in personal life and in work situations.

TA offers a theory of *child development.* The concept of *life-script* explains how our present life patterns originated in childhood. Within the framework of life-script, TA develops explanations of how we may continue to re-play childhood strategies in grown-up life, even when these produce results that are self-defeating or painful. Thus TA gives us a *theory of psychopathology.*

In the area of practical applications, TA does indeed offer us a system of psychotherapy. It is used in the treatment of all types of psychological disorders, from everyday living problems to severe psychosis. It provides a method of therapy for use with individuals, groups, couples and families.

Outside the therapeutic field, TA is used in educational settings. It helps teachers and learners to stay in clear communication and avoid setting up unproductive confrontations. It is particularly suitable for use in counselling.

TA is a powerful tool in management and communications training and in organizational analysis. Among the many other applications of TA are its uses by social workers, police and probation authorities, and ministers of religion. TA can be used in any field where there is a need for understanding of individuals, relationships and communication.

Key ideas of TA

There are a few key ideas that form the foundation of TA theory. They serve to distinguish TA from any other psychological system. In the coming chapters, we shall examine all these ideas in detail and illustrate them by examples. Here they are first in summary. We suggest you simply read this section through to become acquainted with the terms and general ideas.

The ego-state model (PAC model)

Most basic of all is the *ego-state model*. An *ego-state* is a set of related behaviours, thoughts and feelings. It is a way in which we manifest a part of our personality at a given time.

The model portrays three distinct types of ego-state.

If I am behaving, thinking and feeling in response to what is going on around me here and now, using all the resources available to me as a grown-up person, I am said to be in an *Adult ego-state*.

At times, I may behave, think and feel in ways which are a copy of one of my parents, or of others who were parent-figures for me. When I do so, I am said to be in a *Parent ego-state*.

Sometimes I may return to ways of behaving, thinking and feeling which I used when I was a child. Then I am said to be in a *Child ego-state*.

Note the initial capital letters. They are always used when we want to indicate that we are referring to the ego-states (Parent, Adult, Child). A small letter beginning the word shows we mean a real-life parent, adult or child.

The ego-state model is often known alternatively as the *P-A-C model*, after these three initial letters.

When we use the ego-state model to understand various aspects of personality, we are said to be employing *structural analysis*.

Transactions, strokes, time structuring

If I am communicating with you, I can choose to address you from any one of my ego-states – Adult, Child or Parent. You can reply in turn from any of your ego-states. This exchange of information is known as a *transaction*, which is the basic unit of social discourse.

The use of the ego-state model to analyse sequences of transactions is referred to as *transactional analysis proper*. The word 'proper' is added to show that we are talking about this branch of TA in particular, rather than TA as a whole.

When you and I transact, I signal recognition of you and you return that recognition. In TA language, any act of recognition is called a *stroke*. People need strokes to maintain their physical and psychological well-being.

When people are transacting in groups or pairs, they use time in various specific ways which can be listed and analysed. This is the analysis of *time structuring*.

Life-script

Each of us, in childhood, writes a life-story for himself or herself. This story has a beginning, a middle and an end. We write the basic plot in our infant years, before we are old enough to talk more than a few words. Later on in childhood, we add more detail to the story. Most of it has been written by the age of seven. We may revise it further during adolescence.

As grown-ups, we are usually no longer aware of the life-story we have written for ourselves. Yet we are likely to live it out faithfully. Without being aware of it, we are likely to set up our lives so that we move towards the final scene we decided upon as infants.

This unaware life-story is known in TA as the *life-script*.

The concept of life-script ranks with the ego-state model as a central building-block of TA. It is especially important in psychotherapeutic applications. In *script analysis*, we use the concept of life-script to understand how people may unawarely set up problems for themselves, and how they may set about solving those problems.

Discounting, redefining, symbiosis

The young child decides on a life-script because it represents the best strategy that the child can work out to survive and get by in what often seems like a hostile world. In our Child ego-state, we may still be believing that any threat to our infant picture of the world is a threat to the satisfaction of our needs, or even to our survival. Thus we may sometimes distort our perception of reality so that it fits our script. When we do so, we are said to be *redefining*.

One way of ensuring that the world fits our script is to selectively ignore information available to us about a situation. Without conscious intention, we blank out the aspects of the situation that would contradict our script. This is called *discounting*.

As a part of maintaining our script, we may sometimes get into relationships as grown-ups which re-play the relationships we had with our parents when we were children. We do this without being aware of it. In this situation, one of the partners in the relationship plays the part of Parent and Adult, while the other acts Child. Between them, they function as though they had only three instead of six ego-states available. A relationship like this is called a *symbiosis*.

Rackets, stamps and games

As young children, we may notice that in our family, certain feelings are encouraged while others are prohibited. To get our strokes, we may decide to feel only the permitted feelings. This decision is made without conscious awareness. When we play out our script in grown-up life, we continue to cover our authentic feelings with the feelings that were permitted to us as children. These substitute feelings are known as *rackets*.

If we experience a racket feeling and store it up instead of expressing it at the time, we are said to be saving a *stamp*.

A *game* is a repetitive sequence of transactions in which both parties end up experiencing racket feelings. It always includes a *switch,* a moment when the players experience that something unexpected and uncomfortable has happened. People play games without being aware they are doing so.

Autonomy

To realize our full potential as grown-ups, we need to update the strategies for dealing with life which we decided upon as infants. When we find that these strategies are no longer working for us, we need to replace them with new ones that do work. In TA language, we need to move out of script and gain *autonomy*.

The tools of TA are designed to help people achieve that autonomy. Its components are *awareness, spontaneity,* and the *capacity for intimacy.* It implies the ability to solve problems using the person's full resources as a grown-up.

The philosophy of TA

TA rests upon certain philosophical assumptions. These are statements about people, life and the possibility of change.[2]

The philosophical assumptions of TA are:

- *People are OK.*
- *Everyone has the capacity to think.*
- *People decide their own destiny, and these decisions can be changed.*

From these assumptions there follow two basic principles of TA practice:

- *It is a contractual method.*
- *It involves open communication.*

People are OK

The most fundamental assumption of TA is that *people are OK.*

This means: you and I both have worth, value and dignity as people. I accept myself as me and I accept you as you. This is a statement of essence rather than behaviour.

At times, I may not like nor accept what you *do*. But always, I accept what you *are*. Your essence as a human being is OK with me, even though your behaviour may not be.

I am not one-up to you, and you are not one-up to me. We are on the same level as people. This is true even though our accomplishments may differ. It is true even though we may be of different race, age or religion.

Everyone has the capacity to think

Everyone except the severely brain-damaged has the capacity to think. Therefore it is the responsibility of each of us to decide what he or she wants from life. Each individual will ultimately live with the consequences of what he or she decides.

Decisional model

You and I are both OK. We may sometimes engage in not-OK behaviour. When we do, we are following strategies we *decided* upon as young children.

These strategies were the best ways we could work out as infants to survive and get what we wanted from a world that may have seemed hostile. As grown-ups, we still pursue these same patterns at times. We may do this even though the results are unproductive or even painful for us.

Even when we were young children, our parents could not *make* us develop in one particular way rather than another. They could certainly exert strong pressures on us. But we made our own decisions whether to comply with these pressures, to rebel against them or to ignore them.

For us as grown-ups, the same is true. We cannot be *made* to feel or behave in particular ways by others, or by 'the environment'. Other people, or our life circumstances, may exert strong pressures on us. But it is always our own decision whether to conform to these pressures. We are responsible for our own feelings and behaviour.

Any time we make a decision, we can change that decision later. This is true of the early decisions we made about ourselves and the world. If some of these infant decisions are producing uncomfortable results for us as grown-ups, we can trace the decisions and change them for new and more appropriate decisions now.

Thus, people can change. We achieve change not merely by insight into our old patterns of behaviour, but by actively deciding to change those patterns. The changes we make can be real and lasting.

Contractual method

If you are a TA practitioner and I am your client, then we take *joint responsibility* for achieving whatever change(s) I want to make.

This follows from the assumption that you and I relate on equal terms.

It is not up to you to do things *to* me. Nor do I come to you expecting you will do everything *for* me.

Since we both take part in the process of change, it is important that we both know clearly how the task will be shared. Therefore we enter into a *contract*.

A contract is a statement of the responsibility of each party. As client, I say what I want to change and what I am willing to do in order to bring about that change. You, as practitioner, confirm that you are willing to work with me in this task. You undertake to use the best of your professional skills in doing so, and say what recompense you want from me in return for your work.

Open communication

Eric Berne insisted that the client, as well as the practitioner, should have full information about what is going on in their work together. This follows from the basic assumptions that people are OK and that everyone can think.

In TA practice, case notes are open to the client's inspection. The practitioner encourages the client to learn the ideas of TA. Thus the client can take an equal role in the process of change.

To help in communication, the ideas of TA are expressed in simple language. Instead of the long Latin- or Greek-derived words customary in some other branches of psychology, TA speaks in familiar words: *Parent, Adult, Child, game, script, stroke.*

Some people have assumed that this straightforward language must reflect superficial thinking. Their view is mistaken. Though TA's language is simple, its theory is profound and closely reasoned.

Part II
PICTURING PERSONALITY

The Ego-State Model

Chapter 2
THE EGO-STATE MODEL

Think back over the past twenty-four hours of your life.

Were there moments during that time when you acted, thought and felt just as you did when you were a child?

Were there other times when you found yourself behaving, thinking and feeling in ways you copied long ago from your parents, or from other people who were parent-figures for you?

And were there still other occasions when your behaviour, thoughts and feelings were simply a direct here-and-now response to what was happening around you at that moment? On these occasions, you responded as the grown-up you now are, rather than dipping back into your childhood.

● Take time now to write down at least one example of each of these three ways of behaving plus thinking plus feeling which you recall from the past twenty-four hours. ●

You have just completed your first exercise in using the *ego-state model*.

Let's consider what you have just done. You examined three different ways of being in the world. Each of these consisted of a set of *behaviours, thoughts and feelings*.

When I am behaving, thinking and feeling as I did when I was a child, I am said to be in a *Child ego-state*.

When I am behaving, thinking and feeling in ways I copied from parents or parent-figures, I am said to be in a *Parent ego-state*.

And when I am behaving, thinking and feeling in ways which are a direct here-and-now response to events round about me, using all the abilities I have as a grown-up, I am said to be in an *Adult ego-state*.

Often in everyday TA practice, we say simply that I am 'in (my) Child', 'in (my) Parent', or 'in (my) Adult'.

Putting the three ego-states together, we get the three-part *ego-state model* of personality which is at the heart of TA theory. It is conventionally pictured as the set of three stacked circles shown in Figure 2.1. Because the three ego-states are often labelled with their initial letters, the model is alternatively known as the *PAC model*.

This simple version of the diagram, in which the three ego-state circles are not subdivided, is called a *first-order structural diagram*. We shall meet the more detailed second-order diagram in a later chapter.

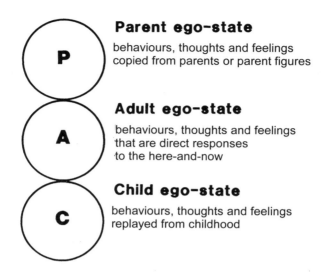

Parent ego-state

behaviours, thoughts and feelings
copied from parents or parent figures

Adult ego-state

behaviours, thoughts and feelings
that are direct responses
to the here-and-now

Child ego-state

behaviours, thoughts and feelings
replayed from childhood

**Figure 2.1 First-order structural diagram:
The ego-state model**

The process of analysing personality in terms of ego-states is called *structural analysis.*[1]

Examples of ego-state shifts

Jane is driving her car along a road crowded with traffic. Second by second, she is observing the position and speed of other vehicles around her. She is looking out for road signs. She controls her own car in response to what is going on around her, in the here and now. Jane is in her *Adult ego-state.*

Just then, another driver passes Jane and cuts in sharply in front of her. For a fraction of a second, Jane feels scared that the two cars will crash. She flashes a glance at her driving mirror, sees the road behind is clear and slows slightly so that the crash is avoided. All the time, she has stayed in her *Adult* ego-state. Her feeling of scare was an appropriate response to the here-and-now danger, helping her body react more quickly in order to avoid a collision.

Now, with the other driver vanishing up the road ahead, Jane shakes her head and purses her lips in disapproval. Turning to her passenger, she says: 'Drivers like that ought not to be allowed on the road!' At this moment Jane has moved into her *Parent ego-state.* When she was little, she had often sat beside her father as he drove his car and watched him as he showed his disapproval of other drivers' errors by shaking his head and pursing his lips in just this way.

A minute or two later, Jane pulls off the road at her office. Looking at her watch, she sees that because of the heavy traffic, she is late for an important meeting with her boss. Her heart sinks and for a moment she feels panic-stricken. Now Jane has shifted into her *Child ego-state*. She has contacted old memories of arriving at school late and feeling scared of the punishment she imagined she might get from her schoolteacher. Her feeling of panic is a response to these old memories, not to anything that is likely to happen in her grown-up situation.

At this instant, Jane is not consciously *aware* that she is re-playing her childhood. If you were to ask her 'Does this situation remind you of anything in your childhood?' she might then bring that old schoolroom scene back to conscious memory. Alternatively, she might have buried those painful recollections so thoroughly that she would not be able to remember them immediately. She might have to take longer, even perhaps go into therapy, if she wanted to bring those deeper memories back into consciousness.

As she now re-experiences her childhood feelings and thoughts, Jane also shows some behaviours which she first showed all those years ago as a schoolgirl. Her heart races. She lifts her hand to beside her mouth, and widens her eyes. From close up, you would be able to see that she has broken out into a light sweat.

Then after a moment or two, Jane thinks to herself: 'Wait a minute! What am I getting scared of? My boss is a reasonable woman. She'll understand why I'm late. Anyway, we can make up the lost time by taking a bit off the coffee break.' Jane is back in her Adult ego-state. Her passenger sees her relax and take her hand away from her mouth. Jane's face breaks into a smile, and she laughs. Her laugh is the laugh of the grown-up woman she is. It sounds quite different from the nervous giggle of a scared child.

● Before reading further, go back to the examples you have noted of when you were in Child, Parent and Adult ego-states during the past twenty-four hours.

Child ego-state

Think of each time you were in a Child ego-state. Note down what feelings you experienced. It may help if you role-play the occasion to yourself.

Record next what you were *thinking*. Often, you can get most easily to Child thoughts by asking yourself: 'What was I saying to myself inside my head?' Explore what you were saying inside your head about yourself, about other people and about the world in general.

Lastly, note down how you were *behaving* while you were in Child. A good way is to role-play yourself in Child while sitting in front of a mirror.

Check that these feelings, thoughts and behaviours were re-plays of how you felt, thought and behaved when you were a child. You may even be able to identify which past occasions you were re-playing. What age were you on each of these occasions?

Parent ego-state

In the same way, note down the set of related feelings, thoughts and behaviours for each time you were in a Parent ego-state. Again, role-play the occasion if you like.

You can often get to Parent thoughts most readily by asking yourself: 'What do I hear my mother or father saying inside my head?' Or perhaps the voice you hear inside your head may belong to another relative like an aunt, uncle or grandparent, or to a schoolteacher.

Check that on those occasions when you were in Parent, you were copying your behaviours, thoughts and feelings from your actual parents or parent-figures. You will probably find it quite easy to identify the specific person you were copying on each occasion.

Adult ego-state

Finally, record the sets of related behaviours, thoughts and feelings that you have identified with the times when you were in an Adult ego-state.

To distinguish Adult from Child or Parent, ask yourself: 'Was this behaviour, or thought, or feeling, appropriate as a grown-up way of dealing with what was going on round me at that present moment?' If the answer is 'yes', then note that response as Adult. ●

You may find that for these occasions when you were in Adult, you are able to list behaviours and thoughts, but not feelings. For much of the time, we can deal effectively with here-and-now reality without experiencing feelings. However, we can and do feel emotions at times while in Adult.

How can you tell Adult from Child feelings? *Adult feelings are appropriate as a way of dealing with the immediate situation.* Recall Jane's moment of scare as the car cut too close in front of her. Her emotional reaction sharpened her responses, helping her to avoid an accident.

If you have not met the idea of ego-states before, you may be in doubt whether some thoughts, feelings or behaviours you listed were Adult as compared to Child or Parent. If so, don't worry. As you read on and complete more of the exercises, you will have plenty of opportunity to develop this important skill of distinguishing between ego-states.

For a healthy and balanced personality, we need all three of our ego-states. We need Adult for the here-and-now problem-solving that enables us to tackle life in a competent, effective way. To fit comfortably into society, we need the sets of rules we carry in our Parent. In our Child ego-state, we have access again to the spontaneity, creativity and intuitive power we enjoyed in our childhood.

Definition of ego-states

Eric Berne defined an ego-state as *a consistent pattern of feeling and experience directly related to a corresponding consistent pattern of behaviour.* [2]

Berne was exact in his choice of words. It's worth while taking some time now to be clear what he was conveying in this definition.

First, Berne is saying that each ego-state is defined by a combination of feelings and experience that *consistently* occur together.

For instance, when Jane realized she was late for her meeting, she began to *experience* memories of feared punishment from her childhood. As she did so, she *felt* panicky. If you were to ask Jane about this, she would confirm that while re-experiencing her childhood in this way, she consistently also feels these childhood emotions. All the memories Jane has of her childhood experiences, plus the feelings that go with them, are classed as belonging in Jane's Child ego-state.

Next, Berne is suggesting that the *behaviours* typical of each ego-state are consistently shown together. If I observed Jane over some time, I would be able to confirm that she shows three separate sets of behavioural signals. One set defines her Adult, another her Parent, and another her Child. The signals making up each set are consistently shown together. There is a clear and consistent difference between one set and another.

For instance, when Jane widens her eyes and begins to sweat lightly, while her heartbeat speeds up, it's predictable that she will also lift her hand to somewhere near her mouth. These signals make up part of the set that defines Jane's Child ego-state. Were I to observe Jane for some time, I would be able to list a whole range of other behaviours that also belong in that set. For instance, Jane may also tilt her head to one side and start waggling her foot. When she speaks, her voice may be high and quavering.

I could go on to make up similar lists of the behaviours that consistently signal Jane's Adult and Parent ego-states.

Now let's return to Berne's definition, and focus on the phrase 'directly related to'.

Berne is saying that when I am in touch with the feelings and experience defining a particular ego-state, I will also be showing the behaviours that define that same ego-state. For instance, while Jane is *experiencing* her childhood memories of being late for school and *feeling* the panic she felt then, she will also show the set of *behaviours* she showed as a child. The behaviours are directly related to the feelings and experience, and together they mark off Jane's Child ego-state.

The whole point of the ego-state model is that it allows us to make reliable connections of this kind between behaviour, experience and feelings. If you see me showing the consistent set of behaviours that mark off my Child ego-state, you can reliably suppose that I am also re-playing experiences and feelings from my childhood. If you see me change my behaviour and begin showing the signals that define my Adult ego-state, you can reasonably assume that my experience and feelings are those of a grown-up person responding to the here-and-now. When I outwardly show behaviours that I copied from my parents, you can predict that I will internally be re-playing feelings and experience I also copied from them.

● Go back now to the personal examples you noted of being in your own Child, Parent or Adult ego-states during the past twenty-four hours.

Check whether the feelings and thoughts you noted for your Child ego-state make up a set which hangs together consistently for you.

Check whether the behaviours you noted for your Child ego-state also make up a consistent set.

Check whether your Child behaviours are consistently associated with your Child feelings and thoughts.

Carry out the same three steps for your Parent and for your Adult behaviours, thoughts and feelings.

Compare the three sets of behaviours, thoughts and feelings you have noted as defining your three ego-states. Check whether the three sets are distinctively different one from another. ●

Are ego-state distinctions real?

By completing the exercises in this chapter so far, you have been able to check whether your own behaviours, feelings and experiences hang together in the way the ego-state model suggests. But what evidence is there that the model applies to people generally?

To collect this evidence, we need to use methods of observing people that keep the observer's pre-conceived ideas out of the picture as far as possible. We need to analyse the results in a way that allows us to judge whether they could have arisen by mere chance. When we have chosen appropriate methods of observation and analysis, we need to use them to investigate two questions.

(1) Do people show three consistent and clearly distinguishable sets of behaviours that correspond to our definitions of the three ego-states?

(2) Do the person's reported experience and feelings correlate with the sets of behavioural clues in the way we would expect from the model?

There is now a substantial body of research that supports the answer 'yes' to both these questions. It's outside the scope of this book to describe these studies in detail. You can follow them up, if you wish, from the References list for this chapter.[3]

Ego-states and superego, ego, id

The three-way division of personality in the ego-state model reminds us of another famous three-part model. Sigmund Freud suggested the existence of three 'psychic agencies': superego, ego and id.

It's obvious that the two models are similar. At first sight, the Parent looks like the judgmental superego, which 'observes, orders, corrects and threatens'. The Adult has similarities to the reality-testing ego. And the Child seems to resemble the id, home of uncensored instincts and drives.

The resemblance between the two models is not surprising, given that Berne was trained initially as a Freudian analyst. But some commentators have gone further and suggested that Berne's Parent, Adult and Child are merely trivialized versions of Freud's three psychic agencies. In this they are mistaken. In his early writings, Berne was at pains to point out the differences between his model and that of Freud.

First and most important: the Parent, Adult and Child ego-states are each defined in terms of *observable* behavioural clues. By contrast, the superego, ego and id are purely theoretical intrapsychic concepts. (By 'intrapsychic', we mean 'experienced only inside the mind'.) You cannot look at me or listen to me and judge whether I am 'in my superego'. But you can judge by observation whether I am in my Parent ego-state.

Next, the ego-states relate to persons with specific identities, while Freud's three psychic agencies are generalized. When a person is in her Parent ego-state, she is not just acting in a way that is generally 'parental'. She is re-enacting the behaviours, feelings and thoughts of one of her *own* parents or parent-figures. When she is in Child, she will not simply be behaving in a 'childlike' manner. She will be reproducing behaviours she performed during her *own* childhood, along with their accompanying feelings and experience.

The Parent, Adult and Child ego-states will each *include* influences from superego, ego and id. Berne pointed out that someone in Parent will be reproducing the parent's 'total behaviour, including her inhibitions, her reasoning, and ... her impulses'. Adult and Child ego-states likewise entail their own inhibitions, reasoning and impulses.

Berne built upon Freud's model by adopting Paul Federn's idea of ego-states, i.e. distinct states in which the ego is manifested at a given time. He further classified these into three behaviourally observable ego-states, which he labelled Parent, Adult and Child.

Freud's model and the ego-state model are not one and the same thing. Neither do they contradict each other. Berne said that superego, ego and id are best thought of as intrapsychic constructs that act as influences upon the ego-states. The Parent is most heavily influenced by the super-ego but also has elements of ego and id functioning. The Child is most heavily influenced by the id but also has elements of superego and ego functioning. The Adult is pretty much pure ego functioning. So in defining ego-states, Berne includes not only the intrapsychic level but also the observable, social level. The two models are simply different ways of portraying personality; neither is 'more correct' than the other.[4]

Ego-states are names, not things

You cannot put an ego-state in a wheelbarrow. You cannot weigh it nor touch it. You cannot find it in any particular location in the body or brain.

This is because an ego-state is not a *thing*. Instead, it is a *name*, which we use to describe a set of phenomena, i.e. a set of related feelings, thoughts and behaviours. In the same way, Parent, Adult and Child are not things. They are names. We use these three words as labels to distinguish the three different sets of feeling-thinking-behaving that you have met in this chapter.

At the same time, it's worth repeating that the ego-states do represent the behaviour, thoughts and feelings of *real people* who are now alive or have been at some time. When I'm in *Child* I am replaying the behaviour, thoughts and feelings of the real child I once was. In *Parent* I'm reproducing the behaviour, thoughts and feelings of a real person who was a parent-figure to me during my childhood. And in *Adult* I'm showing the behaviour, thoughts and feelings of my real grown-up self, right now.

Quite often in everyday TA practice, people talk about ego-states as if they *were* 'things we have'. You may hear statements like:

'My Kid wants some fun,' or

'You have a strong Adult.'

The trouble with talking this way is that we may slip into believing that ego-states have some kind of existence of their own, separate from the person we are talking about. Of course, this isn't so. It's not that 'my Kid' wants some fun. *I* want some fun, and I may be in my Child ego-state while I want it. It's not that 'I have a strong Adult'. Rather, *I* have a good ability to do the things that are usually associated with the Adult ego-state, like reality-testing and assessing probabilities.

Throughout this book, we avoid the habit of talking as though ego-states were 'things'. We suggest that you do the same.

A matter of words: are there 'just three' ego-states?

So how many different ego-states can any one person move into? If we look at the three circles on the P-A-C diagram, it looks as though the answer is 'three'. Likewise, if we think of phrases like '*my* Child' or '*her* Adult', again it seems as if there are 'just three' ego-states: we're implying that the person has just one of each. And in fact, several times in this book so far, we've actually used the phrase 'three ego-states'. So *are* there just three?

When you think of what you already know about ego-states, you'll realize that the answer to this question is, 'No, there are more than three.'

Why is that? The reasons are different for the three different types of ego-state.

Let's look at Parent first. When you're in Parent, you're reproducing the thoughts, feelings and behaviours of one of your own parents or other authority-figures. Now, very few people have had only one significant parent or authority-figure. Even if you were brought up in a single-parent family, it's very likely that you will also have experienced other people who were in a parent-like role – for example a grandparent, elder sibling or schoolteacher. You will have copied thoughts, feelings and behaviours from each of these different people. Therefore you will show a different set of Parental ego-state thoughts, feelings, and actions for each of your parent-figures. As you do so, you will also experience the thoughts, feelings and actions you copied from the figure concerned.

For the Child ego-state, the point is that everyone has several different *ages* in their own childhood that they may revisit on various occasions in grown-up life. You may already have discovered that this is true of you, when you were doing the exercise earlier in this chapter about tracing your own ego-state shifts. So, for example, I may at times 'move back into' being my twelve-year-old self. At other times I may revisit my experience as a six-year-old. At still other times I may re-live occasions when I was two years old. For each of these different Child ages, I will show different ego-state behaviours, each accompanied by the thoughts, feelings and actions I experienced at the age concerned.

How about Adult? We know that 'being in Adult' means thinking, feeling and behaving as a direct response to the here-and-now. So, for sure, at any one moment in time, we can experience only one Adult ego-state. But there are many moments in time. In fact, how do you catch 'the now'? If a moment in time hasn't happened yet, it's in the future. If it has already happened, it's in the past. To avoid getting caught in an endless philosophical discussion about this, Eric Berne proposed a simple solution: we should define 'now' as meaning 'the present 24 hours, starting at the time you woke up this morning and going on till the time you wake up tomorrow morning'[5]. On that reasoning, you have one Adult ego-state for today; you get a new one tomorrow, and so on. In that sense, you show and experience 'more than one' Adult.

'Three ego-states' – a shorthand

Starting from what we've just said above, some TA writers have suggested that we should always refer to 'three *types*' (or *'categories'*) of ego-states. They further suggest that we should avoid talking about 'three ego-states' or using phrases like '*his* Child'.

These writers have precision on their side. However, in this book we shall usually not be following their suggestions. As you've seen, we've already broken their suggested rules. We have two reasons for using the more relaxed wording. First: it's been the wording used in TA literature for many years, so you would meet it in other books even if you didn't meet it here. Second: if we were to stick to talking about 'categories of ego-state', it would make many discussions uncomfortably 'wordy'. Just imagine, for instance, how our example about Jane's ego-state shifts, earlier in this chapter, would have looked if instead of saying 'Jane was in her Child', we'd written each time: 'Jane had shifted into one of her category of Child ego-states'.

So to sum up: we all have more than 'three ego-states' that we can move into. But it's a useful and much-used *shorthand* to use phrases like '*my* Parent' and to talk about 'three ego-states'. We'll use that shorthand throughout this book.

In Chapter 4, we'll be showing you how the 'multiplicity of ego-states' can actually be illustrated by adding some extra details to the first-order ego-state model.

The over-simplified model

After *Games People Play* became a best-seller in the mid-1960s, TA became in part a 'pop psychology'. Certain writers and speakers jumped on the commercial bandwagon. To make TA an even more marketable commodity, they watered down some of Berne's original ideas. They emphasized features that were striking and immediately obvious. They left out the aspects that required deeper thought or closer observation.

It was in this period that an over-simplified version of the ego-state model became current. That trivialized model is still with us. It has been at the root of endless misunderstanding, both among TA people themselves and among professional observers from other fields.

In this section, we take a look at the over-simplified model. *We do NOT suggest that you use it. It will NOT be used at any point in this book.*

We present it here solely because you are likely to meet it in some earlier TA literature. You will also discover it in the thinking of many people who learned their TA during that heady time of the 1960s.

What does the over-simplified model suggest?

It says merely: 'When I'm thinking, I'm in Adult. When I'm feeling, I'm in Child. When I'm making value-judgments, I'm in Parent.'

And that's it! Small wonder that professional observers from outside TA, hearing this model presented as TA's main building-block, have asked in bewilderment: 'Is *this* all there is?'[6]

Having read this chapter's account of what the ego-state model actually says, you may be wondering whether the over-simplified model bears any resemblance at all to the actual version. The fact is that there are resemblances. The over-simplified model presents *some* of the typical characteristics of each ego-state. But it misses out other characteristics that are essential to the model.

Let's look first at the grains of truth in the over-simplified model. How is it similar to the actual model?

You know that when I am in my Adult ego-state, I am responding to the here-and-now with all the resources available to me as a grown-up. Usually, this entails some kind of problem-solving. I am likely to experience myself as 'thinking'. Someone observing my behaviour would probably interpret it by saying I am 'thinking'.

If I go into Child, I begin re-playing behaviours, feelings and thoughts from my own childhood. Children, especially young ones, deal with the world mainly from a feeling position. Therefore, when I'm in Child, I will most often experience myself as 'feeling'. At these times, anyone observing me would likely confirm I seemed to be 'expressing feelings'.

When I am in Parent, I am copying my behaviours, thoughts and feelings from a parent or parent-figure, as that person appeared to me in my own childhood. To a child, parents appear to spend a lot of their time laying down rules about what ought and ought not to happen, or issuing judgments about how the world is. So for a lot of the time when I am in Parent, I will be doing what my parents did and making value-judgments about 'oughts and shoulds'.

It turns out, then, that the over-simplified model gives us some simple first clues to recognizing ego-states. When I am in Adult, I will *often* be thinking. In Child, I will *often* be into feelings. And when I'm in Parent, I will *often* be making value-judgments.

But these obvious clues to ego-states fall far short of giving us a full description of each ego-state. The over-simplified model completely omits to mention that I can think *and* feel and make value-judgments from *any* of my ego-states.

An even more serious fault of the over-simplified model is that it says nothing about the *time* dimension of ego-states. Again and again, Berne emphasized that Parent and Child are echoes of the *past*. In Child, I am replaying behaviours, thoughts and feelings *from my own past* – my childhood. When I am in my Parent ego-state, I am engaging in behaviours, thoughts and feelings that I copied *in the past* from my parents and parent-figures. Only when I am in my Adult am I responding to situations with all my *present* resources as a grown-up.

With that brief look, we turn away from the over-simplified model. It was fine as a topic for lightweight books and after-dinner speeches. But it did not give much clue to what TA is really about. From now on in this book, we stay with Berne's original version of the ego-state model.

Chapter 3
FUNCTIONAL ANALYSIS OF EGO-STATES

In this and the next chapter, we go on to build more detailed versions of the ego-state model. These view ego-states in terms of either *structure* or *function*.

A structural model shows *what* there is in each ego-state. A functional model divides the ego-states to show us *how* we use them. Putting the same idea in more formal language: a structural ego-state model is concerned with the *component parts* of ego-states. A functional model is concerned with their *description*.

- STRUCTURE = 'WHAT' = COMPONENT PARTS.

- FUNCTION = 'HOW' = DESCRIPTION.

The functional model is probably easier to understand at first acquaintance, so we will look at that first.[1] It is pictured in Figure 3.1.

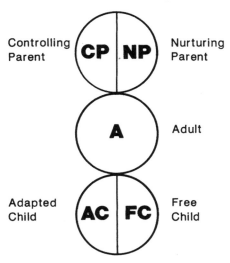

Figure 3.1 Functional analysis of ego-states

Given that in the functional model we are looking at *how* people use and express their ego-states, that means that we need to focus on their observable *behaviour*. For that reason, the subdivisions of the model shown in Figure 3.1 are sometimes called *behavioural descriptions*. (This is the label used in the most recent version of the 'TA 101' syllabus: see Appendix F).

Adapted Child and Free Child

Imagine that I am in my Child ego-state. I am behaving, thinking and feeling just as I used to in my childhood.

For a lot of the time when I was a child, I was adapting to the demands of parents or parent-figures. I had learned that in order to get by, I had better be polite to the neighbours even though I might not have liked them very much. When I needed to wipe my nose, I used my handkerchief instead of my sleeve, even though the sleeve might be more convenient. Very early on in my life, I had worked out that Father liked me better when I was quiet, so when he was around I was mostly quiet. Mother liked me to laugh and didn't seem to like me crying or getting angry. So when I was with Mother I laughed most of the time, even when sometimes I was sad and wanted to cry, or angry and wanted to shout at her.

Now as a grown-up, I often re-play these ways of behaving that I decided on as a child so as to fit in with what my parents expected. When I do so, I am said to be in *Adapted Child*.

There were other times in my childhood when I rebelled against these rules and expectations that my parents seemed to be setting for me. When Father's back was turned, I made rude faces at the neighbour's little girl next door. And sometimes when I was on my own, I gave my nose a really good wipe on my sleeve, just because I was so tired of using that handkerchief. There were even days when I felt so bad about always having to laugh when Mother was around that I made a point of sulking all day, just to show her.

When I behaved in these ways, it was as if I was taking my parents' rules and turning them around backwards. Instead of adapting to their expectations, I was doing as much of the opposite as I could.

In grown-up life, I may still be rebelling in ways like these. Quite often, I may not be aware that my behaviour is a rebellion. When the boss gives me a tough work assignment, I may discover that I 'don't have enough time' to get it finished by the deadline. In fact, I have as much time as anybody ever has, twenty-four hours in each day. Telling the boss I didn't get the job finished, I may feel an obscure satisfaction that says 'That'll show you!' When I was four years old, I may have felt the same rebellious satisfaction as I showed Mother she couldn't make me eat that last potato on my plate.

When I engage in this kind of rebellion, I am nevertheless still responding to childhood rules. Therefore I am said to be still in *Adapted Child*.

Some earlier TA writers portrayed rebellion in a separate ego-state division, which they called the *Rebellious Child*. You may still find the name in some modern sources. In this book, we shall follow the more usual current practice and regard rebellion as part of the Adapted Child set of behaviours.

There were times in my childhood when I behaved in ways that were independent of parental pressures. At these times, I was neither adapting to my parents' expectations, nor rebelling against them. I was simply acting as I myself wanted to. When my pet mouse died, I cried because I was sad. When my little sister pushed me, I got angry and pushed her back. I enjoyed many hours of reading stories and learning how to do jigsaw puzzles, not to please my parents but just for myself.

When I am in my Child ego-state as a grown-up, I may sometimes behave in these uncensored childhood ways. At these times I am said to be in *Free Child*. Sometimes the alternative name of *Natural Child* is used to describe this style of behaviour. .

In the functional model, then, the Child ego-state is divided into *Adapted Child* and *Free Child*. In the picture of the ego-state model, we show this by dividing the Child circle in two (see Figure 3.1).

Positive and negative Adapted Child

As grown-ups, we are all in Adapted Child a fair amount of the time. There are thousands of rules we follow about how to live and be accepted in the world. In everyday living, we don't think consciously about these rules before deciding to follow them. Before I cross the road, I look right and left in the way my father and teachers insisted I do when I first went to school on my own. When I'm at table during a dinner party and want the vegetables, I say 'please'. As a child I learned to do this as if it were automatic, because I correctly learned that people would judge me 'rude' if I didn't. And if they judged me rude, I would take longer to get the vegetables.

Our Adapted Child behaviours may work for us in ways like these. By replaying these rule-following patterns, we often get what we want comfortably for ourselves and other people. And we save a great deal of mental energy. Just imagine what it would be like if you had to think out your table manners afresh every time you sat down at the table!

We can speak of *positive Adapted Child* to describe these productive ways of behaving in our Adapted Child. Some writers use the alternative phrase *OK Adapted Child*.

By contrast, we are said to be in *negative (or not-OK) Adapted Child* when we replay childhood patterns of behaviour which are no longer appropriate to our grown-up situation. As a young child, I may have learned that a powerful way to get attention from Mother and Father was to sulk. Now as a grown-up, I may sometimes still sulk in the hope of getting what I want. When I do so, I ignore my grown-up option of simply asking for what I want directly.

Or I may have decided as a child that it wasn't safe to make any kind of show of myself in front of people. Maybe I got slapped down by Mother for 'showing off'. Perhaps my playmates teased me when I had to recite in class. Now as a grown-up, asked to speak in public, I may turn red, stammer and stutter, while I feel embarrassed and think to myself 'I'm no good as a speaker!' In here-and-now reality, I am perfectly capable of speaking and the situation carries no risk for me.

All of us, for some of the time, display negative Adapted Child patterns of behaviour. Later in the book, you will learn why this is. An aim of personal change in TA is to replace these old outdated patterns with new ones that make full use of our grown-up options.

Positive and negative Free Child

Free Child behaviours too can be classed as positive (OK) or negative (not-OK). To say I am 'in Free Child' means I am engaging in behaviours from my childhood that pay no attention to Parental rules or limits. Sometimes these can be productive and life-enhancing for me as a grown-up, and so are classed as positive. For instance, when I'm at a pleasant party, or when playing with a child or with a pet, I may 'let myself be a child again' and freely show my playfulness and enjoyment in just the same way as I did in my childhood.

Or suppose that as a child I decided to adapt to my parents by never showing I was angry. In grown-up life, without realizing it, I may have been following the same strategy. Bottling up my anger, I may have become depressed or physically tense. Then, perhaps in the course of therapy, I decide to let myself express how angry I feel. Beating furiously on a cushion, I at last mobilize the uncensored Free Child energy I have been hanging on to for all these years. I'm likely to find afterwards that I feel better and more relaxed physically.

In a similar way, many of us reach grown-up life still hanging on to unexpressed Child feelings of grief, scare or desire for physical contact. When we express these emotions in a safe situation, we engage in positive Free Child behaviour.

There are other times when Free Child behaviour is clearly negative. If I belch loudly at a formal dinner-party, I am satisfying my uncensored Child urges. But the social consequences will probably be more uncomfortable for me than if I had held down the belch.

● Think back through the past twenty-four hours. Make a note of occasions when you were in positive Adapted Child. What were your behaviours on each occasion? Do you recall what childhood situations you were replaying?

Do the same for occasions when you were: in negative Adapted Child; in positive Free Child; in negative Free Child.

Take one minute to write down all the words you can think of to describe the behaviours of someone in positive Adapted Child. (If you are working in a group, brainstorm for a minute with someone writing the words up).

Do the same for someone in: negative Adapted Child; positive Free Child; negative Free Child. ●

Controlling Parent and Nurturing Parent

For some of the time when I was a child, my parents were telling me what to do, controlling me or criticizing me. 'Go to bed! Don't run out into the road! Blow your nose! That's clever, silly, good, naughty, fair, not fair...' When I behave in ways which copy my parents in this role, I am said to be in *Controlling Parent* (sometimes called *Critical Parent).*

At other times, my parents were caring for me or looking after me. Mother might cuddle me. Father might read me bedtime stories. When I fell and cut my knee, one of my parents would comfort me and bring the bandages. When I replay the behaviours my parents showed when they were looking after me, I am said to be in *Nurturing Parent.*

We diagram this two-way division in the functional Parent by dividing the ego-state circle in two, in the same way as we did for Child (see Figure 3.1).

Positive and negative Controlling and Nurturing Parent

Some TA writers distinguish positive and negative subdivisions in each of these parts of the Parent. (Again, the terms 'OK' and 'not-OK' are sometimes used instead). They would say we are in *positive Controlling or Critical Parent* when our Parental directives to others are genuinely aimed at protecting them or promoting their well-being. A doctor might command his patient: 'Stop smoking! It's bad for you.' He is re-playing the kind of command he got from his parents when he was small: 'Don't walk out on the road in front of the cars!'

Negative Controlling or Critical Parent describes Parental behaviours that entail a put-down (discount) of the other person. The boss who snarls to his secretary: 'You've made a mistake again!' may be reproducing the tones and gestures of the irritable schoolteacher who said the same to him when he was in class at six years old.

Positive Nurturing Parent implies caring which is provided from a position of genuine regard for the person helped. *Negative Nurturing*

Parent means that 'help' is given from a one-up position that discounts the other person. A positive Nurturing Parent behaviour might be to say to a workmate: 'Do you want help with that job? If you do, let me know.' The negative counterpart might be to walk up to him and say: 'Here, I'll help you with that,' take the work out of his hands and complete it for him. The 'smother-mother' is the classic example of negative Nurturing Parent behaviour.

● Thinking back through your day, note occasions when you showed Controlling Parent towards others. On which of these occasions were you coming from positive Controlling Parent? Negative Controlling Parent? Do you recall which parent or parent-figure you were copying each time?

Do the same for times in the day when you were showing positive or negative Nurturing Parent.

Take one minute to write down all the words you can think of to describe the behaviours of someone in positive Controlling Parent. (In a group, brainstorm for a minute).

Do the same in turn for: negative Controlling Parent; positive Nurturing Parent; negative Nurturing Parent. ●

Adult

The Adult in the functional model is usually not subdivided. We class any behaviour as Adult that is a response to the here-and-now situation, using all the person's grown-up resources.

We have now assembled the whole of the functional model. You can review it in Figure 3.1.

Egograms

How important is each of these functional ego-state descriptions in your personality? Jack Dusay has devised an intuitive way of showing this. He calls it the egogram.[2]

To make an egogram, you begin by drawing a horizontal line. Label it along its length with the names of the five main functional ego-state descriptions. To save spelling them out in full, use their initial letters. Thus Controlling Parent becomes CP, Free Child becomes FC, and so on. Draw them in the order shown on Figure 3.2.

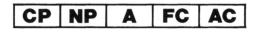

Figure 3.2

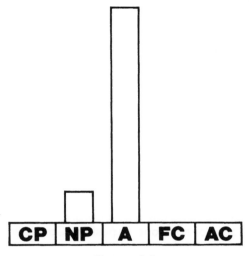

Figure 3.3

The idea is to draw a vertical bar above each ego-state label. The height of the bar shows how much of the time you use that functional ego-state.

Start with the one you judge you use most, and draw its vertical bar. Next, take the one you think you use least and draw its bar. Make the

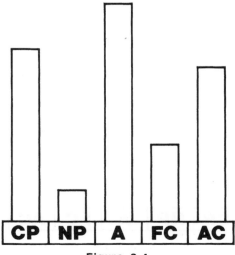

Figure 3.4

relative heights of the two bars fit your intuitive judgment of the relative amounts of time you spend in each functional ego-state.

For instance, if I judge I am in Adult most and Nurturing Parent least, I might draw my first two bars as in Figure 3.3.

Now complete the egogram by drawing in the other three bars. Make the height of each one represent the relative time you spend in that functional ego-state. My completed egogram might look like Figure 3.4.

The exact height of each bar is not important. What matters is the relative height of each bar as compared to the others.

Jack Dusay did not suggest dividing up the bars into positive and negative parts, but it can be interesting to do so. You can shade in a part of the bars for CP, NP, FC and AC to show 'negative'. This leaves the rest of the bar showing 'positive'. For instance, I believe that most of my time in Adapted Child is spent in positive rule-following. When I behave in uncensored Free Child ways, most of these behaviours also lead to comfortable and productive outcomes. I am not often in Nurturing Parent, but when I am, I hardly ever 'smother' people in a negative way. I am often in Controlling Parent. Most of this Controlling Parent time is spent in positive ways of directing others. My final egogram looks like Figure 3.5.

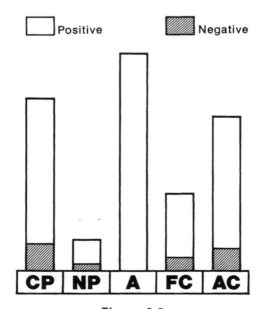

Figure 3.5

● Go ahead and draw your own egogram.

If you are working in a group, share your ideas with another group member as you draw. Work quickly and by intuition.

What do you learn about yourself?

Some people find that one egogram fits them in every situation. Others find they need to draw two or even more different egograms. Perhaps they will have a 'work' and a 'home' egogram. If this is true of you, go ahead and draw each one. What do you learn?

Explain egograms to someone who knows you well. Ask this person to draw *your* egogram. What do you learn by comparing their version with your own? ●

The constancy hypothesis

Jack Dusay suggested a constancy hypothesis:

'When one ego-state increases in intensity, another or others must decrease in order to compensate. The shift in psychic energy occurs so that the total amount of energy may remain constant.'

The best way to change my egogram, says Dusay, is to set about raising the functional ego state I want to have more of. When I do so, energy will automatically shift out of the other functional ego states I want to have relatively less of.

Suppose I look at my egogram and decide I would like to be more in Nurturing Parent and less in Controlling Parent. I begin practising more Nurturing Parent behaviours. Perhaps I offer someone a back-rub once each day. Or at work I experiment with making open offers of guidance instead of ordering people to do things. I don't make any attempt to cut down on my Controlling Parent behaviour. By the constancy hypothesis, I can expect this will go down anyway as I put more energy into Nurturing Parent.

● Is there anything you want to change about your egogram?

If there is, decide which bar you need to raise to achieve this change.

List at least five new behaviours that you can practise to increase this ego-state. Make a point of doing these behaviours in the week following.

Then re-draw your egogram. If possible, get a re-drawn egogram from the person who knows you well. (Do not tell them which changes you aimed to make in the egogram.) Does your new egogram fit the constancy hypothesis? ●

The functional model describes only behaviour, not thinking or feeling

You'll recall from Chapters 1 and 2 that each type of ego-state is defined as a 'consistent set of thinking, feeling and behaviour'. From what you've read in this chapter, you'll realize that the functional model describes only one of these three defining features – namely, behaviour. To that extent, you could say that the functional model 'tells only one-third of the story' about ego-states. But that one-third is an important part of the story: of the three defining features of an ego-state, only behaviour is directly observable.

The functional model is designed for use when we are interested purely in *how* people behave, rather than in *why* they behave that way. It describes what we can see and hear a person doing 'on the outside', and makes no attempt to judge what is happening 'on the inside'. This focus is particularly useful when we are studying patterns of communication between people. It helps us when we want to observe objectively: 'What does one person do and say? What does the other person do and say?'

However, this close focus on behaviour carries its own possible pitfalls. The functional model is immediately appealing. Everybody who meets this model 'knows' intuitively what's meant by labels like 'Controlling Parent', 'Free Child' and so on. From there, it's a very short and tempting step to supposing that behaviours *define* each ego-state. For example: 'She's looking and sounding like a child having a good time – *therefore* she's in Free Child'. Or: 'That man is acting in a really caring way, *so that means* he's in Nurturing Parent'.

As you'll realize, these suppositions are inaccurate. To get the 'full story' on which ego-state a person is in, we don't only need to consider their behaviour. We need also to take into account the thoughts and feelings that go with that behaviour.

Should we talk about 'functional *ego-states*' at all?

In recent years, some TA writers have suggested that because the functional model does not take into account feeling and thinking, it would be better if we didn't use the term 'ego-states' at all in talking about functional analysis. They've suggested also that it would be better if we didn't use the familiar three-circles diagram to draw the functional model on paper, because the three circles are so closely bound up with the idea of ego-states.

Various writers have put forward suggestions on what we might use instead of the ego-state labels and the three circles. One of us (IS) has suggested a 'Five Behaviours Model' made up of five rectangles, with the labels Controlling, Nurturing, Information Processing, Adapting and Free Expression. Susannah Temple, also using a rectangular model, refers to 'Nine Modes of Behaviour', taking into account the 'negative' and 'positive' aspects that we described above in the traditional functional model.[3]

However, at the date of writing, these alternative diagrams and labels have not caught on in mainstream TA theory. Perhaps they will figure in a future edition of this book. Meantime, we invite you to keep clearly in mind that the functional model, with its sole focus on behaviour, does not 'tell the whole story' about ego-states. In the coming two chapters, we'll fill in the 'story' and describe how you can get evidence on all three of these defining features of an ego-state: on thinking and feeling as well as on behaviour.

Chapter 4
THE SECOND-ORDER STRUCTURAL MODEL

In the last chapter's functional model, we divided the ego-states up to indicate *how* they were shown in behaviour – their *description*. Now in looking at the second-order *structural* model, we examine *what* the ego-states have in them – their *component parts*.

Right from the moment I am born, I am experiencing the world. I store those experiences away in memory.

Do we actually record every moment of our life experience somewhere in memory? Have we the potential to recall all of it? Nobody knows for sure but the unconscious seems to retain it all. It is also not clear yet how the storage is accomplished. We do know that everyone retains memories of their past. Some can be brought easily back into awareness. Others are more difficult to recover. Memories of early childhood especially may only come back to us in dreams and fantasies and other ways of accessing the unconscious like hypnosis or muscle testing (a technique from energy psychology).

Throughout this chapter, we will be using the word 'memories' in a sense that is wider than its usual conversational meaning. In everyday conversation, a 'memory' is simply some event or experience that we recall from the past. Here we'll be using the word to mean more than just recall. For sure, recall is part of the process. But as well as storing away the recall itself, we are able also to store the emotions, thoughts and recalled actions that took place at that past time. When we retrieve the recall of the event in question, we re-live also the feelings, thoughts and behaviours that we first experienced when the event was actually taking place. In other words, these second-order ego-states are experiential realities. We can feel and think and behave like our parents did, or like we did as a child.

Each one of us has an uncountable number of experiences of thoughts, feelings and behaviours stored away as memories, in the sense we've just described. The purpose of the second-order structural model is to *classify* these memories in a useful way, within our familiar framework of ego-states.

If you like, you can think of the second-order structural model as a kind of *filing system*. Imagine a businessman sitting at his desk. Each day he deals with many different pieces of paperwork – letters in, replies out,

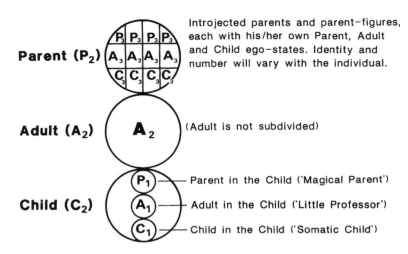

Parent (P₂) — Introjected parents and parent-figures, each with his/her own Parent, Adult and Child ego-states. Identity and number will vary with the individual.

Adult (A₂) — A_2 — (Adult is not subdivided)

Child (C₂)

P_1 — Parent in the Child ('Magical Parent')

A_1 — Adult in the Child ('Little Professor')

C_1 — Child in the Child ('Somatic Child')

Figure 4.1 Second-order structural model

bills, staff records and so on. At the end of the day's work, he doesn't just throw all these bits of paper randomly into a sack on the floor. He stores them away systematically in his filing system.

It's obvious why he does so. By means of the filing system, he can *organize* his records in a way that is useful to his business. Suppose for instance that he needs to draw up his financial accounts. He simply needs to go to the file labelled 'bills', and there are the records of all his outgoings ready for the accountant.

In just the same way, the TA practitioner uses the second-order structural model to 'file away' a person's memory traces of thoughts, feelings and behaviours in a way that will be useful in his understanding of personality through structural analysis.[1]

The second-order structural model is pictured in Figure 4.1. How does it operate as a 'filing system'?

As children, all of us receive messages from our parents. For each message we receive, we have a certain way of thinking about it and certain fantasies we form in relation to that message. We also have feelings we experience about the message, and we make a decision about what we will do in response. In addition, our parents may give us reasons why the message is important. They may convey feelings that imply a covert message in addition to the one they are conveying overtly.

In the second-order structural model, the messages we received from our parents or parent-figures are 'filed away' in P_3. The reasons they gave us for why they are important are stored in A_3. Any secret or covert implications are stored in C_3.

Our own thinking about the messages becomes part of our A_2 content.

The fantasy we formed about what would happen if we did or did not follow these messages becomes part of P_1. The feelings we have in response to our fantasy are stored in C_1, and our early decision about what we will do comes from A_1.

In the following sections, we look in more detail at each of these 'filing compartments' in the model.

Second-order structure: Parent

You already know that the Parent ego-state represents the entire set of thoughts, feelings and behaviours which you have internalized from parents and parent-figures. Thus in the structural model, the *content* of the Parent is defined as the set of memory traces of these parental thoughts, feelings and behaviours.

In formal language, we say that these are parental *introjects*. To introject something is like swallowing it whole instead of chewing and digesting it. Typically this is what children do with their parental modelling.

A child experiences her parents for a lot of the time as issuing commands and defining the world. So the content of the Parent will consist largely of these commands and definitions. 'Don't put your hand in the fire.' 'It's wrong to steal.' 'The world is a good, bad, beautiful, scary place.' Along with the words go memories of the gestures, tones and emotional expressions that went with them.

In the second-order structural model, we first divide the Parent according to whom each remembered message came from. For most people, this will be Mother or Father. Maybe grandparents were also important figures. Teachers often play a part. The number and identity of the people who gave you your Parent content are unique to you.

Next we register that each of your parent-figures had a Parent, Adult and Child ego-state. This gives us the second-order picture of the Parent shown in Figure 4.1.

Notice that the whole Parent ego-state is conventionally labelled P_2 in this diagram. Different TA writers have used different ways of labelling the P, A and C subdivisions in P_2. Here, we call them P_3, A_3 and C_3.

Parent in the Parent (P_3)

My father had a whole set of slogans and commands which he had introjected from his own parents. He passed some of these on to me, and I stored them away in my Parent, along with those I got from my mother. In this way the Parent in the Parent is a storehouse of messages which may be passed down through generations. For instance, Scottish parents may tell their children: 'Porridge will make you strong and you should eat all of it up every morning.' You can imagine their remote ancestors, dressed in skins, saying the same to *their* children as they stirred the pot in their cave each morning.

Adult in the Parent (A₃)

We picture the Adult in the Parent as being the collection of statements about reality which a person has heard from the figures in her Parent and has copied from them. Many of these statements will be true in objective fact. Others will reflect the parents' misapprehensions or fantasies about the world. Still others will be statements about things that were once factually true but are no longer so. For instance, the statement 'You can't walk on the moon' used to be a reality.

Child in the Parent (C₃)

Mother, Father and teacher each had a Child ego-state. When I introjected them into my own Parent, I included my perception and experience of their Child as part of the introject. Accessing my stored memories of them, I may come in contact with their Child feelings, thoughts or behaviours. I can experience myself feeling or reacting as that parent did when I was little.

When my mother was a little girl, she decided she could get what she wanted from people by sulking and looking sour. Later on when I was a child and she wanted something from me, she would often sulk and look sour in the same way. Now in my own Parent ego-state, I carry a message that when I'm in charge of people I can get them to do what I want by sulking and looking sour.

Second-order structure: Adult

The content of my Adult is defined as the thinking, feeling and behaving which I engage in as a response to the here-and-now. This implies that the Adult is the 'filing compartment' in which is placed the whole set of strategies for reality-testing and problem-solving which I have available to me now as a grown-up person.

In the Adult we locate not only the reality-testing we apply to the world outside ourselves, but also our grown-up evaluation of the content of our own Parent and Child ego-states. For instance, I carry a Parent command in P_2 that says: 'Look right and left before you cross the road!' As a grown-up I have assessed this message and have concluded that it makes sense in reality. This conclusion is filed in A_2.

For much of the time I am in Adult, I and others will experience that I am 'thinking'. But you'll recall from Chapter 2 that Adult content is defined to include here-and-now *feeling* responses, as well as here-and-now thinking. You may wonder: how can feelings be a way of problem-solving? Imagine that at this moment a tiger, escaped from a zoo, were to leap through the window of your room. If you are like most people, your here-and-now feeling would be scare. And that emotion would be a great help to the speed at which you ran away.

If I feel here-and-now sadness, that is my way of resolving a different kind of problem: namely, the loss of someone or something important to me.

In the second-order structural model, we usually make no divisions in the Adult. We show A_2 on the diagram as simply a plain circle.

Second-order structure: Child

We define any stored experience from the person's own childhood as being part of the content of the Child ego-state.

There are many different ways in which these millions of memories could be classified. One obvious way would be to group them according to the age they date from. Some TA writers, notably Fanita English, have done just this.[2]

More often, we divide the structural Child ego-state in a different way, pictured in Figure 4.1. The reasoning behind it is simple. When I was a child, I already had Parent, Adult and Child ego-states.

Every child has basic needs and wants (Child). She has fantasies about how best to get these met (Parent). And she possesses intuitive problem-solving skills (Adult).

To signal this, we draw circles for Parent, Adult and Child *within* the larger circle showing the Child ego-state.

These three internal divisions of the Child ego-state are conventionally labelled P_1, A_1 and C_1. The whole Child ego-state in the second-order model is given the label C_2.

Parent in the Child (P_1)

Every child learns early in life that there are rules which must be followed. These rules are laid down by Mother and Father.

Unlike a grown-up, the young child doesn't have the reasoning power to examine the rules and check whether it makes sense to follow them. Instead, she simply knows they must be followed. But often she doesn't feel at all keen on following them. So she finds ways of scaring or seducing herself into obedience.

'If I don't say my prayers at night, the Devil will come out of the fire and get me.'

'If I don't eat all of my dinner, Mother will go away and leave me and never come back.'

'If I act nice, everybody will love me.'

It is in this magical form that younger children store away their own version of messages from their parents. Since these impressions are the child's fantasies of the implications of his parents' messages, they are grouped together in the model as the content of the child's Parent ego-state. Later as a grown-up, I may go back into Child and access these magical messages, which make up the Parent in my Child, P_1.

This magical thinking Parent may often be far more threatening than the actual parent. Even when parents love their child and are parenting him as well as they are able, the young child may perceive them as giving him destructive messages like:

'Drop down dead!'

'Never enjoy anything!'

'You aren't supposed to think!'

To reflect this quality of harshness, P_1 was given several different scary nicknames by earlier TA writers. It has been called the Witch Parent, the Ogre and the Pig Parent.

But the child's grandiose fantasy may be positive as well as negative. The Parent in the Child is also associated with the Fairy Godmother, the Good Fairy and Santa Claus. For this reason we prefer the term 'Magical Parent' for P_1.

Berne called P_1 the 'Electrode'. This refers to the way the Child responds almost compulsively to these magical images of reward and punishment.

Adult in the Child or 'Little Professor' (A_1)

A_1, the Adult in the Child, is a label for the whole collection of strategies the child has available for solving problems. These strategies change and develop as the child grows. Researchers into child development have studied these changes in detail. Their work is necessary reading if you want thorough understanding of the Adult in the Child.[3]

As a young child, I was certainly interested in checking out the world around me. But my ways of doing so didn't entail the processes grown-ups call 'logical'. I relied more on intuition, instant impressions. At the same time, I learned new things far faster than any grown-up can learn. This stored capability earns A_1 its alternative name of 'Little Professor'.

In grown-up life, I can still go back into my Child ego-state and access the intuition and creativity which I hold in A_1.

Child in the Child (C_1)

Six-year-old Jean is lying on the floor, busy reading the book she has just been given at school. In comes the cat. Jean looks up from her book, reaches out to stroke him. But the cat has had a bad day that day. He swipes Jean on the arm, and blood wells up from the scratch.

In the next second, Jean's six-year-old thinking is forgotten. She rolls herself up in a ball, and her wordless scream brings Mother running from the next room. Until the scratch is bandaged and Mother has given comfort, Jean is a baby again. As a child of six, she is back in her one-year-old Child ego-state.

As a grown-up, Jean will have a stored memory of this scene. If she recalls it, she will contact first the Adult in her six-year-old Child ego-state (reading the book). Then she will shift into C_1, the earlier Child within the Child, as she re-lives her pain and panic on being scratched.

Very young children experience the world mainly in terms of body sensations. These will form the bulk of the memories stored in the Child in the Child. For this reason, C_1 is sometimes called the *Somatic Child* or the *Infant*.

Have you ever seen one of those sets of Russian dolls? You unscrew the top of the outside doll and find another smaller one inside. Then you unscrew the top of the second doll and see an even smaller doll inside. You unscrew that one and...

The second-order model of the Child is like that. In the structure of my six-year-old Child I have an earlier Child of, say, three. Inside that in turn is an even earlier Child, and so it goes on. When we draw the diagram for the model, we don't usually bother showing this in full detail. But particularly if you are a therapist, keep this feature in mind. It is often important to track the various ages of the Child that a client may move through in therapy.

Putting C_2 together with the pictures we developed of the Adult and Child, we get the complete second-order structural diagram shown in Figure 4.1.

How the second-order structure develops

(Authors' note: the discussion in this section is above 'TA 101' level. We nevertheless think it is worth including at this point, because it offers you an in-depth understanding of how the ego-states develop from infancy through to adulthood. If you are new to TA, you may wish to read through the section, then come back and consider it in more detail later).

When a child is born, the only ego-state that exists is C_1 (the Infant). If we 'look inside' C_1, we see an even earlier structure: P_0, A_0, and C_0. These represent the personality structure at birth. This structure consists of innate functioning plus adaptations we made have made *in utero*. The ego-state label C_0 represents our instinctual drives and hungers. P_0 means the infant's instinctual programs for getting needs met, while A_0 represents an instinctual problem-solving mechanism. For example, C_0 registers hunger, P_0 cries to signal the environment, A_0 cries louder if no-one responds. If put to the breast, P_0 instinctually sucks to get milk, A_0 roots to find the nipple. There are numerous examples of such instinctual functioning. The child operates with these ego-states until about 6 months when A_1 (the Little Professor) begins to develop.

A_1 represents the intuitive, creative, ingenious part of the child who has a tremendous curiosity about the world and how things work, and figures things out on the basis of feeling and intuition (right-brain processing). The child experiences great pleasure in mastering the world around her: learning to stand, walk, climb, feed herself, etc. This continues until about 18 months when A_2 (the Adult) begins to develop.

The ego-state label A_2 indicates the logical, rational thinking (left-brain processing) part of the personality. This type of thinking is based on language and is therefore not possible until the child begins to use language, at around 18 months to 2 years. The child begins to assert his will and say 'no' in an attempt to establish his own autonomy. In doing so, he often runs headlong into the will of his parents. Thinking is required in order to figure out how to get what he wants in cooperation with what his parents want. A moderate amount of frustration is required in motivating the child to think. Too much frustration and the child rebels. Too little frustration and the child remains passive and lets the parents do it for him. Clear parental expectations and limits are necessary on the part of the parents in assisting the child to learn to think. Around 3 years, P_1 (the Magical Parent) begins to develop.

P_1 represents the child's fantasy of how the world works based on A_1's intuitive perceptions, experience, and interpretations up until that point. Many of the child's interpretations are based on the magical world of the child: witches, ogres, Santa Claus, fairy godmothers, etc. The child's beliefs at that time are grandiose in a positive or negative direction. 'If I do "x" the whole world will love and adore me. If I do "y" the whole world will hate me and reject me.' The child uses that magical thinking to control her behaviour during that time by scaring herself out of doing things the parents have told her not to do. Between 3 and 6 years is also when the child first formulates her script based on this magical thinking. By about 6 years of age, the Child ego-state (C_2) is fully developed and P_2 (the Parent) begins to develop based on A_2 thinking (reason rather than intuition).

The ego-state label P_2 stands for the Rational Parent as opposed to the Magical Parent, although P_2 does contain some non-rational, magical thinking from mother and father's Child. The content of P_2 is mostly internalized from mother and father and other authority figures rather than developed by the child. It contains all three of the parents' ego states (P_3, A_3, and C_3). It is also contains the child's A_2 decisions about the best way to do things and why you do them. The child learns to integrate Adult thinking along with the Parent information if he is allowed to question and argue with the parents about why certain things are important and should be done. The P_2 information operates mostly as an internal influence on the child's behaviour until about 8-10 years when the child has developed enough power and authority in his Parent to use it socially with others. By 12 years of age both the Adult (A_2) and Parent (P_2) are fully developed and the individual has a complete second-order personality structure. The person will continue to have new experiences, learn new information, and develop new values, but the basic structure and potential is already in place.

This is a very brief overview of the development of the second-order structure. If you would like to pursue the topic in more detail, you can follow it up in the sources given in the References list for this chapter, notably in the work of Pam Levin, the Schiffs, and Babcock and Keepers.[4]

Distinguishing structure from function

To use the ego-state model effectively, you need clear understanding of the differences between structure and function. Confusion between the two has been a longstanding problem in the development of TA theory.

Yet the differences themselves are easy to understand. They all arise from one simple fact, which you already know about.

The functional model classifies observed behaviours, while the structural model classifies stored memories and strategies.

So long as you keep this in mind, you will distinguish accurately between structure and function.

One of us (VJ) explained the distinction more fully in a 1976 *TA Journal* article.[5] He wrote:

'Berne was careful in his presentations to differentiate structural and functional diagrams. I believe he had a solid logical basis for being so. Many present-day writers are attempting to equate these two modifying categories. This is like attempting to equate a "wheel" with "revolving". The two categories refer to different aspects of reality. In analysing ego-states, "structural" refers to the component parts of the personality while "functional" or "descriptive" refers to the way in which the personality is functioning at a given point in time. An analogy would be the different ways to look at a heat pump used to heat and cool a house. One could look at the heat pump "structurally" and point to its various components such as the compressor, the air ducts, the thermostat, etc. One could also look at the heat pump "functionally" or "descriptively" and talk about it heating the house, cooling the house transferring air from one place to another, using electricity, etc. These are descriptions of how the total system is functioning at a given point in time.'

Any time you want to clarify the difference between structure and function, think of that wheel and that heat-pump.

You also know another way of wording the distinction:

- STRUCTURE = 'WHAT' = COMPONENT PARTS.

- FUNCTION = 'HOW' = DESCRIPTION.

What is so important about making the correct distinction?

Any time we are talking about interactions between people, we must think in terms of *function*. When we are considering what goes on inside the individual, we need to think *structurally*.

Saying the same things in technical language: *interpersonal* aspects of TA work require a functional approach. *Intrapsychic* matters need to be studied in structural terms.

In this book, our discussion of 'Communicating' in Part III will be almost entirely about function. The account of 'Life-script' in Part IV will relate principally to structure.

When I look at you and listen to you and judge what ego-state you are in, I can make my judgment only in terms of the functional model. Perhaps I see you put your head to one side, crease your brow and put the end of one finger in your mouth. From these observations I judge that you are probably in your Adapted Child.

There is no similar way I can observe you and try to judge whether you are 'in your Little Professor' or 'coming from your Parent-in-the-Parent'. These names define collections of memories, not sets of behaviours. Only by listening to the *content* of what you are saying can I begin to get evidence about second-order structure.

If I do want to know about the content of your Little Professor or Parent-in-the-Parent – the *what* rather than the *how* – I need to do some detective work. Principally, I need to ask you a lot of questions. I may also use my general knowledge about different kinds of personality and about how children develop.

In the next chapter, we shall list Eric Berne's four ways of diagnosing ego-states and relate them to the structure-function distinction.

Relationship between structure and function

It is possible for two things to be *different*, yet to be *related* to each other. This is true of structure and function. Obviously, the way I behave at any moment will depend partly on the set of memories and strategies I am contacting internally.

Suppose I am showing a set of behaviours typical of the negative Adapted Child functional ego-state division. Let's say I am sitting scrunched up with arms and legs tightly folded. I'm clenching my teeth and my face is going red, while sweat breaks out on my brow. If you looked at me then, what could you tell about the structural ego-state part I might be contacting internally?

You might reasonably guess I am experiencing body sensations of the sort which fit with the definition of Somatic Child, C_1. And so I may be. But perhaps I am also accessing internal images of the scary ogre or witch parent figures I built for myself at the age of three and stored away to make up my P_1.

It's also possible that I am replaying the way my father used to scrunch up and go red when he felt under threat as a child. If so, I am accessing part of my own Parent ego-state, the Child in my Father Parent (C_3 of Father).

And for all you know, I may be a skilful actor and be setting up the whole charade for some grown-up purpose that you don't know about yet. If so, then I am likely to be switching internally between the content of my Adult, A_2, and Little Professor, A_1.

To repeat: when you look at me and listen to me, you can *observe* function. But you can only *infer* structure.

The first-order model shows both structure *and* function

In Chapter 2 you met the plain, three-circles diagram of ego-states. You learned that this is often called the 'first-order model' because the circles are not subdivided. Eric Berne called this diagram the 'first-order *structural* model', and this full name is often used in the TA literature. And, of course, the three-circles model does show structure: each circle symbolizes the content of ego-states, in terms of feelings and experience.

However, when you think about it, you'll realize that the plain three-circles model *also* shows function. That follows from Berne's own definition of an ego-state, 'a consistent pattern of feeling and experience *directly related to a corresponding consistent pattern of behaviour'*. (Our italics). In other words, behaviour – function – is an essential part of the make-up of each ego-state. Thus, the first-order model turns out to be both structural and functional.

That means, among other things, that you can think functionally while using the plain three-circles model. You don't necessarily need to draw out Chapter 3's full picture of the 'functional model' with its five subdivisions. Berne himself used the plain first-order model almost all the time when analysing transactions – that is, communications between people. In this book's discussion of transactions (Chapter 7), we'll be doing the same.

Chapter 5
RECOGNIZING EGO-STATES

Eric Berne listed four ways of recognizing ego-states. He called them:

- *Behavioural diagnosis*
- *Social diagnosis*
- *Historical diagnosis*
- *Phenomenological diagnosis.*

Berne stressed that it was best to use more than one of these ways at a time. For a complete diagnosis, all four should be used, in the order shown above. Behavioural diagnosis is the most important of the four. The other three act as checks upon it.[1]

Behavioural diagnosis

In behavioural diagnosis, you judge which ego-state a person is in by observing his behaviour. As you do so, you can see or hear:

- *words*
- *tones*
- *gestures*
- *postures*
- *facial expressions.*

You would diagnose the person's functional ego-state by observing several of these at one time. Are the various clues consistent with each other?

For instance, suppose you see me sitting upright in my chair. My body is balanced evenly round a vertical mid-line. Both feet are planted firmly on the floor. From these body clues, you would form a first judgment that my behaviour is Adult.

You look at my face and see that my gaze is even, my facial muscles relaxed. As I begin speaking, you hear a level tone of voice. Now you have consistent clues from expression and voice tone that help confirm your behavioural diagnosis of Adult.

No one clue is sufficient in itself. Perhaps I am sitting there discussing the philosophy of the ego-state model. If you wrote my words down, they would seem Adult. But as you look at me, you note that I have now shifted my feet so that the toes of one are resting on the toes of the other.

I have tilted my head to one side. With the fingers of my left hand I am rapping on the arm of my chair. The clues from gestures and postures let you know that I am most likely in my Adapted Child, despite my Adult-sounding words.

Are there 'standard clues' to ego-states?

It's traditional for books about TA to give tables of standard clues for behavioural diagnosis. For instance, a wagging finger is said to fit with Controlling Parent. A whining voice is supposed to show Adapted Child. Shouting 'Wow! Yippee!' is given as a clue to Free Child, and so on.

But this idea of 'standard clues' raises a cautionary point, concerning the fundamental nature of the ego-state model.

The tables of 'standard clues' rely on the suggestion that when I am, for instance, in Adapted Child, I will be behaving *like a child* complying with the demands of his parents. Likewise, in Nurturing Parent I will be behaving *like a parent* looking after a child.

But this is not what the ego-state model says. What do I mean when I use the model's language accurately? When I say I am 'in my Child', I mean I am behaving, thinking and feeling as the child *I* once was – not just like *any* child. When I am 'in Nurturing Parent', I am behaving, thinking and feeling as one of *my* parents did, not just like 'parents generally'.

It follows that for a reliable behavioural diagnosis of my Adapted Child, you would need to know how *I* looked and sounded back in my childhood when I was obeying my parents. To recognize me in Nurturing Parent, you would need to have observed my mother or father as they looked after me all these years ago.

The set of behavioural clues that define my Adapted Child or Free Child will be different from yours, because we were different children. Because we had different parents, we will each have our own unique set of behaviours to mark Controlling or Nurturing Parent.

Does this mean that tables of 'standard clues' are useless?

Luckily, the answer is 'no'. There are some kinds of behaviour that are typical of *children in general* when they are obeying their parents or acting spontaneously. There are behaviours that *parents in general* will often show when they are controlling or nurturing their children. So if we look for these typical behaviours, we can make a useful start in diagnosing functional ego-states. We simply need to be aware that it is only a start.

To firm up our diagnosis, we need to get to know the person. Over time we can draw up a list of their own unique sets of behaviours signalling ego-state changes.

In this book we prefer not to give a table of 'standard clues'. Instead we invite you to draw up your own.

● Take a big sheet of paper and draw six vertical columns on it. Head the left-hand column 'Clues from – '. Head the other five columns with the five functional ego-state labels you used in the egogram – CP, NP, A, FC, AC.

Go back to the column headed 'Clues from – '. Evenly spaced down it, write five headings:

- *Words*
- *Tones*
- *Gestures*
- *Postures*
- *Facial expressions.*

Draw in horizontal lines so that you finish up with five empty boxes down each column. One box will be for 'Words', one for 'Tones', and so on.

The idea is that you fill in the behavioural clues *for yourself* in each column.

Let's take the Controlling Parent column. In it you enter behavioural clues that you show when you copy your parents' ways of controlling or commanding others. Think of situations when you typically get into CP. Maybe this will be when you are in charge of subordinates at work. If you are a parent, consider the behaviours you show when you are telling your children what to do.

Here are a few examples of what I might enter for myself under CP.

Words: 'Don't! Stop! Do! Here's how it is. That's good. That's bad. You should. You must.'

Tones: deep, resonant, harsh.

Gestures: chopping the air with right hand. Propping fingers together in a 'steeple' shape. Linking hands behind head.

Postures: leaning far back in chair. Tilting head back, 'looking down nose'.

Expressions: corners of mouth pulled down slightly. Eyebrows raised.

You may find that some of these clues fit for you too. The main thing is to draw up your own unique list. Go ahead with it now.

List only what people can see and hear. Do not interpret. For instance, under 'expressions', put down only what people see you doing with your face. Do not enter words like 'condescending, bossy, supercilious...'. These would be interpretations. As you look at me and listen to my voice, maybe you do feel I'm being bossy. But the bossiness is not something you are observing. It is an interpretation you are making inside your own head. Practise awareness always of what you observe. If you then go on to interpret your observation, stay aware that the interpretation is something separate from what you are observing.

When you have filled in the column for Controlling Parent, go on to fill the other columns in the same way. For Nurturing Parent, list the behaviours you show when you are copying your parents' ways of looking after people. Again, if you are a parent yourself, you are likely to do this some of the time when you are caring for your children.

For Adapted Child, put down behavioural clues you show when you are re-playing ways you had of following other people's rules when you were a child or rebelling against them. You may do this when you are conforming or rebelling in relation to your partner, to the boss at work, and so on.

For Free Child, think of a recent time when you acted like the child you once were, neither conforming to others' rules nor rebelling against them. Maybe you were on the roller-coaster, hid your face and shrieked as it shot down the slope. Perhaps you joined your kids in the paddling-pool, and before long you were yelling and giggling along with them as you splashed water over each other.

Recall that the functional divisions of Parent and Child can be shown in negative ways as well as positive ways. Are there behaviours you show when you're squashing people from negative Controlling Parent? If you're a parent, do you sometimes smother your kids? If so, how do they see and hear you in negative Nurturing Parent? Talking to the boss, do you sometimes crawl to him while wishing he were a hundred miles away? If you do, how would you see and hear yourself on a video film in negative Adapted Child?

In the Adult column, enter behaviours you show when you are acting as your here-and-now grown-up self. This might be a recent situation when you were at work exchanging information with a colleague. You might be in the supermarket buying what you had down on your shopping list. Perhaps you were reading this book and learning about ego-states. Remember that the Adult ego-state relates to here-and-now feeling as well as to thinking. Therefore, Adult behaviours may include expressions of emotion, where the feelings expressed are appropriate responses to the present situation.

Keep the Free Child column for behaviours you show when you are acting as though you were a spontaneous child again instead of a spontaneous grown-up. ●

Sometimes when you are observing my behavioural clues, you may need to ask more questions to help you judge which of my ego-states a particular behaviour fits with. Suppose you see me sitting in a drooping pose. I'm leaning forward, head in hands. The corners of my mouth are turned down. I'm sighing deeply, and my eyes are filling with tears.

From all these clues, you gather that I'm expressing sadness. But what ego-state am I in? Have I perhaps just heard that a close relative has died?

My sadness then would be an appropriate response to the here-and-now, hence Adult. Or have I got back in contact with some memory of a loss I experienced when I was a child, and which I've never let myself be sad about until now? In that case, my feeling expression is from Free Child. Still another possibility is that I am replaying a negative Adapted Child pattern, in which I droop and get sad as a way of manipulating the people around me.

To back up your assessment of my behavioural clues, you may want to ask questions about how other people relate to me. You may ask about my personal history and what my parents were like. And you may explore what I can re-experience from my own childhood.

● As we now look at Berne's other three ways of diagnosis, use them to check back on the behavioural list you have made up for yourself. Alter and add to your list according to what you learn. ●

Social diagnosis

The idea behind social diagnosis is that other people will often relate to me from an ego-state that complements the one I am using. Therefore, by noting the ego-state they respond from I can get a check on the ego-state I have come from.

For instance, if I address you from my Parent ego-state, chances are you will respond to me from your Child. If I open communication with you from my Adult, you will likely come back also in Adult. And if I approach you from my Adapted Child, you may well respond from your Parent.

Thus if I realize that people often seem to be giving me Child responses, I have reason to think that I may often be addressing them from Parent. Maybe I am a manager and find my team members either crawl to me or find ways of sabotaging my orders behind my back. Both of these look like Adapted Child responses. Possibly, then, I am being more of a Controlling Parent with them than I had realized. If I want to change the situation, I can list the Controlling Parent behaviours I have been using in the work situation. Then I can experiment with Adult behaviours instead. My team members' ego-state responses to me will give me a social diagnosis of how far I have managed to change from my Parental approach.

● Think of a recent occasion when someone seemed to be responding to you from their Child. What behavioural clues did the other person show that you interpreted as indicating they were in Child?

Did you invite this response by coming from your Controlling Parent or Nurturing Parent? If so, look at your list of behavioural clues and pick out how the other person saw and heard you in Parent.

How might you have altered your own behaviour to invite them to respond from a different ego-state?

Do the same exercise for recent occasions when someone seemed to be responding to you from their Adult; their Parent. ●

Historical diagnosis

In historical diagnosis, we ask questions about how the person was as a child. We ask about the person's parents and parent-figures. This lets us double-check on our impressions of the person's functional ego-states. It also lets us know about ego-state structure. *Historical diagnosis deals with both process and content.*

I might see you in a group, hunching forward with a frown on your face. Your hand is up covering your eyes. I hear you say: 'I'm confused. I can't think.' Behaviourally, I diagnose you to be in Adapted Child.

For historical diagnosis, I might ask you: 'How did you feel as a child when somebody asked you to think?' Or perhaps I might say: 'To me, you look like you're about six right now. Do you connect with anything in your childhood?' You might recall: 'Yes, Dad used to badger me to read books, then laugh because I couldn't get all the words right. So I used to play stupid just to spite him.'

At another moment you may be leaning back in your chair. Tilting your head back, you look down your nose at your neighbour. You tell her: 'What you've just said isn't right. Here's how things really are...' Perhaps she cowers down, hunches her shoulders and raises her eyebrows in Adapted Child style. Now I have both behavioural and social clues that you are in Controlling Parent. For a historical check, I might ask: 'Will you freeze your position a second? Did either of your parents sit like that when they were telling you how things were?' Maybe you burst out laughing and reply, 'Yeah, it's Dad again!'

Your reports thus give me a double-check on my behavioural diagnosis. Seeing you showing the sets of behaviours that I think fit with your Adapted Child ego-state, I have confirmed that your internal experience is a replay of the way you responded to parental pressures in your childhood. As you show Parent clues behaviourally, you report to me that you are copying the behaviours of one of your own parents.

● Look back at the list of behavioural clues you have drawn out for yourself. Use historical diagnosis to check the clues for each ego-state.

As you go through the Controlling Parent and Nurturing Parent clues, find if you recall what parent or parent-figure you are copying with each behaviour. What are the copied thoughts and feelings that accompany the behaviour?

For Adapted Child and Free Child clues, recall situations in your childhood when you behaved in that same way. How old were you? What were you thinking and feeling at these times?

For Adult, check that the behaviours you have listed are *not* a replay of your childhood nor a parental behaviour you have swallowed whole.

You may find that you want now to shift some of your behavioural clues to a different column. For instance, some of the clues you first listed for Adult may turn out to fit better in Adapted Child. ●

Phenomenological diagnosis

There are rare occasions when I may re-experience a past situation as if it were genuinely happening now. Berne wrote that '...phenomenological validation only occurs...if the individual can re-experience the whole ego state in full intensity with little weathering.'

Suppose you had just recalled that time when Dad badgered you to read and then laughed at you for getting the words wrong. If you and I were working in therapy, I might invite you to get back into that child-hood scene. Perhaps you put Dad in front of you in imagination and tell him what you couldn't tell him when you were six. You might find your-self first whining to Dad. Then you might re-contact furious anger and start yelling 'It's not fair!' while beating on a cushion in the way you would have liked to beat on Dad. You and I have a phenomenological diagnosis of part of the content of your Child ego-state.

Berne used the word 'phenomenological' here in a sense that is differ-ent from its usual dictionary definition. He never explained why he had chosen to do this. Simply register Berne's technical meaning as described above.

Ego-state diagnosis in practice

Ideally, we would use all four ways of diagnosis. But in practice, this is often impossible. When it is, we simply diagnose as best we can.

When we use TA in work with organizations, education or communi-cations training, or simply to help our own everyday relations with others, we need to rely mainly on behavioural diagnosis. Social diagnosis gives us some back-up. Even in TA therapy, behavioural diagnosis is the first and most important way of recognizing ego-states.

● To develop your effectiveness in using TA, practise continually refining your behavioural diagnosis. Keep referring back to the table of ego-state clues you have made out for yourself, revising it as you become more and more aware of your own ego-state shifts.

If you have the equipment, make audio or video recordings of your-self. Analyse your ego-state clues second by second. Relate your changes in words, voice tone, and body signals if you have video, to what you were experiencing internally.

Get into the habit of doing behavioural diagnosis when you are communicating with others. Do it when you are in meetings or classes. Do it when you are talking with your spouse, your boss, your employees. Keep track of the other person's ego-state shifts and your own. This may feel awkward at first. Persist until it becomes second nature.

Keep your analysis to yourself unless you are sure the other person wants to know about it!

Take every available chance to check your behavioural diagnosis against historical and phenomenological evidence. *But only do this with others if you have their explicit agreement in advance.* The more often you check in this way, the more accurate will your behavioural diagnosis become. ●

The executive and the real Self

For simplicity in our discussion of ego-states, we have assumed until now that a person can be in only one ego-state at a time. In reality, the position is less straightforward. It's possible for someone to *behave* in a way that fits one ego-state, while he *experiences himself* as being in a different ego-state.

For example, imagine that I am at work, discussing a planned assignment with a colleague. For the first few minutes of the discussion, I have my attention fully on the task in hand. If you were watching my behavioural signals, you would make an accurate assessment that I am in Adult. My own internal experience also is that I am in Adult – responding to the here-and-now, exchanging and assessing information.

But as the talk goes on longer and longer, I begin to feel bored. I say to myself in my head: 'I wish I were out of here. It's such a nice day outside – I'd rather be taking in a walk in the fresh air. But I don't suppose I can...' Now I am experiencing myself in Child. I am replaying times from my schooldays when I had sat indoors in class, feeling bored with the lesson and wishing I could go out and play.

Bored though I feel, I keep on with the job in hand. As you observe my behaviour, you see me continuing to exchange information. Thus outwardly, I am still behaving in Adult. But my behaviour no longer fits with the ego-state I am experiencing.

To describe this situation, Eric Berne suggested a distinction between the *executive* and the *real Self*.[2]

When an ego-state is dictating a person's behaviour, that ego-state is said to *have executive power*.

When a person experiences himself to be in a particular ego-state, we say he is experiencing that ego-state as his *real Self*.

Most often, the ego-state with executive power will also be experienced as the real Self. In the example above, as I began my work discussion, I had executive power in Adult and simultaneously experienced Adult as my real Self.

But then, as I began to feel bored, I shifted my experience of real Self into my Child ego-state. Nevertheless, I continued to act in a way that was consistent with Adult. Thus I kept executive power in the latter ego-state.

Suppose my work colleague had kept up the discussion for even longer. I might then have yawned and lost track of what he was saying. As he waited for me to reply to one of his points, I might have blushed and said 'Oh, sorry, I'm afraid I wasn't with you.' The other possibility is that I might have said, 'I need some fresh air,' excused myself, and gone outside. Now I would have executive power in Child, while also experiencing Child as my real Self.

● Make up at least three more examples that illustrate someone having executive power in one ego-state while experiencing a different ego-state as her real Self.

Do you recall any examples of this from your own experience in the past week? ●

Incongruity

This division between the executive and the real Self obviously poses extra problems for ego-state diagnosis. Since the ego-state with executive power is the one that determines behaviour, you would expect that the person's behavioural clues would indicate that ego-state. So long as that ego-state is being experienced also as real Self, your behavioural diagnosis will give you an accurate view of the person's internal experience.

But what if the person then switches into a different ego-state as real Self, while still keeping executive power in the original ego-state? How can you detect this using behavioural diagnosis?

The fact is that sometimes you can't detect it. This is most likely at moments when the person's overall behaviour is relatively inactive. For instance, you may see me sitting listening to a lecture. I'm sitting upright, not moving much and not saying anything. At first guess you might judge me behaviourally to be in Adult. But internally, I might be in a Child daydream. Without further enquiry, you have no means of knowing this.

More often, however, the person does show behavioural clues to indicate what is going on. You'll realize that when someone has executive power in a different ego-state from that experienced as real Self, there is a split between his behaviour and his internal experience. Externally, he usually shows this in the following way: his most obvious behavioural signals will indicate the ego-state that has executive power. But at the same time, he will exhibit other, more subtle signals that do not match those of the executive ego-state. Instead, they fit the ego-state he is experiencing as real Self.

In technical language, we say then that his behaviour shows *incongruity*.

When I was having the discussion with my colleague at work, my most obvious behaviours matched the ego-state I had in executive throughout, i.e. Adult. But if you had watched and listened to me with close attention, you would have noted some changes at the moment I became bored and shifted into Child as my real Self. Up to that point, the pitch of my voice had varied noticeably through my sentences. Now, it became monotonous. My gaze, which until then had been switching regularly between the work document and my colleague's face, now lost focus and stared at one point on the table. These incongruities would help you judge that I had shifted my experience of real Self out of Adult and into Child. If Child takes over as executive, you would see congruity again.

Recognizing incongruity is one of the most important skills you can develop as a user of TA. We shall return to this topic when we look at transactions in Chapter 7.

Berne's energy theory

Eric Berne developed a theoretical explanation of what happens when we shift executive power and our sense of real Self between one ego-state and another. It is outside the scope of this book to discuss his theory in detail. We will sketch it out in this section, and you can follow it up if you wish from the References list.

Berne followed Freud in hypothesizing the concept of psychic energy, or *cathexis*. He suggested that this energy exists in three forms: bound, unbound and free. The additional term 'active cathexis' is applied to the sum of unbound plus free cathexis.

To illustrate the difference between these three forms of cathexis, Berne used the metaphor of a monkey in a tree. When the monkey is sitting on a high branch, it possesses *potential* energy – the energy that would be released if the monkey fell to the ground. This potential energy is analogous to bound cathexis.

If the monkey then does fall off the branch, the potential energy is released as *kinetic* energy. This illustrates the nature of unbound cathexis.

However, a monkey is a living organism. Rather than just falling off the branch, it can exercise the choice to jump to the ground. Berne suggests that this spontaneous use of energy is analogous to free cathexis.

Each ego-state is envisaged as having a boundary. Free cathexis can move readily between one ego-state and another across these boundaries. In addition, each ego-state contains a certain measure of energy that is resident within its boundary. If that energy is not being used at any given moment, it corresponds to bound cathexis. When the resident energy is brought into use, the bound cathexis is converted to unbound cathexis.

For instance, when I began my conversation at work, I was actively using the energy that resides in my Adult ego-state. The cathexis in that ego-state was unbound. By directing my attention to the task at hand, I was also shifting free cathexis into Adult.

Throughout the scene in the example, I *could* have been employing some of the energy resident within the boundaries of my Parent ego-state. For example, I might have begun replaying Parental judgments in my head about whether I was working hard enough. However, I did not do so. The cathexis within the boundary of my Parent ego-state remained bound.

Berne hypothesized that an ego-state will take over executive power when it is the one in which the sum of unbound plus free cathexis (i.e. active cathexis) is greatest at a given moment. The ego-state experienced as real Self will be the one that at a particular moment has the greatest amount of free cathexis.

At the beginning of my discussion at work, I had executive power in Adult and also experienced Adult as my real Self. We can infer, therefore, that I had the highest active cathexis *and* highest free cathexis in Adult during this time.

When I started paying attention to feeling bored, I moved some free cathexis into Child. I continued doing so until that ego-state came to contain higher free cathexis than either my Adult or my Parent. At that point I began experiencing Child as my real Self. But I kept executive power in Adult, showing that I still had the highest total of active cathexis in my Adult ego-state.

If the discussion had gone on much longer, I might have unbound more and more of the bound cathexis resident in Child, until finally that ego-state had more active cathexis than Adult and so took over executive power.

You'll realize that it is possible at times for a person to have some active cathexis in *all three* ego-states at once. For instance, I might continue to keep executive power in Adult, exchanging technical information with my colleague. While doing so, I might also unbind some cathexis in Parent and start criticizing myself internally for not understanding the task well enough. At the same time I might unbind some Child cathexis and begin feeling ashamed that I was not complying with those Parental demands.

If you found this section's theoretical exposition tough going at first sight, don't worry – most people do. You may wish to return and read the section again when you are more familiar with the practice of recognizing ego-state shifts. If you like theory, you'll want to pursue the more detailed treatment of the topic in the writings of Berne and other theorists.

Chapter 6
STRUCTURAL PATHOLOGY

So far we have assumed that you can always tell the content of one ego-state clearly from that of another. We have assumed also that people can move at will between ego-states.

But what happens if the content of two ego-states gets jumbled up? Or if a person cannot get into or out of a particular ego-state? Eric Berne named these two problems *contamination* and *exclusion*. Together they go under the heading of *structural pathology*.[1]

Contamination

At times, I may mistake part of the content of my Child or Parent ego-states for Adult content. When this happens, my Adult is said to be *contaminated*.

It is as though one ego-state intrudes into the boundary of another. On the ego-state diagram, we picture this by drawing the circles overlapping

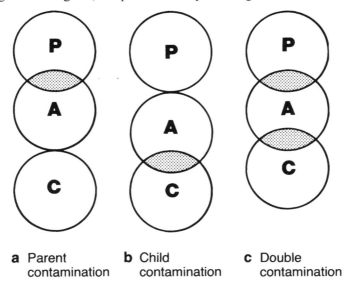

a Parent   **b** Child   **c** Double
contamination   contamination   contamination

Figure 6.1 Contamination

and shading in the overlap. The shaded area stands for the contamination.

Figure 6.1a shows Parent content intruding into the Adult, a *Parent contamination*. Figure 6.1b shows *Child contamination*. And Figure 6.1c shows *double contamination*, with both Parent and Child overlapping the Adult.

Parent contamination

I am in Parent contamination when I mistake Parental slogans for Adult reality. These are taught beliefs that are taken as facts. Berne called this *prejudice*. For example:

'All Scotsmen are mean.'
'Blacks are idle.'
'Whites exploit you.'
'The world is a bad place.'
'People can't be trusted.'
'If at first you don't succeed, try, try, try again.'

If I believe that a statement like this is an expression of reality, I am in contamination.

When a person is speaking about herself and says 'you' instead of 'I', it's likely that the content of what follows will be Parent-contaminated. For instance, Madge is describing her life:

'Well, you've just got to keep on going come what may, haven't you? And you can't let people see your feelings.' Chances are that Madge learned these two slogans from her parents. Probably, her parents also believed they were statements about reality.

The type of thinking involved in Parental contamination of my Adult is called *justification*. I use my contaminated Adult in the service of my Parent to gather only the information that would allow me to justify my prejudice.

Child contamination

When I am in Child contamination, I cloud my grown-up thinking with beliefs from my childhood. These are fantasies, evoked by feelings, that are taken as fact. Maybe I am leaving a party and hear people laughing as I walk out of the door. I say to myself: 'They're laughing at me behind my back!'

At that moment I am re-playing a time from my early childhood when I decided without words: 'There's something wrong with me. Everybody knows what it is except me. But nobody will tell me.'

I am not aware that it is a re-play. In contamination, I mistake that childhood situation for grown-up reality.

If I chose, I could go back into the room and check whether the party-goers had actually been laughing at me. If they truthfully said 'No', I might move out of contamination. Doing so, I would separate my Adult appraisal of the present situation from my outdated Child interpretations of the world. I might realize the people in the room had been laughing at a joke that had nothing to do with me. Perhaps I might also recall the childhood memories of being teased, but now would identify them as being from the past.

Suppose even that the people in the room had been having a good laugh at my expense. I might move out of contamination by realizing 'So what? If they choose to laugh at me, that's their affair. I'm still OK.'

But I might not be ready that day to move out of my Child contamination. In that case, when the revellers told me 'No, we weren't laughing at you,' I might say to myself internally: 'Huh! Bet they're lying just to be nice to me.'

Berne sometimes used the word *delusion* to describe the kind of belief that typically arises from Child contamination. Some common delusions are:

'I'm no good at spelling/arithmetic/languages.'
'People just don't like me.'
'There's something wrong with me.'
'I was born fat.'
'I can't stop smoking.'

When the content of a Child contamination comes from earlier childhood, the delusion is likely to be more bizarre. This is especially likely if the person's childhood was full of traumatic events.

'I can kill people just by being around.'
'If I drop dead, then Mother will love me.'
'People are trying to kill me with cosmic rays.'

The type of thinking involved in Child contamination of my Adult is called *rationalization*. I use my contaminated Adult in the service of my Child to gather only the information that would allow me to rationalize my delusion.

Double contamination

Double contamination occurs when the person re-plays a Parental slogan, agrees to it with a Child belief, and mistakes both of these for reality. For instance:

(P) 'People can't be trusted,' paired with:
(C) 'I can never trust anyone.' Or:
(P) 'Children should be seen and not heard,' paired with:
(C) 'To get by in the world, I have to keep quiet.'

Some modern TA writers see all contamination as being double. To them, the content of the double contamination consists of all the outdated, distorted beliefs a person holds about himself, other people and the world. In TA language, these are the *script beliefs*.[2]

● Take a piece of paper and head it: 'I am the sort of person who....'
Then take two minutes to write down all the ways you think of to finish
the sentence.

At the end of the two minutes, relax, breathe and look round the
room for a while. Help yourself get into Adult by sitting vertically balanced in your chair. Plant both feet flat on the ground. Look at what you
have written. For each of the ways you finished the sentence, check
whether it is a statement about reality or a Child contamination.

If you decide any of the statements about yourself do come from
Child contamination, think what the reality of the matter is. Strike out
the Child-contaminated words and put in the Adult up-date. For instance, if you had put:

'I am the sort of person who can't get along with people,'
you could strike it through and write instead:

'I am intelligent and friendly and I'm very well able to get along with
people.'
Update all Child-contaminated statements in this way.

Now take another piece of paper. Take two minutes to write down
all the slogans and beliefs you remember hearing from your parents and
parent-figures.

Get into Adult as before. Look through your list of Parental slogans
and beliefs. Check whether each one is a statement about reality or a
Parent contamination. If you decide there are any you want to up-date
to fit with grown-up reality, strike them out and substitute your new
version. For example, you might strike out:

'If at first you don't succeed, try, try, try again,'
and write instead:

'If at first you don't succeed, change what you're doing so that you
do succeed.'

This exercise is fun and useful. You can do it in moments of leisure. ●

Exclusion

Sometimes, Berne suggested, a person will shut out one or more of her
ego-states. He called this *exclusion*.

Figures 6.2a – 6.2c show the three possibilities for exclusion of one
ego-state. In the diagrams, we show the excluded ego-state by crossing
it through and drawing a line between it and the neighbouring circle.

People who *exclude Parent* will operate with no ready-made rules
about the world. Instead, they make their own rules afresh in every situation. They are good at using Little Professor intuition to sense what is
going on around them. These people are often 'wheeler-dealers'. They
may be top politicians, successful executives, or Mafia bosses.

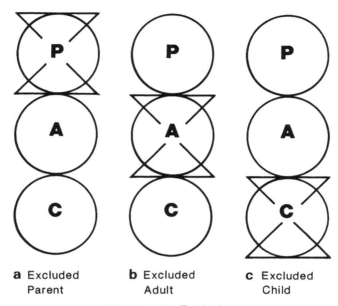

a Excluded Parent   **b** Excluded Adult   **c** Excluded Child

Figure 6.2   Exclusion

If I *exclude Adult*, I switch off my grown-up power of reality-testing. Instead, I hear only an internal Parent-Child dialogue. My resulting actions, feelings and thoughts will reflect this constant struggle. Because I am not using my full Adult powers of reality-testing, my thoughts and actions may even become bizarre, with the possibility that I may be diagnosed psychotic.

Someone who *excludes Child* will shut out any recall of experiences from his own childhood. He will also block out the related thoughts, feelings and actions that went with those experiences. Asked 'How was life for you as a child?', he will reply 'I don't know. I don't remember anything about it.' When we express feelings as grown-ups, we are often in our Child ego-state. Therefore the person with excluded Child will often be regarded as a 'cold fish' or 'all head'.

If two out of the three ego-states are excluded, the one operational ego-state is labelled *constant* or *excluding*. It is shown on the diagram as a thicker circle. Figures 6.3a – 6.3c show the three possibilities.

A person with *constant Parent* will deal with the world solely by accessing a set of Parental rules. Asked 'How do you think we could develop this plan?', she might answer 'Well, I think it's a good plan. Keep at it, that's what I say.' In response to 'How do you feel?', her reply might be 'At times like this, you've got to keep calm, haven't you?'

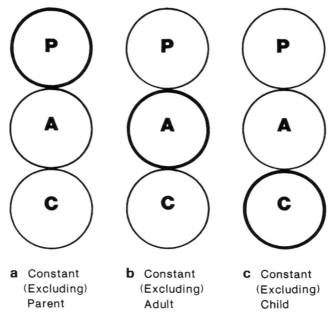

a Constant   **b** Constant   **c** Constant
   (Excluding)   (Excluding)   (Excluding)
   Parent   Adult   Child

Figure 6.3   Constant (excluding) ego-states

According to Berne, someone with *constant Adult* is 'unable to join in the fun'. Instead he functions 'almost solely as a planner, information-collector, and data-processor'.[3]

We'd add here: there are some points in Berne's writing when his illustrative examples don't seem to fit with his own definitions of ego-states, and we think this is one of them. His reference to the person with constant Adult as being 'unable to join in the fun' seems inconsistent with his own definition of the Adult. In terms of Berne's original ego-state model, the Adult is defined as that set of behaviours, thoughts and feelings that are a direct response to the here-and-now. It follows that a person *can* 'have fun' while in Adult, though the activities the person counts as 'having fun' are likely to be different according to whether he is in Adult or in Child.

● You may like to think how this applies to yourself. How does your 'Adult fun' differ from your 'Child fun'? Are there any ways of having fun that you enjoyed as a child and still enjoy as a grownup? ●

Anyone in *constant Child* will at all times behave, think and feel as though they were still in childhood. Meeting a problem, this person's strategy will be to escalate feelings. They will shut out both grown-up reality-testing and sets of Parental rules. This person is likely to be seen by others as 'immature' or 'hysterical'.

In our experience, exclusion is never total. Instead, it is specific to particular situations. For instance, if we talk of someone as 'having an excluded Child', what we really mean is that they seldom get into their Child ego-state, except in some select situations.

People cannot function without having some Child ego-state. They cannot function outside of institutions without some Adult. They don't get along in society very well without having some Parent.

Part III
COMMUNICATING

Transactions, Strokes and Time Structuring

Chapter 7
TRANSACTIONS

You are sitting reading this book. I come into the room and say 'Hi there!' You look up and reply 'Hi!' We have just completed a simple *transaction*.

A transaction takes place when I offer some kind of communication to you and you reply to me. In formal language, the opening communication is called the *stimulus*. The reply is called the *response*.

This gives us the formal definition of a transaction as *a transactional stimulus plus a transactional response*. Berne referred to the transaction as the 'basic unit of social discourse'.

You and I might continue our conversation. In response to your 'Hi!' I might ask 'Had a good day?' and you might reply in turn. Now we have a chain of transactions. The response of each one serves as stimulus to the next. Communication between people always takes the form of such chains of transactions.

In the *analysis of transactions*, we use the ego-state model to help explain how communication takes place – or, sometimes, fails to take place. We also consider how people may communicate on more than one level at the same time.[1]

Complementary transactions

I ask you 'What's the time?' You reply 'One o'clock.' We have exchanged here-and-now information. Our words are Adult. Our voice tones and body signals confirm the Adult ego-state.

Figure 7.1 pictures this Adult-Adult transaction. The arrows show the direction of each communication. In formal language, these arrows are known as *vectors*. The label S stands for 'stimulus', R for 'response'.

Asking you for information, I was in my Adult ego-state. We show this by having the 'S' vector start from the Adult circle on my PAC diagram. I intended my communication to be heard by you in your Adult. Thus the vector ends up at the Adult on your diagram.

With your matter-of-fact reply, you also were coming from Adult and expected me to receive the information in my Adult. Hence the 'R' vector comes back from your Adult circle to my own.

This illustrates one kind of *complementary transaction*. We define such a transaction as follows:

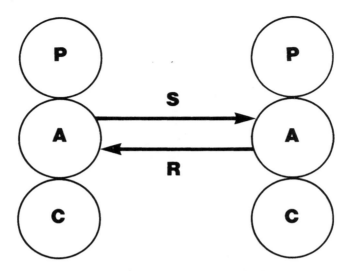

Figure 7.1 Adult-Adult complementary transaction

A complementary transaction is one in which the transactional vectors are parallel and the ego-state addressed is the one that responds.

Check how this definition applies to the Adult-Adult transaction in our example. Because a complementary transaction always has the vectors parallel in the diagram, it is often called by the alternative name *parallel transaction.*

Figure 7.2 shows another kind of complementary transaction. This time it features Parent and Child ego-states.

The store manager looks up as her assistant comes through the door, ten minutes late. Shifting into Parent, the manager growls: 'Late *again*! This just won't do!' Cowering and blushing in Child, the assistant mutters: 'Sorry. I'll try not to do it again.'

With her Parental growl, the manager means her stimulus to be heard by the assistant in Child. So the 'S' vector starts from her Parent circle and goes to the assistant's Child circle. Sure enough, the assistant does go into Child. His muttered apology is for the benefit of the manager in Parent. This is shown by the placing of the 'R' vector.

You'll see that this example also fits the definition of a complementary transaction.

● Two other possibilities for complementary transactions are Parent-Parent and Child-Child. Go ahead and draw a transactional diagram for each. Think of words to fit the stimulus and the response in each case. ●

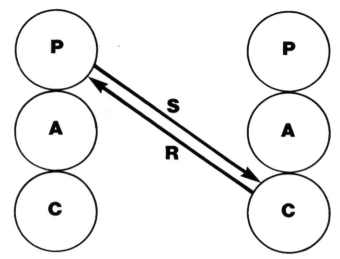

Figure 7.2 P→C, C→P complementary transaction

First rule of communication

A complementary transaction has a quality of expectedness about it. Asking you for information about the time, I expected you to respond from your Adult, and you did. When the manager told off her assistant, she expected a Child apology and she got it.

A conversation may consist of a chain of complementary transactions. If so, the whole chain will have this feel of something predictable happening.

Manager: 'I should think you would be sorry, too! This is the third time this week.'

Assistant (whines): 'I said I was sorry, boss. Anyway, I was held up in the traffic.'

Manager: 'Huh! Don't come that stuff with me! You should have left earlier...'

An exchange like this can go on 'in a groove' until the transactors run out of steam or decide to do something else.

This is formalized in the *first rule of communication*:

- *So long as transactions remain complementary, communication can continue indefinitely.*

Notice we don't say 'will continue', but 'can continue'. Obviously any conversation will draw to a close after a certain time. But as long as the transactions stay complementary, there is nothing in the process of communication to break the smooth flow of stimulus and response.

● Make up an imaginary conversation consisting of a chain of Adult-Adult complementary transactions. Do the same for Parent-Child, Parent-Parent and Child-Child exchanges. Check that each fits with the first rule of communication.

If you are working in a group, get into pairs and role-play each kind of exchange. See how long you can keep going in a chain of parallel transactions. ●

Crossed transactions

I ask you 'What's the time?' You stand up, go red in the face, and yell: 'Time! Time! Don't ask me about the time! You're late *again*! What on earth do you think you're doing?'

This is not the Adult response I had invited with my Adult question. Instead, you have moved into an angry Parent ego-state. With your scolding, you invite me to move out of my Adult and into my Child. The transactional diagram for our exchange is given in Figure 7.3.

This is an example of one kind of *crossed transaction*. It is so called because the vectors on the diagram for this type of transaction usually cross.

Also, 'crossed' is an apt description for the feel of this sort of exchange. When you cross our transaction by yelling at me, I feel as though you had cut across the flow of our communication.

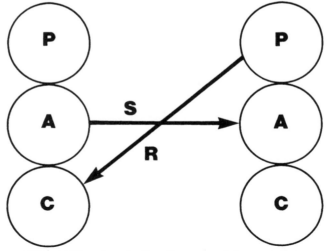

Figure 7.3 A →A, P →C crossed transaction

Formally, *a crossed transaction is one in which the transactional vectors are not parallel, or in which the ego-state addressed is not the one that responds.* Let's re-run the scene between the manager and the late-arriving assistant. The assistant comes in and the manager growls at him Parentally. But instead of cowering and apologizing, the assistant looks evenly at the boss. He replies in a level voice: 'I can hear that you're angry. I understand why you may feel that way. Please tell me what you want me to do about this now.'

He has crossed the manager's P – C stimulus with an A – A response. We see it in Figure 7.4. Once again the response cuts across the flow of communication that had been expected by the person sending the stimulus.

Second rule of communication

When a transaction is crossed, chances are that the person receiving the cross will shift into the ego-state that the crosser has invited. He will likely then move into a parallel transaction from that new ego-state.

When I ask you the time and you yell at me for being late, I will probably get into Adapted Child and apologize. Or I may be rebellious from that same ego-state: 'Well, I couldn't help it. Don't know what you're making so much fuss about.' My original Adult request for information is forgotten for the time being.

The *second rule of communication* says:

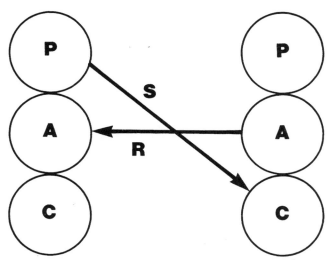

Figure 7.4   P → C, A → A crossed transaction

> • *When a transaction is crossed, a break in communication results and one or both individuals will need to shift ego-states in order for communication to be re-established.*

The 'break in communication' may be felt as only a mild jolt. At the other extreme, it may entail the two people storming furiously out of the room, slamming the doors and never speaking to each other again.

Eric Berne calculated that in theory there are 72 possible varieties of crossed transaction. Luckily, two of those are by far the most common in practice. They occur when an A – A stimulus is crossed either by a C – P response or by a P – C response.

● Make up your own example of an A – A stimulus crossed by a C – P response. How might the conversation continue if the person receiving the response moved into Parent and opened a parallel transaction from that ego-state?

Do the same exercise for an A – A stimulus crossed by a P – C response.

Make up an example of an A – A stimulus crossed by a C – C response. Draw the transactional diagram. Notice from this example that parallel vectors do not *always* mean a parallel transaction.

If you are working in a group, get into pairs and role-play a conversation in which every transaction is crossed. Each time the other person speaks, decide which ego-state she was inviting in you. Get into a different ego-state and respond. She then crosses you in return. See how long you can keep up the sequence without slipping into parallel transactions. When you finish, discuss your experience during this exercise. How was it different from the earlier one in which you kept all the transactions parallel? ●

Ulterior transactions

In an *ulterior transaction*, two messages are conveyed at the same time. One of these is an overt or *social-level* message. The other is a covert or *psychological-level* message.

Most often, the social-level content is Adult-Adult. The psychological-level messages are usually either Parent-Child or Child-Parent.

Wife: 'What did you do with my car key?'

Husband: 'I put it in your drawer.'

Simply looking at the written words, we'd say this was an Adult-Adult complementary transaction. And so it is, at social level. But now let's re-run it with sound and visuals.

Wife (harshly, voice tone dropping at end of sentence; tense facial muscles, drawing brows together): 'What did you do with my car key?'

Husband (voice quavering, rising tone; hunches shoulders, drops head forward, looks out from under raised eyebrows): 'I put it in your drawer.'

The psychological level is a parallel P – C, C – P exchange. If we put words to the messages conveyed at this level, they might read:

Wife: 'You're always messing with my things!'

Husband: 'You're always unjustly criticizing me!'

This gives the transactional diagram shown in Figure 7.5. We show the social-level stimulus and response as solid arrows and label them 'Ss' and 'Rs'. The dotted arrows stand for the psychological-level stimulus and response, 'Sp' and 'Rp'.

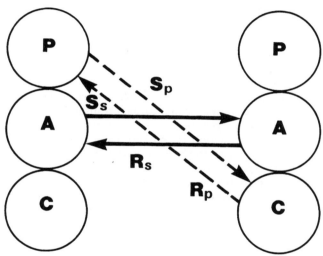

Figure 7.5 Duplex ulterior transaction: social level A → A, A → A; psychological level P → C, C → P

Any ulterior transaction like this, in which an A – A social message overlies a psychological-level exchange between P and C (less often, C – C or P – P), is called a *duplex transaction*.

Eric Berne pictured another kind of ulterior, which he called the *angular transaction*. Here, I may address you with a social-level stimulus from Adult to Adult. But my secret message is from my Adult to your Child. I hope you will take my invitation and come back with a Child response. The textbook example is that of a salesperson hoping to hook a customer into an impulse purchase.

Salesperson: 'Of course, Sir, that camera is the top of our range. But I guess it's probably beyond your budget.'

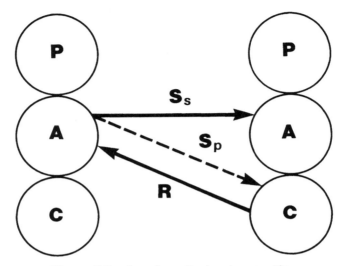

Figure 7.6   Angular ulterior transaction

Customer (defiantly): 'I'll take it!'

The transactional diagram at Figure 7.6 shows the angle between the 'Ss' and 'Sp' vectors which gives this transaction its name.

It's always possible that the exchange might have gone differently:

Salesperson: '...it's probably beyond your budget.'

Customer (thoughtfully): 'Well, now you mention it, you're right. It is beyond my budget. Thanks anyway.'

Here, the salesperson's manoeuvre has not succeeded in 'hooking' the customer into Child.

The example illustrates an important general point about transactions. *When I offer you a transactional stimulus, I can never MAKE you go into a particular ego-state. The most I can do is INVITE you to respond from that ego-state.*

Third rule of communication

Berne's *third rule of communication* says:

- *The behavioural outcome of an ulterior transaction is determined at the psychological and not at the social level.*

Berne wrote 'is determined', not 'may be determined'. He is suggesting that when people communicate on two levels, what actually happens is *always* the outcome of the secret messages. If we want to understand behaviour, we must pay attention to the psychological level of communication.

In TA language, we talk of this as *'thinking Martian'*. Berne pictured a little green man from Mars coming down and observing Earthlings. This Martian has no preconceptions of what our communications are supposed to mean. He simply observes how we do communicate, then notes the behaviour that follows.

● Practise being that Martian. Be aware always of the psychological as well as the social level. Check on Berne's striking claim. Was he right in believing that the behavioural outcome is always determined at the psychological level? ●

Transactions and non-verbals

In an ulterior transaction, the social-level message is conveyed by the words. To 'think Martian' at the psychological level, you need to observe non-verbal clues. These are found in voice tones, gestures, postures and facial expressions. There are also more subtle clues in breathing, muscle tension, pulse rate, pupil dilation, degree of sweating and so on.

We have referred to psychological-level messages as 'secret messages'. In fact they are not secret at all if you know what to look for. The non-verbal clues are there for you to read.

Young children read these clues intuitively. As we grow up, we are systematically trained to blank out this intuition. ('It's not polite to stare, dear.') To be effective in using TA, we need to re-train ourselves in noting body clues. You have made an important start by practising behavioural diagnosis of ego-states.

The truth is that every transaction has a psychological as well as a social level. But in an ulterior transaction, the two do not match. The messages conveyed by the words are belied by the non-verbal messages.

You learned in Chapter 5 that *incongruity* is the technical name for this kind of mis-match. To 'think Martian', practise watching for incongruity.

And this leads us to a more general point. *To analyse ANY transaction accurately, you need to consider non-verbal clues as well as the words.*

Recall our example of the wife asking her husband where her car key was. Simply reading the words, it looked Adult-Adult. With non-verbal clues, it turned out to be a Parent-Child exchange. We could have re-run the same words with different sets of non-verbals to give a different kind of transaction each time.

● Test this out. Keep the same words between wife and husband. Find out how many different kinds of transaction you can generate by putting in different non-verbals.

In a group, role-play the wife-husband transaction with different sets of non-verbal clues. ●

Options

No one kind of transaction is 'good' or 'bad' in itself. If you want to maintain a smoothly predictable flow of communication, keep your transactions parallel. If you find that your communication with someone is often jerky and uncomfortable, check whether you and she cross your transactions frequently. If so, decide whether to smooth out your interchanges by avoiding the crosses.

But suppose the office's prime bore is only too keen to set up a smooth flow of communication with you? Or imagine that your next-door neighbour has just settled down to start her daily tale of woe while drinking your coffee? In these cases you might be glad to interrupt their flow by deliberately crossing transactions.

In his article *Options*, Steve Karpman developed the idea that we can choose to transact in whatever way we like. In particular, we can choose new ways of transacting so as to break out of familiar, uncomfortable 'locked' interchanges with others.[2]

At work, Jack always seems to be apologizing or justifying himself. His supervisor takes the other end of this set-up by continually criticizing Jack and telling him how things should be.

Supervisor: 'You should have printed out this report in a bigger type size. It's too small for me to read.'

Jack: 'Oh, sorry. My mistake.'

Supervisor: 'Well, I suppose you couldn't help it. But I did put round an email about this.'

Jack: 'I do try to keep up with my emails, but honestly, I've been so busy lately…'

The two seem locked into this Controlling Parent – Adapted Child groove. If Jack finally decides to break loose, how does he use Options?

Karpman writes: 'The object is "to change what is going on and get free in whatever way you can." To get this you have to get the other person out of their ego state, or change your ego state, or both.' He sets out four conditions that need to be met for this strategy to work:

- *One or both ego-states must actually change.*
- *The transaction must be crossed.*
- *The subject must change.*
- *The previous topic will be forgotten.*

We would suggest that the first and second of these conditions are the essential ones. We think the other two are 'optional extras', though they will usually apply.

Supervisor: 'You should have printed out this report in a bigger type size.'

Jack (feigns falling off his chair. Lies on his back on the floor, waving arms and legs in the air): 'Aaargh!! Mean to say I've done it *again*? What on earth are you going to do with me, boss?'

Supervisor: (Cracks up laughing).

Jack has switched into Free Child playing instead of Adapted Child apologies. The supervisor in turn accepts Jack's invitation into Free Child.

Crossing from Free Child is only one option. Maybe Jack would first test out a more conventional cross from Adult:

Jack (takes his memo pad): 'Please tell me what size of type you want me to use for these reports in future?'

Any time you feel locked into an uncomfortable set of transactions, you have the option of crossing from any of your five functional ego-state parts. And you can address any of those five parts in the other person. Karpman even suggests that you can choose to use negative as well as positive ego-state divisions. Jack might have chosen to cross his supervisor's negative Controlling Parent scolding by coming back with a negative Controlling Parent squelch of her own:

Supervisor: 'You should have used a bigger type size.'

Jack (draws self up, frowns; speaks in harsh tone): 'Now just wait a minute. This is *your* fault. You should have made sure we all knew about this.'

We suggest that in beginning practice with Options, you keep to positive ego-state parts. In any case, use Adult to decide which way of crossing is most likely to get the results you want safely and appropriately.

You can never guarantee that your cross will succeed in inviting the other person into a new ego-state. If it doesn't, test shifting your own ego-state and issuing a different cross.

● Think of a situation where you have felt 'locked' into a familiar, uncomfortable groove of parallel transactions with someone. Maybe this will be a work situation. Perhaps it will be happening in a closer relationship. Using the functional model, locate the ego-states you and the other person have been coming from.

Now work out at least four ways you could use your ego-state Options to cross this flow of transactions. For the moment, list any possible cross even though it may seem 'way-out'.

From this list of possibilities, pick one or several that seem likely to get results safely and appropriately. If you have excluded any Options as being 'inappropriate', look at them again. Remember that you have the ability to use any of your ego-states. Sometimes an unconventional cross is the one most likely to work. Use Adult to separate the unconventional from the genuinely unsafe.

If you want to, go ahead in the situation to test out your Options and discover the results.

In a group, anyone who wants to can describe a 'locked' situation he wants to get free from. The other group members brainstorm possible Options, role-playing the cross in each case. The person who brought the problem should take note of each brainstorm idea but not pass comment on any until all suggestions have been given. It's then up to him to choose to take one, several or none of the suggestions. If he acts on a suggestion, the outcome is his own responsibility. ●

Chapter 8
STROKES

You are walking along the street. You catch sight of a neighbour of yours coming in the other direction. As you and the neighbour pass, you smile and say: 'Nice day!' Your neighbour smiles back and replies: 'Yes, it is.'

You and your neighbour have just exchanged *strokes*. A *stroke* is defined as *a unit of recognition*.[1]

We are all so familiar with this kind of exchange that we usually don't give it a thought. But suppose this scene were re-run with only a slight difference. As your neighbour approaches, you smile and say: 'Nice day!' Your neighbour makes no response whatever. He or she walks past as if you weren't there. How would you feel?

If you are like most people, you would be surprised at your neighbour's lack of response. You might ask yourself: 'What's gone wrong?' We need strokes, and we feel deprived if we don't get them.

Stimulus-hunger

Eric Berne described certain *hungers* that are experienced by all of us. One of these is the need for physical and mental stimulation. Berne called this *stimulus-hunger*.

He pointed to the work of researchers in human and animal development. In a well-known investigation, René Spitz had observed babies reared in a children's home.[2] They were fed well, kept clean and warm. Yet they were more likely to experience physical and emotional difficulties than were children brought up by their mothers or other direct caretakers. Spitz concluded that what the children in the home lacked was stimulation. They had little to look at all day except the white walls of their rooms. Above all, they had little physical contact with those who looked after them. They lacked the touching, cuddling and stroking that babies would normally get from their caretakers.

Berne's choice of the word 'stroke' refers to this infant need for touching. As grown-ups, he said, we still crave physical contact. But we also learn to substitute other forms of recognition in place of physical touching. A smile, a compliment, or for that matter a frown or an insult – all show us that our existence has been recognized. Berne used the term *recognition-hunger* to describe our need for this kind of acknowledgement by others.

Kinds of strokes

We can classify different kinds of strokes. They can be:

- *Verbal or non-verbal*
- *Positive or negative*
- *Conditional or unconditional.*

Verbal v. non-verbal strokes

In the example at the beginning of the chapter, you and your neighbour exchanged both verbal and non-verbal strokes. You spoke to each other, and you smiled.

You could have traded many other verbal strokes, ranging all the way from 'Hello!' to a full-scale conversation.

Different non-verbal strokes might have been to wave, nod, shake hands or hug each other.

Referring back to the last chapter, you'll realize that *any transaction is an exchange of strokes*. Most transactions involve both verbal and non-verbal exchanges. They may be wholly non-verbal. It's difficult to imagine a transaction that is purely verbal and has no non-verbal content, except perhaps a telephone conversation.

Positive v. negative strokes

A *positive stroke* is one that the giver of the stroke intends to be pleasant. A *negative stroke* is one that is intended to be painful. In our opening example, you and your neighbour exchanged positive strokes, both verbal and non-verbal.

If your neighbour had responded to your greeting by frowning at you instead of smiling, he would have given you a negative non-verbal stroke. He could have given you a more intense non-verbal by punching you in the eye. To give you a negative verbal stroke, he might have responded to your cheerful 'Nice day!' with 'Huh!', or even 'It was until *you* came along.'

In general, positive strokes help you feel good while negative strokes help you feel bad. You might imagine that people would always seek positive strokes and avoid negatives. In reality, we work by a different principle: *any kind of stroke is better than no stroke at all*.

This idea is supported by various gruesome studies of animal development. In one, two sets of baby rats were kept in identical featureless boxes. One group were given electric shocks several times a day. The other group were not. To the experimenters' surprise, the group receiving the shocks developed better than those left without this stimulation, painful as it was.[3]

We are like those rats. To satisfy our stimulus-hunger, we can use negative strokes just as readily as positives.

As infants, we know this instinctively. For almost all of us, in early childhood, there were times when we experienced not getting the positive strokes we needed or wanted. At such times, we figured out ways to get negative strokes. Painful as they were, we preferred them to the dreaded alternative of being left stroke-deprived.

In grown-up life, we may re-play this infant pattern, and continue to seek out negative strokes. This is the source of some behaviours that seem on the face of it to be self-punishing. We shall meet this idea again when we discuss games, rackets and script.

Conditional v. unconditional strokes

A *conditional stroke* relates to what you do. An *unconditional stroke* relates to what you are.

- *Positive conditional:* 'That was a good piece of work you did.'
- *Positive unconditional:* 'You're lovely to have around.'
- *Negative conditional:* 'I don't like your socks.'
- *Negative unconditional:* 'I hate you.'

● Make up five examples each of these four kinds of strokes – positive conditional and unconditional, negative conditional and unconditional. Think of non-verbal as well as verbal examples of each.

In a group, have a round in which each person gives a positive conditional stroke to the person on his or her left. Notice each time how the stroke is given and how it is received. When the round is finished, discuss what you observed. Then do a round in the other direction. Again discuss how the strokes were given and taken. ●

Stroking and reinforcement of behaviour

As infants, we test out all sorts of behaviours in order to find out which ones yield us the strokes we need. When a particular behaviour does turn out to earn strokes, we are likely to repeat that behaviour. And each time we get a further stroke from it, we become even more ready to use that behaviour in future.

In this way, stroking *reinforces* the behaviour that is stroked. Grown-ups, needing strokes just as much as infants, are just as ready to mould their behaviour in whatever ways seem most effective to keep the strokes coming.

Recall that we work by the principle 'any kind of stroke is better than no stroke at all'. If there do not seem to be enough positive strokes to fulfil our need for stroking, we will go ahead and seek out negative strokes.

Suppose I decided as a child that I had better seek negatives rather than risk being stroke-deprived. Then when I receive a negative stroke as a grown-up, that negative will act as a reinforcement of my behaviour *just as effectively as a positive stroke*. This helps us further in understanding why people may tenaciously repeat patterns of behaviour that appear to be self-punishing.

The same knowledge gives us guidance on how we can break free from these negative patterns. We can do so by changing our ways of seeking strokes. Instead of setting up to get painful negative strokes, we can set up to get enjoyable positive strokes. And each time we do get a positive stroke for a new behaviour, we become more ready to repeat that new behaviour in future.

Here, the *quality* and *intensity* of strokes are important. Neither of these concepts can be measured numerically. But it's common sense to suppose that people will attach different subjective values to strokes according to who those strokes come from and how they are given.

For instance, suppose we two authors get a positive stroke for the value of this book from a respected practitioner in TA who has just read it from cover to cover. We will certainly experience that stroke as higher in quality than one we might get from someone not interested in TA who has merely scanned the Preface and the chapter titles.

Again, imagine a child getting a negative stroke from his father for behaving in some way the parent doesn't like. That stroke may be conveyed by a stern voice and wagging finger. Or it may be accompanied by furious yelling and a physical assault. Clearly, the child is likely to experience the latter negative as more intense than the former.

Giving and taking strokes

Some people have a habit of giving strokes that start off sounding positive, but have a negative 'sting' at the end.

'I can see you understand this, more or less.'

'That's a lovely coat – did you buy it in the second-hand shop?'

Strokes like these are called *counterfeit strokes*. It's as though they give something positive, then take it away again.

There are also people who are very liberal in doling out positives, but do so insincerely. This person will spot you across the room, rush up and smother you in a bear-hug. Grinning from ear to ear, he says: 'Wow! I'm touched that you're here! The room just lit up since you came in! And you know, I read that article you wrote and I just thought it was *so* inspired, *so* insightful...' And so on.

Eric Berne described this as *marshmallow-throwing*. Other writers use the term *plastic strokes* to describe these insincere positives.

There are other people who go to the opposite extreme, and have trouble in giving any positive strokes at all. Typically, this person comes from a family where positive stroking was scarce. Cultural background also plays a part. Someone from Britain or Scandinavia is likely to be sparing with positives, especially positive physical strokes. Persons from a Latin or Caribbean culture, more liberal in positive stroking, may experience these northern people as cold and reserved.

When it comes to taking strokes, we all have our own preferences. I may like to hear strokes for what I do rather than what I am. You may prefer strokes that are unconditional. Maybe I am quite ready to take a fair number of negatives, while you feel upset at even a slight negative stroke. You may revel in being stroked physically, whereas I squirm at anything more than a handshake.

Most of us have certain strokes that we are used to getting. Because of their familiarity, we may devalue these strokes. At the same time we may secretly want to receive other strokes that we seldom get. Perhaps I am used to getting positive verbal conditional strokes about my ability to think clearly. I do like these, but I feel they are 'small change'. What I may really want is for somebody to tell me: 'You look great!' and give me a hug.

I may even go a step further, and deny *to myself* that I want the strokes I most want. Suppose that as a small child I wanted Mother to give me big hugs and she seldom did. To ease the pain of this, I might decide to blank out my longing for hugs. As a grown-up, I may keep up this strategy without being aware I am doing so. I may steer clear of physical strokes, denying to myself the need for them that is still unsatisfied.

In TA terms, we say that everybody has their preferred *stroke quotient*. The proverb 'Different strokes for different folks' is another way of saying this. We see, too, why the quality of a stroke can't be measured objectively: a high-quality stroke to you may be a low-quality stroke to me.

Stroke filter

When someone gets a stroke that doesn't fit in with her preferred stroke quotient, she is likely to ignore it or belittle it. We say that she *discounts* or *filters out* the stroke. When she does this, you are likely to observe some incongruity in the way she receives the stroke.

For instance, I may sincerely say to you: 'I admire your clear thinking in the way you've written this report.' But suppose when you were a child, you decided: 'I'm good-looking and I'm fun, but I'm no good at thinking.' My stroke doesn't fit with your preferred stroke quotient. Hearing my stroke, you may say 'Thanks.' But as you say it, you curl up your nose and twist your mouth as if something tasted bad. Another frequent way of discounting a stroke is to laugh or giggle: 'Thanks, huh huh!'

It's as if each of us holds up a *stroke filter* between ourselves and incoming strokes. We filter out strokes selectively. We let in those strokes that fit with our preferred stroke quotient, and keep out those that don't. In turn, our stroke quotient serves to maintain our existing picture of ourselves.

Some people decide as children that positive strokes are scarce or untrustworthy, and decide to survive on negatives instead. In grown-up life, they may continue to filter out positives and take in negatives. These people prefer the stick to the carrot. Offered a compliment, they are likely to discount it.

'I do like your hair.'

'Huh! Yeah, well, must remember to wash it sometime.'

Persons who have had an especially painful childhood may decide it is unsafe to let in any strokes at all. These people keep up a stroke filter so tight that they turn aside virtually all the strokes they are offered. In doing so they maintain their Child security, but deprive themselves of the strokes they could get quite safely as grown-ups. Unless they find ways of opening up their stroke filter, they are likely to end up withdrawn and depressed.

● In a group: think back to the rounds of the group in which you gave and took strokes.

Of the strokes given, which were straight and which were contaminated? Did anybody throw marshmallows?

When people were taking strokes, who received the stroke with open appreciation? Who discounted the offered stroke? How did you see and hear them doing so?

Did anyone openly refuse a stroke they did not want, rather than discounting it?

Now get into sub-groups of four. Decide whether, in the coming exercise, you will work with positive strokes only, or with both positives and negatives. If anyone in the group wants positives only, their want must be respected.

Take turns at being the 'stroke receiver'. For three minutes, the ' receiver' listens while the other three deliver verbal strokes. The strokes can be conditional or unconditional.

When the three minutes is up, the 'receiver' shares her or his experience with the others. Consider these questions:

Which of the strokes that I got did I expect to get?

Which strokes didn't I expect?

Which strokes did I like?

Which strokes did I dislike?

Are there any strokes I'd have liked to get and didn't?

Then go on to the next 'stroke receiver' and repeat. ●

The stroke economy

Claude Steiner suggests that as children, we are all indoctrinated by our parents with five restrictive rules about stroking.

- *Don't give strokes when you have them to give.*
- *Don't ask for strokes when you need them.*
- *Don't accept strokes if you want them.*
- *Don't reject strokes when you don't want them.*
- *Don't give yourself strokes.*

These five rules together are the basis of what Steiner calls the *stroke economy*.[4] By training children to obey these rules, says Steiner, parents ensure that '...a situation in which strokes could be available in a limitless supply is transformed into a situation in which the supply is low and the price parents can extract for them is high.'

Steiner believes parents do this as a way of controlling their children. By teaching children that strokes are in short supply, the parent gains the position of stroke monopolist. Knowing that strokes are essential, the child soon learns to get them by performing in ways that Mother and Father demand.

As grown-ups, says Steiner, we still unawarely obey the five rules. As a result we spend our lives in a state of partial stroke-deprivation. We use much energy in seeking out the strokes we still believe to be in short supply.

Steiner suggests that we are readily manipulated and oppressed by agencies that manage to set themselves up in the role of stroke monopolists. These may be governments, corporations, advertisers or entertainers. Therapists, too, may be seen as stroke purveyors.

To re-claim our awareness, spontaneity and intimacy, Steiner urges, we need to reject the restrictive 'basic training' our parents imposed on us regarding stroke exchange. Instead, we can be aware that strokes are available in a limitless supply. We can give a stroke whenever we want. No matter how many we give, they will never run out. When we want a stroke, we can freely ask for it and we can take it when it is offered. If we don't like a stroke we are offered, we can reject it openly. And we can enjoy giving ourselves strokes.

Not everyone in TA would go all the way with Steiner in his stark portrayal of the 'stroke economy' as a basis for commercial and political oppression. You can arrive at your own view.

What is certain is that most of us restrict our stroke exchange in accordance with our early childhood decisions. These decisions were made in response to our infant perceptions of pressure from parents. As grown-ups we can re-assess these decisions and change them if we want to.

● In a group: think back over the stroking exercises you have already done. In the whole group or in sub-groups, discuss how you experienced giving, accepting and rejecting strokes. Which were you comfortable with? Uncomfortable? When you were uncomfortable, do you trace that back to rules you remember your parents setting for you as a child? These rules are likely to have been have been modelled rather than expressed in words. ●

Asking for strokes

There is one myth about stroking that almost all of us are taught. The myth is: 'Strokes that you have to ask for are worthless.'

Here is the reality: strokes that you get by asking are worth just as much as strokes you get without asking.

If you want a cuddle, ask for it and get it, it is just as good a cuddle as one you get by waiting and hoping.

You may object: 'But if I ask, maybe the other person will give me the stroke just to be nice.'

Appraising from Adult, we can see this is a possibility. Alternatively, the stroke may be sincere. There's a good chance that others may have been wanting to stroke you but had been hearing their own Parent proclaiming 'Don't give strokes.'

You always have the option of checking with the other person whether or not their stroke was genuine. If it was not, you have further options. You can choose to take it anyway. Or you can reject their marshmallow and ask for a stroke that is genuine, from the same person or from someone else.

● In a group: get into sub-groups of four. If you like, they can be the same fours as for the exercise in which three people stroked and the fourth listened.

This will be an exercise in asking for strokes. Again, take turns to be the 'stroke receiver'. This time, the 'receiver' takes three minutes to ask the others for strokes.

The three strokers respond by giving the stroke asked for *if they are genuinely willing to give it.* If you are a stroker and are not willing to give the stroke genuinely, say to the person asking: 'I'm not willing to give you that stroke right now.' Do not offer any explanation.

When time is up, the 'receiver' shares his or her experience with the others.

Then go on to the next 'stroke receiver' and continue.

If you are working individually: write down at least five positive strokes you want but don't usually ask for. They can be verbal, non-verbal or a mixture of both. In the following week, ask at least one person for each of these strokes.

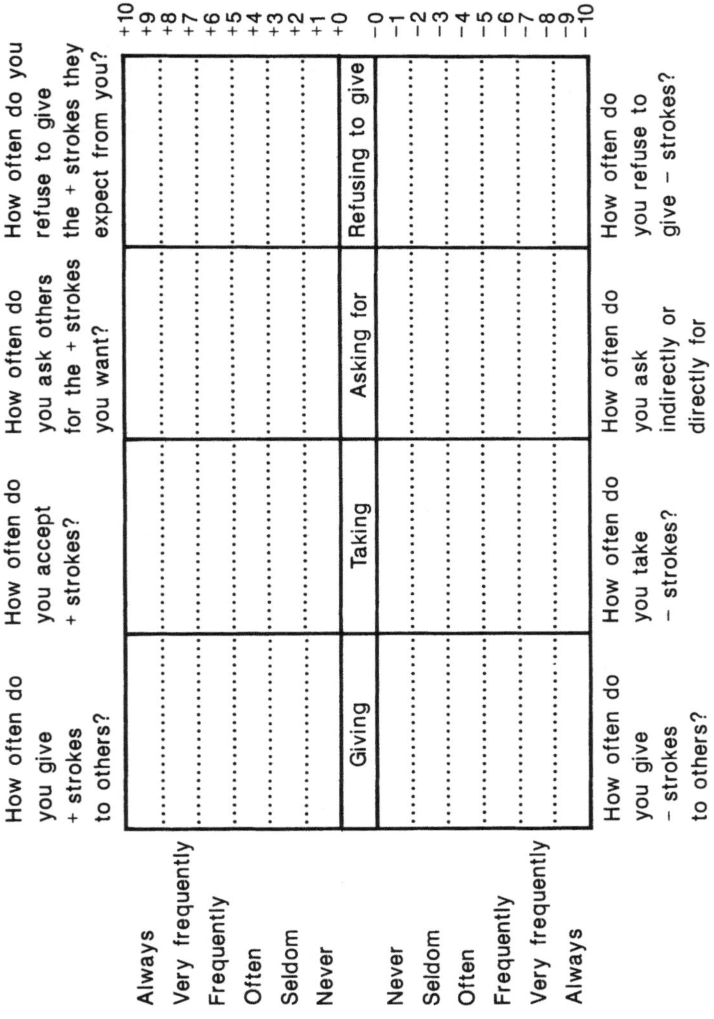

How often do you give + strokes to others? — Giving
How often do you accept + strokes? — Taking
How often do you ask others for the + strokes you want? — Asking for
How often do you refuse to give the + strokes they expect from you? — Refusing to give

How often do you give − strokes to others?
How often do you take − strokes?
How often do you ask indirectly or directly for − strokes?
How often do you refuse to give − strokes?

Scale: +10 +9 +8 +7 +6 +5 +4 +3 +2 +1 +0 −0 −1 −2 −3 −4 −5 −6 −7 −8 −9 −10

Top labels: Always, Very frequently, Frequently, Often, Seldom, Never
Bottom labels: Never, Seldom, Often, Frequently, Very frequently, Always

Figure 8.1 The stroking profile

If you get the stroke, thank the stroker. If you do not, it's OK to ask for Adult information about why the other person did not want to give the stroke you asked for.

The exercise is complete when you have *asked for* the strokes, whether or not you got all of them. When you have asked for all the strokes on your list, give yourself a stroke for doing the exercise. ●

The stroking profile

Jim McKenna has devised a diagram that he calls the *stroking profile*.[5] It analyses stroking patterns in rather the same way as Dusay's egogram analyses the use of functional ego-states, by use of a bar-chart.

To make out a stroking profile, you begin with the blank diagram shown in Figure 8.1. You draw bars in each of the four columns to represent your intuitive estimate of how frequently you: give strokes; take them when they are offered; ask for strokes; and refuse to give strokes.

You make separate estimates under each heading for positive and for negative strokes. The frequency for positives is shown by drawing a bar upwards from the central axis of the diagram. For negatives, draw the bar downwards.

Figure 8.2 shows one possible example of a completed stroking profile. This person doesn't give many positive strokes, but is liberal with negatives. She is keen to take positives from others, and often asks for them. She perceives herself as seldom taking or asking for negatives. Frequently she refuses to give positive strokes that other people expect, but she is not so ready to refuse giving negatives. How would you feel about relating to the person who drew this stroking profile?

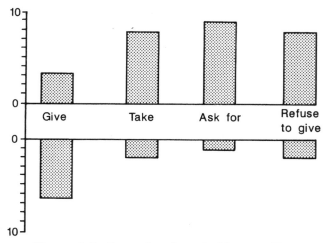

Figure 8.2 Example of a stroking profile

● Go ahead and draw your own stroking profile. Work rapidly and intuitively.

Under 'asking for strokes', in the negative column, include times when you set up in some indirect way to get attention from others that was painful or uncomfortable for you. At these times, you would be re-playing a Child belief: 'any stroke is better than no stroke at all'. In the same way, when you are completing the negative column under 'refuse to give', include occasions when you refused to give others negatives that they were setting up indirectly to get from you.

Jim McKenna suggests that the negative and positive scales under each heading show an inverse relationship. For instance, if a person is low in taking positive strokes, he will likely be high in taking negatives. Does this pattern apply to your completed stroking profile?

Discover if there is anything about your stroking profile that you want to change.

If so, the way to proceed is to increase the bars you want more of. This, says McKenna, is more likely to work than aiming to reduce the bars you think you have too much of. In Child, you are likely to be un-willing to give up old stroking patterns until you have something better to replace them.

If you do want to change your stroking profile, note down at least five behaviours designed to increase any bar you want more of. Carry out these behaviours in the coming week. For instance, if you decide you want to give more positive strokes to others, you might note down one compliment you could genuinely give to each of five of your friends, but have never given. Then go ahead and give those compliments during the week.

Is McKenna right in suggesting that as you increase the bar you want more of, the bar you want less of in the same column decreases auto-matically? ●

Self-stroking

There's no doubt that many of us as children were taught Steiner's fifth rule: 'Don't give yourself strokes.' Parents told us: 'Don't show off! It's rude to boast!' School continued the indoctrination. When we came out at the top of the class or won prizes on sports day, it was OK for others to say how good we were. But we ourselves were supposed to shrug and say modestly: 'Oh, it was nothing.'

As grown-ups, we may continue this Adapted Child behaviour. By the time we reach adulthood, most of us are so used to it that we belittle our own achievements even to ourselves. By doing so, we restrict an impor-tant source of strokes: *self-stroking*.

We can stroke ourselves at any time. Here are some ways of practising this pleasant skill.

● In a group: do a round of the group in which each person tells the group one good thing about himself or herself. Anyone who isn't willing to do this should simply say 'pass' when their turn comes.

It's OK for you to brag openly and sincerely during this exercise.

When each person is giving their brag, the rest of the group listen closely and show their appreciation of whatever good thing the boaster is sharing.

When you have the feel of telling the group one good thing about yourself, go on to a more extended brag exercise. In this, each member of the group in turn goes into the centre of the circle and brags non-stop for an agreed length of time. The bragger should talk directly to various people around the circle, loudly enough so that everyone can hear. If you run out of ideas, simply repeat yourself.

The rest of the group encourage the bragger by good-natured comments like: 'Yeah! Great stuff! Tell us more!'

A variant of this is the 'self-stroking carousel.' The group splits into two. Sit down in two circles, one inside the other. The inside circle face out, so that people are facing each other in pairs.

The group leader or a volunteer needs to keep time. For three minutes, the inside person of each pair brags continuously to the outside person, who listens and appreciates. When the time-keeper calls 'Change', the outside partner takes over as bragger while the inside person listens.

After another three minutes, the time-keeper calls 'Move.' Everybody in the inside circle shifts round one place to the left so that they get a new partner, and begins bragging again for another three minutes. Then the new outside partner brags for three minutes. The inside circle moves round one place again, and so on.

Continue until each person has bragged to everyone in the other circle, or as long as time and energy last.

Working individually: get a large sheet of paper. On it write everything good about yourself. Take as much time to do this as you want. If appropriate in your living circumstances, pin the paper up where you can see it often. Otherwise, keep it somewhere readily at hand. Each time you think of another good thing about yourself, add it to the list on the paper.

Make a list of at least five ways you can stroke yourself positively. Maybe you will take time to relax in a warm bath with your favourite music playing. Perhaps you will treat yourself to a special meal or a trip away somewhere. Don't regard these strokes as 'rewards' for anything. Give them to yourself for your own sake.

Use Adult appraisal to check that these strokes are really positives. Confirm that they are affordable, safe and healthy for you. Then go ahead and give yourself each one. ●

The 'stroke bank'

Though self-stroking is an important stroke source, it is never a complete replacement for the strokes we get from other people. It's as if each of us has a *stroke bank*.[6] When we get a stroke from someone, we not only take that stroke at the time it is given, but store the memory of it away in our stroke bank. Later we can go back to the bank and pull the stroke out to use again as a self-stroke. If the stroke was one we specially appreciated, we may re-use it many times over. But eventually these saved-up strokes lose their effectiveness. We need to top up our bank with new strokes from others.

Are there 'good' and 'bad' strokes?

It's tempting to assume that positive strokes are 'good', negative strokes 'bad'. In the literature of TA, this assumption has often been made. People have been urged to get and give unlimited numbers of positives, preferably unconditional. Parents have been advised that if they dole out a diet of positive strokes, their children will grow up OK. In reality, the matter is not so simple.

Recall that our need for strokes is based on recognition-hunger. Recognition in itself is a stroke. By censoring out whole areas of another person's behaviour that we regard as 'negative', we give only partial recognition to that person. A selective diet of unconditional positive strokes may not fit the person's internal experience. And so, curiously, he may feel stroke-deprived while apparently surrounded by positive strokes.

Conditional strokes, both positive *and* negative, are important to us because we use them as a way of learning about the world. This is true in our childhood and in our grown-up lives. As a child, I threw my bowl of strained carrots all over the floor. Mother yelled at me, and I didn't like that. I learned that if I wanted Mother to smile instead of yelling, I could do it by keeping my carrots in their bowl. Negative conditional strokes let me know what the limits are so I don't act in inappropriate ways. They are like having guard-rails on a bridge so I don't run off the sides.

For me as a grown-up, conditional strokes perform the same signalling function. A negative conditional tells me that someone doesn't like the way I am behaving. I can then take my own option of whether or not to change my behaviour so that they do like it. A positive conditional stroke signals that someone else does like what I am doing. Getting positive conditional strokes helps me feel competent.

If negative conditionals are absent, I don't know what the limits are and have no motivation to change a behaviour even though it may be counter-productive for me. This is what happens when people are 'too polite' to tell someone he has bad breath or needs to wash his shirts more often. This person may be avoided by others but not know why.

I do not need negative unconditional strokes, but even they carry messages that I can use for my own good. If someone tells me 'I can't stand you', I know that no change in my behaviour is going to alter their view. To look after myself, I need to withdraw from their company.

There is some evidence that when parents actually manage to rear children on an unchanging regime of positive strokes, the child eventually becomes unable to distinguish positives from negatives.[7] He has consistently had part of his internal experience denied or not recognized by his parents. This may lead to a range of problems in later life. Luckily, most parents follow their urges and enforce rule-setting by a mixture of negatives and positives.

A healthy stroke quotient thus will include both positives and negatives, conditionals and unconditionals.

This said, there are some good reasons for the traditional TA emphasis on positive stroking. Especially in northern cultures, people tend to be miserly with positives. In the office, the boss may tell his employees off when they come in late. He's less likely to praise them when they arrive on time. The schoolteacher, marking Johnny's spelling test, may point out the one word he got wrong and say nothing about the other nine words he got right.

Both boss and teacher would improve the effectiveness of their feedback by giving positives for what is good as well as negatives for what is bad. Overall, we need more positives than negatives if we are to feel consistently good about ourselves.

Strokes v. discounts

A *straight negative stroke* must be clearly distinguished from a *discount*.[8] A discount always entails some distortion of reality. In the context of stroking, I discount you if I criticize you in a belittling or distorting way. Unlike a straight negative stroke, the discount takes away from the reality of what you are or what you do.

We shall take a detailed look at discounts in a later chapter. For now, here are some examples of straight negatives contrasted with discounts.

- *Negative conditional stroke:* 'You spelled that word wrong.'
- *Discount:* 'I see you can't spell.'

- *Negative conditional stroke:* 'I feel uncomfortable when you do that.'
- *Discount:* 'You make me feel uncomfortable when you do that.'

- *Negative unconditional stroke:* 'I hate you.'
- *Discount:* 'You're hateful.'

Unlike a straight negative stroke, a discount gives me no signal on which I can base constructive action. It cannot, because the discount itself rests on a distortion of reality.

Chapter 9
TIME STRUCTURING

Whenever people get together in pairs or groups, there are six different ways in which they can spend their time. Eric Berne listed these six modes of *time structuring* as:

- *Withdrawal*
- *Rituals*
- *Pastimes*
- *Activities*
- *Games*
- *Intimacy.*[1]

These, Berne suggested, are all ways of satisfying *structure-hunger*. When people get into a situation where no time-structure is placed upon them, the first thing they are likely to do is to provide their own structure. Robinson Crusoe, arriving on his desert island, structured his time by exploring and setting up living quarters. Prisoners in solitary confinement make themselves out calendars and daily timetables.

If you have ever taken part in a group dynamics exercise where the group's time was initially completely unstructured, you'll know the discomfort of this situation. Typically, people will ask: 'But what are we here to *do*?' Eventually each group member will resolve this question by engaging in one of the six ways of time-structuring.

As we look at each of the six ways, we can relate it to what we already know about ego-states and strokes. The intensity of stroking increases as we move down the list from withdrawal to intimacy.

In TA literature, it has sometimes been suggested that the degree of psychological *risk* also increases as we go down the list. Certainly, the unpredictability of stroking does tend to increase. In particular, it becomes less predictable whether we will be accepted or rejected by the other person. From Child, we may indeed perceive this unpredictability as a 'risk' to ourselves. When we were children, we depended for our OK-ness on the stroking we got from our parents. We perceived possible rejection by them as a threat to our survival, hence as a genuine and immediate risk.

For us as grown-ups, there is no such risk in *any* of the ways of time-structuring. Nobody can 'make' us feel. If another person chooses to act in a rejecting way towards me, I can enquire why and ask them to change.

If they do not, I can leave the relationship with that person and find another relationship where I am accepted.

Withdrawal

Let's suppose I am taking part in that group dynamics exercise. A dozen people, including me, have turned up in a room. We have no agenda other than to be there. For a time, we sit in silence.

I may turn my attention inward. Perhaps I carry on a monologue in my head. 'Wonder what we're here for? Ah well, I suppose somebody else knows. Ouch, this chair is uncomfortable! Maybe if I asked that woman over there, she'd tell me what this exercise is for...'

Maybe I go away from the room in my imagination. While I sit there in body, I'm off in spirit to next year's holiday or yesterday's row with the boss.

I am engaging in *withdrawal*. When a person withdraws, she may stay with the group physically, but does not transact with other group members.

While I withdraw, I may be accessing any ego-state. It may not be possible for others to make a behavioural diagnosis of my ego-state at this time, because of the lack of external clues. During withdrawal, the only strokes I can get or give are self-strokes. Since I do not engage with others, I avoid the psychological 'risk' of rejection that I may perceive in my Child. Some people habitually withdraw in groups because they decided as children that it was risky to exchange strokes with others. They may develop a large and well-used *stroke bank*. Like a camel in the desert, these people may be happy to go for long periods without any external stroke input. Nevertheless, if I withdraw for a lot of the time, I run the eventual risk of drawing down my stroke bank and becoming stroke-deprived.

Rituals

As we sit there in the group room, a man across from me in the group breaks the silence. Turning to his neighbour, he says: 'Well, I suppose we might as well introduce ourselves. I'm Fred Smith. Nice to meet you.' He offers his hand for a handshake.

Fred has chosen to structure his time with a *ritual*. This is a familiar social interaction that proceeds as if it were pre-programmed.

All children learn the rituals appropriate in their family culture. If you are from a Western country and someone holds out their hand for a handshake, you know you are supposed to take the hand and shake it. An Indian child learns the *namaste* gesture in the same way. British girls and boys learn that when somebody says 'How do you do?,' you respond by asking the same ritual question. Rituals vary in complexity. Simplest of all is the American one-stroke exchange: 'Hi!' 'Hi!' At the other extreme are some religious rituals. Here, the sequence actually is written down, and the priest and worshippers follow detailed directions during a ritual that may last for hours.

Structurally, the programme for rituals belongs in the Parent ego-state. In carrying out a ritual, we are in Child listening to these Parent directions or operating from Parent directly. Functionally, rituals are usually performed in Adapted Child. Most often, a ritual brings comfortable results in terms of our adapting to expected norms, and so will be classified as positive Adapted Child behaviour. Because of the stereotyped words, tones and body signals used in rituals, it may be difficult to confirm this with behavioural diagnosis.

Rituals are perceived from Child as involving more psychological 'risk' than withdrawal. If you say 'hello' the other person may or may not respond. However, rituals do provide familiar positive strokes. The participants in a ritual will often keep a close count of the strokes exchanged. Though low in intensity, these strokes can be important as a way of topping up our stroke bank. If you doubt this, imagine how you might feel if you held out your hand for a handshake and the other person ignored you. The predictability of ritual strokes may be a plus for people who decided in childhood that it was risky to exchange strokes within a closer relationship.

Pastimes

Back in the group, the ice has been broken. Now several people are chatting about their experiences in groups.

'I did a group like this before, in high school. We never did get to know what it was about.'

'Yes, I know what you mean. What I don't like is the long silences.'

'Tell you what, I think it's easy money for the people who set these things up. Why, when I enrolled for this group I expected that...' And so on.

The speakers have moved into a *pastime*. Often, we use the verb and say they are *pastiming*.

A pastime, like a ritual, proceeds in a way that is familiar. But the content of a pastime is not programmed so strictly as that of a ritual. The pastimers have more leeway to make their own embellishments.

In any pastime, the participants talk *about* something but engage in no action concerning it. The pastimers in the group exercise are discussing the group and groups generally. They give no sign that they are going to do anything about what is happening in the group.

A frequent clue to pastiming is 'pastime = past time'. Most often, pastimers will be discussing what happened yesterday somewhere out there, rather than now and here. Pastiming is typified by the light superficial conversation heard at cocktail parties.

Berne gave witty names to some familiar pastimes. Men may pastime around 'General Motors', while women may prefer 'Kitchen' or 'Wardrobe' if they are comfortable in traditional sex roles. When parents get together, there's usually a session of 'P.T.A.' (Parent-Teacher Association):

'Johnny's just getting his second set of teeth through. We were up most of the night last night.'

'Oh, yes, I remember when our two were that age...'

For Britishers, the best-known pastime of all is one that Berne didn't name: 'The Weather'.

Pastimes are usually conducted from Parent or Child ego-states. In a Parental pastime, people voice sets of pre-judged opinions about the world.

'The young people today, don't know what they're coming to.'

'Yes, I know. Why, only yesterday...'

Child pastimers go back and re-play thoughts and feelings from when they were children.

'This silence is making me feel really uncomfortable.'

'Mm. I wonder what we're supposed to be doing here?'

Some pastimes sound on the social level as though they were Adult. But when you 'think Martian', they turn out to be Child.

'You know, as we sit here, I'm experiencing that we may all be in our Adapted Child. What do you think?'

'Well, I think I'm in my Adult now. But maybe I was in Child a few minutes ago.'

This is the pastime that Berne called 'TA Psychiatry'. The social-level exchange of information is covering the real agenda, which is a Child avoidance of what is really going on between the group members. Obviously, we would need to check this assessment by observing tones and non-verbal signals.

Pastiming yields mainly positive strokes, with some negatives. By comparison with strokes from rituals, pastime strokes are more intense but somewhat less predictable. Therefore we perceive them from Child as carrying a slightly greater 'risk'.

In social interchanges, pastiming serves an additional function. It is a way in which people 'sound each other out' as possible partners for the more intense stroke exchanges that take place in games or intimacy. We will say more about these below.

Activities

A woman across the group from me speaks up. 'So far, we've been spending our time talking about what we might be supposed to do here. But I'm wondering what we *are* going to do. Here's a suggestion. How's about we brainstorm for two minutes on things we could do, then take a vote and do one of those things?'

Her neighbour responds: 'I think that's a good idea. I'll stand by the board and be the recorder.' People all round the group agree, and start calling out their suggestions.

Now we are in *activity*. The communication between the group members is directed at achieving a goal, not just talking about it. This is the difference between activities and pastiming. In activity, people are directing their energy towards some material outcome. We are likely to be in activity for much of the time at our workplace. Other examples would be repairing an appliance, changing the baby or writing a cheque. Someone who plays a sport 'seriously', or works hard to become a skilful player of a musical instrument, is engaging in an activity.

The Adult is the predominant ego-state in activity. This follows from the fact that activities are concerned with achieving here-and-now goals. Sometimes in activity we may follow appropriate rules. At such times we switch into positive Adapted Child or positive Parent.

Strokes from activity can be both conditional positive and conditional negative. They are usually delayed strokes, given at the end of the activity for a job well or poorly done. Both the intensity of stroking and the degree of psychological 'risk' perceived in activity can be greater or less than in pastiming, depending on the nature of each.

Games

In the group room, the brainstorm is over. A dozen or so suggestions are scribbled on the board. 'OK, now let's vote,' says the recorder. 'I'll call out each suggestion. Hold your hand up if it's one you want to do.'

Voting completed, the recorder counts. 'Well, that's clear,' he says. 'We start by having a round of the group. Each of us is going to say who we are and what we want to get from being here.'

'Just a minute,' comes another voice. Everybody looks round at the speaker, a man who has told us his name is John. Right now he is leaning forward, elbows on knees. He scrunches his brows together in a frown. 'I'm utterly confused by all this. Who said the vote was to be binding on everybody?'

The recorder screws his mouth up into a tense smile, tilts his head back and looks down his nose at John. 'Ah, well, you see,' he says, 'that's just how things are with votes. The minority have to go with the majority. It's called democracy. Clear now?'

'No, sorry, I'm not,' John says. 'In fact, you've confused me even more. What's democracy got to do with it?' He screws up his brow even tighter and squints across the room.

The recorder sags and gives out a sigh. Shrugging his shoulders, he looks around the group. 'Well, so much for that idea,' he says sadly.

But now John, too, changes his position. Sitting up straight, he widens his eyes, while his mouth falls open. He slaps himself on the side of the head. 'Oh, *no*,' he says. 'This is the story of my life. Look, I'm afraid I've messed up this exercise for all you people. I'm *sorry*, I really am.'

John and the recorder have each just played a *game*.

The analysis of games is a major part of TA theory. We shall look at games in detail in later chapters. For now, simply notice the main features of that interchange between John and the recorder.

They exchanged a sequence of transactions. At the end of that sequence, they both felt bad.

Immediately *before* they got into those bad feelings, they seemed quite suddenly to switch roles. John had started by protesting his confusion and sounding irritable. He switched into self-blaming and sounding apologetic. At the same moment the recorder switched from patronising explanation into drooping helplessness.

For both parties, there was a split second just before the switch when each had a sense that something unexpected was happening. Had they had time to express this sense in words, each might have asked: 'What on earth is going *on* around here?'

Despite this sense of the unexpected, both John and the recorder will actually have run similar sequences many times before. The surroundings and the people may be different from one occasion to the next. But each time, the nature of the switch will be the same, and so will the bad feelings that each person experiences.

In fact, John and the recorder had signalled their willingness to play the game with each other right at the beginning of their interchange. They did this by exchanging ulterior transactions. Their social-level messages sounded like an exchange of information. But at psychological level, John invited the recorder to play the game, and the recorder accepted.

We all play games from time to time. When you are identifying your own time-structuring patterns in the exercises below, label as 'Games' the time you spend in the kind of interchange we have just described. It's repetitive for you. It ends up with you feeling bad. And at some point, it entails a moment when you ask yourself 'What just happened?' and get a sense of having switched roles in some way.

All games are re-plays of childhood strategies that are no longer appropriate to us as grown-ups. Therefore, by definition, games are played from any negative ego-state part: negative Adapted Child, negative Controlling Parent or negative Nurturing Parent. Also by definition, games cannot be played from Adult.

Games always entail an exchange of *discounts*. These discounts are on the psychological level. At social level, the players experience the game as an exchange of intense strokes. In the opening stages of a game, the strokes experienced may be either positive or negative. At the close of the game, both players experience intense negative strokes. The degree of psychological 'risk' perceived is greater than in activities or pastimes.

Intimacy

As I listen to John protesting his confusion then switching to apology, I start to feel angry. Instead of holding down my anger, I express it. Turning to John, I tell him: 'I'm really angry at you for what you've just said. You can think just as well as anybody else. I want you to get on and do it.' I speak these words in a harsh, loud voice. Leaning over toward John, I feel myself going red in the face. My tones and body signals are congruent with what I am expressing.

John's face goes as red as mine. Leaning towards me and almost rising from his chair, he waves his arms above his head. 'Well, I'm angry too!' he yells. 'I've been feeling that way since I came in here. Yes, I can think, and right now I want some space to myself to do that without you shouting at me.'

John and I have been in *intimacy*. We have expressed our authentic feelings and wants to each other without censoring.

In intimacy, there are no 'secret messages'. The social level and the psychological level are congruent. That is an important difference between intimacy and games.

Just as important is that in intimacy, the feelings expressed are appropriate to finish the situation. When John and I got angry with each other, each let the other know what he wanted through emotions as well as words. Neither of us could *make* the other behave in a particular way. But we had each made as clear as possible what we wanted, on a feeling as well as a thinking level.

By contrast, the feelings experienced at the end of a game do nothing to resolve the situation for the players. We know this because games are played over and over again.

When we come to look in more detail at games and rackets, we shall return to this distinction between productive and unproductive feelings.

Berne's choice of the word *intimacy* here should be understood as a specialized technical usage. Intimacy as a time structure may or may not have much to do with 'intimacy' in the usual dictionary sense. When people are being sexually or personally 'intimate', they may perhaps also be sharing their feelings and wants openly with each other. In that case, they are structuring their time in intimacy. But it's common also for intense emotional relationships to be founded mainly on game-playing.

Games are sometimes used as a substitute for intimacy. They involve a similar intensity of stroking (though game strokes are mainly negative) but without the same degree of perceived 'risk'. In a game, each person shifts the responsibility for the outcome to the other. In intimacy, each accepts his own responsibility.

Writing of the ego-states concerned in intimacy, Berne said:

'Intimacy is a candid Child-to-Child relationship with no games and no mutual exploitation. *It is set up by the Adult ego-states of the parties concerned*, so that they understand very well their contracts and commitments with each other...'

We have supplied the italics in this quotation to emphasize the importance of the Adult in intimacy. Some TA writers since Berne have simplified his presentation and portrayed intimacy as being *purely* a Child-Child interchange. As usual, Berne's original idea turns out to be more subtle and significant. To relate in intimacy, we first need to establish the relationship with our full Adult powers of thinking, behaving and feeling. Within this protective framework, we can go back into Child if we want to, sharing and satisfying some of the unmet needs we carry from our early years.

Some TA writers have suggested that intimacy also entails mutual caring and protection from Parent.[2] The message from this ego-state is: 'I won't discount you, and I won't allow you to discount me.'

Stroking in intimacy is more intense than in any other form of time-structuring. Either positive or negative strokes may be exchanged. But there will be no discounting, since intimacy is by definition an exchange of authentic wants and feelings.

When we were describing intimacy earlier in this section, we deliberately chose an example in which the strokes exchanged were straight negatives. This was to counter the impression, given by some TA writers after Berne, that intimacy must *always* be a kind of seventh-heaven of positive stroking.

When intimacy does entail an exchange of positive strokes, they are experienced as especially pleasant and gratifying. For example, we can imagine one way in which that scene in the group might continue. Having let fly my anger against John, I relax, look him in the eye and smile. I say: 'Hey, I feel I know you better now. I'm glad you were open with me about how you felt.' John looks back at me just as directly. He smiles and says: 'I'm glad too. And I like that you listened to me.' We lean towards each other and clasp hands.

Because intimacy is not pre-programmed, it is also the most unpredictable of all the ways of time-structuring. Thus from Child, I may perceive intimacy as being the most 'risky' way to relate to another person. My fear may be if I'm fully open and honest, the other person may not be. Paradoxically, when it is reciprocated, it is actually the *least* risky. When I and the other person are in intimacy, we are communicating without discounting. Therefore, the outcome of intimacy must always be constructive for the people concerned. Whether or not they will always find it *comfortable* is another matter. It is likely to depend on whether the strokes exchanged are straight positives or straight negatives.

● Make a 'time-structuring pie chart'. To do this, draw a circle. Divide the circle into slices representing the amounts of your typical waking day that you spend in the six different forms of time structuring.

Find out whether you want to change the look of your time-structuring pie. If so, draw the version you want to achieve. Write down at least five ways in which you will increase the amount of the time-structure you most want to increase. In the coming week, carry out these behaviours. Then re-draw your time-structuring pie.

Be alert each day to how you and others structure time. Analyse time-structuring during meetings, at work, in conversations with neighbours, at parties, or wherever. Do not tell others what you are doing unless you are sure they want to know.

In a group: make up sub-groups of six. Choose any topic of conversation. Talk about it for three minutes, with each person role-playing one of the six ways of time-structuring. At the end of time, discuss your experience. Choose another topic, shift time-structuring roles and repeat.

In the large group, count off round the room from 'one' to 'six'. All the 'ones' are to role-play withdrawing, the 'twos' rituals, the 'threes' pastiming, and so on. Then mill around and have a 'time-structure cocktail party' for five minutes, with everyone in role. At the end of time, share your experience with the rest of the group. ●

Part IV
WRITING OUR OWN LIFE-STORY

Life-Scripts

Chapter 10
THE NATURE AND ORIGINS OF LIFE-SCRIPT

You have written your own life-story.

You began writing it at birth. By the time you were four years old, you had decided on the essentials of the plot.

At seven, you had completed your story in all its main details. From then until you were about twelve years of age, you polished it up and added a few extras here and there. In adolescence you revised your story, updating it with more real-life characters.

Like all stories, your life-story has a beginning, a middle and an end. It has its heroes, heroines, villains, stooges and walk-on characters. It has its main theme and its sub-plots. It may be comic or tragic, enthralling or boring, inspiring or inglorious.

Now that you are an adult, the beginnings of your story are out of reach of your conscious memory. You may not have been aware, until now, that you wrote it at all. Yet without that awareness, you are likely to live out the story you composed all those years ago. That story is your *life-script*.

● Suppose for now that you have, indeed, written the story that is your own life.

Take pencil and paper and write down answers to the following questions. Work quickly and intuitively, accepting the first answers you bring to mind.

What is the title of your story?

What kind of story is it? Happy or sad? Triumphant or tragic? Interesting or boring? Use your own words, putting them down just as you bring them to mind.

In a few sentences, describe the closing scene: how does your story end?

Keep your answers. You can refer to them again as you read more about the nature of life-script. ●

In everyday TA language, we usually refer to life-script simply as *script*.

Nature and definition of life-script

The theory of script was first developed by Eric Berne and his students, notably Claude Steiner, in the mid-1960s. Since then many writers have built on those original ideas. The concept of script has grown in importance as a part of TA theory, until now it ranks with the ego-state model as a central idea of TA.[1]

In *Principles of Group Treatment*, Berne defined life-script as 'an unconscious life plan'. Later, in *What Do You Say After You Say Hello*, he gave a more complete definition: 'a life plan made in childhood, reinforced by the parents, justified by subsequent events, and culminating in a chosen alternative'.

To develop understanding of script, it's worth taking time to explore the detail of these definitions.

Script is a life plan

The notion that people's grown-up life patterns are affected by childhood experience is central not only to TA but to many other psychological approaches. Where TA script theory is distinctive is in its suggestion that the child lays down a *specific plan* for her life, rather than simply a general view of the world. This life plan, the theory suggests, is laid out in the form of a drama, with a clear-cut beginning, middle and end.

Script is directed towards a payoff

Another distinctive assertion of script theory is that the life plan 'culminates in a chosen alternative'. When the young child writes his life drama, he writes the closing scene as an integral part of it. All the other parts of the plot, from the opening scene onwards, are then planned to lead up to this final scene.

In the technical language of script theory, this closing scene is called the *payoff* of the script. The theory suggests that when as adults we play out our script, we are unawarely choosing behaviours that will bring us closer to our script payoff.

Script is decisional

Berne defines the script as 'a life plan *made* in childhood'. This is to say that the child *decides* upon the life plan. It is not determined solely by external forces such as the parents or by the environment. In technical TA language, we express this by saying that the script is *decisional*.

It follows that even where different children are brought up in the same environment, they may decide upon quite different life plans. Berne relates a story of two brothers who were both told by their mother: 'You'll finish up in an asylum.' One of the brothers became an in-patient in a mental hospital; the other became a psychiatrist.

In script theory, the term 'decision' is used in a technical sense, different from the usual dictionary meaning of the word. The child's script decisions are not made in the deliberate thinking way that we associate with adult decision-making. The earliest decisions result from feelings, and are made before the child has words. They depend also on a different kind of reality-testing from that used by adults.

Script is reinforced by the parents

Though the parents cannot determine a child's script decisions, they can exert a major influence upon them. From a child's earliest days, her parents are giving her messages, on the basis of which she forms conclusions about herself, others and the world. These *script messages* are non-verbal as well as verbal. They form the framework in response to which the child's main script decisions are made. In Chapters 13 and 14 we shall look at the various kinds of script message and how they relate to script decisions.

Script is outside of awareness

In grown-up life, the nearest we come to a memory of our earliest years is in dreams and fantasies. Unless we take time to work with and discover our script, we are likely to remain unaware of the early decisions we made, even though we may be living them out in our behaviour.

Reality is redefined to 'justify' the script

When Berne wrote that the script is 'justified by subsequent events', he might have done better to put quotation marks around 'justified'. What we often do is to interpret reality in our own frame of reference so that it *appears* to us to justify our script decisions. We do this because, in our Child ego-state, we may perceive any threat to our script-based view of the world as a threat to the satisfaction of our needs or even a threat to our survival. When we look at *discounting, redefining and frames of reference* in later chapters, we shall see how this distortion occurs and how it relates to life problems.

Origins of the script

Why do we make these sweeping infant decisions about ourselves, others and the world? What function do they serve? The answers lie in two crucial features of script formation.

(1) Script decisions represent the infant's best strategy for surviving in a world that often seems hostile, even life-threatening.

(2) Script decisions are made on the basis of an infant's emotions and reality-testing.

In our discussion of these in the following sections, we acknowledge our debt to the work of Stan Woollams.[2]

Response to a hostile world

The infant is small and physically vulnerable. To her, the world is populated by lumbering giants. An unexpected noise may signal that her life is in immediate danger. Without words or coherent thinking, she knows that if Mother and Father go away, she will die. If they get too angry with her, they may annihilate her. And the infant does not have grown-up understanding of time. If she is hungry or cold, and Mother does not come, then perhaps Mother will never come, and that means death. Or it could mean what is worse than death – being left alone for ever and ever.

When the child is two or three years old, perhaps a brother or sister is born. The toddler, now that she is bigger, knows she will probably not die because of this. But all Mother's attention seems to be taken up by the new arrival. Maybe there is not enough love to go around? Will the baby take it all? The threat now is the loss of Mother's love.

Right through the years of script formation, the child is in a one-down position. She perceives her parents as having total power. In her infancy, that power is of life or death. Later, it is to satisfy her needs or leave them unsatisfied.

Her response is to decide upon strategies for staying alive and getting her needs met as best she can.

Early reality-testing and emotion

A young child does not think like a grown-up. Nor does she experience emotion in the same way. Script decisions are made on the basis of a child's distinctive ways of making sense out of the world, which until about age six are based primarily on feeling and intuition.

The baby's emotional experience is of rage, utter misery, terror or ecstasy. He makes his early decisions in response to these intense feelings. Thus it is not surprising that the decisions are often extreme. Say for instance he has to be in hospital for an operation. This is not a pleasant experience even for a grown-up. But for the infant it may be a terrifying disaster. As well as his scare, he feels abject sadness that Mother is not there and perhaps never will be again. And he is filled with rage because she has let this happen to him. He may decide: 'These people want to kill me. Mother let it happen, so she wants to kill me too. I'd better kill them all before they get me.'

In the logic of the infant, the rule is to reason from the particular to the general. For instance, suppose the child's mother is inconsistent in responding to his demands. Perhaps she comes sometimes when he cries but ignores him at other times. The child doesn't just conclude 'Mother is untrustworthy.' Instead he may decide 'People can't be trusted,' or perhaps 'Women can't be trusted.' A girl of four or five may feel furious at Father for ceasing to give her the warm attention he lavished on her when she was a toddler. She is likely to decide not just 'I'm furious at Father,' but 'I'm furious at men.'

The child may compensate for his feeling of powerlessness by imagining he is omnipotent or can work magic. Maybe he senses that Mother and Father get along badly with each other. Particularly if he is an only child, he may decide 'It's my fault.' If his parents get into physical fights, he may believe it is his job to protect one parent from the other or to resolve their conflict.

If the child senses he is being rejected by a parent, he may attribute the fault to himself, deciding 'There's something wrong with me.'

Young children have difficulty in distinguishing between urges and deeds. A toddler may feel 'I want to kill this new baby who's getting all the attention!' To her, this amounts to saying 'I have killed the new baby.' She may then conclude: 'As a murderer, I am bad and horrible.' In grown-up life, this person may carry a vague feeling of guilt for the 'crime' she never committed.

A central skill of TA is to develop a sense for this kind of infant logic or magical thinking. Linguists talk of *Sprachgefühl*, the 'feeling for a language'. Particularly if you want to use TA in therapy, it pays to acquire a feeling for the child's language of script.

To improve your understanding of this language, you can read the work of Erikson, Piaget and other investigators of child development.[3] To get a feel of what it means for *you*, pay attention to your dreams. They are the nearest we come in grown-up life to a memory of what that hostile world was like to us as infants.

● EXERCISES: DISCOVERING YOUR OWN SCRIPT

Dreams, fantasies, fairy-tales and childhood stories can all give us clues to our script. Here are some exercises using these.

When you are doing the exercises, let your imagination run free. Don't bother thinking what they are for or what they mean. Don't censor or try to figure out what you are supposed to say. Just accept your first images and the feelings that may come with them. You can do your interpreting and deciphering afterwards.

You will get the most from the exercises if you find a group or partner to work with. Whether in a group or working individually, it's also a good idea to record your responses on tape. Just turn the recorder on and let it run during the exercise. Afterwards, play it back several times and let your intuition bring meanings to the surface. You will be amazed at the amount you learn about yourself and your script.

While doing any of these exercises, it is possible that you may begin to experience strong emotions. These will be childhood feelings that you are bringing to the surface along with your script memories. If you do have this experience, you can decide at any point to stop or continue the exercise. If you choose to stop, cease the exercise and fix your attention on some prominent object in the room. Tell yourself (or your partner) what the object is, what colour it is, and what it is used for. Think of some routine grown-up topic such as what you will be having for your next meal, or when you next need to be at your workplace. While doing this, stand or sit up straight with your head and body balanced around a vertical mid-line.

Hero or heroine

Who is your favourite character? It may be someone from a childhood story. Perhaps it is a hero or heroine from a play, book or film you remember. Maybe it is a real person.

Choose the first character you bring to mind.

Now turn on your recorder and/or get attention from your partner or group. Become your chosen character. Talk about yourself for as long as you like. Use the word 'I...'

For example: suppose my story hero is Superman. I may start off: 'I'm Superman. My job is to help people with problems. I fly in from nowhere, do all sorts of miraculous things, then disappear again. Most of the time, nobody knows I'm Superman, because I go around in disguise...'

Whoever your chosen character is, now go ahead, be him or her and talk about yourself.

Story or fable

A variation of the first exercise is to tell a story or fable. Again, choose any one you like – the first one you bring to mind is best. It may be a childhood fairy-tale, a classic myth, or anything else you want.

You might begin: 'Once upon a time, there was a beautiful girl who was sent to sleep for ages and ages by her evil stepmother. She lay in a room deep inside a castle. Round the castle was a prickly hedge. Kings and princes came looking for the girl, but none of them was strong enough to hack through the hedge...'

To get even more from the story, you can go on and become each one of the people and things in the story. Each time, talk about yourself. From the story above, you could choose to be the girl, the stepmother, the room, the castle, one of the princes, and the hedge.

As the hedge, you might say: 'I'm a hedge. I'm sturdy, rough and prickly. All my prickles point outwards, so that people can't hack me around. My job is to protect that young girl who's asleep inside me...'

Dream

Choose a dream of yours. You are likely to learn most from a recent dream or one that recurs, but any dream will do.

Tell the dream. Relate it in the *present* tense, not the past.

Then, just as you did with your story, become each of the people and things in the dream and talk about yourself.

Recall how you felt immediately after you awoke from the dream. Was it a pleasant or unpleasant feeling?

Did you like how the dream ended? If you did not, you can continue the exercise by re-writing your dream ending. Tell the re-written ending just as you told the dream, using the present tense.

Test whether you're now fully satisfied with the dream's ending. If not, re-write it again, as many times as you want to.

Object in the room

Look around the room. Choose any object you see. The best one is the first one you think of. Now be that object and talk about yourself.

For example: 'I'm the door. I'm hard, square and wooden. Sometimes I get in people's way. But when I do, they just push me to one side...'

To get even more from this exercise, ask a partner to conduct a conversation with you as the object you have chosen. The partner is *not* to make interpretations. He is just to talk with you as the door, the fireplace or whatever you have chosen to be. For instance:

'I'm the door. When I stand in people's way, they push me aside.'

'Well, door, how do you feel when people push you aside?'

'I feel angry. But I'm a door and I can't talk. I just let them do it.'

'Aha. So is there anything you want to change, door, to feel better?'

See your life as a play

For this exercise, you need someone to act as a 'guide' and talk you through it while you relax. Alternatively, record the cues on tape and listen to them while relaxed. One guide can lead a group of people through the exercise.

The guide need not follow the cues as written here word for word. In fact it is better if she simply jots down a few reminders of the sequence to follow, then improvises the wording. She should allow plenty of pauses between sentences. This gives the participants time to develop their visualizations.

Get relaxed in a chair or on the floor. It may help to close your eyes. The guide then goes ahead on these lines:

'Imagine you're in a theatre. You're waiting for a play to start. This play is your very own life story.

'What kind of play is this you're going to watch? Is it a comedy, a tragedy? Is it a high drama or a kitchen-sink opera? Is it interesting or boring, heroic or matter-of-fact – or what?

'Is the theatre full, half-empty, empty? Are the audience going to be enthralled or bored? Happy or sad? Are they going to applaud or walk out – or what?

'What's the title of this play of yours – your very own life-story?

'So now the lights are going down. The curtain is opening. Your very own play is just beginning.

'And you see the first scene. This is the very first scene of your life. You are very, very young in this scene. What do you see round you? Who is there? Do you see faces or parts of faces? If you see a face, see the expression on that face. What do you hear? Be aware of what you feel. Maybe you feel some feeling in your body. Maybe you feel some emotion. Do you smell or taste anything? Give yourself time now to be aware of this very first scene in your play.' *(Pause)*

'Now the scene changes. In this next scene of your play, you are a young child – maybe three to six years old. Where are you? What can you see round about you? Are there any other people there? Who is there?

Are they saying anything to you? Are you saying anything to them? Do you hear any other sounds?

What do you feel in this scene? Do you feel any sensations or feelings in your body? Do you feel any emotions?

Maybe you smell something or taste something?

Take time now to be aware of all you see, hear, feel, taste or smell in this second scene of your play – the scene when you are three to six years old.' *(Pause)*

Then the 'guide' runs through the same cues for the following scenes in the play, one after the other:

Teenage scene, about ten to sixteen years old;

Present scene, the age you are now;

Scene ten years in the future;

The last scene of your play – your death scene. In giving the cues for this scene, the 'guide' should also ask 'How old are you in this last scene of your play?'

Finally the 'guide' asks you to come back to the present, taking all the time you need.

Share as much of your experience as you want to with the group or a partner. ●

Chapter 11
HOW THE SCRIPT IS LIVED OUT

Having written our infant life-story, we are likely to go ahead and live it out for at least some of the time in our adult life.

In this chapter, we describe how you may live out your script as a *winner, loser* or *non-winner*. We show how people may move into and out of script-determined behaviour, and explain why knowledge of script is important in understanding people's life patterns.

Your script has both *content* and *process*. You'll remember that content refers to *what*, while process refers to *how*.

The content of your script is different from anyone else's. It is as unique as a fingerprint. Script process, on the other hand, seems to fall into a relatively small number of distinctive patterns. We shall look at these in a later chapter.

Winning, losing and non-winning scripts

In terms of content, we can classify scripts under three headings:

- *winning*
- *losing or hamartic*
- *non-winning or banal.*[1]

Winning script

Berne defined a 'winner' as 'someone who accomplishes his declared purpose'. (Robert Goulding added: 'and makes the world a better place as a result.') 'Winning' also implies that the 'declared purpose' be met comfortably, happily and smoothly. If I decide as a child that I am going to be a great leader, and eventually I become a successful, fulfilled general or politician basking in public praise, I am a winner. If I decide to be a millionaire, then I win if I grow up to be a happy, comfortable millionaire. If I decide to become a penniless hermit, and go on to become that hermit living happily in my cave, I am a winner. 'Winning' is always relative to the goals I set for myself.

Losing script

By contrast, a 'loser' means 'someone who does not accomplish a declared purpose'. Once again, it's not just the accomplishment or otherwise that matters, but the degree of comfort that goes with it. If I decide to become a great leader, join the army and finish up being drummed out in disgrace, I am a loser. If my political life is ended by a scandal over which I am thrown out of office, I am a loser. If I decide to be a millionaire and finish up as a penniless hermit, I am a loser.

But I am also a loser if I decide to be a millionaire, become one, and feel perpetually miserable because of my ulcer and the pressure of business. If I get my hermit's cave and live there complaining of my poverty, the dampness and the lack of company, I'm a loser.

Berne was careful to define 'winner' and 'loser' in relation to 'accomplishing declared purposes' because he wanted to emphasize that 'winners' were not simply to be equated with people who piled up material goods and money. Nor were 'losers' necessarily those people who were short of material things.

The fact is, though, that some of us in childhood may decide to achieve a purpose that *cannot* be attained without misery, self-limitation or even physical harm. For example, the infant may decide without words: 'I'm supposed to fail at whatever I do', and then go ahead to live out that script decision. To achieve his declared purpose, he fails at things. Another child may decide early in life: 'To be loved by Mother and Father, I have to drop dead', and go on to achieve that tragic purpose. Scripts with this kind of payoff would be called 'losing' by everyone, even though they do not fit the letter of Berne's definition.

Losing scripts can be broadly classified as first-, second- and third-degree, according to the severity of the payoff. A first-degree losing script is one where the failures and losses are mild enough to be discussed in the person's social circle. Examples might be repetitive quarrels at work, mild depression with out-patient treatment, or failure at college examinations.

Second-degree losers experience unpleasant script outcomes that are serious enough to be unacceptable topics for social conversation. This might mean being fired from a series of jobs, being hospitalized for severe depression, or being expelled from college for misconduct.

A third-degree losing script culminates in death, serious injury or illness, or a legal crisis. Third-degree payoffs might be imprisonment for stealing the firm's funds, lifelong hospitalization for a psychiatric disorder, or suicide after failing final examinations.

We often use the term *hamartic* to describe third-degree losing scripts and their payoffs. The word is derived from the ancient Greek *hamartia*, meaning 'a basic flaw'. It reflects the way in which a losing script, like an ancient Greek drama, seems to lead inexorably from the early negative decision to the tragic final scene.

Non-winning script

Someone with a non-winning script is a 'middle-of-the-roader'. He plods along from day to day, not making any big wins but not making any big losses either. He doesn't take risks. This kind of script pattern is often called *banal*.

At work, a non-winner will not become the boss. He will not be fired either. Instead, he will likely serve out his working years, be awarded a marble clock, and go into quiet retirement. He may sit in his rocking-chair reflecting: 'I *could* have been the boss if only I'd been in the right place at the right time. Ah well, I didn't do so bad, I suppose.'

Winners, losers and non-winners

Berne suggested that you could tell a winner from a loser by asking him what he would do if he lost. He said a winner knows but doesn't talk about it. A loser doesn't know, and all he can talk about is winning: 'When I make my first million...', 'When my horse comes in....' He stakes everything on one option, and that is how he loses.

A winner always has additional options, and that is how he wins. If one thing doesn't work out, he does something else until he is successful.

A non-winner sometimes wins and sometimes loses, but never very big in either direction, because he doesn't take risks. He plays it safe, and that is how he remains a non-winner.

Cautions on classification

This classification of scripts as winning, non-winning and losing is only approximate. What may count as a non-winning payoff to you may be a winning payoff to me. What is unacceptable in my social circle may be OK in yours.

In fact, most of us decide on scripts that are a mixture of winning, non-winning and losing. In my unique set of childhood decisions, I perhaps set myself up to be a winner at brainwork, a non-winner at physical activity, and a first-degree loser at personal relationships. Your personal combination of decisions may be entirely different.

Most important of all is to realize that *any script can be changed*. By becoming aware of my script, I can discover any areas in which I made losing decisions, and change them to winning decisions. The winning-nonwinning-losing classification is useful information about the past. It gives me a valuable road-map for present changes. In no way is it an unchangeable statement about the future.

● Review what you discovered about your own script when you did the exercises in the last chapter.

Would you say your script has been mainly winning, mainly losing, or mainly banal?

Do you identify specific areas in your life where you have set yourself up to be a winner, a loser, a nonwinner?

Are there areas in which you have so far been a loser or nonwinner and would like to be a winner?

If so, for each of these areas, write down how you would *know* you were winning instead of losing or nonwinning in that area. What would be your winning outcomes?

Then for each area, write down at least five actions you can take to bring about your winning outcomes. Do one of these actions each day. If you are working in a group, report back on your successes. ●

The script in adult life

As grown-ups, we sometimes re-play the strategies we decided upon as infants. At these times we respond to here-and-now reality as if it were the world we pictured in our early decisions. When we do so, we are said to *be in script*. Another way of saying this is that we are engaging in *scripty* behaviour or feelings.

Why do we do this? Why don't we just leave our infant decisions behind as we grow up? The primary reason is that we are still hoping to re-solve the basic issue that was left unresolved in our infancy: how to get unconditional love and attention. Thus as adults, we frequently react as if we were still infants. In common with many other therapies, TA sees this fact as the source of most life-problems.

When we get into script, we are usually not aware that we are re-enacting infant strategies. We can develop this awareness by understand-ing our script and discovering our own early decisions.

It is not possible to predict accurately whether someone will get into script at a particular moment. But there are two factors that make it more likely:

(1) When the here-and-now situation is perceived as stressful.
(2) When there is some resemblance between the here-and-now situa-tion and a stressful situation in childhood.

These two factors reinforce each other.

Stress and the script

Stan Woollams has suggested the idea of a *stress scale*.[2] The greater the stress, the more likely the person is to get into script. If we grade stress, say from 1 to 10, I may get into script in a situation that is stressful at level 6 or higher. You may be able to go up to 8 before moving into script.

Say I have a disagreement with my immediate line manager. This represents only a level 3 stress. So I stay out of script. I discuss our differences in an Adult way. I reason that my manager and I will either work out a compromise, or have to agree to differ. If it's the latter, then no disaster.

But say now the line manager calls in the Director. An argument with the boss counts as level 6 on the stress scale. I flip into script. Faced with the Director, I activate the same physical reactions, feelings and thoughts I used to have as a child when my angry father loomed over me like a giant, shouting words of abuse I couldn't understand. Without realizing it consciously, I have made the Director 'become' my father. And I respond as if I were a terrified kid of three again.

The 'stress scale' is a good way of pointing up the relationship between stress and scripty responses. It does *not* mean that stress can 'make' anyone go into script. The movement into script is decisional, even though the decision is out of awareness.

It's probable that simply by learning about script, I will become able to take greater stress before I move into scripty behaviour. If I undertake personal therapy, I can further improve my ability to problem-solve rather than reverting to scripty behaviour.

Rubberbands

When I went into script in my argument with the Director, it wasn't just because the situation was stressful. It was also that the here-and-now scene *resembled* a painful scene from my childhood.

In TA language, we say that the present situation is a *rubberband* back to the early situation.

This expresses graphically how we respond at times as though we had been catapulted back to early childhood scenes. Imagine a gigantic rubber band stretching through time. It hooks on to some feature of the present that recalls childhood pain, and twang! – off we go into the past.

Usually we have no conscious memory of the childhood scene. Thus we also don't recognize the point of resemblance. For me, the rubberband stretched from the Director back to my angry father. But while I was quailing before the Director's wrath, I didn't consciously realize my father was there behind him.

Because Mother and Father are such important figures in our early life, they are often to be found at the far end of rubberbands. So are our siblings, and other parent-figures like grandparents, aunts and uncles. Whenever we join a group of people, we are likely to cast each of the group in the role of a parent or sibling. Talking to anyone with whom we relate significantly, we identify them some of the time with figures from the past. We do so without conscious awareness.

This is the phenomenon that Freudians call *transference*. In TA, we refer to it colloquially as 'putting a face on someone'. When I went into script in my argument with the boss, I was putting my father's face on him.

Rubberbands do not always stretch back to people. We can also hook back to sounds, smells, particular surroundings, or anything else that reminds us unawarely of stressful situations in childhood.

One of the goals of change in TA is to *disconnect rubberbands*. Through script understanding and personal therapy, I can resolve the original trauma and free myself of the pull back to old childhood scenes. By doing so, I allow myself to tackle here-and-now situations with all the grown-up resources at my command.

● Think of a recent situation in which you were under stress and which ended unpleasantly or unsuccessfully for you. In particular, think what bad feeling you experienced during that situation. You need not actually experience that feeling again while you do this exercise.

Now recall a situation during the past year that turned out badly for you in a similar way, and in which you felt the same bad feeling.

Go back about five years and recall a similar situation in which you felt that same bad feeling.

Now bring back the memory of a similar unpleasant situation, with the same bad feeling, from your teenage years.

Recall now a similar scene, with a similar bad feeling, from your childhood. What age were you?

If you can, think back to a similar scene or scenes from even earlier in your childhood. What age were you? Who was there? What was happening?

The aim of this exercise is to trace the far end of the rubberband. What was the similarity between the recent experience and your childhood experience? If another person was involved in the recent experience, what 'face' from the past were you putting on him or her?

Once you are aware what past situation you were replaying, you can begin disconnecting the rubberband. Use Adult awareness to remind yourself that people in the here-and-now are in fact different from Father, Mother or others whose faces you may have put on them. If you begin experiencing that same bad feeling, let yourself be aware that the present situation is different from that in the past. You now have the resources and options of a grown-up person, as well as those of the child you were in the early scene. ●

Script and the body

It seems that we make some of our earliest decisions with our body as well as our mind. Perhaps the infant wants to reach out for Mother. But he discovers that Mother often draws away from him. To quell the pain of this rejection, he suppresses his bodily urge. To stop himself reaching out, he tenses his arms and shoulders.

Many years later as a grown-up, he may still hold this tension. But he will be unaware he is doing so. He may experience aches and pains in his shoulders or his neck. Under deep massage or in therapy, he may feel the tension and then release it. With that release, he is likely to release also the flood of feeling he had repressed since infancy.

Eric Berne wrote of *script signals*. These are bodily clues that indicate a person has moved into script. Perhaps she will sigh deeply, change position, or tense up part of her body. Berne drew attention especially to tensions in the sphincters, the muscles that close the various body openings.

Some TA therapists have specialized in this area of *bodyscript*.[3]

Why script understanding is important

Why is the life-script such an important concept in TA theory?

The reason is that it gives us a way of understanding why people behave in the ways they do. We specially need this understanding when we are examining ways of behaving that seem on the face of it to be painful or self-defeating.

For instance, when we look at *games* later in the book, we shall find people getting into painful interchanges that they repeat over and over. Why do we keep doing this sort of thing when it is so uncomfortable?

Script theory suggests an answer: we do it to reinforce and further our script. When we are in script, we are clinging to infant decisions. For us as infants, these decisions seemed the best possible way of surviving and getting needs met. As grown-ups, we still hold this belief in our Child ego-state. Without conscious awareness, we seek to set up the world so that it appears to justify our early decisions.

When in script, we attempt to meet adult problems by re-playing infant strategies. Necessarily, these bring the same results as they brought when we were infants. When we get those uncomfortable results, we can say to ourselves in our Child ego-state: 'Yes. The world *is* like I decided it was.'

And each time we 'confirm' our script beliefs in this way, we can take a step closer to our script payoff. For example, I may have decided as a baby: 'There's something wrong with me. People reject me. The ending of my story will be to die sad and alone.' In grown-up life, I may further this life-plan by setting up to be rejected time and time again. With each rejection, I tick up another 'confirmation' that my closing scene is a lonely death. Outside of my awareness, I may be holding the magical belief that if I play out this ending, Mother and Father will change and love me at last.

The script as 'magical solution'

The script offers a magical solution for resolving the basic issue that was unresolved in childhood: how to get unconditional love and acceptance. As adults we have a hard time letting go of that magic, because as kids we often identified with a fairy-tale and our fantasy is that if we can make our life go like the fairy-tale we too can end up living 'happily ever after'.

The only problem is that fairy-tales perpetrate a hoax on kids. They teach that if you want to have something good happen to you, you first have to be a big enough victim to deserve it.

For example, if you want to marry a prince you have some interesting choices. You can work hard, suffer, sit in the ashes and weep, and wait for your fairy godmother to come along and send you off to the ball. Or you can eat a poisoned apple, or prick your finger on a poisoned spindle and wait for some guy to come along who has an investment in kissing dead women. Or you can get locked up in a tower, grow long hair and wait for somebody to come by who has an investment in finding women who are institutionalized. Or you can go around kissing toads or trying to turn beasts into princes.

If you want to marry a princess, the choices are equally appealing. You can go around kissing dead women, or looking for women who are locked up. Or you can try to find women who run away from you, or go around acting beastly or froggy. If you want to end up being successful and well liked, you first have to start out being ugly and made fun of.

The positive thing that fairy-tales do is to give kids a sense of power and control over their lives at a time when they feel powerless. The only problem is that the solution offered is magical and does not work in reality, but at least it enables the child to survive in a situation that might otherwise seem hopeless.

Later, in adult life, the Child in us continues to hold on to that magical belief and keeps trying to make it work. If it hasn't worked yet, then maybe we haven't suffered enough to deserve the rescue. A part of moving out of the script is to give up the belief in a perfect world. Instead, we can begin to use our Adult to problem-solve and figure out how to get our needs met in a world that won't ever be perfect, but can be beautiful and enjoyable.

The script as 'protection against disaster'

There is still another reason why people cling so tenaciously to script beliefs. Suppose I am faced with the possibility of behaving, thinking or feeling in some way that does not fit with my script. To me in Child, this would mean having to give up the 'magical solution', and that seems bad enough. But it would also mean I had to face up to what I feared might happen *instead* of the magical outcome I had been hoping for.

When I made my script decisions as an infant, it seemed to me that the only alternative to following these decisions would be some terrible, unspeakable disaster. I had no clear conception of what that disaster might be. I knew only that I was terrified of it. At all costs, it had to be avoided. And the only way I knew of avoiding it was to cling to the decisions I had made about myself, others and the world. Each time I could 'confirm' these decisions, I made it seem less likely that the catastrophe would overtake me.

When we play out our script in grown-up life, we are still following this infant motivation. That is why people will often report that they feel 'more comfortable' continuing to follow ways of behaving which, at the same time, they recognize as self-damaging. Without being aware of it, they are acting out the belief: 'The way I'm behaving now is painful. But it's not nearly as bad as the unknown disaster that would happen if I changed my behaviour.'

All this helps us see why script understanding is so important to the process of personal change. To move out of script, I have to identify the needs I did not have met as a child. I have to find ways of getting those needs met now, using my grown-up resources instead of relying on the script's 'magical solution'. And I have to assure myself that I can break free of my script patterns without having to face the disaster I so much dreaded when I was an infant.

The script and the life course

Berne wrote: 'The script is what the person planned to do in early childhood, and the life course is what actually happens.'

Your life course is the result of four interacting factors:

- *heredity*
- *external events*
- *script*
- *autonomous decisions.*

My inheritance of genes largely determines my physical make-up. It may also help determine my mental characteristics, though there is still no agreement in the 'nature vs. nurture' argument. Perhaps I decide as a child that my destiny in life is to be a famous athlete. If heredity has given me a body that is only moderately fast and strong, then I may do better to find a different way of fulfilling myself.

Perhaps my early decision was to live to a healthy old age. I may be unfortunate enough to be caught in a fire, earthquake or plane crash, even though I have not set up in any way for such an outcome. A chance external event has cut across my decision to live.

Sometimes, external influences disrupt negative script patterns. For instance, when a country's population is 'pulling together' during wartime, fewer people suffer from neurotic complaints than in peacetime.

(This is not an argument in favour of war. There are more comfortable ways of curing neurosis.)

Whether or not I undertake formal therapy, many of my life decisions can be taken with full use of my grown-up resources. We say that these decisions are *script-free* or *autonomous*. When I make an autonomous decision, I am dealing with here-and-now reality as the adult I now am.

How do you know whether you are acting in script or autonomously? As you continue to read this book and work through the exercises, you will develop ways of judging this. If in doubt, assume that you are in script. Especially if you get into a situation that repetitively seems to 'go wrong' for you, take it as your first assumption that you have been setting that situation up without being aware you were doing so. Then test out ways of setting up to make the situation go right instead of wrong.

Chapter 12
LIFE POSITIONS

Berne suggests that the young child, early in the process of script formation, '...already has certain convictions about himself and the people around him... These convictions are likely to stay with him the rest of his life, and may be summarized as follows:

(1) I'm OK, or
(2) I'm not-OK;
(3) You're OK, or
(4) You're not-OK.'

By putting these together in all their possible combinations, we get four statements about self and others:

(1) I'm OK, you're OK;
(2) I'm not-OK, you're OK;
(3) I'm OK, you're not-OK;
(4) I'm not-OK, you're not-OK.

These four views are known as *life positions*.[1] Some writers call them *basic positions*, *existential positions*, or just *positions*. They represent fundamental stances a person takes up about the essential *value* he perceives in himself and others. This means more than simply having an opinion about his own and other people's *behaviour*.

Once the child has adopted one of these positions, she is likely to construct all the rest of her script to fit in with it. Berne wrote: 'Every game, script and destiny is based on one of these four basic positions.'

The child who chooses 'I'm OK, you're OK' is likely to build a winning script. He views himself as lovable and good to have around. He decides that his parents are lovable and trustworthy, and later extends this view to people generally.

If the infant takes up the position 'I'm not-OK, you're OK', she is more likely to write a banal or losing life-story. To fit with her basic position, she will construct her script round themes of being victimized and losing out to others.

'I'm OK, you're not-OK' may form the basis for a script that seems on the face of it to be winning. But this child will have the conviction that he needs to be one-up and put others one-down. He may manage to do this for some of the time, achieving his wants but only with a continual struggle. At other times, the people around him will get tired of being one-down and reject him. Then he will switch from apparent 'winner' to heavy loser.

The position 'I'm not-OK, you're not-OK' is the most likely foundation for a losing script. This child has become convinced that life is futile and full of despair. She views herself as being one-down and unlovable. She believes no-one will help her because they are not-OK as well. Thus she will write her script around scenes of rejecting and being rejected.

Origins of life position

There's some disagreement among TA authorities on how life positions originate, and at what age.

Berne believed that '...the position is taken in early childhood (third to seventh year) in order to justify a decision based on early experience.' In other words, for Berne, the early decisions come first, and the life position is adopted later in childhood to make the world appear to justify what has been decided.

For instance, the infant might decide without words: 'Never again will I risk loving anyone, because Mother showed me I was unlovable.' Later he justifies this by adopting the conviction 'I will never be loved', which translates to 'I'm not-OK.' If a little girl is physically abused by her father, she may decide 'Never again will I trust a man, because of Father's ill-treatment.' She then generalizes to the conviction 'All men are untrustworthy', or 'You (they) are not-OK.'

In the view of Claude Steiner, life position is adopted much earlier. He sees its origins in the earliest months of nursing. For Steiner, the position 'I'm OK, you're OK' reflects the comfortable, mutual interdependence between the feeding infant and her mother. He equates this to the position of 'basic trust' described by child development authority Erik Erikson. This is '...a state of affairs in which the infant feels that she is at one with the world and that everything is at one with her.'

Steiner suggests that all children begin in the position 'I'm OK, you're OK'. The child shifts to another position only if something interrupts the mutual interdependence between child and mother. Maybe the child perceives Mother as withdrawing the protection and acceptance she had offered in earlier days. For some infants, birth itself may be felt as such a threat. The baby may respond to these discomforts by deciding that she is not-OK or that others are not-OK. She has moved from Erikson's state of 'basic trust' into 'basic mistrust'. The child then goes on to build her script upon this fundamental view of self and others.

Thus Steiner agrees with Berne in suggesting that the life position 'justifies' script decisions. But in Steiner's version, the life position is adopted first in time and the decisions come later.

Life position can be defined as one's basic beliefs about self and others, which are used to justify decisions and behaviour.

Life position in adulthood: the OK Corral

Each of us arrives in adulthood having written a script based on one of the four life positions. But we don't stay in that position every hour of the day. Minute by minute, we shift between positions.

Franklin Ernst has developed a way of analysing these shifts. He calls it the *OK Corral* (Figure 12.1, overleaf).[2]

Ernst uses the phrase 'OK-with-me' instead of just 'OK'. This helps emphasize that OKness is a matter of *my* convictions about *me,* and *my* convictions about *you.*

The vertical axis of the Corral indicates 'You're OK' in the upwards direction, 'You're not-OK' going downwards. On the horizontal axis, we get 'I'm OK' on the right, 'I'm not-OK' on the left. Each of the four quadrants then corresponds to a life position.

Often, TA writers shorthand 'OK' by a '+. sign, and 'not-OK' by a '-'. Sometimes the word 'You' is shortened to 'U'. The four life positions are then written simply I+U+, I-U+, I+U- and I-U-.

On the version of the Corral shown in Figure 12.l, each of the four positions is given a name. These names were not on Ernst's original diagram, but are often used by other writers.

Franklin Ernst points out that each of the childhood positions is reflected in grown-up life by a particular kind of social interaction. He calls this an *operation.* The names for the four operations are shown on the Corral. If we get into one of these operations without awareness, from our Child ego-state, we are likely to create a scripty 'justification' for the corresponding life position. But we also have the choice of getting into Adult and using any of the operations with awareness. By doing so we can invite the social outcomes we desire.

I'm OK, You're OK: Get-On-With

I've just arrived at my workplace. In comes the boss with a stack of papers. 'Here's the report we've been waiting for,' she says. 'I've marked points for your action. Will you see to these and report back, please?' 'Right,' I say, 'I'll do that.'

In agreeing to the boss's request, I have checked with myself that I am competent to do what she asks and feel good about doing it. I see her as being fair and reasonable in asking me to do it. Thus I am in the position of 'I'm OK, you're OK'. In our social interaction, the boss and I are *getting-on-with* what we are both there to do.

Each time I have an interaction from this position, I reinforce my belief that I and others in the world are OK.

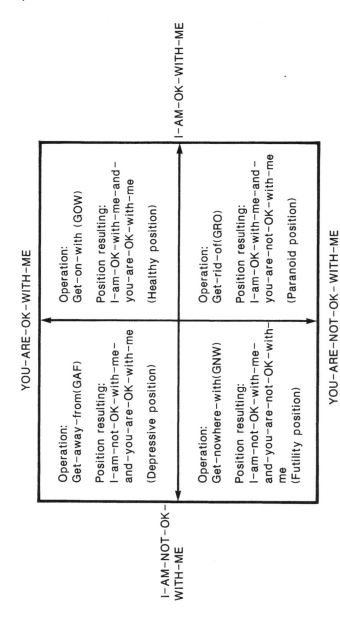

Figure 12.1 The OK Corral: Grid for What's Happening

I'm not-OK, You're OK: Get-Away-From

I've just settled down and opened the report at the first page. From the corner of my eye, I see somebody bearing down on me. It's one of my workmates. He's wearing a worried frown. Having seen that look before, I can make a good guess what he's coming for. He wants to spend a lot of time moaning about his work situation, asking my advice and then not taking it. As he arrives at my desk and opens his mouth, I have two choices. I can get into script or respond from Adult.

Scripty operation: Suppose I get into script and adopt the position 'I'm not-OK, you're OK'. I say to myself: 'I just can't cope with this fellow's complaints. I'm not up to it. But he's somebody who just seems to keep on talking no matter what I do. I have to get out of here!' I tense up my stomach and start sweating. Not really hearing what my workmate is saying, I mumble: 'Sorry, Jim, have to go out to the bathroom a minute!' and make for the door. Only when I'm outside do I relax and heave a sigh of relief. I have *got-away-from* Jim in a scripty way. In doing so, I have reinforced my Child conviction that I am not-OK while others are OK.

Adult operation: If I choose to stay in Adult, I say to myself: 'Right now, I'm not willing to listen to Jim. He's got problems, but it's not my job to settle them. Once he gets started talking, it's difficult to stop him. I think the best thing I can do is move out of range.' As Jim opens his mouth and gets halfway through his first complaint, I say: 'Hey, Jim, that sounds bad. Can't stop now, though. I've got to get down to the library and check some sources on this report. Hope you manage to solve your problems.' I pick up the report and walk out. With Adult awareness, I have chosen the operation of *getting-away-from*.

I'm OK, You're Not-OK: Get-Rid-Of

Ten minutes later, I'm back in my office with a cup of coffee, well into the report. The door opens again. This time it's my assistant. He looks downcast. 'Afraid I've got some bad news,' he says. 'You know that printing job you gave me to set up? I was busy and forgot to get it off. We've missed the printer's deadline. What do I do?'

Scripty operation: I may respond from a position of 'I'm OK, you're not-OK'. I go red in the face and snarl at my assistant: 'What do you *do*? What you do is you sort this out right away! So get a move on – I don't want to hear a word more from you till you've got that job done, understand?'. As I say this my heart-rate soars and I literally 'go hot under the collar'. When my assistant has disappeared back through the door, I say to myself: 'Can't trust anybody to do a job these days unless I do it myself!' I have *got-rid-of* my assistant, while creating a scripty 'justification' for believing that I am OK while others are not.

Adult operation: I reply to my assistant: 'Well, it's your job to get this sorted out. Right now I'm doing something urgent. So please go and find some ways of getting this job finished as soon as possible. Come back at four o'clock and report to me.' I look back down at the report to signal that our interview is finished. Here, I've *got-rid-of* my assistant in a way that lets me look after myself and leaves us both OK.

I'm not-OK, You're not-OK: Get-Nowhere-With

The phone rings. It's my partner calling from home. 'Something awful has happened! A water-pipe burst and the whole carpet got soaked before I could turn the water off!'

Scripty operation: at this, I may go all the way into 'I'm not-OK, you're not-OK'. I say to myself: 'I've had enough. I can't take this any longer. And my partner's no help either. It's hopeless.' I sigh into the phone: 'Look, I just can't take this. It's just too much after the day I've had.' Without waiting for an answer, I hang up the phone. I feel drained and depressed. Internally, I have reinforced my view that I and others are not-OK.

Adult operation: Deciding to stay in Adult, I reply: 'Look, the harm's done now. Just go on hold till I get home. Then we'll see what we can do.' I have chosen the operation of *getting-nowhere-with*.

Personal change and the OK Corral

Though we switch between quadrants on the Corral, we each have one 'favourite' quadrant where we spend most of our time while in script. This will be the one we decided on in childhood as our basic position.

'I'm OK, you're OK' is the *healthy* position. Here, I get-on-with living and problem-solving. I act to achieve the winning outcomes I desire. This is the only position based on reality. If my childhood position was 'I'm not-OK, you're OK', I am likely to play out my script mainly from the depressive position of feeling one-down to others. Unawarely, I will choose my bad feelings and repetitive behaviours to 'confirm' that this is my rightful position in the world. If I experience psychiatric problems, I am likely to be diagnosed neurotic or depressed. Should I have written a hamartic script, my probable payoff is self-harm or suicide.

An early position of 'I'm OK, you're not-OK' will mean that I live my script mostly from the defensive position of trying to stay one-up on others. Those around me are likely to experience me as overbearing, insensitive, aggressive. Though the name *paranoid* is often applied to this position, it also corresponds to the psychiatric diagnosis of character-disorder. In a third-degree losing script, my closing scene may entail killing or harming others.

If I took up a basic position of 'I'm not-OK, you're not-OK' as an infant, my script will be played through principally from the *futility* position. Here, I am believing that the world and others are no good, and neither am I. If I wrote a banal script, my pattern will be to get-nowhere-with most of the things I set out to do in life. If my script is hamartic, the likely payoff is 'go crazy', with a psychotic diagnosis.

Like all aspects of the script, life position can be changed. This is likely to happen only as a result of script insight, therapy or some powerful external experience.

The process of change often entails a movement through the Corral in a specific sequence. If the person starts off by spending most time in I-U-, her next move is likely to be into I+U-. After some time with that as her most important quadrant, she will shift to I-U+. The final goal is to increase the time spent in I+U+ until it becomes the favourite position.

It may seem strange that people often need to shift through I-U+ in order to get from I+U- to I+U+. But the experience of therapy shows that I+U- is often a *defence* against I-U+. The infant who concluded 'I'm OK and all those others are not-OK' took up that position to defend against the painful realization of being one-down and powerless in the face of her parents. To change as a grown-up, she needs to face that infant pain and then let it go.

● EXERCISES WITH THE OK CORRAL

Draw the axes of the OK Corral and label the quadrants.

Now draw an enclosure on the axes to show how much time you spend in each quadrant during an average day. For instance, if you think you spend most time in I-U+, next most in I+U+, third most in I+U- and least of all in I-U-, your enclosure would look like Figure 12.2. Franklin Ernst called this picture the *Corralogram*.[3]

What are the circumstances in which you are likely to get into each quadrant? What do you typically do and say, and how do you feel, when you are in each one?

What ego-states do you come from in each quadrant? (Use the functional model). What ego-states are you inviting in others?

What kinds of stroke do you give and get in each quadrant?

Now that you have drawn your Corralogram, is there anything you want to change about it?

If you do want to make changes, think how you could choose any of the four Adult operations to use instead of getting into scripty responses. Decide on at least one occasion when you will test out an Adult operation in the coming week, and do it. If you are working in a group, report back on the results. ●

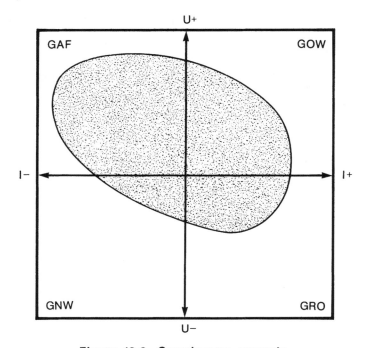

Figure 12.2   Corralogram example

Chapter 13
SCRIPT MESSAGES AND THE SCRIPT MATRIX

You know that the life-script consists of a set of *decisions*. These are made by the child in response to *script messages* about self, others and the world. The script messages come mainly from the child's parents.

In this chapter we look at the nature of script messages and the ways in which they can be transmitted. We meet a model, the *script matrix*, which gives us a standard method for analysing the messages underlying each individual's script.

Script messages and the infant's perception

It's important to recall that the infant makes her script decisions in response to her own *perception* of what is going on around her. This perception is founded on an infant's ways of feeling and reality-testing. Therefore the messages that the infant perceives as coming from the parents and the world around her may be quite different from any that a grown-up would perceive. The young baby, startled by a sudden loud noise, may conclude without words: 'Somebody out there is trying to kill me!' At that same moment her loving parents may be congratulating themselves on the safe environment they are providing for her.

Kinds of script message

Script messages may be conveyed *verbally*, *non-verbally*, or in these two ways combined.[1]

Both verbal and non-verbal messages may contain an element of *modelling*. Verbal script messages can be transmitted in the form of *commands* or *attributions*.

Verbal v. non-verbal messages

Before the infant has words, he interprets other people's messages in terms of their non-verbal signals. The young baby has acute perception of expressions, body tensions, movement, tones and smells.

If Mother holds him close and warm, letting him mould to the shape of her body, he is likely to perceive her message to him as 'I accept and love you!' But if she tenses up and holds him stiffly a little away from her, he may read her as conveying: 'I reject you and don't want you close!' The mother herself may be quite unaware of her tension and distancing.

Sometimes the infant may construe script messages from events around her that are not of the parents' making. Loud noises, sudden movements, separations from the parents such as a stay in hospital, may all appear to the baby as life-threatening. Because she assumes that her parents are in charge of reality, she may conclude that the threats also come from them.

Later in childhood, when the child understands language, non-verbal communication is still important as a component of script messages. Physical abuse, or the threat of it, may mean to the child that his parents reject him or possibly want him dead. When parents speak to the child, he will interpret the script meaning of what they say according to the non-verbals that go with it. Recall Berne's Third Rule of Communication: when transactions are ulterior, the significant message is on the psychological level.

Picture the young schoolchild coming home with the new reading book she's just been given by teacher. She starts reading it to her parents and stumbles over a word she hasn't met before. Father says: 'You got that word wrong.' With those words could go many different sets of non-verbals. Each of these would carry its own meaning to the child in terms of possible script decisions.

Father might speak in a harsh, loud voice, while curling his lip and screwing his face up. At the same time he might knock the book out of her hand or even deal her a blow. To the child, his message reads: 'I don't want you around and would prefer you dead.'

He might say the words in a flat voice, without looking up from the newspaper he himself is reading. Reading the non-verbals, his daughter interprets his message as: 'You're not important to me.'

He might accompany his words with a wink and a giggle. Using Little Professor strategy, the little girl tests out giggling back. Sure enough, Father smiles even more. She reads his message: 'To please me, you have to act stupid.'

Father might say the words in an even voice, while sitting beside her pointing the words out in her book. He then gives her time to look at the word again. His 'Martian' conveys to the child: 'It's OK for you to think.'

Modelling

Young children are perceptive observers of the way people behave. Particularly, they note how Mother and Father relate to each other and to other family members. Using Little Professor strategies of reality testing, the child continually tries out solutions to the question: 'How do I best get what I want around here?'

Maybe a little girl notes that when Mother wants something from Father, she usually gets it by starting a fight and then bursting into tears. The child forms the conclusion: 'To get what I want from people, especially men, what I need to do is start a fight and then burst out crying.'

Perhaps a little boy had a brother who died. He notes that his parents go to the cemetery each week with flowers. They seem to be sad most of the time and to be thinking more of the one who died than the other who is still alive. The child concludes: 'People who die get all the attention.' He doesn't have the grown-up capacity to understand the finality of death. So he may then decide: 'In order to get the attention I want from my parents, I need to die like my brother did.'

Commands v. attributions

Script messages can be in the form of direct commands. 'Don't bother me! Do what you're told! Get lost! Hurry up! Don't be naughty! If at first you don't succeed, try, try, try again!' Most parents bombard their children with hundreds of commands like these. Their potency as script messages will depend on how often they are repeated and on the non-verbals that go with them.

At other times, the child may be told not just what he should *do*, but what he *is*. This kind of message is called an *attribution*.

'You're stupid!'

'You're my little girl!'

'You'll end up in jail.'

'You'll never make it.'

'You're good at reading!'

These are examples of attributions spoken directly to the child. Their content may be positive or negative. As always, their power as script messages will be affected by the non-verbal signals that accompany them. 'You're stupid', spoken harshly along with a blow, conveys a different script message from the same words spoken in a light tone accompanied by a smile and a cuddle.

Sometimes attributions may be delivered indirectly. This means that the parent speaks *about* the child to someone else, either when the child is present or in a way that will be communicated back to the child.

'This one is the quiet one.'

'Jill is so cute!'

'He's not strong, you know.'

'She worries us because she's so naughty.'

'Father says you're just a nuisance!'

Indirect attributions like these are especially likely to be read by the child as potent script messages. She views her parents as determining reality. Hearing them talking to other people about how she is, she takes it for granted that what they say has to be fact.

In some families, attributions are passed on from one generation to the next by psychological-level messages. These may be based on such features as position in the family or the giving of names. For example, Ellen came into therapy because she feared she might be going mad. Through script analysis, she registered that two other women in her family had been christened Ellen: her aunt and her grandmother. Both had become psychotic at about Ellen's present age. The psychological-level message, never spoken in words, was: 'Anybody in our family christened Ellen goes mad at 35.'

Traumatic event v. repetition

The child may make a central script decision in response to a single event that she experiences as especially threatening. Perhaps a little girl is sexually abused by her father. She may read that single episode as an overpowering script message, and decide: 'Never again will I trust men.' Earlier in life, a period of separation from the mother may often form the basis for non-verbal decisions like 'I can't trust anyone' or 'People want me dead.' Some TA therapists believe that the single traumatic event of birth is itself a potent influence on script decisions.

Probably more often, decisions are arrived at over a period of time, in response to script messages that the child experiences repetitively. Perhaps the infant reaches out to Mother and she turns away from him. He reaches out again, and again gets no response. Not until he has done this many times may he begin to form the conclusion: 'Mother doesn't want me close.' The little boy who hears the attribution 'This is the shy one' may need to hear it repeated for months and years before deciding firmly that he is indeed shy.

Eric Berne compared the build-up of script messages to a pile of coins, stacked one on the other. A few of the coins in the stack are skewed. The more skewed ones there are, the more likely is the whole stack to go off line and fall over. One badly skewed coin can throw the stack off true. So can a number of slightly skewed coins, particularly if they are all arranged to lean the stack in one direction. This is a graphic picture of the way in which traumatic events and repeated messages combine to form the basis for the life-script.[2]

The script matrix

Your mother and father both had their own Parent, Adult and Child ego-states. They transmitted script messages to you from all three of these ego-states. You received these messages and filed them away in your own three ego-states. From this realization, Claude Steiner developed what is now one of the central models of TA: the *script matrix*. It is shown in Figure 13.1.[3]

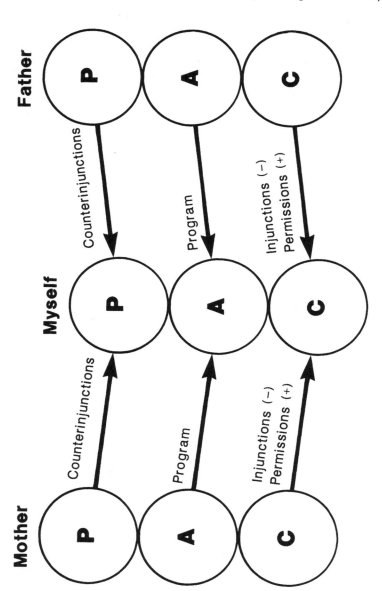

Figure 13.1 The script matrix

Messages that originate from mother's and father's Parent ego-states are called *counterinjunctions*. You file them away as part of the content of your own Parent.

Modelling or 'here's how' messages from the Adult of the parent to the Adult of the child make up what is called the *program*. They may also come from the Little Professor of the parent to the Little Professor of the child.

Messages sent from the Child ego-state of mother and father can be of two kinds: *injunctions* or *permissions*. We picture these as being filed away in the content of your own Child ego-state.

Different TA writers have drawn script matrix diagrams that differ from each other in minor details. The one we show here is a collated version.

Counterinjunctions

These Parent-to-Parent messages were originally called *counterinjunctions* because they were thought to 'run counter to the injunctions'. We know now that these messages *may* sometimes contradict injunctions, but may just as often reinforce injunctions or be irrelevant to them. Still, the name 'counterinjunctions' has stuck.

The *counterscript* is the set of decisions made by the child in compliance with the counterinjunctions.

Counterinjunctions consist of commands about what to do or not do, plus definitions of people and the world. We all get thousands of these from our parents and parent-figures. Typical ones are:

'Be good!'
'Don't be naughty!'
'Be my princess!'
'Work hard!'
'Come top of the class!'
'It's bad to tell lies.'
'Keep things in the family.'

Most of the time, we use our counterscript in a positive way, to look after ourselves and fit in comfortably with society. As grown-ups, we don't need to think whether we should belch at the table or whether it's polite to throw unwanted food over our shoulder; the knowledge is already there in our positive counterscript. In the same way, we don't run out in the road in front of traffic or stick our hand into the fire.

Most of us, though, have a few counterscript messages that we have decided to use as part of a negative script set-up. Suppose I carry the Parental command 'Work hard!' around in my head. I may use it to win success at school and college. In my career I may go on working hard and get a good promotion. But I may also work so hard that I overstress myself. I may sacrifice leisure, relaxation and friendships to the demands of work. If my script is hamartic, I may use my 'Work hard' message to further a payoff of ulcer, high blood-pressure or heart attack.

There are five commands in particular that play a special role in the counterscript. They are:

- *Be Perfect*
- *Be Strong*
- *Try Hard*
- *Please (people)*
- *Hurry Up.*

These are called *driver messages* or simply *drivers*. The name 'driver' is used because the Child feels a compulsion to follow these commands. He believes he can stay OK only so long as he obeys the driver.

All of us carry these five messages around in our counterscript, though in varying proportions. When I replay a driver message internally, I exhibit a set of behaviours that typically accompany that driver. These *driver behaviours* are consistent from person to person. By studying someone's driver behaviour, we can reliably predict some important features of their script. In a later chapter, we look at drivers in more detail.

Program

The *program* consists of messages about how to do things. In compiling the script matrix, we phrase these as sentences beginning: 'Here's how to...' Each of us learns many thousands of program messages from parents and parent-figures. For instance, 'Here's how to...

count to 10
write your name
make porridge
tie your shoes
be a man (a woman)
be cute
come top of class
hide your feelings.'

As with counterscript, we use most of our program messages in a constructive, positive way. But we may also carry around some negative program. For instance, a boy may learn from his father's modelling: 'Here's how to work hard, overstress yourself and die young.' A little girl may learn from Mother: 'Here's how to sit on your feelings and end up depressed.'

These negative program messages might be shown more accurately in the matrix diagram as coming from the *contaminated* Adult in the parent, and being filed away in the *contaminated* Adult of the child. Also, many of the 'here's how' messages in the program might better be seen as forming part of the content of the Little Professor (A_1) of the parent and being stored in A_1 of the child, rather than A_2. However, the diagram is not always drawn with this detail.

Injunctions and permissions

Picture a mother with her new baby. As she looks after her child, the mother may be replaying messages from her own Parent ego-state, such as: 'Children need to be protected. Their needs come first.' For much of the time also she may be in her Adult ego-state, practising techniques of child-care she has read up in books. But what's going on in her Child ego-state?

As the mother goes back and replays her own infancy, she may be feeling: 'Great! Now there's another kid to play with around here!' She may be enjoying the physical interchange of strokes between the baby and herself, just as she enjoyed stroking and being stroked when she was the infant. Picking up her non-verbal messages, the baby is likely to conclude: 'Mother wants me and likes me being close to her.'

In script language, we say that the mother is giving her baby *permissions* – here, permission to exist and permission to be close.

But the Child in another mother may feel instead: 'This is dangerous. Now this new baby is around, she is going to get all the attention. When am *I* going to get attention? Maybe there isn't enough attention to go round?' Replaying the uncensored feelings and urges of her own infancy, the mother may be scared and furious at the new arrival. She may want, deep in her Child ego-state, to reject the baby or even kill him.

She is likely not to have the slightest conscious awareness of these feelings. In her own consciousness and to any outside observer, she is a loving and caring mother.

But the baby knows. With his acute awareness of nonverbal cues, he picks up Mother's scare and anger. Little by little he may form the conclusion, without words: 'Mother doesn't want me close to her. In fact, she would rather I weren't around at all.'

These negative messages from the parent's Child are examples of *injunctions*. In this case, the injunctions are 'Don't exist' and 'Don't be close'.

As grown-ups, we each carry around a set of injunctions and permissions, filed away in the content of our Child ego-state. The decisions we made in response to these messages are the principal foundations of our life-script. This whole complex of injunctions and permissions, plus the decisions made upon them by the child, is sometimes called the *script proper*.

Distinguishing injunctions/permissions from counterinjunctions

How do you tell the difference in practice between a negative counterinjunction and an injunction? Or between a positive counterinjunction and a permission? There are two ways of distinguishing them.

(1)   Counterinjunctions are verbal, injunctions / permissions are (originally) preverbal. If you listen inside your head, you will be able to hear your counterinjunctions being spoken in words. Often you will be able to hear the actual parent or parent-figure who originally spoke them to you.

If you go against a counterinjunction, and listen again in your head, you are likely to hear verbal scolding from the parent-figure who gave the command.

Injunctions and permissions, by contrast, are not necessarily heard in words. Instead, you feel them in emotions and body sensations, and reflect them in behaviour.

If you defy an injunction, you are likely to experience bodily tension or discomfort. Your heart may race, you may get a headache or start sweating or feel 'knots in the stomach'. You are likely to find all sorts of ways of avoiding the behaviour that goes against the injunction. These ways may seem Adult to you, but are actually rationalizations.

For instance, suppose I received the injunction 'Don't be close' from my mother and made the early decision that, indeed, I had better not get close to anybody. Now as a grown-up, I am taking part in an encounter group. The leader invites us to close our eyes, find a partner by touch alone, and get to know that person by feeling their hands. I start sweating gently and my pulse-rate goes up. As I feel another person reach out for my hand, I open my eyes and say: 'Hm. Don't see the point in this exercise. What do you think it's for?'

Sometimes injunctions are heard in words also. For instance, a person who has been given the injunction 'Don't exist' may recall his parents saying things like 'I wish you had never been born!' or 'Drop dead!'

(2)   Injunctions / permissions are given in early childhood, counterinjunctions later. Developmentally, injunctions and permissions are earlier than counterinjunctions. This of course is related to the 'verbal – preverbal' distinction. As a general rule, the child takes in injunctions and permissions in the years before she has command of language. There is no one age that marks a sharp end-point to this period. In our experience, injunctions may continue to be given until the child is between six and eight years old. Counterinjunctions are usually given between the ages of three and twelve.

Chapter 14
INJUNCTIONS AND DECISIONS

In their work as therapists, Bob and Mary Goulding found that twelve themes emerged again and again as the basis for people's negative early decisions. They developed the list of these twelve injunctions which we give below.[1]

Each injunction has its corresponding permission. Traditionally in script analysis, injunctions are written beginning with the word 'Don't...' and permissions with the phrase 'It's OK to...'

Notice that 'Don't...' and 'It's OK to...' are not simple opposites. 'Don't...' conveys a blanket prohibition, a command not to do something. But 'It's OK to...' is not a command to do something. Instead, it invites the receiver of the message to *choose* whether to do something or not do it.

Realize too that these names for the injunctions and permissions are only verbal labels we apply for convenience in script analysis. The injunctions and permissions themselves are conveyed to the child in ways that are mainly non-verbal.

Twelve injunctions

Don't Be (Don't Exist)

If you have ever contemplated suicide, it's most likely that your script messages include a Don't Exist injunction. The same is probably true if you have ever felt worthless, useless or unlovable.

You may remember a parent saying things to you like: 'I'll kill you for that!', or 'I wish I'd never had you!' These verbal messages help confirm the presence of this injunction, though its main impact will have been through non-verbal signals earlier in your life.

Why should parents deliver Don't Exist to a child? It's likely to be because the parent, in his or her own Child ego-state, feels deprived or threatened by having the child around. Maybe a young man marries and becomes a father. Seeing his wife give most of her energy and attention to the new baby, the father may experience a rubberband back to his own childhood. Without awareness, he re-lives the time when he was two, and a new baby had just arrived in his family. As that two-year-old, he was profoundly scared in case there would never again be enough attention for him. How could he ever get Mother's love back? The only hope seemed to be if he could get the baby out of the way, and preferably dead. Now as a grown-up, he may signal these same homicidal urges non-verbally to his own baby.

Or perhaps a woman already has several children and doesn't want more. Because of family pressures, or 'by accident', she does have a new child. In her own Child ego-state, she is screaming: 'No! Not another one! I want attention to *my* needs for a change!' She will likely suppress her Child fury, denying it even to herself. But in subtle ways, she conveys rejection to the baby. Maybe she never smiles and seldom talks to him, even as she does all the right things to look after him materially.

Where a parent physically or mentally abuses a child, the Don't Exist message is being conveyed overtly.

The Don't Exist injunction turns up frequently during script analysis. This may seem surprising, considering its death-laden implications. But recall that it is quite easy for an infant to read a threat of death into all sorts of parental behaviour or external events which to a grown-up might appear quite harmless. Remember also how the young child may confuse deeds with urges. Perhaps wanting a younger sibling dead, she may decide 'I'm a murderer and so I deserve to die.' She delivers Don't Exist *to herself*.

The same may happen where a mother subtly conveys to her child 'You hurt me badly when you were born.' (Berne called this the 'Torn Mother script'). The child may decide 'Just by being born, I harmed Mother or maybe even killed her. Therefore, I'm dangerous and can harm or kill people just by being around. So I deserve to be hurt or killed myself.'

Parents may also say things like: 'If it weren't for you, I could have gone to college, or taken that trip to foreign countries, or wouldn't have had to marry that so-and-so...'

If Don't Exist is a common injunction, why don't most people commit suicide? Luckily, people are extremely ingenious at staying alive. In his early years, the child carrying a Don't Exist is likely to make *compound decisions* to defend against its fatal outcome. These decisions will be of the form: 'It's OK for me to go on existing *so long as I...*' The blank can be completed in many ways, such as: '...keep on working hard' or '...don't get close to people.' In a later section we shall look at compound decisions in more detail.

Don't Be You

This injunction can be conveyed to a child by parents who have a boy when they wanted a girl, or *vice versa*. Their non-verbal message is 'Don't be the sex you are'. This may be reflected in their choice of a name for the child. Maybe a girl is called Jacky or a boy is christened Vivian. Parents may dress their daughter in 'butch' clothes or their son in frilly collars and bows. In grown-up life, the person carrying 'Don't be the sex you are' may continue to cultivate dress or manners that suggest the opposite sex.

Don't Be You may be more general, and simply convey 'Don't be you, be some other child'. Parents may prefer a younger to an elder child, or a brother to a sister. A mother who feels rejecting towards her child may continually compare him with other children: 'Little Johnny down the road can ride a two-wheel bicycle – isn't he clever? And he's a year younger than you are, too.' Here, the parent may be holding an image of the 'ideal child' she wishes. She reacts positively only to the aspects of her actual child which resemble that image, and discounts the rest.

Parents may also make statements like: 'You're just like your no-good Uncle Harry.' Then, the more the child acts like Uncle Harry the more strokes he gets.

Don't Be a Child

This is another injunction handed out by parents who, in their Child ego-state, feel threatened by having their child around. But instead of wanting the baby right out of the way, the Child in the parent says: 'There's only room for one kid around here – and that's me. But I'll put up with you, so long as you behave like a grown-up instead of a child.' This may be reflected later on by verbal messages like 'You're too old to...', or 'Big boys don't cry'.

Don't Be a Child is also given out by parents who were never allowed to be child-like themselves and feel threatened by child-like behaviour. They may have been reared in times of depression or in a stern home where worth and value were related to doing.

Sometimes eldest or only children give themselves this injunction. Seeing Mother and Father arguing, an only child may decide: 'The only other person around here is me. So I must be the cause of the fight. Therefore, it's up to me to do something about it. I'd better grow up quickly so I can take charge.' An eldest child may decide similarly that she is responsible for her younger brothers and sisters.

If you feel awkward relating to children, you probably carry Don't Be a Child. The same is probably true if you stiffen up when you are at parties or in similar 'fun' situations among other adults. 'Don't have fun' and 'Don't enjoy' are sometimes listed as variants of Don't Be a Child. For sure, we don't need to be in our Child ego-state in order to have fun or enjoy. But if you decided as a child that having fun and enjoying were things children did, and that *you* were supposed to be a solemn little grown-up, you may well rubberband to that decision when the chance arises of having fun at your present age.

In some families, if you are having too much fun you are labelled lazy or sinful. There may be a magical belief that if you feel *too* good, something bad will happen. So the way you magically ward off evil is to not feel too good.

Don't Grow Up

It is often the youngest child who gets a Don't Grow Up injunction. The parents, in their Child ego-state, may not want to let go of having a young kid around in the family. They may define their whole worth in terms of being a good father or good mother. If their child grew up, they would no longer feel valuable. Alternatively, this injunction may be given out by parents who never grew up themselves. Their message is 'stay my little playmate'.

Sometimes Don't Grow Up is read as 'Don't leave me'. The woman who stays at home into her middle age, caring for a demanding aged mother, may be carrying this message.

Another variant of Don't Grow Up is 'Don't be sexy'. This is often given by a father to his daughter, at the stage of her childhood when she is old enough to become noticeably feminine. In his Child, her father is scared of his own sexual response to her. He puts out non-verbal messages of physical distancing, which the little girl may read as an injunction against growing up and becoming a sexual woman.

Don't Make It

This injunction is given by a parent who, in his own Child, is jealous of the accomplishments of his son or daughter. Suppose a father comes from a poor family. He had to go out to work when he was fifteen years old, and he never got the chance to go to college. Now, as a result of his hard work, he and his children are financially comfortable. He is paying for his daughter to go to a good school, so that one day she will have the chance to go on to a university.

Seeing her excel at her lessons, the father may feel parental pleasure. But outside of his awareness, in his Child ego-state, he is bitterly jealous that his daughter is getting chances that he never got. What if she does succeed in her studies? Maybe that will prove she is better than he is? Non-verbally, he may convey the Don't Make It injunction to his daughter, even while on an overt level he is urging her to work hard and do well.

A student who has made a script decision to obey a Don't Make It injunction will typically work hard in class and do all her assignments competently. But come the examinations, she is likely to find some way of sabotaging herself. Maybe she will panic and walk out of the exam. Maybe she will 'forget' to hand in a crucial piece of work. She may even come down with a psychogenic illness, or find she has suddenly become unable to read.

Don't (Don't Do Anything)

The blanket message 'Don't!' implies: 'Don't do anything, because anything you do is so dangerous that you're safer doing nothing at all'. If someone in adult life continually dithers between courses of action, always feeling he's getting nowhere but never taking any action to change this, he may be carrying this script message.

The 'Don't' injunction is given by a parent who, in Child, is terrified that her child will come to harm if he is allowed to run free of the parental apron-strings. The grounds for the terror lie in the parent's own script rather than in reality. A parent with this fear may say things like: 'Johnny, go see what your little sister is doing and tell her not to.'

Don't Be Important

People carrying this message may become panicky when they are asked to take on any kind of leadership role. They may 'dry up' when called upon to speak in public. In her career, the person complying with Don't Be Important may work excellently in a subordinate post, but either not seek promotion or sabotage herself when there is a chance of getting it. A variant of this injunction is 'Don't Ask For What You Want'.

This is another script message arising from parents' impulse of rejection towards their child. Non-verbally, the parent conveys from his Child ego-state: 'I'll put up with having you around, kid, just as long as you realize that you and your wants are not important around here.'

Don't Belong

The Indian statesman Pandit Nehru used to say: 'When I am among Europeans, I feel like an Indian. When I am among Indians, I feel like a European.' The chances are that Nehru had received a Don't Belong injunction from his parents. The person complying with Don't Belong feels 'out of it' in groups, and so is likely to be seen by others as a 'loner' or 'unsociable'.

This message may be conveyed as an attribution by parents who continually tell their child he is 'different from other children', 'shy', or 'difficult'. Or the parents may model the injunction through their own social ineptitude. The message may be conveyed either by scapegoating the child or by continually telling him how special he is.

Don't Be Close

The injunction Don't Be Close may imply a ban on physical closeness. In this form it is often modelled by parents who seldom touch each other or the child. Alternatively, it may signify 'don't be emotionally close'. This form of the message may be passed down through the generations in families who never talk to each other about their feelings.

A child may give herself Don't Be Close as a response to continual physical distancing by the parent. The child may reach out time and again, only to get no response. Eventually she may decide that her seeking for closeness is not worth the pain of rejection.

A variant of Don't Be Close is 'Don't Trust'. This message is sometimes read by the young child when a parent abruptly goes away or dies. Unable to understand the true reason for the parent's disappearance, the infant may conclude: 'Never again will I trust anyone to be here when I want them.' 'Don't Trust' can also be picked up if the parent is abusive or tries to trick or take advantage of the child. The decision is: 'I'll stay away from you in order to protect myself.'

Carrying decisions like these in adult life, the person may be continually suspicious of others he relates to. Even when they warmly accept him, he may have his feelers out for signs of rejection. If the other person refuses to reject him, he may 'test the relationship to destruction' and then say: 'I told you so!'

Don't Be Well (Don't Be Sane)

Imagine that Mother and Father are two busy people, both out all day working. They love their daughter but don't have much energy to give her attention when they get home in the evenings and she comes back from the day-care centre.

Then she gets ill. Mother takes time off work to look after her sick daughter. Father does what he's seldom done before and reads her stories while she falls asleep at night.

In her astute Little Professor, the little girl stores away the conclusion: 'To get the attention I want around here, I have to be ill.' Without realizing it or intending it, her parents have given her the injunction Don't Be Well. If she complies with this message in grown-up life, their daughter may use the scripty strategy of getting sick whenever things go wrong in her relationships or at work.

Sometimes Don't Be Well is given by attribution, as when parents continually tell a child's relatives and neighbours: 'This one isn't strong, you know.'

The variant Don't Be Sane is often modelled for the child by a psychotic parent or relative. The child may only get attention if he acts crazy enough. This injunction may be made more potent by unspoken rules about how insanity is to be passed on in a particular family.

Don't Think

The Don't Think injunction may be given by a parent who consistently belittles his child's thinking. Little James proudly shows Father his first efforts at writing his own name. Father snorts: 'Huh! Clever-pants, you are!' Sometimes Don't Think may be modelled, as by a hysterical mother who models for her daughter: 'When women want to get something from men, they can do it by switching off their thinking and escalating feelings.' Don't Think may also convey: 'Obsess about everything in creation except the immediate problem at hand.'

An adult complying with a Don't Think injunction is likely to respond to problems by getting confused, or by feeling bad about the problem instead of thinking how to solve it.

Two variations of Don't Think are 'Don't think about *x*' (where *x* stands for something that is treatening to the family, e.g. dad's drinking) and 'Don't think what *you* think, think what *I* think.'

Don't Feel

Don't Feel may be modelled by parents who themselves bottle up their feelings. Sometimes there is an embargo on any show of feeling in the family. More often, particular feelings are prohibited while others are allowed. Thus the Don't Feel injunction may be interpreted as 'Don't feel anger', 'Don't feel fear', and so on.

Sometimes the message is read as 'experience the feeling but don't show it'. Other children receive a more extreme version that enjoins them not even to experience a particular emotion. Little boys, for instance, are often instructed time and time again by their fathers: 'Big boys don't cry', or 'Be a brave soldier!' These mottoes translate to 'Don't experience sadness' and 'Don't experience fear'.

In some families the Don't Feel message implies 'Don't experience physical sensations'. This injunction is often given early in infancy. If given powerfully, it can be the source of some severe problems in adulthood. For instance, a child enjoined against feeling hunger may later develop an eating disorder. In the opinion of some TA therapists, the 'Don't feel sensations' message lies at the root of certain kinds of psychosis.

Some parents convey a version that goes: 'Don't feel what *you* feel, feel what *I* feel'. Mother says to young son: 'I'm hungry. What do you want to eat?' or 'I'm cold, go put on your sweater.'

Episcript

Fanita English has described an especially virulent kind of script message that she calls *episcript*.[2] Here, a parent conveys an injunction and adds to it the non-verbal message: 'I hope this happens to you, so that it won't have to happen to me.'

For instance, a mother scripted with Don't Exist during her own childhood may pass a Don't Exist on to her son or daughter. In her Little Professor, the mother may believe that this buys a magical release from her own injunction. At the psychological level she conveys to her child:

'If you drop dead, maybe I won't have to.' Thus the injunction here is like a 'hot potato', passed on from generation to generation.

Sometimes an episcript may take the form of a family task or family curse, with every generation supposed to end up the same way. Fanita English gives the example of a young man who at one time had been taking psychedelic drugs. He became interested in psychology, came off the drugs and started working as a therapist. However, it soon became apparent that he was sabotaging some of his clients, giving them covert messages that said: 'Crack up and go into a madhouse!'

His supervisor detected this set-up, and the young man came back into therapy for himself. Through script analysis, he realized he had received the command 'Go into a madhouse!' (Don't Be Sane) as a 'hot potato' passed on by his mother. He had sought to obey her injunction by taking drugs. In becoming a therapist, he had been trying to pass on the same 'hot potato' to his clients. When he and his therapist explored his family history, they found that the same 'go crazy' episcript had been handed down through at least two previous generations. Nobody had actually gone into a madhouse. Each generation believed it had avoided that outcome by the magical device of passing the 'hot potato' along to someone else.

How decisions relate to injunctions

We have emphasized that a parent's injunctions cannot *make* the child write her script in a particular way. It is the child who *decides* what to do with the injunctions she receives. One child may accept an injunction as it stands. Another may modify it ingeniously to ease its impact. Still another may simply refuse to accept the injunction at all.

For instance, suppose a little boy picks up Don't Exist from his mother. He may simply take on board the whole impact of the injunction, and commit suicide either as a child or in adulthood. The suicide may be overt or may take the form of an 'accident', as where someone drives his car fast while drunk.

Another possibility is that the child may make a magical early decision to shift the impact of Don't Exist by deciding to kill someone else instead of killing himself. This results in a hamartic script in which the payoff is homicide instead of suicide.

Alternatively, the magical belief may be of the form: 'If I can stop existing as a sane person, maybe I won't actually have to die.' This gives the script the hamartic payoff of 'go-crazy'.

At the other extreme from these tragic decisions, the infant may already be able to realize: 'This message is my mother's problem, not mine,' or have a supportive grandparent and thus reject the Don't Exist injunction altogether. Children who do this may, in the Gouldings' words,

'...become little psychiatrists or priests, as they study the family and attempt to cure it, while saving their own lives by recognizing the pathology is not of their doing.' Many of these 'little psychiatrists or priests' go on to become big psychiatrists or priests, and good ones too.

The child always has the option of turning an injunction around in this way to create positive instead of negative outcomes. For instance, a little boy who gets 'Don't be the sex you are' may grow into a man rich in positive qualities that are conventionally pictured as 'feminine' – sensitivity, physical warmth, openness to feelings.

Another way of avoiding the impact of injunctions is to make *compound decisions*. This means that the child uses Little Professor ingenuity in combining different script messages, with the objective of staying alive and getting her needs met as well as she can. These compound decisions come up frequently in script analysis, and are important in understanding how the script works. In the sections below, we look at various kinds of compound decision and see how they are used to defend against harmful injunctions. Practical experience suggests that Don't Exist is one of the messages most often defended against, and so we use it in most of the examples.

Counterinjunction covering an injunction

Consider the script matrix shown in Figure 14.1.

You'll notice Jack has been given the Don't Exist injunction by his mother. To Jack in his Little Professor, the main priority is to work out a way of staying alive. How might he do this?

One way is to take a counterinjunction and use it to cover up the Don't Exist. Jack might take his mother's 'Work Hard!' counterinjunction and make the compound decision: 'So long as I work hard, it's OK for me to stay alive.'

What is this likely to mean for Jack as a grown-up? He is likely to grow into a man who drives himself hard at whatever he does. At his job, he will be seen as a glutton for work. When he plays sports, he may work hard at being good at them. In personal relationships he may work hard to be good company, and when having sex he is likely to work hard to satisfy his partner.

Now suppose Jack starts getting high blood pressure, ulcers or other stress symptoms. He decides to work less hard. Maybe he takes extra holidays or starts delegating work to other people. Everything seems fine for a while. But strangely enough, Jack finds it very difficult to stick to his new pattern. Almost without knowing it, he fills his new-found leisure time with commitments. Maybe he takes up a voluntary position, and within a week or two is taking it so seriously that he's pressuring himself more than he was before. What's going on?

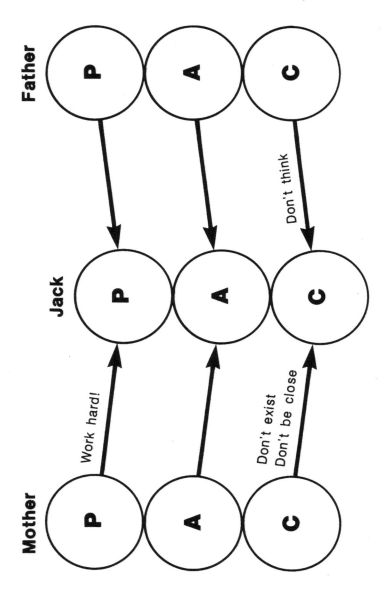

Figure 14.1 Partial script matrix for Jack

The clue is that Jack has disturbed the dynamic balance of his script. In his conscious awareness, he sees himself as having taken a positive step by dropping some of his workload. But in his unaware Little Professor, he perceives this same change as a threat to his life. His scripty belief is: 'Now I've stopped working so hard, I have to listen to Mother telling me to drop dead.' It's no wonder that he soon finds ways of starting to overwork again.

We say that Jack has been *covering* Mother's Don't Exist with the counterinjunction Work Hard. When he starts to work less hard, he *uncovers* the injunction.

This kind of script set-up sometimes has a paradoxical and particularly unpleasant outcome. In keeping on working hard, Jack is following a Little Professor strategy for staying alive. But after years of overwork, he may drop dead from a heart attack, or become disabled by ulcers or high blood pressure. The very set-up that is designed to *defend* against a hamartic payoff has resulted in that payoff being reached.

To see how Jack can make changes that truly release him from this negative set-up, we need to understand the dynamics of his compound decision. If he sets out to drop his overworking but does nothing about the underlying Don't Exist message, the chances are great that he will soon slip back into working too hard. This may appear like 'self-sabotage' to an outside observer. But to Jack in his Little Professor, it's the exact opposite of sabotage; it appears to be his only way of avoiding Mother's death threat.

To dismantle this part of his script, Jack needs to defuse the Don't Exist message *first*. Once he has given himself permission to keep on living despite Mother's curse, he can go ahead and reduce his work commitments. Now he will find he can keep the pressure off comfortably and permanently.

One injunction covering another injunction

Don't Exist was not the only injunction Jack got from his mother. She also gave him Don't Be Close. Jack might use this lighter injunction to defend against the heavier one. As an infant he might make the compound decision: 'It's OK for me to go on living, so long as I don't get close to anyone.'

When in his script as an adult, Jack, outside of his awareness, will play out this early decision. He will appear to others as physically distant and unwilling to share his feelings. He will likely find it difficult to give or take strokes, especially physical ones.

Jack may not be comfortable with this pattern. He may feel stroke-deprived or lonely, and set out to get closer to someone in a relationship. But it's probable that he will prevent himself from doing this for more than a short time. Then he is likely to find a way of drawing away from the other person, perhaps setting up to reject or be rejected.

Consciously, Jack feels sad and upset about being alone again. But in his unaware Little Professor, he is breathing a sigh of relief. Had he kept on being close, thus breaking Mother's Don't Be Close injunction, he would have had to face her homicidal command 'Don't Exist.'

Here again, if Jack wants to abandon this scripty set-up and enjoy closeness, he needs to begin by taking the sting out of the Don't Exist injunction. He can do this by deciding to live, no matter what.

Playing one parent against the other

Father did not hand Jack a Don't Exist message. Instead, he gave the lighter injunction Don't Think. This afforded Jack yet another infant strategy for staying alive. He might decide: 'So long as I play stupid for Father, I won't have to drop dead for Mother.'

In adult life, Jack may sometimes seem to 'switch off' his thinking. At these times he plays confused and says things like: 'I can't get my thoughts together. My mind must be going.' Outside of his awareness, he is seeking to keep Father around to protect him from Mother's lethal injunction.

Antiscript

Some people may take one of their script messages and turn it around to its opposite. They then follow this opposite instead of the original message. Most often, this is done with counterscript. When we act in this way we are said to be in *antiscript*.[3]

A person may go into and out of antiscript at different times in her life in response to any one script message. Teenage is a common time for antiscript. An example is the girl who has gone through childhood obeying the counterscript 'Be quiet and do what parents say'. At fourteen she suddenly switches, becoming brash and loud, staying out late, going around with what her parents call 'bad company'.

It might seem that she has broken free of her counterscript. In reality, she is following it just as much as she did before. She has merely turned her script message around, as you might turn a colour slide around to view it from the back.

Antiscript may be thought of as what the rebellious child decides to do when she has had enough of the script and counterscript. At this point, she stops caring what happens if she no longer follows these early decisions.

Later on, when she gets married, this same girl might move back out of antiscript and revert to her script and counterscript. Once again she would become quiet and conventional, this time acting the 'little woman' for her husband.

● DRAWING YOUR OWN SCRIPT MATRIX

Take a big sheet of paper and draw a blank script matrix like that in Figure 13.1. On it you can enter script messages you received from your parents.

This self-analysis is not meant to be an exact exercise. Nor does it give answers that are graven in stone. You should regard your script matrix as an important source of *information about your past*. It gives you a road-map of the ways in which you can *change your own future*. Like any map, your matrix can be revised and made more complete as you get more information. And like a map also, it can be changed as new roads are built and broadened, old ones done away with.

Work quickly and rely on your intuition.

Injunctions
Look through the list of 'twelve injunctions'. Consider whether you have experienced the living problems or discomforts associated with each one.

Note the injunctions you think have been important for you. Enter them on the matrix according to the parent they came from. Some may have come from both parents. Do you remember the parent modelling the injunction for you? Giving you injunction-laden commands or attributions? If in doubt, go on your hunches.

When entering up your injunctions, keep to the twelve standard names used in the Gouldings' list. If you think a variant name fits best, put it in brackets after the standard name. An example might be: 'Don't Be a Child (Don't Enjoy)'.

Counterscript
Recall the do's and don'ts, slogans and mottoes, your parents frequently gave you as a child. When was each parent pleased with you? Angry with you? What words did they use to let you know they were pleased or angry? What advice did they give you for how to be a success and bring credit to the family?

From this evidence, enter your counterscript messages. You will likely find it quite easy to remember which parent gave you which command. Listen for the voice in your head. If in doubt, simply guess. Some counterscript may come from other relatives, older siblings, or school-teachers.

Program
When compiling the script matrix, we conventionally only include the parts of the program that are negative. (There would not be space to enter all the thousands of positive 'How to's' all of us learn from our

parents). Recall that the negative program comes from the contaminated Adult of the parent, though on the diagram it is shown as coming simply from the Adult circle.

Did either parent model for you how to achieve some scripty outcome? Frequently, one parent models how to obey an injunction or counterinjunction you have got from the other parent. For instance, Mother may have handed you a Don't Feel message, while Father models: 'Here's how to deny your feelings'.

Enter your negative program as a set of statements beginning 'Here's how to...' Some people do not have any obvious negative program messages. If you cannot identify any, leave that part of your matrix blank.

Using fantasy, story and dream data

Now look back through the material you gathered while you were doing the exercises with fantasies, stories and dreams in Chapter 10. This will be in freehand form, just as you brought it to mind.

Look at it now in terms of the formal script matrix. Use your thinking and intuition to check how it relates to what you have already entered on the matrix diagram. Alter or fill out your matrix entries accordingly. ●

It has been traditional in TA to use formal *script questionnaires* to identify script data of the kind you have been discovering in the exercise above. We do not include a script questionnaire here, since we think formal questionnaires are more suitable for interview use than for self-directed script exploration. If you want to look at examples of formal questionnaires, follow up the References list for this chapter.[4]

Chapter 15
PROCESS SCRIPTS AND DRIVERS

So far in Part IV, we have been discussing the 'what' of the life-script – its *content*. Now in this chapter, we turn to look at the *process* of the script – how we live it out over time.

Study of the life-script has revealed a fascinating fact. It is that there seem to be only six main patterns of script process. Whether I am Chinese, African or American, I will live out my script according to one or more of these six patterns. The same is true whatever my age, sex, education or culture. These six *process scripts* are the subject of the first main section in this chapter.

In the chapter's second section, we go on to look at five distinctive, short-lived behaviour patterns called *driver behaviours*. These are closely related to process scripts. Like process scripts, they are universal across cultures, nationalities, religions or ages. Also in common with process scripts, the detection of driver behaviours is concerned only with *how* the person says or does things – the *process* of their behaviour or communication. You can observe someone's driver behaviours no matter what the *content* of their communication may be. You don't need to be in a counselling session with them; they don't even need to be talking about themselves.

By observing someone's driver behaviours, you can accurately predict their process script. Indeed, driver observation allows us you to predict a whole additional range of features of someone's personality – for example their main personal characteristics, their preferences about how to communicate with others and be communicated with, and their most likely script beliefs, typical games and rackets. This cluster of personal characteristics makes up the individual's *personality adaptation*. We shall go on to look at personality adaptations in more detail in the next chapter.

Process scripts

The six types of process script were originally described by Berne.[1] Some alterations to his classification have since been suggested by other TA theorists, notably Taibi Kahler.[2]

Here are the six patterns of script process, as listed by Eric Berne:

- *Until*
- *After*

- *Never*
- *Always*
- *Almost*
- *Open-ended.*

Each of these has its own theme, describing the way in which the person lives her script over time. Berne, always fond of the classics, listed a Greek myth illustrating each of these process themes.

Until script

If I live out my script according to the Until pattern, my motto in life is: 'I can't have fun *until* I've finished my work.' There are all sorts of possible variants of this, but they all share the notion that 'something good can't happen *until* something less good has been finished.'

'I have to understand myself fully before I can change.'

'Life begins at forty.'

'After I retire, I'll be able to travel.'

'My reward is in the next world.'

Like all the process themes, the Until pattern is lived out both short-term and long-term. Jonathan believes: 'Once the children grow up and leave, I'll have time to relax and do all the things I've been wanting to do.' Day by day as he waits for his lifetime Until, he lives out the same pattern over shorter time-spans. He says to his wife: 'OK, I'll come and have a drink with you, but just wait a minute until I've finished washing the dishes.'

Jonathan shows the Until pattern even in the structure of the sentences he uses. Frequently he will put in a *parenthesis*. He says things like: 'I told my wife – *and, mind you, I said the same to my daughter only yesterday* – that we'd have to do something about the house.' He interrupts himself in mid-sentence to put in the extra thought. With this sentence pattern, Jonathan is reflecting the Until belief: 'I have to cover everything before I can finish.'

The Greek hero Hercules had an Until script. Before he could be promoted to become a demi-god, he had to complete a set of arduous tasks – not least of which was cleaning a mountain of manure out of the King's stables.

After script

The After pattern is the obverse of Until. The person with an After script follows the motto: 'I can have fun today, but I'll have to pay for it tomorrow.'

'This is a great party! But oh, dear, what a headache I'm going to have in the morning.'

'After you're married, life is just one round of obligations.'

'I like to start the day bright and early, but I get tired by evening.'

Frequently, the After-script person will use the sentence pattern illustrated in the first and third of these examples. The sentence begins with a 'high'. Then comes a fulcrum, often represented by the word *but*. After that point, all the rest is a 'low'. A sentence like this is a miniature re-play of the After script.

The After pattern is illustrated by the myth of Damocles. This Greek potentate lived a round of eating, drinking and being merry. But all the time, above his head there hung a sword suspended on a single horse-hair. Once he looked up and saw it, he could never be happy again. He lived in constant dread of when it would fall. Like Damocles, the person with an After script believes he can have a good time today, but only at the cost of the sword falling tomorrow.

Never script

The theme of Never is: 'I can never get what I most want.' Andrew often says he would like to get into a steady relationship with a woman. But he has never done so. In fact, he never seems to get started going to places where he might meet new women. He's often thought he would like to go back to college and study for a degree. But he hasn't got round yet to submitting application papers.

In his Never script pattern, Andrew is like Tantalus, who was condemned to stand eternally in the middle of a pool of water. To one side of the pool was a store of food, to the other side a crock of water. But both were just out of Tantalus' reach, and he stayed hungry and thirsty.

In the myth, Tantalus didn't seem to realize that he could get hold of food and water by just taking a step to either side. A person in the Never script pattern is like this. He could get what he wanted by simply taking a step, but he doesn't take it.

No distinctive sentence pattern has been discovered for the Never script. However, people with a Never script often talk about negative script content in a repetitive, 'broken-record' manner. They tell you their troubles one day, then next day they tell them again as if the first time hadn't happened.

Always script

The person with an Always script asks: 'Why does this always happen to me?' The Greek myth for Always is that of Arachne, who was good at embroidery. She was unwise enough to challenge the goddess Minerva to an embroidering contest. The outraged deity changed Arachne into a spider, condemned to spin her web for all eternity.

Martha follows the Always pattern. She's been married three times and divorced twice. Her first marriage was to a man who was quiet, retiring and not very sociable. Martha broke with him, she told her friends, because she really wanted someone more dynamic. But to the surprise of those same friends, she was soon announcing her engagement to another man who seemed to them like a carbon-copy of the first one. That marriage didn't last long either. Martha's third husband is retiring, quiet and not very dynamic, and she's already complaining to her friends about him.

People with the Always pattern may play it out like Martha, by going from one unsatisfactory relationship, job or locality to another. A variant is to stay with the original unsatisfactory choice instead of moving on to a better one. The person with an Always script may say: 'I've not got much out of working with this therapist. But, well, I suppose I'll keep on and just hope we get somewhere.'

Martha often uses a sentence pattern that typically accompanies an Always script. She begins the sentence, then goes off on a tangent. She switches to another tangent and goes off on that one, and so on. 'Well, what I've come to see you for is...huh, when I was on the way here I saw my friend and she – oh, by the way, I've got some money with me and...'

Almost script

Sisyphus was another character to fall foul of the touchy Greek gods. He was condemned to spend eternity pushing a huge rock up a hill. Every time he almost got to the top, he lost his grip on the rock and it rolled all the way down to the bottom again. Like Sisyphus, the modern-day person with an Almost script says: 'I almost made it this time.'

Fred borrows a book from his friend. Giving it back, he says: 'Thanks for the book. I've read it all except the last chapter.' When Fred cleans his car, he gets it almost clean, except for a few patches of mud that he's missed.

Living his Almost pattern over the longer term, Fred has almost been promoted at work. But though he's got near the boss's chair, he's not quite made it in there. Each time he gets to the short-list, and each time he somehow fails to perform at the interview.

Berne called this script pattern 'Over and Over'. However, later writers have pointed out that *all* the patterns are lived over and over, and so the title 'Almost' has been adopted instead.

Taibi Kahler has suggested that there are two types of Almost pattern. He calls the one we have just described 'Almost Type 1'. In his 'Almost Type 2', the person actually *does* make it to the top of the hill. But instead of parking his rock and sitting down with a sigh of relief, this person hardly even notices he's got to the top. Without a pause, he looks around for an even higher hill to push the rock up, and off he goes. At the top of that one in turn, he looks around to spy a still higher mountain to tackle.

The person with Almost Type 2 will often be a material high achiever. Janet, for instance, sailed through her examinations at school. She went straight on to win a scholarship to college. By the time she graduated with a first-class degree, she had already decided to begin her PhD studies. Now holding her doctorate, she is working hard for a Fellowship to her learned society. Though the envy of her colleagues, Janet herself does not feel she has 'made it'. Once she's a Fellow, she tells her friends, she's got her eye on a Professorship. Of course it will mean still more hard work, and she never seems to have time to socialize.

There are two different sentence patterns that signal the Almost script. The speaker may start a sentence, then go off on one tangent which he finishes. 'What I'm lecturing to you about today is – oh, by the way, I have a page of notes that I'll give you.'

Alternatively, the person with an Almost script may come out with a string of positives followed by a single negative. 'Aren't the trees lovely in Autumn? It's really warm, too, and such bright sunshine. Mind you, the air's cold.'

Open-ended script

This pattern resembles the Until and After scripts in having a particular cut-off point after which things change. But for the person with an Open-ended script, the time after that point is just one big void. It's as if the closing pages of a theatrical script had gone missing.

Alfred has just retired after 40 years' service to his firm. Now he's at home with his tributes and marble clock. He had been looking forward to his extra leisure. But instead of enjoying it, he feels strangely uneasy. What's he going to do with himself? How will he fill his time?

Margery says goodbye to the youngest of her four children as he leaves home for the last time, now a young adult. She heaves a sigh of relief. After all these years, no more child-rearing chores! But a day or two later, Margery is feeling a bit down. Without the extra washing-up, the dirty clothes lying around for her to tidy away, she's at a loss what to do with her time.

The Open-ended script pattern may be lived out over the short as well as the long term. Some people typically set only short-term goals. Once they have completed these, they flounder, not knowing what to do until something else comes along. Then they set another short-term goal, and the process is repeated.

The motto of the Open-ended script is: 'Once I get to a certain point in time, I won't know what to do with myself afterwards.' It recalls the myth of Philemon and Baucis. This elderly couple welcomed the gods in the form of travel-worn strangers when others would not. As a reward for their kindness, the gods extended their lives by turning them into trees planted beside each other with their branches entwined.

Combinations of process themes

We all show all six of the process script patterns. But for most of us, one of the patterns is predominant. Jonathan shows mainly the Until script, Martha clearly lives out the Always pattern, and so on.

Some people combine two of the patterns. Usually one of these will be the main one, with a second one also important. For instance, people with Almost Type 2 may also show the Until pattern. This is true of Janet in our example. Her unspoken motto is: 'I can't rest until I've made it to the top. And I never really make it to the top, because there's always an even higher top somewhere. Therefore, I can never rest.'

A person who combines the Until and Never scripts will follow the belief: 'I can't have fun until I've finished my work. But I never finish my work. Therefore, I can never have fun.'

Other frequent combinations are After plus Almost Type 1, and Always plus Never. You may care to work out the scripty 'mottoes' that go with each.

● YOUR PROCESS SCRIPT PATTERN

Look through the descriptions given above for the different process script types. Pick out the pattern or patterns that you think have been typical of you.

If your partner, or a friend who knows you well, is willing to work with you on this exploration: ask them to read through the descriptions of the various process script types, then ask them to give their opinion on the main process script pattern(s) that you show. ●

Origins of process script

Why are there only these six process themes? Why are they so uniform across cultures? Nobody knows. Finding the answers to these questions is a challenging task for TA research.

We do have some idea about how process script is transmitted from parents to children. It seems to be part of the counterscript, passed on mainly by parental modelling.

Driver behaviours

Working in the early 1970s, clinical psychologist Taibi Kahler made an intriguing discovery. He had followed up Berne's idea that the script may be played out over very short time periods. Second by second, Kahler noted his subjects' words, tones, gestures, postures and facial expressions. He found that there were certain distinctive sets of these behaviours that people consistently showed *just before* they moved into any kind of scripty behaviour or feelings.

Kahler and his co-workers listed five of these second-by-second behaviour sequences. They called them *driver behaviours.*[3]

These five patterns of behaviour also turned out to be distinctively related to the six process script types. By observing someone's driver patterns, you can predict reliably what her process script will be. You can also predict many other features of her life-script and of her personality generally, as the following chapter will show.

Thus by learning how to detect the five driver behaviours, you can tell a lot about a person in a short space of time. In this section we describe how you can observe these behaviours.

How to detect driver behaviour

The five driver behaviours are:

- *Be Perfect*
- *Be Strong*
- *Try Hard*
- *Please (others)*
- *Hurry Up.*

Each of these is signalled by a distinctive set of *words, tones, gestures, postures and facial expressions.*

You have already learned to use these clues in making a behavioural diagnosis of ego-states (Chapter 5 above). In looking for driver behaviours, you need to shrink your time-scale. Driver behaviours are typically shown within half-a-second to one second. Observing within this short time-span takes some initial practice if you are not used to it. But it soon becomes second nature.

The caution 'don't interpret' applies here, just as it did when we were discussing behavioural diagnosis in general. Stay with the behaviours you can actually see and hear. For instance, as you look at me you may be tempted to say I 'look stern'. But what am I doing with my face, body and voice that you interpret as 'sternness'? Where do you see muscle tension? Is my voice low, high, loud, harsh? Are my eyebrows up or down? In what direction am I looking? What hand gestures do you see me making? To become skilful at detecting drivers, stay with observable clues like these. Following is a list of the clues for each driver.

Be Perfect

Words: the person in Be Perfect will often use *parentheses.* For example:

'I'm here today, *as I said*, to teach you about drivers.'

'TA is, *we might say*, a theory of personality.'

The wording for Be Perfect frequently includes words and phrases like these, whether in parentheses or not. They act as qualifiers but add no new information to what's being said. Typically: *as it were, probably, possibly, certainly, completely, one might say, as we have seen.*

Another clue is that the speaker may count points off by numbers or letters. 'Our topics today are – *one* – to discuss drivers; and – *two* – to study their relationship to script.'

Tones: often sound Adult. Well-modulated, neither high nor low.

Gestures: counting on the fingers to accompany the points counted off by letters or numbers in the wording. Hand may stroke chin in the traditional 'thinker's' gesture. Fingertips may be placed together in a V shape, the gesture called 'steepling'.

Postures: often looks like Adult. Upright, evenly balanced round midline.

Facial expressions: eyes look upwards (less often, downwards) and to one side, usually while the person is making a pause in speech. It's as though the person were trying to read the 'perfect answer' written somewhere on the ceiling or floor. At the same time, the mouth is often slightly tensed, with the corners drawn a little outwards.

Be Strong

Words: a person in Be Strong will typically distance from their feelings and use words that convey: 'my feelings and actions are not my responsibility, but are caused by agencies outside me.'

'You're making me angry.'

'This book bores me.'

'The thought strikes me that...'

'His attitude forced me to fight back.'

'The inner-city environment brings about violence.'

Often, too, he uses distancing words like *one, you, people, it, that,* when he is talking about himself.

'It feels scary' (meaning 'I feel scared').

'That feels good' (meaning 'I feel good').

'You have to keep your feelings to yourself' (meaning 'I have to').

'Situations like this put pressure on one.'

Tones: flat, monotonous, usually low.

Gestures: Be Strong is marked by an absence of gesture.

Postures: frequently the posture is 'closed'. The arms may be folded or crossed in front of the body. Legs may be crossed, or placed in the 'figure-four' position, with the ankle of one leg resting on the knee of the other. The whole body conveys immobility.

Facial expressions: the face is expressionless and immobile.

Try Hard

Words: the word patterns most typical of Try Hard are interrogative grunts like *huh? uh?,* and vocalizations such as *can't, what? what's that again? don't get you, it's hard to....*

The person in Try Hard may sometimes use the word *try:*

'What *I'm trying* to tell you is...'

'*I'll try* and do what we agreed.'

However, in our experience, the use of 'try' is not in itself highly diagnostic of the Try Hard driver. When used in this driver fashion, 'try' always conveys 'I'll try to do it instead of doing it.' And, as listener, you may not know until afterwards whether or not this was the meaning being conveyed.

Tones: the person will often tense up the throat muscles so that the voice sounds muffled or strangled.

Gestures: often one hand is placed beside the eyes or beside one ear, as though the person were straining to hear or see something. Fists may be clenched.

Postures: with Try Hard as with Please Others, the person often strains forward. Hands may be placed on the knees. General impression is of a hunched-up pose.

Facial expressions: a distinctive clue for Try Hard is that the person crunches his brow up so that two vertical lines appear above his nose. The eyes and sometimes the whole face may be screwed up into tight wrinkles.

Please Others

Words: the person in Please Others often uses the 'high-*but*-low' sentence structure we have already met as a clue to the After script.

'I've really enjoyed your teaching, but I don't know if I'll remember what you said.'

'What a terrific party! But, by golly, I'm going to regret it in the morning.'

Frequently she will put in querying words and phrases like *OK? hmm? all right by you? kind of...? sort of...?*

Tones: high voice, squeaky tone, typically rising at the end of each sentence.

Gestures: reaching out with the hands, usually palms up. Head nodding.

Postures: shoulders hunched up and forward. Leaning towards the other person.

Facial expressions: the person in Please Others will very often look at you with her face turned slightly downwards. Thus she needs to look up at you with her eyebrows raised. This in turn means that she crinkles her brow up into horizontal lines. At the same time she shapes her mouth in an expression similar to a smile. However, as compared to a non-driver genuine smile, the Please Others expression is more tense. The upper teeth are bared, and sometimes the lower teeth are shown as well.

Hurry Up

Words: hurry, quick, get going, let's go, no time to...

Tones: staccato, machine-gun-like. Sometimes the person in Hurry Up will rush the words out so quickly that she scrambles them up.

Gestures: finger-tapping, foot-tapping or wagging, wriggling round in the chair, repetitive checking of watch.

Postures: no specific posture, but the overall impression is of agitated movement.

Facial expressions: frequent, rapid changes in direction of gaze.

In our experience, it's unusual for someone to show several Hurry Up clues at any one time. Much more often, *one* of the clues to Hurry Up is shown, while at the same time the person is showing several clues to a different driver. For example, I may be in Be Strong, stony-faced, holding an immobile position with arms and legs tightly crossed... while down below, I incessantly waggle my left foot.

No one clue necessitates a driver

For reliable diagnosis of a driver, you need to look for *several clues for that driver occurring together.* Do not go on just one clue. For instance, hearing me say 'I'll try to...', you may conclude: 'Aha! He's in Try Hard driver.' But that does not necessarily follow. Were you to look at my other behavioural clues, you might see me tensing my mouth, looking upwards at the ceiling, and ticking off points on my fingers. These signals would make it more likely that I was actually in the Be Perfect driver. Alternatively, I could speak the words 'I'll try to...' while my other behavioural clues signalled that I was in Adult, not in any driver. (As we have just said, the Hurry Up driver is an exception to this advice to 'look for several clues').

Caution: you cannot detect drivers by observing content

To detect drivers effectively, you must focus on *process.* You cannot detect drivers by just observing the *content* of the person's behaviour.

For example, suppose you get the impression that your friend Andy 'wants to do things perfectly'. You may have noticed that he isn't comfortable to go out to work without putting a perfect shine on his shoes. Or he may present written work that is always impeccably laid out on the page. Features like these may be of interest to you in themselves. But they alone are *not* diagnostic of the Be Perfect driver. 'Wanting to get things perfect' has to do with the content of the person's behaviour, not its process. If you did want to know whether Andy showed the Be Perfect driver, you would check from second to second whether he often used parentheses in his speech patterns, looked upwards during pauses, or counted out points with his fingers.

Likewise, suppose Jeanette answers 'Yes' when asked in a research questionnaire: 'Do you find it important to please others?' Again, this tells you something about her personality. But it is *not* a way to discover whether she shows the Please Others driver. That driver, like all the others, consists in a package of quite specific, short-lived behaviours. To detect Please Others, you would not look for general 'pleasingness'. You would check from second to second whether Jeanette momentarily raised her eyebrows, bared her upper teeth, turned her face down while looking upwards, hunched her shoulders around her ears, and said *anything* in a high and rising voice tone.

Unfortunately, some writers and researchers in TA have fallen into the tempting trap of assuming that drivers could be detected from content. Entire books have been written, entire research projects carried out, starting from this misconception. We earnestly invite you not to share in their mistake. If you would like to be a skilful 'driver detective', your guiding principle always is: *stay with the process.*

Primary driver

Each of us shows all five of the driver behaviours. But most people have one driver that they show most frequently. Often this will also be the driver they show *first* when they respond to a transactional stimulus. This is called their *primary driver*.

Some people have two main drivers that are about equal in frequency. Much less often, you meet someone who shows an even spread of three or more drivers.

● PRACTICE IN DETECTING DRIVER BEHAVIOURS

If you have a television set, watch an interview program. Use it as practice in detecting the second-by-second clues of driver behaviour.

If you have a video recorder, record the program while you are doing this. Later, play back the recording in slow motion or with stop-frames. Check your second-by-second observations against this.

Experiment to see whether different TV personalities typically show different primary drivers. Does your favourite comedian have a different primary driver from your least favourite politician?

What do you think is your own primary driver? Write your answer down.

Now get an objective check. Either have someone observe you who knows driver clues, or record yourself on video and play back the recording. Were you right in your initial guess of your own primary driver?

If you are working in a group, get into sub-groups of three. Decide who will be 'client', who will be 'counsellor' and who will be 'observer'. The client talks to the counsellor for three minutes on any light topic. The counsellor listens and responds in any way she wishes, and is also responsible for timekeeping. The observer, with pencil and paper, notes down which drivers he detects in the behaviour of client and counsellor. (To simplify the exercise the first time through, the observer can concentrate on the client's driver behaviours only). When the three minutes is up, the observer feeds back what driver clues he observed. Then switch roles and repeat the exercise.

Look out for driver behaviour in all sorts of everyday interaction. Practise detecting drivers as you work, shop, travel, have casual conversations with friends. *Do not tell people you are doing this* unless you know for sure they are interested. ●

Drivers and process script types

By noting someone's primary driver(s), you can tell their main process script type.[4] The correspondences between the two are shown in Table 15.1.

Main driver(s)	Process script(s)
Be Perfect	Until
Be Perfect + Be Strong	Until + Never
Be Strong	Never
Try Hard	Always
Please Others	After
Please Others +Try Hard	Almost 1
Please Others + Be Perfect	Almost 2
Please Others + Be Perfect	Open-Ended

Table 15.1: Drivers and Process Scripts

The two types of Almost script are shown by people who have Please Others ranking first-equal with Try Hard and Be Perfect respectively. For the Open-ended script, the person will also show Please Others plus Be Perfect, but both drivers will be shown more intensely than for Almost Type 2.

● YOUR PRIMARY DRIVER AND SCRIPT PROCESS

You have already noted which process script was most typical for you. You have noted also your primary driver. Do the two correspond in the way we have described in the section above?

What if they do not seem to correspond? The listed connections be-tween driver and process script are generalizations, and it is conceivable they may simply not apply to you. But they have proven to apply reliably in thousands of observed cases. If they appear at first not to fit for you, it is worth while to review your initial judgment on your primary driver and your process script type. In our experience, the most common rea-son for an apparent mis-fit is that the person has not identified her pri-mary driver accurately. ●

Driver *behaviours* and driver *messages*

If you are reading through this book in chapter order, you may already have been thinking: 'I've seen these five driver names before. They were mentioned in Chapter 13. They were described there as "five commands in particular that play a special role in the counterscript". So when we talk about "drivers", are we talking about counterscript messages, or are we talking about observable behaviours?'

The fact is we are talking about both. There are indeed five driver messages, which are listed on the script matrix among the counterinjunc-tions. And, as we said in Chapter 13: 'When I replay a driver message internally, I exhibit a set of behaviours that typically accompany that driver.' That 'set of behaviours', shown externally, is the driver behav-iour.

As with any script message, if the child decides to obey it, she or he will make a corresponding *script decision*. Decisions around the driver messages will form part of the counterscript. The content of each of these counterscript decisions is shown in Table 15.2.

Drivers and life position

You'll see from this table that the driver messages in the counterscript carry a special implication about life position. The Parental message is: 'You're OK *if* you...are perfect, please others, etc.'

Thus when I am in script and listening to this Parental message in my

Adapted Child, my position is: 'I'm OK *as long as* I...am perfect, please others, etc.'

We say that drivers reflect a position of *conditional OKness*.

Driver	Counterscript decision
Be Perfect	I'm only OK if I get everything right (therefore, I've got to cover every detail before I can finish anything)
Be Strong	I'm only OK if I disown my feelings and wants
Try Hard	I'm only OK if I keep on trying hard (therefore, I won't actually do what I'm trying to do; because if I did it, I wouldn't be trying to do it any more)
Please Others	I'm only OK if I please other people
Hurry Up	I'm only OK if I hurry up

Table 15.2: Counterscript decisions underlying the five drivers

Drivers and life position

You'll see from this table that the driver messages in the counterscript carry a special implication about life position. The Parental message is: 'You're OK *if* you...are perfect, please others, etc.'

Thus when I am in script and listening to this Parental message in my Adapted Child, my position is: 'I'm OK *as long as* I...am perfect, please others, etc.'

We say that drivers reflect a position of *conditional OKness*.

Why drivers are related to process scripts

Why is driver behaviour related so closely to process script type? The answer is that the driver behaviours themselves are miniature versions of the process scripts. Each time I go into a driver behaviour, I play out the corresponding process script pattern within the space of half-a-second.

As Taibi Kahler expresses it: 'The five drivers are the functional manifestations of not-OK (structural) counterscripts.'

For instance, suppose I am teaching a class about TA. I say: 'TA – which was first developed by Eric Berne, in approximately the years from the late 1950s onwards – is a system, or should we say model, for understanding personality; that, at least, is a beginning definition.' As I come out with this mouthful of parentheses, I am looking upwards at the ceiling, as though I expected to see the perfect definition written there. I am ticking off with my fingers the two concepts 'system' and 'model', to make sure I've said it in every way possible.

In the instant I carry out this set of Be Perfect behaviours, I am obeying an internal Parental voice that says: 'You're only OK around here if you get everything right.' Listening to this voice from my Adapted Child, I am believing that I can't finish my sentence *until* I've covered the entire waterfront. Otherwise, says my Child belief, I'll be not-OK.

Thus, in those few seconds, I have lived out my main script process of Until. In doing so, I have reinforced that process.

This driver-script relationship holds also for three of the other drivers. Each time I show the Please Others driver, I am living out the After script pattern. The Parental voice in my head repeats the counterscript: 'You're only OK around here if you please people.' With raised eyebrows and toothy smile, I hope from Adapted Child I am being pleasing enough. *But* I'm scared that sooner or later I'll run out of energy to please, and then will come the 'downer' as the sword of Damocles falls on my head.

In showing Be Strong, I am tuning in a counterscript message: 'You're only OK if you hide your feelings and wants from people. Don't let them see you're weak.' Listening to this in Adapted Child, I obey by shutting down external signals. I keep my face impassive, move little, speak in a flat voice.

As I show this set of Be Strong behaviours, I live out and reinforce the Never script process pattern. I may want contact and strokes from the others around me. But by keeping up my expressionless front, I give them no clue of this. Like Tantalus, I stop myself from making the move I would need to make to get what I want.

Suppose my primary driver is Try Hard. As you ask me a question, I hunch forward, crunching my brow into two vertical lines above my nose. I squint my eyes. My hand is up beside my head, as though I had difficulty in hearing you. I say: 'Huh? What? Didn't get you.' Actually my hearing is fine. I am in the Try Hard driver. During those few seconds, I am listening to a Parental voice from the past. It tells me: 'To be OK around here, you have to keep trying hard to do things.' In order to obey this command, I 'know' in Adapted Child that I can't let myself actually get around to doing anything. If I did do it, I couldn't keep on trying hard to do it any more.

As I try to do things but don't, I continue to go round and round in the Always script pattern. Maybe I don't much like where I am at the moment. I try hard to get somewhere else, but don't actually do what I'd need to do to get there.

The connections between script and driver for the two Almost scripts and the Open-ended script are not so clear. By conjecture, it isn't difficult to see how the combined counterscript mottoes for the drivers might add up to the script patterns. You may care to work out what the combined mottoes are, and do your own conjecturing.

You'll notice that there is no direct driver-script connection for the Hurry Up driver. In many ways, Hurry Up is an odd-man-out among the drivers. It seems to turn up most often along with another driver as primary, and to act as a reinforcer of that primary.

Driver behaviour is a 'gateway into script'

One of Taibi Kahler's earliest discoveries about driver behaviours was that, just before a person experiences a racket feeling or internally 'hears' an injunction, she will *always* show driver behaviour.[5] It is as though the person moving into script must unavoidably do so by going through a driver 'gateway'.

The usefulness of this for you is clear. There are many situations where you may want to get some indication whether a particular item of behaviour, or a particular reported feeling, is scripty or is not scripty. For example, suppose you are in conversation with somebody and he laughs. Is this a gallows laugh or an autonomous laugh? Or suppose she expresses anger. Is this racket or authentic anger?

Here is the clue that driver behaviour gives you: did the person engage in driver behaviour *just before* he laughed, or just before she expressed the feeling? If the answer is 'no', then you know that the person has *not* moved into script.

Note, however, that the reasoning does not necessarily work in the converse direction. As we have said, the person who goes into script will always show driver behaviour just before doing so. But it is also possible for the person to show a driver behaviour and then *not* go into script. She may, instead, simply move back out of the driver behaviour into non-scripty feelings and behaviours. The 'gateway into script' is just like any other gateway. There are times when you can come to the gateway, take a look through, but then not go through it. Other times, you can come to the gateway, open it, and go on through to the other side.

This reflects the fact that the Child sees the driver as a 'condition for OKness'. Suppose I get into my Be Perfect driver. I start hearing the Parental voice in my head: 'You're OK *as long as* you get things perfect enough.' For my Child, either of two things can happen after that. One is that I do experience myself as 'getting things perfect enough' to satisfy my internal Parent. In that event, I let myself stay OK. From the outside, you'll see me dipping into my Be Perfect driver behaviour for an instant, then moving back into driver-free Adult. I have momentarily opened up the driver 'gateway', taken a look through, then shut it again.

The alternative outcome is that I don't 'get things perfect enough' for my internal Parent. Then my Child belief is, 'I'm no longer OK.' And with that, I go on through the driver 'gateway' and into my negative script. In my external behaviour, you typically might see me following up the driver with a racket, a gallows laugh, or a move on to the Drama Triangle.

So in summary, here's how driver observation helps you to judge whether or not someone has gone into script:

- If *no* driver behaviour: subsequent feeling or behaviour is *not* scripty.
- If driver behaviour: subsequent feeling or behaviour *may or may not* be scripty.

Origins of drivers

Why are there five and only five driver behaviours? Why are they the same for everybody, regardless of culture, age, or education? Why does each driver consistently accompany its own specific counterscript message? Nobody knows.

Taibi Kahler himself has suggested that the drivers may be partly in-born, a result of 'nature' as well as 'nurture'.[6] This would certainly help to account for their apparently 'automatic' quality. There is also some interesting work emerging from current neuroscience, drawing attention to the fact that certain facial expressions, gestures etc. are universally recognised across cultures as conveying particular social messages.[7] Perhaps driver behaviours belong in that category.

But these ideas are still in the realm of conjecture. One of the most challenging tasks of current TA research is to produce a convincing account of the origins of driver behaviour.

Should we set out to 'cure' drivers and process scripts?

When the awareness of process scripts and drivers was first being developed, during a decade or so from the late 1970s, it seemed almost as though TA practitioners had found a 'magic bullet' to help cure their clients. Since drivers are a 'gateway into script', the reasoning went, then if we confronted driver behaviours we would help the client to keep that 'gate' shut. Hence they would never go into their script in the first place. For example, if a therapy client screwed up her face and said 'I'll try…, the therapist might retort: 'Will you relax your face, look me right in the eye, and say "I will…"?'

And when it came to moving out of one's process script, that seemed equally straightforward. You could do it as a self-help exercise. All you needed to do, it seemed, was first to get aware of whatever process pattern you had been living out. If you decided you wanted to change it, you simply made an Adult decision to act in ways that contradicted the pattern. For instance, if you had been living according to an After script, you might make a contract with yourself to enjoy a party *and* feel good the morning after. (An interesting variation of this was, 'I'll decide to feel bad about something before the party, so I can go ahead and feel good after it.'). Several textbooks on TA published around that time – including the first edition of this book – included detailed lists of suggestions on how to change one's process patterns in this way, by Adult thought and action.

However, time and experience have moved on since then. It turns out that there is one big problem with these seemingly obvious ways of changing one's script. That is: they don't work. Or at least, they don't work all the time, and for most people they don't produce permanent change.[8]

The first casualty of experience was the notion that it was therapeutically useful to confront driver behaviours. For sure, it is possible to confront each and every driver behaviour that someone shows. But if you do, the outcome most often is that they quickly start feeling bad. Far from staying out of their script, they get right into it. And if you consider the possibility that driver behaviour may be a 'hard-wired' social signal from their Child that says 'I'm beginning to get into distress here', then what signal might you be sending to the other person by continually confronting every driver? In Child they may experience you as conveying: 'I'm not "hearing" you, no matter what you say.' If that's the case, no wonder they feel bad.

In present-day TA practice, therefore, we don't invite clients to 'get rid of' their driver behaviours. Instead, we observe these behaviours and *use* them diagnostically. We take from them the rich information they give us about a person's script and personality style, and work from there.

As for the suggestion that someone can extinguish their process script by deliberately acting in ways that contradict it: for some people, this may succeed in producing permanent change. More often, it works for a while, but then the old process pattern 'creeps up on' the person again. For example, take the individual with the After script who contracts to enjoy the party and feel good the next morning. She may do so once, or a few times. But then she goes to another party, enjoys herself, then feels awful the next morning and says: 'What happened that time?'

Why so? The clue here is a point that we first mentioned in Chapter 14. That is: within the dynamic balance of the life-script, it's often the case that one script decision may be used as a defence against another. In particular, a counterscript decision may be used as a defence against a decision in the script proper. For example, the Child may make the *compound decision:* 'It's OK for me to exist *as long as* I please people.'

As you've learned in this chapter, process script patterns themselves are part of the counterscript. Recall Jonathan, whose main process script pattern is Until. It's possible that Jonathan may have taken the compound decision: 'It's OK for me to exist – *as long as* I keep on putting off enjoying myself until I've got all my work finished.' If so, Jonathan would be using the Until script pattern as a defence against a Don't Exist injunction.

Now suppose Jonathan decided from Adult to break out of his Until pattern. To his Child, this would mean he was taking away his defence against a death sentence. But, as always with defences against Don't Exist, it's extremely unlikely that he would simply go off and commit suicide. Instead, his Child would find ways of 'sabotaging' the behavioural change. So we might soon find Jonathan saying: 'I know I've decided to get out of my Until script, so I'll be knocking off work shortly – but just a minute, I need to clear my email Inbox.'

To summarize: if someone is using a process script pattern as a defence against another more harmful part of the script, then any Adult decision to change the process script pattern is likely to fail. In a worst-case scenario, it might even be dangerous.

So if you have a process script that you don't like, what do you do? Our suggestion is that if it's practicable for you, you go to a competent therapist or counsellor and explore your script to discover whether the process pattern is a defence against any 'heavier' script decision. If it turns out not to be a defence, then you can go ahead and contract for behavioural changes to counteract your unwanted process script. If, on the other hand, it emerges that your process pattern has been defending against a more harmful decision in your script proper, then you can work with the practitioner to defuse that heavier decision. Once that's done, you'll discover that the unwanted process pattern is much easier – and safer – to shift.

Chapter 16
PERSONALITY ADAPTATIONS

One of the most useful concepts in current TA is the model of *personality adaptations*. These represent six ways in which a person may deal with the world, based on what worked best in their family of origin. In this chapter we show how you can recognize the six adaptations. Throughout the chapter we include exercises that you can use to help discover your own adaptations.

Why is it useful to know personality adaptation?
When you know someone's personality adaptation(s), you can key in directly to a whole body of extra information that is likely to apply to that person. First of all, you get a general description of their personality – 'the kind of person they are'. You can make a reliable prediction of their main *process script,* which we described in the previous chapter. Each adaptation also carries with it a typical set of *script beliefs* about self, others and the world. Along with these go typical emotions and patterns of behaviour that the person is likely to show while in script – that is, their typical *games, rackets* and *racket feelings*. This information is invaluable as a starting point for personal change in therapy (including self-therapy) and counselling. It also helps in the everyday task of understanding oneself and others and knowing how best to get along with the people in your life.

Each personality adaptation has typical positive traits that the person can use constructively. This knowledge helps individuals to build on their strengths. It is also useful in the organizational field, as an aid to successful team-building.

By knowing someone's personality adaptation, you also gain guidance on how best to make and keep contact with that person. To do this, you make a systematic choice of the sequence in which you address the person's three *contact areas* of thinking, feeling or behaviour. This is the *Ware Sequence.* We shall describe it in detail below.

The six personality adaptations
The concept of personality adaptations was first developed by psychiatrist Paul Ware and clinical psychologist Taibi Kahler.[1] Further contributions to theory and practice in the area have been made by one of the present

authors, Vann Joines.[2] As part of the process of script-formation, say these writers, every child decides on a set of basic strategies for surviving, and a set of strategies for dealing with the parents' expectations. The person replays these strategies in grown-up life, particularly in stressful situations. The strategies then represent various ways of *adapting to* the world. Research has shown that there are six main sets of these strategies.[3] These six correspond to the six core personality adaptations.

All 'normal' people display most of the six adaptations to some degree, since they each represent the very best option for dealing with a particular situation. However, most of us have one adaptation that is more prominent than any of the others. Some people have two adaptations that are first-equal in importance.

As a psychiatrist, Paul Ware noted that the six personality adaptations corresponded broadly to certain formal diagnostic categories. In his original work, he labelled them with names drawn from clinical psychodiagnosis. However, Ware stresses that his use of these labels *does not necessarily imply psychopathology in a clinical sense*. Each adaptation is defined by a set of characteristics and behaviours, some of which would typically be regarded as positive and others that would usually be viewed as negative. Therefore, a person can show the characteristics of any of the adaptations while still being clinically 'normal'. In other words, we will see the adaptations across the spectrum from healthy to dysfunctional. A formal clinical diagnosis will only be attached if a person shows a particular adaptation at such high intensity as to interfere with his day-to-day functioning. When that is true, the person is using predominantly the negative behaviours of that adaptation.

To underline that the adaptations comprise positive as well as negative behaviours, we shall give an alternative set of names for the personality adaptations, suggested by Vann Joines.[4] We list these names below, each following the traditional diagnostic label that was applied to the adaptation by Paul Ware. (In place of Ware's original label 'Hysteric', we have used the term 'Histrionic' that is now more usual).

- Obsessive-compulsive *(Responsible-Workaholic)*
- Paranoid *(Brilliant-Skeptic)*
- Schizoid *(Creative-Daydreamer)*
- Passive-aggressive *(Playful-Resister)*
- Histrionic *(Enthusiastic-Overreactor)*
- Antisocial *(Charming-Manipulator)*.

By the adjective he adds to each name, Joines underlines the important point that each adaptation has its advantages as well as its problems.

Table 16.1 lists the personality traits that define each personality adaptation.

Adaptation	Characteristics	Description
Responsible-Workaholic (*Obsessive-Compulsive*)	Conforming, conscientious, responsible, reliable	Perfectionist, overly inhibited, dutiful, tense (hardest thing to relax), dependable, neat
Brilliant-Skeptic (*Paranoid*)	Rigidity of thought, grandiosity, projection, brilliant thinkers, very alert, keep on top of things, pay attention to details	Hypersensitive, suspicious, jealous, envious, knowledgeable, careful
Creative-Daydreamer (*Schizoid*)	Withdrawn passivity, day dreaming, avoidance, detachment, artistic, creative thinking, concerned about others	Shy, overly sensitive, eccentric, caring, supportive, pleasant, kind
Playful-Resister (*Passive-Aggressive*)	Aggressive passivity, demonstrates resentment, overly-dependent, determined to think for themselves, weighs both sides of an issue	Obstructive, pouting, stubborn, loyal, energetic, playful, tenacious
Enthusiastic-Overreactor (*Histrionic*)	Excitable, over-reactive, emotionally unstable, dramatic, attention getting, seductive, high energy, concerned about others' feelings, imaginative	Immature, self-centred, vain, dependent, playful, attractive, fun
Charming-Manipulator (*Antisocial*)	Conflict (with rules of society), low frustration tolerance, seek excitement and drama, high energy, goal oriented, think well on their feet	Selfish, callous (tough), irresponsible, impulsive, charming, charismatic, aggressive, articulate, promoting, manipulating

Table 16.1: The six personality adaptations in summary

● Look through the list of personality features shown in Table 16.1. For each adaptation, consider the 'Characteristics' and the 'Description' together, as making up the overall cluster of features defining that adaptation. Working down the list of adaptations, mark the items in the Characteristics and the Description for each adaptation that you think apply especially to you.

For example, looking at the features shown under Characteristics for the Workaholic, I say to myself: 'Conforming? No, that's not really "me".' So I don't mark that item. I look at the next three words – 'conscientious, responsible, reliable' – and think, 'Oh yes, all these fit me OK.' So I mark all three. Looking next at the Description column for Workaholic, I mark off 'perfectionist, dutiful, dependable', since all these are words I'd apply to myself. But I don't identify myself as 'overly inhibited' or 'tense', so I leave these unmarked. And as for being 'neat' – I could wish! So I don't mark that one either.

When you've worked all the way down the list, take a look at the different numbers of features that you've marked within each adaptation. Is there one adaptation that you've marked noticeably more than any other? If so, which one is it? Perhaps you'll find there are two adaptations that have about the same number of marks. Much less likely, but still a possibility, is that that you've marked three or more adaptations just about equally.

It can be very useful to get a 'second opinion' on this exercise. If you want to do that, make a copy of the list. Ask somebody who knows you well – partner, friend, workmate – to mark up the adaptation features in the way you've just done for yourself. Don't show them your own list until they've done that. Then compare their list with yours.

If you're working in a group, you can do this as a pair-work or small-group exercise, with each member of the group marking up their own list and also marking up the list for the other member(s) of the pair or group.

What you get from this exercise is a *subjective* view – your own or somebody else's – of the degree to which you show the qualities of each adaptation. As the chapter goes on, you'll see how this initial 'take' on your adaptations can be cross-checked against other evidence.

THE JOINES PERSONALITY ADAPTATIONS QUESTIONNAIRE (JPAQ)

If you would like an accurate and objective assessment of your adaptations, using a validated questionnaire, you can take the Joines Personality Adaptation Questionnaire (JPAQ) for a small fee on-line at *www.seinstitute.com*. An administrative, scoring, and interpretative kit for the JPAQ can also be purchased at the same web address. ●

'Surviving' v. 'performing' adaptations

Three of the adaptations are called 'surviving adaptations', since they involve how the child learns to take care of himself when he feels he can't rely on others to keep him safe. These surviving adaptations are the *Creative-Daydreamer, Charming-Manipulator,* and *Brilliant-Skeptic.*

The three others are called 'performing adaptations', because they involve how the child tries to take care of himself in light of the parents' expectations. The performing adaptations are *Playful-Resister, Responsible-Workaholic,* and *Enthusiastic-Overreactor.* Everyone has at least one of the surviving adaptations and at least one of the performing adaptations that are most prominent, although some people may have more than one of each.

How drivers indicate personality adaptations

You can also assess someone's personality adaptation within a few minutes of first meeting her, without the need for extensive 'history-taking'. You do this by observing the person's driver behaviours.

By noting a person's *primary driver* (recall the previous chapter) you can make a reliable diagnosis of her main personality adaptation. Table 16.2 shows the correspondences between drivers and personality adaptations. For each adaptation, the primary driver may often be accompanied by secondary drivers. These are shown in brackets.

Primary Driver(s)	Personality Adaptation
Be Perfect (+ Be Strong)	Responsible-Workaholic (Obsessive-Compulsive)
Be Perfect = Be Strong	Brilliant-Skeptic (Paranoid)
Be Strong (+ Try Hard or Please Others)	Creative-Daydreamer (Schizoid)
Try Hard (+ Be Strong)	Playful-Resister (Passive-Aggressive)
Please Others (+ Try Hard or Hurry Up)	Enthusiastic-Overreactor (Histrionic)
Be Strong or Please Others	Charming-Manipulator (Antisocial)

Table 16.2: Correspondences between primary drivers and personality adaptations

The Brilliant-Skeptic adaptation is marked by a combination of Be Perfect and Be Strong driver behaviours, shown with about equal intensity. The Charming-Manipulator swings between two drivers, Be Strong and Please Others, according to the way his Child ego state experiences the situation. If his Kid senses that there's going to be opportunity for excitement, seduction or other personal gain, then he will show Please Others. On the other hand, if his Child sees the situation as unpromising or dull, this person will switch to showing Be Strong as his main driver.

● From the exercises in the last chapter, you have already got a reading of your own primary driver and any secondary drivers that you show. You have also assessed your personality adaptation(s) using the descriptive list in Table 16.1. The model predicts that your main adaptation should match your primary driver, in the way shown in Table 16.2. How well do these two readings match?

If they match exactly, that gives you further evidence that your assessment of your primary driver and your main adaptation are accurate. If they don't match, then one possible reason is that the model just doesn't apply to you. But in view of the large amount of research evidence that supports this model, we suggest that if you do get what appears to be a mis-match between driver and adaptation, you take a further look at either or both. You may wish to get further opinions on your primary driver or your main adaptation. Another possibility to consider is: do you shift from one adaptation to another in different situations? Some people do. If that is true of you, then you will find that when you shift adaptation, you will *also* shift the main driver that you show. ●

Personality adaptations and process scripts

In the last chapter, you learned about process scripts – that is, the various patterns by which a person may live out their script over time. You saw also how someone's driver behaviours reliably predict their process script. Since driver behaviours also predict personality adaptation, it follows that there is a tie-up between your personality adaptation and your process script. The correspondences between the two are shown in Table 16.3. In the right-hand column of the table we repeat the main drivers that go with the adaptations, to give a three-way aide-memoire.

● In the last chapter you assessed your process script patterns as well as your driver behaviours. So now you can make a three-way comparison between:

- your personality adaptation(s), as indicated by the list of features in Table 16.1;
- your driver behaviours (Table 16.2); and
- your process script(s) (Table 16.3).

In the same way as you did for the driver-adaptation pairings in Table

16.2, now you can check out the pairings that the model suggests between adaptation and process script. In just the same way as before, an exact match further supports your assessment of your primary driver, personality adaptation and process script. A mis-match may simply mean that the model does not work for you. But we nevertheless suggest that you look further into all three of the variables, checking out the same possibilities as for your driver-adaptation pairing. ●

Adaptation	Process script(s)	Main driver(s)
Responsible-Workaholic *(Obsessive-Compulsive)*	Until (Almost II, Open-Ended)	Be Perfect
Brilliant-Skeptic *(Paranoid)*	Until + Never	Be Perfect = Be Strong
Creative-Daydreamer *(Schizoid)*	Never (Always)	Be Strong
Playful-Resister *(Passive-Aggressive)*	Always Almost I	Try Hard
Enthusiastic-Overreactor *(Histrionic)*	After (Almost I and II)	Please Others
Charming-Manipulator *(Antisocial)*	Never (Always, Almost)	Be Strong *or* Please Others

Table 16.3: Process script types for different personality adaptations
(Note: Brackets indicate likely subsidiary process script types)

Making and keeping contact: the Ware Sequence

Paul Ware distinguished three possible areas of contact that you can address whenever you are communicating with another person. These *contact areas* are *thinking, feeling* and *behaviour*.[5]

He suggests that to make and maintain effective contact with any given individual, you need to address these three areas in a particular sequence. This *Ware Sequence* varies according to the individual's personality adaptation.

Paul Ware's work was first developed for application in the fields of counselling and psychotherapy. However, the Ware Sequence applies equally well to any area of communication. It can be applied in work settings, in education, and in personal relationships.

Three 'doors to contact'

Each person, says Ware, has three contact 'doors':

- open door
- target door
- trap door.

Each person's contact doors correspond to the three contact areas of thinking, feeling and behaviour. However, the *order* of correspondence between contact doors and contact areas differs from one personality adaptation to another.

For example, for a person whose main adaptation is Brilliant-Skeptic, the Ware Sequence looks like this:

- open door: thinking
- target door: feeling
- trap door: behaviour.

By contrast, the Creative-Daydreamer's open door is behaviour, his target door thinking, and his trap door feeling.

In making first contact with someone, says Ware, you need to address the area that corresponds to their *open door*. Once you have established communication and rapport at the open door, you can move to their *target door*. In counselling or therapy, this is often the area in which most of the overt 'work' gets done.

The *trap door* is the area in which the person is most heavily defended and is most likely to get stuck. However, it is also the area in which you will see the greatest change, but the change is accomplished by working with the target area rather than the trap area.[6]

If you address the doors out of order, the person is likely to block you. This is especially probable if you attempt to make first contact at their trap door. How do you know if they are 'blocking' you? The answer is that you look for driver behaviour. If you have addressed the wrong contact area for that client at that moment, the chances are that she will show a driver. She may then follow this by experiencing a racket feeling, and/or engaging in some form of scripty behaviour or thinking.

The Ware Sequence and personality adaptation

Table 16.4 shows the different orders of the contact areas in the Ware Sequence for the six personality adaptations.

You'll see from the table that three of the adaptations have behaviour as the open door. However, the nature of this behaviour is different for each adaptation.

Adaptation	Open door	Target door	Trap door
Responsible-Workaholic (Obsessive-Compulsive)	Thinking	Feeling	Behaviour
Brilliant-Skeptic (Paranoid)	Thinking	Feeling	Behaviour
Creative-Daydreamer (Schizoid)	Behaviour (Inaction)	Thinking	Feeling
Playful-Resister (Passive-Aggressive)	Behaviour (Reaction)	Feeling	Thinking
Enthusiastic-Overreactor (Histrionic)	Feeling	Thinking	Behaviour
Charming-Manipulator (Antisocial)	Behaviour (Manipulation)	Feeling	Thinking

Table 16.4: The Ware Sequence for different personality adaptations

The Creative-Daydreamer's typical *inaction* means that if you are to open effective communication, *you* need to make the first move, because the Creative-Daydreamer will not.

The Playful-Resister shows *reaction:* she tends to wait for you to start up communication, then to do or say something that 'cuts across' you. For example, she may interrupt you and tell you she doesn't agree with a word you've said. The best way to address this behaviour is with a playful response. In this case, it might be: 'Well, sounds like we're both stuck, doesn't it?'

The Charming-Manipulator will oftentimes open communication by saying or doing something that is designed to trick, bamboozle or corner you. You have the choice of two different kinds of response. If you're good at trickery, you can out-trick the Charming-Manipulator. (Eric Berne gave the example of a client who asks the therapist: 'Can you cure me, doctor?' The appropriate answer, Berne recommended, was 'No.') Alternatively, you can be completely transparent. For example, in answer to the question from Berne's client, you might launch into an honest detailed discussion as to the meaning of 'cure'.

Example: using the Ware Sequence with the Enthusiastic-Overreactor adaptation

Imagine you have a work colleague whose main adaptation is Enthusiastic-Overreactor. You and she are meeting to discuss a planned project. You would make contact most effectively by first addressing her open door of feeling. As she comes into the room, after the initial 'Hello', you might open with a warm enquiry: 'So, how are you feeling today?' You would not begin by asking her: 'So what have you been thinking about this project since we last met?' If you wanted to know that from her, you would wait until she had had a chance to expand to you about how she was feeling, then put your question.

An even more ineffective opening would be: 'What do you think we need to do to get this project rolling?' The Overreactor is likely to respond to that by beginning to feel bad. A person with this adaptation decided in childhood that her role in life was to please others by doing what they wanted. She decided also that she needed to read other people's minds to find out what she needed to do to please them.

Thus when you ask her what *she* wants to do, she may re-play this childhood pattern. If so, she will begin wondering what you expect her to do. Then she may feel inadequate or confused because she fears she may not be doing the right thing to please you. If you persist in addressing her trap door of behaviour, she in turn will most likely escalate her racket feelings.

With this colleague, you will only make good contact in the area of behaviour if you have first gone through her open and target doors of feeling and thinking. You need to do this at her own pace, taking care that she is moving with you. You can check this by watching out always for driver behaviour. If she gets into a driver, or shows other script signals, your best option is to back-track and make good contact again at the previous contact door.

Testing for contact area

If you are in doubt about your diagnosis of someone's personality adaptation, you can simply apply the Ware Sequence in trial-and-error style, by addressing one of the contact areas and observing the other person's response. If he responds to you in a way that is free of driver behaviour or racket feelings, the chances are good that you have addressed the correct contact area for that individual. By contrast, if he gets into a driver or shows a racket, you have most probably chosen the wrong contact area.

For example, suppose you are a counsellor and are at the beginning of a counselling session with a new client. You decide to test whether the client's open door is behaviour. You might open by saying:

'If there's anything you want to do to get comfortable, please go ahead and do it.'

If the client simply goes ahead and does things to get comfortable – takes off his shoes, rearranges the cushions, or whatever – you have probably made the right judgment.

However, suppose that instead of this, he arranges himself carefully on his chair, body vertical round the mid-line. He pauses and looks up at the right-hand corner of the ceiling, while pressing the fingers of both hands together in front of him. He replies: 'Well, I think, actually, I'm comfortable enough already, thanks very much.'

Noting these Be Perfect driver signals, you might judge that his main adaptation was Responsible-Workaholic or Brilliant-Skeptic, not Creative-Daydreamer. This would mean that his open door is thinking, not behaviour. You therefore shift back and re-test with:

'OK, good. So, will you tell me what your thinking is in coming to counselling?'

Using the Ware Sequence in the long and short term

The Ware Sequence gives you guidance to the long-term 'strategy' as well as the short-term 'tactics' of communication. Over the longer perspective of any relationship – whether it be in therapy, in a work setting, or in personal life – the other person's main adaptation indicates the contact areas in which you will be likely to communicate most effectively with her in the early, middle and late stages of the relationship.

For example, if you are a therapist and you are working with a client whose main adaptation is Creative-Daydreamer, you might centre your early sessions on the fulfilment of behavioural contracts. Once the therapeutic relationship is well established, you can move with the client into exploring and clarifying his thinking. As he does so, he will become clearer about the actions he needs to take to get his needs met. This in turn will help him to become more effective and proactive in dealing with the world. Later still, the client is likely to do his most significant change work in the area of experiencing and expressing feelings. This can happen even though you and he may never address the area of feelings directly.

● By now, you have had the chance to assess your own personality adaptation(s) on the evidence of several different clues. You can check this information further now by exploring what Ware Sequence applies to you. Using Table 16.4, run through some recent or imagined scenarios in which another person makes first contact with you in each of the contact areas. How do you respond when someone *first* approaches you in the area of your feelings? of your thinking? of your behaviour? For example, are you like the work colleague in our example above, who feels good when she's first approached at the area of feelings? Or would your response be to 'crunch up inside' and say to yourself: 'What's all this business about how I'm *feeling*? Aren't we here to get something done on this project?' ●

Personality adaptations and script content

Each personality adaptation is accompanied by a 'cluster' of typical *in-*

junctions, games and *racket feelings*. These of course are features of script content (the 'what') rather than script process (the 'how'). But they can still be detected from the same process clues that allow you to judge someone's main adaptations, notably by observation of their driver behaviour. We summarize this information on typical script content in Table 16.5, given at the end of the chapter. (You'll find full descriptions of the various *games, rackets* and *racketeering themes* in coming chapters).

You'll note that we use the word 'typical' to describe these features of script content. What we mean is that these characteristics are more variable, for any given adaptation, than the process features that we've described above. For example, an individual showing the Enthusiastic-Overreactor adaptation is likely to show a 'cluster' of injunctions, games and racket feelings that look very much like the ones listed in the table. But she may not show all the listed features, and she may show some features that are not listed. In other words, the lists in Table 16.5 give you a good starting point for diagnosing script content, but for a precise reading you have to get to know the individual.

'Pen-portraits' of the six adaptations

We've covered a lot of information in this chapter, and a lot of it has been in the form of tables and lists. For those of you who prefer your information in stories, we'll close the chapter with 'pen-portraits' of the six adaptations.[7]

Responsible-Workaholic (Obsessive-Compulsive)

People with a Responsible-Workaholic adaptation tend to be withdrawing in their orientation to other people. They are happy to be on their own. When they socialize, they prefer to relate one-to-one, or at most with two or three other people. They are active in their approach to problem solving. In social situations, too, they are happy to initiate relationships, rather than waiting for others to approach them.

Workaholics are responsible individuals who are as good as their word. They make wonderful employees who do what they say they will do. They are the people who become the pillars of society and keep things running.

Their difficulty lies in knowing when to quit being responsible. They often become workaholics. The problem is that they have difficulty enjoying what they have accomplished because they don't let themselves relax, play, and have fun.

They contact the world through thinking (open door). They need to integrate their feelings (target door) with their thinking. The greatest change occurs in their behaviour (trap door) as they integrate feelings with thinking. They stop working all the time and learn to relax, play, and have fun.

Their relaxation cannot be achieved by addressing their behaviour directly, because behaviour is the area in which they feel the most vulnerable. The message they received in childhood was that they would be OK if they were 'perfect', so they are doing everything they possibly can to be perfect.

The way to make contact with them is by engaging their thinking. The next step is to elicit their feelings by being nurturing or playful. Avoid addressing their behaviour, since that is where they tend to get stuck.

Important issues for them in personal change are: accepting that they can be 'good enough' even if they are not perfect, and learning how to 'be' as opposed to 'do'. They need to learn how to feel good about themselves apart from what they do so they can relax and have time to enjoy themselves and others.

Brilliant-Skeptic (Paranoid)

Individuals with a Brilliant-Skeptic adaptation are withdrawing in relation to other people, in much the same way as the Workaholic. That is, they prefer to be on their own or with one or two others. However, the Brilliant-Skeptic person tends to take a more neutral stance when it comes to problem solving and to initiating relationships. They are equally ready to be proactive or to wait for others to make the moves. When there is a problem, they initially pull back, size up the situation, figure out what to do and then take decisive action to control the situation.

They are brilliant thinkers who attend to every detail. People with a Brilliant-Skeptic adaptation do well in accounting, management, law, and other positions that involve detailed thinking. They are wonderful organizers because they seldom miss anything. They are concerned with maintaining control.

Their difficulty is they sometimes misperceive stimuli while assuming their perception is true. They then act on these misperceptions without confirming them.

They contact the world through thinking (open door). They need to integrate feelings (target door) with thinking. Integrating feeling with thinking produces change in their behaviour (trap door). They stop being so suspicious of others and begin to relax and feel safe.

Relaxation cannot be achieved by working with their behaviour directly, because behaviour is the area in which they feel most vulnerable. As children they received the message that they had to 'be perfect' and to 'be strong' to be OK. They are already doing everything they know how to be both perfect and strong and behave in a way that is beyond reproach.

The way to make contact with them is through engaging their thinking. The next step is to elicit their feelings in order to problem-solve. Avoid addressing their behaviour, since that is where they tend to get stuck.

Important issues for them in personal change are: learning to trust, and experiencing that they can relinquish some control without being 'out of control'. They also need to learn to check out their perceptions with others rather than assume they are true, in order to get accurate information with which they can feel safe.

Creative-Daydreamer (Schizoid)

Individuals with a Creative-Daydreamer adaptation are withdrawing in relation to other people. They are happy to be on their own. Creative-Daydreamers take a passive stance with regard to problem solving and social interaction, preferring others to 'make the first move'.

They are creative thinkers and often involved in artistic pursuits, for example as artists, playwrights, poets, and architects. They make good workers since they have a lot of endurance and generally do what they are told. They are kind, supportive people who are easy to be with and are respectful of other people's space.

The difficulty is that they sometimes get lost in their daydreams and do not put their thoughts into action.

They contact the world through their behaviour (open door). The behaviour they use is withdrawn passivity. They tend to keep a low profile and stay in the background. They need to integrate their thinking (target door) with their behaviour. As they integrate their thinking with their behaviour, they take action to get their needs met. This in turn produces a change in their feelings (trap door). They become animated, energetic, and feel good.

Feeling good cannot be achieved by working with their feelings directly, because feelings are their most vulnerable area. The message they received as a child was that in order to be OK, they had to 'be strong' (that is, distance from their feelings and wants). They are already doing everything they know how to be strong and not feel. So if one attempts to work with their feelings directly, they will quickly feel not-OK.

The way to make contact with them is by addressing their behaviour (withdrawn passivity). You can best do this by initiating contact and bringing them out. The next step is to invite them to share their thinking; then, get them to bring their thinking to closure by taking action to get their needs met. Avoid focusing on their feelings, since feeling is where they tend to get stuck.

Important issues for them in personal change are: learning to be as supportive of themselves as they are of everyone else, and claiming their right to take up as much space in the world as everyone else. They need to learn that it is OK for them to have feelings and needs, and to expect others to take their feelings and needs into account so they can rejoin the world of human interaction and closeness.

Playful-Resister (Passive-Aggressive)

Individuals with a Playful-Resister adaptation are engaging of other people: they enjoy being one of a group. However, they take a passive stance with regard to problem solving. This means, among other things, that they prefer others to initiate relationships and solve problems.

Thus in order to get themselves included socially, Playful-Resisters tend to be aggressively passive by reacting to things. For example, they may say, 'Gosh, it sure is hot in here!' and expect someone else to do something about it. They are playful but strongly resist (in an indirect or passive way) others' control.

Playful-Resisters make good detectives, investigative reporters, and critics. If anything is wrong with a situation, they are the first to point it out.

Their difficulty is in engaging in useless power struggles. They fight against others' control even when no one is trying to control them.

They contact the world through their behaviour (open door), which is aggressive passivity. They need to integrate their feelings (target door) with their behaviour. Integrating their feelings with their behaviour produces a change in their thinking (trap door). They stop seeing situations as 'either-or' all or nothing power struggles.

Thinking differently about situations cannot be achieved by working directly with their thinking, because thinking is the area in which they feel most vulnerable. The message they received in childhood was that in order to be OK they had to 'try hard'. (This is shorthand for, 'Try hard, but don't actually do it.') Passive-Aggressives are already doing everything they know how to try hard in their thinking and are struggling as a result.

The way to make contact with them is by being playful. The next step is to access their feelings by being nurturing and then find out what they are wanting. Avoid getting into thinking with them, since that is where they tend to get stuck.

Important issues for them in personal change are eliminating viewing problems in an 'either-or' framework, and realizing that they don't have to struggle to survive. They need to learn to ask directly for what they want and experience that others will be co-operative in helping them get their needs met. They need to experience the freedom to be different (and sometimes difficult) and still be OK with others.

Enthusiastic-Overreactor (Histrionic)

Individuals with an Enthusiastic-Overreactor adaptation are engaging of other people. They are 'people people' *par excellence*, the typical 'life of the party'. They also tend to take an active stance with regard to problem solving. This applies also to their preferred way of socializing: they move proactively towards others.

Enthusiastic-Overreactors are emotionally responsive to other people. They are often experienced as 'warm' or 'fun to be around'. They are sociable, love to entertain and keep people around them happy, and want others to do the same for them. They make wonderful hosts and hostesses and do well in public relations or any position that involves meeting the public. They love attention and tend to equate attention with love.

When they get into difficulty, it stems from being *over*-reactive. They tend to meet problems by escalating feelings, rather than thinking or acting.

Enthusiastic-Overreactors make contact with the world through feeling (open door). They need to integrate their thinking (target door) with their feeling. As they integrate thinking with feeling, they change their behaviour (trap door), in that they stop over-reacting to situations.

Eliminating over-reacting to situations cannot be achieved by working directly with their behaviour, however, because their behaviour is the area in which they feel the most vulnerable and have the greatest defences. Their defensiveness developed because the message they got as a child was that in order to be OK they had to 'please others' and they are doing everything they know how to try to be pleasing.

The way to make contact with Enthusiastic-Overreactors is through their feelings by being nurturing or playful. The next step is to engage their thinking in order to problem-solve. Avoid addressing their behaviour, since that is where they tend to get stuck.

Important issues for them in personal change are: they can be important and be loved even if someone is not paying attention to them, and just because they feel something is true, it does not make it true in reality. They need to learn how to feel good about their thinking and to claim their power.

Charming-Manipulator (Antisocial)

Individuals with a Charming-Manipulator adaptation move back and forth between being engaging with others and active in problem-solving, and withdrawing from others and being passive in problem solving.

Manipulators are actively aggressive with other people. They are also charming. They attempt to intimidate or seduce to get what they want. They feel a great need for external stimulation. They do well in sales and in promotional activities like fund raising and getting new projects off the ground. They are charismatic individuals who often go into politics or other public arenas. They also make good entrepreneurs.

Their difficulty results from being manipulative and taking advantage of others when they can't get what they want in a direct fashion. They also have a hard time being self-starting if there is not some external 'action' to pursue.

They contact the world through their behaviour (open door), which is to be actively aggressive. They need to integrate their feelings (target door) with their behaviour. Integrating their feelings with their behaviour produces a change in their thinking (trap door). They then begin to think about long-range consequences rather than about outsmarting everyone in the present situation.

Thinking long-range cannot be achieved by working with their thinking directly, because thinking is where they feel most vulnerable. The message they got in childhood was that in order to be OK they had to outsmart everyone else. Therefore, they continually try to stay one jump ahead of other people.

The way to make contact with them is by playfully exposing their attempts to fool others. The next step is to find out what they really want but presume they can't get, which has been their motive for trying to outsmart others. Avoid getting caught up in their thinking (which is an attempt to con you), since that is how they manipulate and avoid change.

In personal change, it is important for them to understand that they cannot be abandoned as a grown-up, since they now have the resources to find others in a way that they couldn't as a child. Further, not only others but they themselves can be available to them now (the grown-up part can be available to the child part). They need also to know that it is safe for them to be real rather than having to pretend. They need to learn how to get their needs met co-operatively, in such a way that others also get their needs met. By doing so, they can begin to experience intimacy rather than drama.

● If you would like more information about the adaptations, you'll find it in our book *Personality Adaptations: A New Guide to Human Understanding in Psychotherapy and Counselling*. (Lifespace Publishing, 2002.)

Adaptation	Typical injunctions	Typical games*	Typical rackets
Responsible-Workaholic (*Obsessive-Compulsive*)	Don't Be a Child Don't Feel Don't Be Close Don't Be Important Don't Enjoy	See How Hard I'm Trying If It Weren't For You Harried	Anxiety, depression, and guilt (covering anger, hurt and sexual feelings) Anger (covering sadness)
Brilliant-Skeptic (*Paranoid*)	Don't Be a Child Don't Be Close Don't Trust Don't Feel Don't Enjoy Don't Belong	Now I've Got You Blemish Kick Me	Anger at others (covering scare) Righteous indignation Jealousy Envy Suspicion
Creative-Daydreamer (*Schizoid*)	Don't Make It Don't Belong Don't Be Sane Don't Feel (joyful, sexual, angry) Don't Enjoy Don't Grow Up Don't Think	Do Me Something See What You Made Me Do If It Weren't For You Kick Me	Numbness Blankness Anxiety (covering anger, hurt, joy and sexual feelings)
Playful-Resister (*Passive-Aggressive*)	Don't Grow Up Don't Feel Don't Make It Don't Be Close Don't Enjoy	Why Don't You-Yes But Do Me Something Stupid Kick Me	Frustration (covering hurt) Confusion (covering anger) Righteous indignation
Enthusiastic-Overreactor (*Histrionic*)	Don't Grow Up Don't Think Don't Be Important Don't Be You	Rapo If It Weren't For You Stupid	Anxiety, sadness, and confusion (covering anger)
Charming-Manipulator (*Antisocial}*	Don't Be Close Don't Feel (sad, scared) Don't Make It Don't Think (in terms of future problem solving; think to outsmart, make fools of)	Catch Me If You Can Cops and Robbers	Confusion Anger (covering scare and sadness)

Table 16.5: Typical injunctions, games (*plus racketeering themes), and rackets for each adaptation

Part V

MAKING THE WORLD FIT OUR SCRIPT

Passivity

Chapter 17
DISCOUNTING

In the process of living, I am continually being presented with problems. How do I get across the road without being killed? How do I deal with the work assignment I've just been given? How do I respond to a friendly or an aggressive approach from someone?

Each time I meet a problem, I have two options. I can use the full power of my grown-up thinking, feeling and actions to solve the problem. Or I can go into script.

If I do move into script, I begin perceiving the world so that it seems to fit the decisions I made as an infant. I am likely to blank out my awareness of some aspects of the real situation. At the same time, I may blow up other aspects of the here-and-now problem into giant proportions. Instead of taking action to solve the problem, I rely on the 'magical solution' that my script offers. I hope in Child that by working this magic, I can manipulate the world into providing a solution for me. Instead of being active, I become passive.

In Part V, we look at this contrast between passivity and problem-solving. This area of TA theory is known as *Schiffian* or *Cathexis* theory, after the 'Schiff family' who first developed it, and the Cathexis Institute which they founded.

The Schiffs define *passivity* as 'non-problem-solving behaviour,' i.e. 'how people don't do things, or don't do them effectively'.[1]

Nature and definition of discounting

Discounting is defined as *unawarely ignoring information relevant to the solution of a problem.*[2]

Imagine I am sitting in a crowded restaurant. I begin to feel thirsty and think I'd like a glass of water. I try to catch the eye of the waiter. He pays no attention. I gesture again. Still no response.

At this instant I go into script. Without being aware of it, I begin re-playing a time in my infancy when I had wanted to call my mother to me and she had not come. I put my mother's face on the unresponsive waiter. At the same time I begin acting, feeling and thinking as though I were still a young child. I droop and feel hopeless. I say to myself in my head: 'It's no good. No matter how much I try, he's not going to come.'

To get to this conclusion, I have had to ignore some information about here-and-now reality. I have *discounted* several options I have as a grown-up, options I did not have as a baby. I could have stood up, walked over to the waiter and tapped on his shoulder. I could have gone to the nearest table where there was a water jug, asked for it and poured myself a drink. Had I acted in these ways, I would have been active in problem-solving instead of being passive.

A friend is sitting with me in the restaurant. Seeing the waiter's lack of response to my gestures, my friend gets angry. He snorts: 'That fellow is obviously incompetent. If I had my way, I'd see him fired!'

My friend has also gone into script. But as a child he decided upon the life position I+U-, rather than my own I-U+. Now he sees the waiter through the spectacles of his own script. He discounts the waiter's competence to respond to my call. Like me, my friend is being passive. His sitting there snarling about the waiter will do nothing to get me my glass of water.

Grandiosity

Every discount is accompanied by *grandiosity*. This is an exaggeration of some feature of reality, either minimizing or maximizing. The expression 'making a mountain out of a molehill' aptly describes grandiosity. While a person is discounting, she will 'blow up' some features of the situation out of proportion, while at the same time minimizing other features, again out of proportion. The typical pattern of thinking in grandiosity is one of 'all or nothing'.

Whereas discounting is intrapsychic and outside of conscious aware-ness, grandiosity takes place in the person's conscious thinking. Discounting is the unconscious mechanism the person is using; grandiosity is the conscious justification for doing so.

When I sat in the restaurant feeling hopeless because the waiter wasn't bringing my glass of water, I was discounting my own options. In doing so, I was crediting the waiter with power he didn't have, the power to determine whether or not I got any water. I was also not recognising my own power. My belief was: 'He has all the power; I have none.' Both these statements are grandiose.

As my friend discounted the waiter's competence, he was also being grandiose about himself and the waiter. He was taking on himself the role of judge and jury, when he had neither adequate evidence nor responsibil-ity to do so. He was also seeing the waiter as totally incompetent.

● Think back to a recent situation in which the outcome was unsatisfac-tory for you. That situation represents a problem you didn't solve.

Looking back, do you now identify a feature or features of reality that you were discounting? Could you have acted in a different way that you 'didn't think of at the time'? Were you ignoring somebody else's ability to act in a particular way? Were there resources in the situation that were available but which you didn't think of using?

Do you identify where you were being grandiose? What features of yourself, others or the situation were you blowing up or minimizing out of proportion?

If you are working in a group, or if you have a friend who is willing to help you, get a second opinion on your answers. It is often easier for us to spot other people's discounting and grandiosity than to spot our own.

Whether or not you have got immediate answers to these questions, keep your problem situation in mind. You can refer to it again as background to the further discussion in this chapter. ●

The four passive behaviours

When I discount, I do so by making a statement to myself in my own head.

Thus *a discount itself is not observable*. Since you can't thought-read, you have no way of knowing I am discounting unless I speak or act in some way that indicates the presence of the discount.

There are four types of behaviour that always indicate that the person concerned is discounting. These *four passive behaviours* are:

- *Doing nothing*
- *Overadaptation*
- *Agitation*
- *Incapacitation or violence.*

Doing nothing

The members of a TA group are sitting in a circle. The group leader says: 'Let's go round the group and each person say what he or she appreciates or resents about today's session. If you don't want to take part, it's OK to say "pass".'

The exercise begins. People round the group each give an appreciation or resentment. One or two say 'pass'.

Then comes Norman's turn. There's a silence. People wait for Norman to say something, but he doesn't. He sits unmoving and silent, staring into space. Since he doesn't seem to want to speak any appreciation or resentment, the person next to him waits for him to say 'pass'. But Norman doesn't do that either. He continues to sit as if dumb.

Norman is showing the passive behaviour called *doing nothing*. Instead of using energy to take problem-solving action, he is using it to stop himself from acting. A person exhibiting this passive behaviour feels uncomfortable and experiences himself as not thinking. He is discounting his own ability to do anything about the situation.

Overadaptation

Amy comes into the house after a hard day's work. Her husband Brian is sitting reading a newspaper. Looking beyond him into the kitchen, Amy sees a huge pile of unwashed dishes beside the sink.

'Hi,' says Brian. 'Hope you've had a good day. Just about time for tea, isn't it?' Taking her coat off, Amy goes straight through to the kitchen. She washes the pile of dishes and gets down to making tea.

Neither Brian nor Amy notice that he has not asked her to wash the dishes and make tea. Nor has she asked him if he wants her to. Still less has she paused to think whether she herself *wants* to wash the dishes, or whether it might be more appropriate if Brian washed them.

Amy's passive behaviour is *overadaptation*. When someone overadapts, she is complying with what she *believes* in Child are the wishes of others. She does so without checking with them what their wishes are in reality, and without any reference to what her own wishes are. The person in overadaptation, unlike the person who is doing nothing, experiences herself as 'thinking' during the passive behaviour. Her 'thinking', though, actually proceeds from a contamination.

Someone in overadaptation will often be experienced by others as helpful, adaptable or accommodating. Thus overadaptation is frequently stroked by those to whom the person relates. Because of this social acceptability and because the person appears to be thinking, overadaptation is the most difficult to detect of the four passive behaviours.

The person in overadaptation is discounting her ability to act on her own options. Instead, she follows options she believes others want.

Agitation

The class of students is listening to the lecturer. At the back of the room sits Adam. The lecturer is speaking rather quietly, and Adam has difficulty in hearing him. As the lecture period goes on, Adam has more and more trouble following what the lecturer is talking about. He puts down his pen and starts drumming his fingers on the desk. If we could see underneath that desk, we'd notice that Adam is waggling his foot rapidly up and down in time to his finger-drumming.

Adam is showing *agitation*. In this passive behaviour, the person is discounting his ability to act to solve a problem. He feels acutely uncomfortable, and engages in purposeless, repetitive activity in an attempt to relieve the discomfort. Energy is directed into the agitated activity instead of into action to solve the problem. During agitation, the person does not experience himself as thinking.

If Adam were using his clear Adult, he could simply attract the lecturer's attention and ask him to speak up. As it is, his finger-drumming and foot-waggling do nothing towards solving his problem.

Many common habits entail agitation. Nail-biting, smoking, hair-twiddling and compulsive eating are all examples.

Incapacitation and violence

Betty is in her late thirties. The younger of two daughters, she still lives at home with her aged mother, whom she looks after. The old woman, despite her age, is really in pretty sound health.

Out of the blue, Betty meets a man and they fall in love. Happily she announces to her mother that she intends to move out to live with him and perhaps get married.

A couple of days later, the mother begins having dizzy spells and has to take to her bed. The doctor can find nothing physically wrong with her. But Betty begins to feel guilty about her intention to move out.

Mother's passive behaviour is *incapacitation*. Here, the person disables herself in some way. Discounting her own ability to solve a problem, she hopes in Child that by incapacitating herself she can get someone else to solve it.

Incapacitation can sometimes be in the form of psychosomatic ailments, as here. Alternatively it can be achieved by mental breakdown or by abuse of drugs or alcohol.

Robert has just had a furious row with his girlfriend. He storms out of the house and walks the streets for a long while. He goes down town, has a few beers. Then he picks up a chair and smashes all the plate-glass windows in the bar.

Robert's passive behaviour is *violence*. It may seem strange to refer to violence as a 'passive' behaviour. But it is passive, because it is not directed at solving the problem in hand. When Robert smashes the windows, he does nothing to resolve his differences with his girlfriend.

Incapacitation can be viewed as violence directed inwards. In both incapacitation and violence, the person is discounting his ability to solve a problem. He releases a burst of energy, directed against self or others, in a desperate attempt to force the environment to solve the problem for him.

Incapacitation or violence will often follow a period of agitation. When the person is agitating, he is building up energy which he may then discharge destructively by either incapacitating or getting violent.

The purpose of all the passive behaviours is to get someone else more uncomfortable with the problem than I am, in the hope that that they will take over and solve it for me.

● Review the problem situation you considered in the last section. Do you identify which of the passive behaviours you engaged in?

Now re-run the situation in your mind's eye. When you come to the moment where you began the passive behaviour, imagine yourself instead staying in Adult and using the full power of your grown-up thinking, feeling or behaving to solve the problem. How do you then act differently? ●

Discounting and ego-states

Discounting can be related to what you already know about ego-state pathology (Chapter 6).

Discounting may indicate the presence of *contamination*. That is to say: when I am discounting, I may be mis-perceiving reality to fit Parent or Child script beliefs, which I mistake for Adult thinking.

Exclusion may be another source of discounting. Here, I am ignoring aspects of reality because I am blanking out one or more of my ego-states. If I am excluding my Child, I will ignore the wants, feelings and intuitions I carry from my own childhood, which might in reality be relevant to the problem I have to solve in the present. With excluded Parent, I will blank out the rules and definitions of the world I learned from my parent-figures, though these also can often be useful in problem-solving. An excluded Adult means that I discount my own ability to assess, feel or act in direct response to any feature of the here-and-now situation. As you would expect, excluded Adult is the most disabling of the three exclusions in terms of the person's intensity of discounting.

Often discounting can occur without any ego-state pathology. In these cases, it is simply the result of the person's Adult being uninformed or misinformed. For instance, an over-weight woman decides to go on a slimming diet. She stops eating bread, potatoes and pasta. Instead, she takes nuts and cheese. In fact, the nuts and cheese have more calories per ounce than the foods she's given up. She discounts this fact simply because she doesn't know about it.

Detecting discounts

You know that discounting, not observable in itself, can be inferred by the person's showing any of the four passive behaviours. There are many other ways of detecting discounts.

Driver behaviour always indicates a discount. Remember that when I show a driver, I am internally replaying the script belief: 'I'm only OK *if* I...Try Hard, Please Others, etc.' The reality is that I am OK whether or not I follow these driver messages.

The Schiffs specify certain *thinking disorders* as clues to discounting. One of these is *over-detailing*. Asked a simple question, the person showing this disorder will reply with a long tirade of minute details. *Over-generalization* is the opposite of this, in which the person expresses ideas only in sweeping, global terms. 'Well, my problem is something huge. People are after me. Things are getting me down.'

In Part VI we shall look at *rackets, games* and *behaviours from the*

Drama Triangle. All these also confirm the presence of discounting.

Verbal clues

One of the skills of TA is to identify discounting by listening to the words people use. In the examples we have given in this chapter, we have chosen words that made it clear the speaker was discounting. In everyday conversation, the verbal clues to discounting are usually more subtle.

In theory, what we are listening for is straightforward. We know the speaker is discounting when she says something in which information about reality is ignored or distorted. The difficulty in practice is that everyday speech is full of discounts, so much so that we become desensitized to them. We need to re-learn the skill of listening to what is really being said and testing each statement against reality.

For instance, when someone says 'I can't...' he will most often be discounting. The test is to ask yourself: 'Well, can he, either now or some time?'

'I'll try to...' is usually a discount, since what it implies is usually 'I'll try to, but I won't do it.' The same is true of all other driver wording. Be Strong discounts are particularly common.

'What you say is boring me.'

'I'm baffled by this problem.'

'A thought just crossed my mind.'

Sometimes a discount is signalled by leaving out a part of the sentence. For instance, a member of a TA group may look around the other group members and announce: 'I want a hug.' She doesn't say whom she wants the hug from. She is omitting information relevant to the solution of her problem – how to get the hug she wants – and her request thus entails a discount.

Nonverbal clues

Equally important is the skill of identifying discounts from nonverbal clues. Here, the discount is signalled by a mis-match between the words being said and the nonverbal signals that go with them. You'll recall from Chapter 5 that this mis-matching is called *incongruity*.

For example, a teacher asks his pupil: 'Do you understand the assignment I've given you?' The pupil replies 'Sure.' But at the same time he puckers his brow and scratches his head. If the teacher is alert to 'thinking Martian', he will ask more questions to check whether his pupil is discounting.

Incongruity does not always indicate discounting. For instance, the chairman of a meeting stands up and pronounces: 'Today, we have a lot of work ahead of us.' But as he makes this serious statement, he beams round the table. His 'Martian' signals simply: 'And I'm glad to see you all here.'

Gallows laughter

One frequent indication of a discount is *gallows laughter*. Here, the person laughs when making a statement about something unpleasant.

'Oh! That was silly of me, ha ha!'

'Hee, hee, hee – I sure got the better of *him*.'

'Had a bit of a bump in the car on the way over here, ho ho!'

In gallows there is incongruity between the laugh and the painful content of the words. Whenever someone gives a gallows laugh, smile or chuckle, he is making a non-verbal invitation to the listeners to reinforce one of his script beliefs. The invitation is accepted on psychological level if the listeners join in the gallows laughing. For instance, the person who says 'I'm silly, ha ha' is in script, inviting the listeners to join his laughter and thus 'confirm' his script belief: 'I can't think'.

The straight response to gallows laughter is to refuse to join in the laughing or smiling. You may also say: 'That's not funny', if you are in a situation where it is socially appropriate to do so.

● You have already practised the skill of 'thinking Martian'. Now you can refine this skill by distinguishing the nonverbals that signal discounts from those that do not. In fact, it is not always possible to tell clearly from someone's nonverbal signals whether he is discounting. If it is important for you to know, you may have to check your impressions by verbal questioning. ●

Chapter 18
THE DISCOUNT MATRIX

Discounting results in unsolved problems. Thus if we can devise a systematic way of identifying the nature and intensity of discounting, we will have a powerful tool for problem-solving. Such a tool exists. It is called the *discount matrix*, and was developed by Ken Mellor and Eric Sigmund.[1]

The discount matrix starts from the idea that we can classify discounts according to three different criteria:

- *area*
- *type*
- *level.*

Areas of discounting

There are three *areas* in which people can discount: *self, others,* and the *situation.*

In the example given above, where I was sitting in the restaurant drooping because the waiter wasn't bringing my glass of water, I was discounting myself. I was ignoring my own ability to take action to get what I wanted.

My friend, who got angry and started criticizing the waiter, was discounting not himself but the other person. In judging the waiter 'incompetent', he was blanking out any aspects of the waiter's actions that might have contradicted his criticism.

Suppose that after drooping for a while, I'd turned to my friend and said: 'Well, there we are. It really isn't fair that these other people are getting served and I'm not. But then, this world is an unfair place, isn't it?' Here, I'd have been discounting the situation.

Types of discounting

The three *types* of discounting are of: *stimuli, problems* and *options.*

To discount a *stimulus* is to blank out perception that something is happening at all. As I sat in the restaurant, I might simply not have allowed myself to feel that I was thirsty. I would have been discounting the stimulus of my own thirst. Maybe my friend, in calling the waiter incompetent, had 'not seen' the way in which the waiter had actually succeeded in serving many other customers, even though the evidence was right there in front of him.

The person who discounts a *problem* realizes that something is happening, but ignores the fact that whatever is happening poses a problem. Feeling thirsty there in the restaurant, I might have said to my friend: 'I feel very thirsty right now, but, oh well, it doesn't matter.'

When discounting *options*, the person is aware that something is happening and that it constitutes a problem. But she blanks out the possibility that anything can be done about the problem. This is where I was discounting in the original version of the restaurant scene. As I sat drooping, I knew that I felt thirsty. I was aware that my thirst was a problem to me. But I was unawarely ignoring the many options I had, other than just sitting and hoping the waiter would respond.

Levels (modes) of discounting

The terms *level* and *mode* are interchangeable, but *level* gives a clearer idea of what is meant. The four levels of discounting are: *existence, significance, change possibilities* and *personal abilities*.

Let's apply those four levels to my discounting of my own options in our example. In the original version of the scene, I was discounting the *existence* of my own options to solve the problem. I didn't even consider the possibility of, for example, walking over and speaking to the waiter instead of gesturing to him.

If I had been discounting the *significance* of my options, I might have said to my friend: 'I suppose I could go over and ask him. But I bet asking him wouldn't make any difference.' Here, I'd have realized there was something different I could do, but blanked out the possibility that this action could have any effect.

Discounting my options at the level of *change possibilities*, I might have said: 'Of course, I *could* walk across and collar the fellow. But people just don't do that in restaurants.' In this case I would have let myself realize that the option existed and that it might have results, while ignoring the possibility that anyone could actually put the option into practice.

At the level of *personal abilities*, I might have discounted by saying: 'I know I could go across and ask him for some water. But I just don't have the nerve to do it.' Here, I am aware the option exists and could bring results. I realize that some people in the world might well use that option. But I dismiss my own ability to do so.

The discount-matrix diagram

The discount matrix is compiled by listing all the possible combinations of *types* and *levels* of discount. When we do so, we get the diagram shown in Figure 18.1.

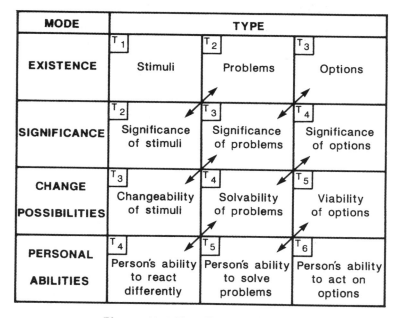

MODE	TYPE		
EXISTENCE	T_1 Stimuli	T_2 Problems	T_3 Options
SIGNIFICANCE	T_2 Significance of stimuli	T_3 Significance of problems	T_4 Significance of options
CHANGE POSSIBILITIES	T_3 Changeability of stimuli	T_4 Solvability of problems	T_5 Viability of options
PERSONAL ABILITIES	T_4 Person's ability to react differently	T_5 Person's ability to solve problems	T_6 Person's ability to act on options

Figure 18.1 The discount matrix

You'll see that the matrix has three columns for the three types of discount, and four rows for the four modes or levels. The wording in each of the resulting twelve boxes indicates the combination of type and level.

Let's take another example to help explain the meaning of the matrix. Suppose two friends are talking. One of them is a heavy smoker. As he lights up yet another cigarette, he is convulsed by a bout of coughing. His friend says to him: 'That's a terrible cough. I'm concerned about you. Please, give up smoking.' What might the smoker reply if he were discounting in each of the twelve different boxes on the matrix?

If the smoker were discounting the *existence of stimuli*, he might reply: 'What cough? I wasn't coughing.'

Discounting the *existence of the problem*, he might say: 'Oh, no, I'm fine, thanks. I've always had a cough.' He is letting himself be aware of his cough, but blotting out the possibility that this may constitute a problem for him.

Notice next that in doing this, the smoker *is also discounting the significance of the stimulus*. In discounting the possibility that his cough may be a problem, he is also discounting the fact that the cough may have some meaning (significance) for him.

This is indicated on the matrix diagram by the diagonal arrow connecting the boxes for 'existence of problems' and 'significance of stimuli'. The arrow means that one of these discounts will always entail the other.

All the diagonal arrows on the diagram have this meaning. The 'T' numbers, entered at the top left of each box, are labels for the different diagonals. For instance, discounts of the existence of problems and of the significance of stimuli correspond to diagonal T_2.

Let's test this out on the next diagonal down, T_3. We can take the top-right box on this diagonal, where the smoker is discounting the existence of options. He might show this by replying: 'Well, yes, but we smokers do cough, you know? A short life and a happy one, that's what I say, ha ha.'

Now he is admitting that he has a cough and that the cough may well indicate a problem, namely that smoking can kill people. But he is blanking out the possibility that anyone can do anything to avoid smokers' cough.

In doing so, he also blanks out any perception that the possibility of being killed by smoking is something he might be concerned about. He discounts the significance of the problem.

And by his denial that anything can possibly be done by anyone to get rid of a smokers' cough, he discounts the changeability of the stimulus.

Check that the same equivalence of discounts also applies along the other diagonals. On T_4, the smoker might say: 'Well, yes, I suppose I should give up really. But I've been smoking so long, I don't think my giving up now is going to make any difference.'

On T_5 he might respond: 'Sure, you're right, I need to give up. But I can't figure out how to do it.'

And on T_6 the smoker might say: 'Yes! I've been telling myself for ages I should throw my cigarettes and lighter away. But I just can't seem to get round to it.'

Another feature of the matrix is that *a discount in any box also entails discounts in the boxes below it and to its right.*

For instance, suppose a person is discounting the existence of a problem. Since he is not allowing himself to be aware that the problem even exists, he's obviously also going to blank out any perception that the problem may be significant. Nor will he be thinking whether he or anyone else can solve the problem. He is thus discounting in the entire column of boxes related to 'problems'.

And since he is ignoring the existence of the problem, why should he consider whether there are options for solving it? Because he thus discounts the existence of options, he will also discount all the other boxes in the 'options' column.

Finally, recall that a discount of the existence of problems is equivalent to discounting the significance of stimuli, along diagonal T_2. Therefore the other two boxes below it in the 'stimuli' column will be discounted also.

To summarize: *a person discounting on any diagonal will also be discounting in all the boxes below and to the right of that diagonal.*

You may wish to go back to the 'smoker' examples and confirm this *hierarchy of discounts.*

● Make up the discount matrix for another imaginary case. Wife and husband have just settled down in bed for the night. Then, in the next room, their baby starts crying. The husband says to his wife: 'Do you think one of us should go and see why the baby's crying?'

Work out the responses his wife might give if she were discounting on each of the diagonals in the discount matrix.

Confirm that the 'hierarchy of discounts' applies. ●

Using the discount matrix

Whenever a problem is not being solved, some information relevant to the solution of that problem is being ignored. The discount matrix gives us a systematic way of pinpointing what information is being missed. This in turn provides guidance to the specific actions we need to take to solve the problem.

You'll recall that if a person is discounting on any given diagonal of the matrix, she will also be discounting in all the boxes below and to the right of that diagonal. This gives us an important clue to the process of problem-solving. When a problem remains unsolved despite efforts to solve it, this is often because the person *is addressing the problem on too low a diagonal of the discount matrix.*

It follows that in using the matrix as a problem-solving tool, we need to begin by looking for discounts *on the highest diagonal first.* We step into the matrix at the top left-hand corner. If we discover a discount there, we need to deal with that discount before going any further downwards or to the right.

Why? Because if we miss that initial discount and try to deal with a discount on any lower diagonal, *our intervention will itself be discounted.*

Let's illustrate this by referring back to the example about the smoker and his concerned friend. Suppose you are that friend. As you listen to the smoker's hacking cough, you say to yourself: 'He's going to kill himself if he doesn't stop smoking. Something needs to be done about this.'

So you say out loud: 'I'm concerned about you. Please give up smoking.'

With your intervention, you have addressed the problem on the lowest diagonal of the box. The issue is whether the smoker is going to act on a specific option.

But suppose the smoker is discounting much higher on the matrix? For example, he may be on diagonal T_2. This will mean he is aware that he has a hacking cough. But he does not regard this as being of any concern to him. He does not perceive it as a problem. In terms of the discount matrix, he is discounting the significance of the stimulus and the existence of the problem.

It's obvious, then, that he will also discount any relevance in what you have just said to him. Why should he have any investment in stopping smoking when, as far as he is aware, his smokers' cough is not a problem?

Since you can't read his mind, you have no way of knowing where he is discounting until he responds to you. And notice here an important point: he may respond from the highest diagonal on which he is discounting, but may also respond *from any diagonal below it*.

For instance, suppose he replies: 'Hm, yes, I know I should give up, but I think once you're hooked on this habit, you're hooked on it.' This is a discount of the solvability of problems, making it look as though he is discounting on diagonal T_4.

The temptation for you then is to start into an exposition of the evidence that people can, in fact, give up smoking. But you will get nowhere with this. The smoker is really discounting on T_2. Thus, outside of his awareness, he is saying to himself: 'So, people can give up smoking. What's that got to do with me? This cough of mine is no problem anyway.'

Suppose now you wanted to help your smoking friend by systematically using the discount matrix. You would begin by checking for a discount on diagonal T_1. 'Are you aware that you've got a really bad cough?'

If he confirms he is aware of the cough, you would go down to the next diagonal. You might ask: 'Is that cough of yours something you're concerned about?' Were he to reply 'No, not really, it's something I just take for granted,' you would have located his discount on T_2. This lets you know that if your smoker friend is to give up his habit, he first needs to become aware that his cough may indicate a problem. He needs to realize too that this problem may be a cause for his concern.

● Use this technique to review your personal example of a problem situation you did not solve at the time.

Beginning at the top left of the discount matrix, check each box, working downwards on successive diagonals, until you identify the box in which you were discounting. As before, if you are working in a group or with a willing friend, it may be helpful if you get a second opinion.

Test whether you were also discounting in all the other boxes on the same diagonal and those below it.

What was the area of the discount? Were you discounting yourself, others or the environment?

When you have identified the discount, consider its ego-state source. Did it come from a contamination? An exclusion? Or were you uninformed or misinformed?

Let yourself be aware of whatever part of reality you had previously been discounting. If you need accurate or new information, get it.

Now re-run the situation in your mind's eye. When you come to the point at which you began to discount, replace the discount with your full awareness of reality. How do you now act, think or feel differently? How does this alter the outcome of the situation? ●

The discount matrix was originally developed for use in psychotherapy. But it provides an equally effective tool for problem-solving in organizations and education. In these settings also, it is common for problems to remain unsolved because they are being addressed on too low a diagonal in the discount matrix. The remedy remains the same: to identify the information that is being missed, start at the top left corner of the matrix and check downwards through the diagonals. Bear in mind that people often discount because they are misinformed or uninformed, rather than because they are getting into script.

For instance, picture a university teacher with a class of his students. He asks them questions to check their understanding of his recent lectures. To his dismay, they can answer hardly any. When the class finishes, the lecturer tells himself: 'These students just haven't been working. What's the trouble? Why have they no motivation?'

By assuming that the students have not been working, he is addressing a discount in the area of 'others', on diagonal T_5 or T_6 of the discount matrix. He has assumed that his students know they may have problems if they don't work, but that they either don't feel they can handle the work or just aren't getting started to it.

If the lecturer were to check through the discount matrix, he would discover that the real problem is quite different. The fact is that when he is lecturing, he mumbles. The students can't hear what he is saying. The discount is on diagonal T_2 of the matrix. To address the problem, the lecturer simply needs to speak up.

Chapter 19
FRAME OF REFERENCE AND REDEFINING

I have my way of perceiving the world. You have your way, and it will be different from mine.

Suppose you and I stand outside a window, and look at the room within. We report to each other what we see.

I say: 'It's a fairly small room. It's square in shape. There are people in it. The carpet is green and the curtains brown.'

You report: 'It's a family scene. The whole atmosphere is warm. There's Mother, Father and two kids, and they're talking and laughing. It's a big room, so they have plenty of space.'

Judging by these reports, a listener might think you and I were looking at two completely different rooms. But the room is the same. It is our perception of it that is different. Were we each to report on what we were hearing, feeling, smelling or tasting as we looked into that room, the chances are that our reports of these perceptions would differ also.

What is more, it's probable that you and I would respond to that scene in different ways. I might feel nothing in particular, and walk away after viewing the room for a few minutes. You might feel happy, knock on the window and open a conversation with the people inside.

Thus, you and I differ in how we perceive the scene and how we respond to it. Your *frame of reference* is different from mine.

The frame of reference

The frame of reference is defined by the Schiffs as *the structure of associated responses which integrates the various ego-states in response to specific stimuli.* It provides the individual with '...an overall perceptual, conceptual, affective and action set, which is used to define the self, other people and the world...'[1]

To help explain this formal definition, the Schiffs say that the frame of reference can be thought of as a 'filter on reality'. As you and I looked at the room, each of us filtered out certain parts of the scene. For instance, I noted the colour of the carpet, but filtered out the identities of the people in the room. From your frame of reference, you did the opposite.

We also *defined* the size of the room differently. To me, it was 'fairly small'. To you, it was 'big'. It so happens that I was brought up in an old house in the country, where all the rooms had been large. You spent your childhood in a city flat where the rooms were pocket-sized. Thus the definition of 'a big room' in our respective frames of reference is different.

You added another definition. You said: 'The whole atmosphere is warm'. I had not defined 'atmosphere', and had not even perceived it as part of the scene.

Now suppose you ask me if I agree with you that the atmosphere is warm. I might reply: 'No, I certainly don't.' You may wonder how I could possibly disagree with you so flatly. Aren't the family in the room talking and laughing openly with each other? How could there be a warmer atmosphere than that?

But then I add: 'Warm atmosphere? No, that carpet is completely the wrong colour. They need an orange or red one. And look at those grey walls!' You and I have encountered another way in which people's frames of reference often differ. We have each used the same words. But the *meanings* we attach to the words are quite different. The definition of 'a warm atmosphere', in this case, differs between your frame of reference and mine.

Frame of reference and ego-states

As a further aid to understanding the frame of reference, the Schiffs suggest that it can be thought of as a 'skin that surrounds the ego-states, binding them together'. As I perceive the world according to my unique frame of reference, I make my own unique set of ego-state responses to that perceived world. It's in this way that the frame of reference 'integrates the various ego-states'.

As you and I looked into the room, I got into Adult and made a comment on shapes, sizes and colours I saw in the here-and-now. You were in Child, re-playing happy memories of family scenes like this which you had enjoyed in your own childhood. Having made these ego-state shifts internally, we transacted with each other externally from the ego-states we had chosen.

Our frame of reference gives us the patterns in which we integrate our ego-state responses so as to express our overall personality.

Role of the Parent

The Parent ego-state plays a particularly important part in the formation of the frame of reference. This is because our frame of reference consists of *definitions* of the world, self and others. It is from our parents and parent-figures that we originally learn these definitions. Depending on the age at which we receive them, they may be filed away as part of the content of our own Parent ego-state (P_2) or of the Parent in the Child (P_1).

Each of us has a personal set of Parental definitions of what is good, bad, wrong, right, scary, easy, difficult, dirty, clean, fair, unfair, and so on. It is on this set of definitions that we base our views of self, others and the world. We choose our responses to situations accordingly.

Frame of reference and the script

What is the relationship between the script and the frame of reference? The answer is that the script *forms part of* the frame of reference. The frame of reference in total is made up of a large number of definitions. Some of these definitions will entail discounts, while others will not. The script consists of *all the definitions in the frame of reference that entail discounts.*

When I get into script, I am ignoring features of the here-and-now situation that would be relevant to the solution of a problem. I am discounting. In doing so, I am replaying outdated definitions of myself, others and the world that include those discounts.

For instance, as a child I may have received messages from my parents telling me I was not able to think. Now suppose that as a grown-up, I am about to take an examination. If I get into script at this point, I begin internally replaying the old Parental definition of myself that says: 'You can't think!' Agreeing with this in my Child ego-state, I accept the discount of my own thinking ability. I begin to feel inadequate and confused.

Nature and function of redefining

In this example, the reality of the situation is that I am able to think. Thus in accepting the old definition of myself as unable to think, I have *distorted my perception of reality so that it fits my script.* This process is called *redefining.*[2]

You learned in Part IV that the child makes script decisions because they seem to be the best way of surviving and getting by in a hostile world. In my Child ego-state as a grown-up, I may cling to these early decisions, because I am still clinging to the belief that they are necessary for my survival. Thus if some feature of reality seems to challenge my script decisions, I am likely to defend against it. Putting this idea into Schiffian language, we say: when my scripty frame of reference is threatened, I defend against the threat by redefining.

As a child, I accepted my parents' definition of me as 'unable to think'. I made this script decision because I believed it was the only way I had of surviving and getting my needs met. Now as I get into script as a grown-up, I re-run this old survival strategy. I redefine reality by discounting my own ability to think.

This does not help me solve the problem, which is to pass the examination. But outside my awareness, in my Child ego-state, I am following a motive that seems more important than any examination could be. That is: to defend against the unspeakable disaster I fear may happen if I challenge my parents' definition.

Redefining transactions

When I redefine, I do so internally. How will you know from my outward behaviour whether or not I am redefining?

The only external clue is that you will see or hear me discounting. Thus, the signals of discounting are the external manifestation that redefining is taking place internally. Every discount represents a distortion of reality.

In Chapter 17, you learned to recognize a whole range of behavioural clues that indicate that someone is discounting. These same clues, then, also tell you that the person is redefining. We also know someone is redefining if he shows grandiosity or a thinking disorder, which are typical accompaniments to discounting.

There are two distinctive transactions that give clear verbal evidence of redefining. They are the *tangential transaction* and the *blocking transaction*.

Tangential transactions

A tangential transaction is one in which the stimulus and response address different issues, or address the same issue from different perspectives.

For example, a therapist asks a group member: 'How do you feel?' She replies: 'Well, when we spoke about this in the group yesterday, I felt angry.' With her response, she addresses the issue of how she feels, but from the perspective of yesterday instead of today.

Or, at a wage negotiation, a union representative asks: 'What do you want from our side so we can conclude this agreement?' The personnel manager answers: 'We're not at all satisfied with the conditions you've proposed so far.' Here, the issue has been shifted from 'wanting' to 'feeling satisfied with'.

Everyday conversation is full of tangential transactions. When people are in situations they perceive as stressful, they are even more likely to redefine in this way. This is not surprising, because in stressful situations people are likely to begin perceiving threats to their frame of reference. The covert purpose of going off on a tangent is to divert the other person away from the issue that constitutes the threat. The person who initiates the tangential transaction will not be consciously aware she is doing so.

Often, the other person will follow the tangent, rather than sticking with the original topic. He may even go off on a further tangent of his own. For example:

Union representative: 'What do you want from our side so we can conclude this agreement?'

Personnel manager: 'We're not at all satisfied with the conditions you've proposed so far.'

U.R.: 'No, and we're not satisfied with what you've proposed either.'

P.M.: 'Oh? So what would you need from us that would satisfy you?'

U.R.: 'Ah, the trouble is, I'm not sure you can deliver what we need...'

When people get into an exchange of tangential transactions, they are likely to have an uncomfortable sense that their conversation is 'getting nowhere', or 'going around in circles'. On the psychological level, that is exactly what is intended. Conversations like these can go on for a long time. The participants may feel they have been working hard, and end up feeling drained. By the close of their discussion, they may have never got back to the original issue they had intended to address.

Blocking transactions

In a blocking transaction, the purpose of raising an issue is avoided by disagreeing about the definition of the issue.

Examples might be:

Therapist: 'How do you feel?'
Group member: 'Do you mean emotionally or physically?'

Union representative: 'What do you want from our side so we can conclude this agreement?'
Personnel manager: 'Are you talking about what we want, or what we think we can get?'

You will seldom hear long exchanges of blocking transactions. It is more likely that after the initial block, the parties will begin detailed arguments over the definition of the issue. Or, if one of the people concerned is a really determined blocker, the conversation may come to a halt in a dumbfounded silence. At the psychological level, the aim of the blocking transaction is the same as that of the tangential: to avoid addressing issues that would threaten the frame of reference of either or both participants.

● In a group: form small groups of three. In each small group, decide who is going to be 'client', who 'counsellor' and who 'observer'.

The client chooses any topic he wishes. He and the counsellor talk about that topic for three minutes. (The observer, or the group leader if there is one, keeps time.)

The client's task is to respond tangentially to *everything* the counsellor says. Each time the client goes off on a tangent, the counsellor is to follow him off on the new topic. The client then takes off on yet another tangent, and so on. The aim is for the client to keep up a continuous chain of tangential transactions for the whole three minutes.

When that time is up, take another two minutes for the client and counsellor to discuss their experience, and for the observer to report what she heard and saw.

Change roles and repeat until everyone has had a turn in each role.

Now re-run the exercise, but with one difference: this time, the counsellor is *not* to go with the client's tangents. Instead, each time the client offers a tangent, the counsellor is to find ways of pulling the client back to the original topic. The client's task is still to entice the counsellor away on as many tangents as he can manage. Repeat as before until everyone has played each role.

Now do a similar two-part exercise, but using blocking transactions instead of tangential transactions. Again, in the first part of the exercise the counsellor is to allow the client to block her. In the second part, the counsellor is to use her ingenuity to avoid being blocked, while the client keeps up his efforts to block every transaction.

Finally discuss how your experience of the exercise using blocking transactions differed from that of the exercise using tangential transactions. ●

Because you are doing this exercise with Adult awareness, your exchanges will be role-plays of tangential and blocking transactions, rather than actual instances of these transactions. But the exercise gives you practice in recognizing and confronting the tangents and blocks that people may use without awareness.

Chapter 20
SYMBIOSIS

In Schiffian theory, a *symbiosis* is said to occur *when two or more individuals behave as though between them they form a single person.*[1]

In a relationship like this, the people concerned will not be using their full complement of ego-states. Typically, one of them will be excluding Child and using only Parent and Adult. The other will take the opposite position, staying in Child while shutting out her other two ego-states. Thus they have access to a total of only three ego-states between them. This is pictured in Figure 20.1.

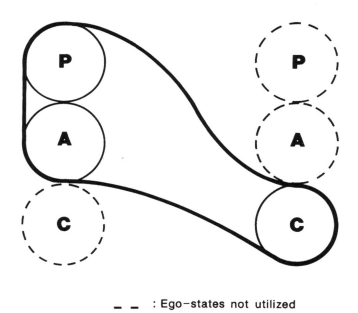

_ _ : Ego-states not utilized

▬▬ : Symbiosis

Figure 20.1 Symbiosis

For instance, imagine a lecturer conducting a tutorial class with his students. They are working through some exercises on theory.

The lecturer writes an exercise up on the board. Turning to one of the students, he asks: 'OK, Jim, will you tell us how you'd work through the next steps of this and get to the solution?'

Jim says nothing. Instead, he sits silent and unmoving for a while. Then he begins to waggle his foot rapidly up and down and rub the side of his head. Still he does not say a word.

The silence drags on. The other students in the class start to fidget as well. Finally the lecturer says: 'Seems like you don't know this one, Jim. Really, you *should* be working harder on your assignments. Now, here's what we do to get the solution...' And he completes the exercise on the board.

Jim relaxes, stops waggling his foot, and dutifully makes notes of the solution the lecturer has provided.

At this point, student and lecturer have moved into a symbiosis. By denying his own ability to reason out a solution, and covertly manipulating the lecturer into taking charge of the situation, Jim has discounted his own Adult and Parent ego-states.

The lecturer, obligingly providing the solution while giving Jim a 'should' about his revision, has stepped into the complementary role of Adult and Parent. In doing so, the lecturer has discounted his own Child ego-state. Had he allowed himself to use his Child resources, he'd have become aware that he was feeling uncomfortable and unsatisfied with the exchange that was going on between Jim and himself. He would have tuned in to an intuition: 'Hey, I've just been conned into doing all the work around here, and I don't like it!' Using that Child perception, he might have been able to find a creative way of facilitating Jim and the other students to work out the problem for themselves.

As it was, the lecturer shut out his own Child feeling of discomfort. Instead, he sought comfort by taking up his familiar symbiotic role of Adult and Parent.

Jim, too, relaxed and felt more comfortable as soon as he had settled into his familiar Child role.

That's the trouble with symbiosis. Once a symbiosis has been established, the participants *feel* comfortable for a while. There's a sense that everybody is in the role that is expected of them. But that comfort is acquired at a price: the people in the symbiosis are each shutting out whole areas of their own grown-up resources. Over time they will both build up resentment from parts of themselves being discounted.

In everyday relating, people move into and out of symbiosis with each other from moment to moment. Sometimes also, a long-term relationship is founded upon symbiosis. This is true of Bill and Betty, who exemplify one picture of a 'traditional' married couple. Bill is the strong, silent type.

With a pipe clamped in his jaw, he expresses himself in grunts. Come joy or disaster, Bill keeps his feelings firmly behind a granite facade. He looks after all the household finances, giving Betty a weekly allowance. When there's a decision to be made, Bill makes it, and tells Betty afterwards.

Betty, for her part, sees her mission in life as being to please her husband. She's happy to go along with his decisions, because, she tells her friends, 'she likes a strong man to lean on'. If a household emergency arises, Betty dissolves into tears, panic or giggles, and waits for Bill to come home and sort it out.

Some of their friends wonder occasionally how Bill manages to get along with Betty's helplessness. Others marvel that Betty can keep relating to Bill when he's so unfeeling. But in fact, their marriage has lasted a good many years, and looks set to last for many more. They gain their stability from being in symbiosis. Bill plays Parent and Adult to Betty's Child. Within that symbiosis, each 'needs' the other. And as always in symbiosis, the stability they experience is bought at the price of discounting a part of each person's capabilities. Over time, they will each build up resentment at having been discounted, which is likely to cause some distancing in their relationship.

● If you are working individually, find someone who is willing to do this pairwork exercise with you. In a group, get into pairs.

For the first part of the exercise, find a way of making contact in your pair so that each of you is propping the other one up physically. For instance, you might turn back-to-back and lean together. Or you might put the palms of your outstretched hands against those of your partner, then both move your feet back so that each person is bearing part of the other's weight.

Once you have found this mutual leaning position, stay in it a while. Be aware what you are feeling and thinking as you do so, but do not put this in words to your partner yet.

Next, one of you should make just the beginning of a movement out of the leaning position. Make the movement large enough to give the other person the feel of how it would be if you moved away completely. (Do not move away so far that the other person actually falls down). Then the one who has moved gets back into the mutual leaning position, and the other person takes a turn to make a move out. Register what you experience when you are the person who remains in the leaning position and the other person begins to move away from you.

For the second part of the exercise, find a way of making contact in your pair so that you are still touching, but each is bearing his or her own weight. For example, you might again place the palms of your hands against your partner's, but this time have each person stand upright instead of leaning on each other. Stay in this self-balanced position for a while. Register to yourself what you experience. How does this differ from what you experienced in the first part of the exercise?

Now have one partner break the contact. For example, if you have been standing with your hands touching, one of you might simply lower his hands. Register your experience when you are the person who is staying still and the other person breaks contact with you. How does this experience differ from that in the first part of the exercise, when the two of you were leaning together and the other person began to move away?

After a while, the partner who has broken contact makes that contact again. Repeat several times breaking and re-making contact, all the while with both partners bearing their own weight.

Run through this sequence again, with the other partner being the one who breaks and makes contact.

Take time to share your experiences with your partner. ●

The first part of this exercise is designed to literally 'give you the feel' of symbiosis. When the two of you are leaning on each other, most people report they feel 'comfortable' or 'supported'. But some also say they feel apprehensive in case the other person will move away and let them fall down. Almost everyone becomes aware of this apprehension when their partner does draw away slightly.

This illustrates another feature of actual symbiosis. When one of the partners perceives that the other is about to withdraw from the symbiotic pairing, she is likely to defend against this withdrawal. Her belief is: 'Without the other, I won't be able to stand on my own'. Paradoxically, it's this belief that gives symbiosis its apparent quality of stability.

Recall Bill and Betty, the strong silent husband and little-woman wife. Imagine that some of Betty's friends tell her about a women's group they have started, and that she joins it. She becomes uncomfortable with her Child role in the symbiosis. She starts questioning some of Bill's decisions. Instead of pleasing him all the time, she starts pleasing herself also. She learns assertiveness techniques, and starts practising some of them on her husband. What do you guess Bill's reaction will be?

The chances are that he will start escalating in an attempt to keep Betty in the symbiosis. He is likely to ignore or ridicule Betty's new assertiveness. He may get coldly withdrawn or openly angry when she fails to have the dinner ready for him or doesn't bring his slippers.

Bill may succeed in his attempts to invite Betty back into the symbiosis. If he does not, their relationship may be in for a stormy period.

Another possibility is that Bill himself will change his attitudes and move out of the symbiosis. Perhaps he will do this on his own, perhaps by joining a group or going into therapy.

If so, the relationship between Betty and himself will change and become more like what you experienced in the second part of the exercise. Now, you were still making contact with the other person, but the two of you were standing up independently instead of leaning on each other. One of you could break contact, and the two of you were still standing. The contact could be made and broken at will, and yet neither person fell down.

There's no guarantee that you will feel more *comfortable* in this independent position than you did in the mutual leaning position. In fact, many people report feeling less comfortable in the second part of the exercise than in the first. They are aware that they have more options – of moving, breaking and making contact – than they had when they were propping each other up. That's how it often is when two people move out of symbiosis in a relationship. They have more options, more flexibility, less predictability, and no guarantee of feeling more comfortable initially.

'Healthy' v. 'unhealthy' symbiosis

There are some situations in which it's appropriate for people to be in symbiosis. For example, suppose I have just come out from under the anaesthetic after an operation. I'm lying on a trolley being wheeled down a hospital corridor. I'm not very sure yet where I am, but I am sure of one thing: I'm hurting. Apart from the pain, the main thing I'm aware of is that a nurse is walking along beside me, holding my hand and telling me: 'You'll be all right. Just hang on to my hand.'

At that point, my Adult and Parent are out of commission. I am in no condition to start assessing here-and-now problems. I don't have the energy to access the messages I got from my parents about how to look after myself. I am doing what is appropriate for me to do: regressing to being a child again, feeling my pain and letting myself be cared for.

The nurse is giving me the Adult and Parent input that I need. She is dealing with current problems while giving me protection and reassurance. This is her job, so she also is appropriately in her symbiotic position.

In Schiffian terms, we say that the nurse and I are in a *healthy symbiosis*. This is contrasted with *unhealthy symbiosis*, illustrated by the examples given earlier in this chapter. When the word 'symbiosis' is used alone, it normally implies unhealthy symbiosis.

How do we distinguish formally between healthy and unhealthy symbiosis? The answer is that a symbiosis will be unhealthy whenever it involves *discounting*. In the examples of symbiosis between the student and the lecturer, and between Bill and Betty, the parties were each discounting reality by acting as though they only had three ego-states between them. By contrast, when I was being wheeled along on that hospital trolley, the reality was that my Adult and Parent were out of action because of the trauma and the effects of the anaesthetic. The nurse was indeed using her Parent and Adult. But she wasn't necessarily discounting her own Child while she did so.

Symbiosis v. normal dependency

One obvious example of a healthy symbiosis is that which exists between a child and his parent. When the baby is born, he is all Child. He doesn't yet have the capacity to solve problems or protect himself. These functions need to be performed by the parent, who will appropriately use Adult and Parent ego-states in doing so. Stan Woollams and Kristy Huige have suggested the term *normal dependency* to denote this healthy parent-child symbiosis.[2]

Recall that in a healthy symbiosis, the parties are not discounting *any* of their ego-states. The infant does not yet have a functioning Parent or Adult, so they cannot be discounted. However, the parent does have a Child ego-state. To avoid slipping into unhealthy symbiosis, she needs to stay aware of her own Child needs and find some way of getting these met, even while she is closely involved in caring for her infant.

Symbiosis and the script

Thus in ideal parenting, the child's caretaker will be employing Parent and Adult resources appropriately, while still not discounting her own Child. As the child grows, the parent will provide him with what is needed to complete each stage of development. At each stage, the child acquires more and more of his own resources, and so has less and less need to lean on the parent. Ideally, the parent encourages the child in this appropriate separation, while continuing to provide support in the areas where the child still needs it.

In this ideal process, the initial intense symbiosis between child and parent is progressively broken.[3] The final result is that by the time the child reaches young adulthood, both parties are relating without symbiosis. Each is able to stand independently, making or breaking contact at will.

The trouble is that there are no ideal parents. No matter how good a job Mother and Father make of parenting, every child goes through the process of development with some needs unmet along the way.

This fact reveals the scripty *function* of symbiosis in adult life. *Every symbiosis is an attempt to get developmental needs met that were not met during the person's childhood.*

As always with scripty behaviour, the person in symbiosis is using outdated strategies in his attempt to get needs met. These strategies were the best he could work out as a young child, but are no longer appropriate in grown-up life. In symbiosis, the person is *discounting* grown-up options. The discounting is outside his awareness.

Whenever we get into symbiosis, we are unwittingly re-playing old childhood situations where we felt an unmet need. We once again set up the relationship that existed in the past between ourselves and a parent or parent-figure, and re-run the situation in an attempt to manipulate the other into satisfying the need that was not met. This is what happens in games, as we will see later.

Choice of symbiotic position

You may be thinking: 'OK, so if symbiosis is a re-play of old childhood situations, I can see why people get into the Child role in symbiosis. But why should anybody choose to be in the Parent role?'

The answer is that some children make an early decision: 'The parenting around here is so ineffective that my best option is to take over as parent myself.' Perhaps Mother, in her own Child ego-state, was scared to set firm boundaries for her children. Instead, she blackmailed them by saying things like: 'If you do that, you'll hurt me', or 'Look – you're making Father angry!' The child was being asked to take responsibility for the parents' feelings and welfare. He might respond by deciding that his job in life was to look after his parents. Thus, in effect, he became a little parent himself. In grown-up life, he may re-enter this role in symbiosis in an attempt to control others or get appreciation for his caretaking.

Other children, who perceive their parents as abusive or oppressive, may take up the life position 'I'm OK, you're not-OK' and fantasize about putting their parents down from a Parental position. This, again, is replayed in their grown-up symbiotic relationships: outside of awareness, their aim is to 'get even' with the abusive parent.

Symbiotic invitations

When people meet, they are adept at signalling to each other what symbiotic role they want to take up. These *symbiotic invitations* are often conveyed without words. Usually, one or more of the four passive behaviours will be shown.

In the example that opened this chapter, Jim made his symbiotic invitation first by doing nothing, then by agitation. When he sat silent and then began to fidget, he was conveying to the lecturer the covert message: 'I need you to think for me and tell me how things are.' His symbiotic invitation was for the lecturer to take up Parent and Adult roles, while he took up Child.

By going ahead and completing the exercise, the lecturer was agreeing on that same psychological level: 'Yes, you're right. You do need me to think for you and tell you how things are.' As he did so, he accepted Jim's symbiotic invitation.

Sometimes a symbiotic invitation may be conveyed in words. When this happens, the person will be heard manipulating for what she wants, rather than asking directly. This is often done subtly. For instance, a member of a therapy group may look forlornly down at the floor and say: 'I need a hug.' The temptation is for other group members to go ahead and give her the hug she seems to have asked for. But if they do so, they will have accepted her symbiotic invitation. Had she asked for the hug in a non-symbiotic manner, she would have looked at one particular member of the group and said: 'Will you give me a hug?'

Competitive symbiosis

But what happens when two people meet who both want to take up the same symbiotic role? If they both want to be Parent, or both seek to act Child?

When this is so, the parties will begin 'jockeying for position' in the hope of taking up their preferred symbiotic role. For example, you may have heard this kind of exchange in a restaurant as two people prepare to pay up after the meal:

'Now, put that money away. I'll pay for this.'

'No, no, come on, *I'll* pay.'

'I absolutely insist! Not another word!'

These transactions may go on for some time, with each party escalating insistence on paying. Each is seeking to be Parent to the other. They are in a *competitive symbiosis* – in this case, competing for the Parent position.

By its nature, competitive symbiosis is unstable. Exchanges like this usually last only for a relatively short time. They may conclude in two possible ways. The parties may storm away from each other, slamming doors as they go. Or one of them may back down and yield the desired symbiotic position to the other. The one who has backed down then takes the complementary position in the symbiosis.

For instance, the exchange in the restaurant might end with one of the parties saying: 'Ah, well, if you insist...' and putting away his wallet with a show of reluctance. He has backed down to the Child position, allowing himself to be 'looked after' by the other person.

People can also compete for the Child position by attempting to prove that they are more needy than the other person. For example, husband says, 'I'm so exhausted I don't think I can move,' to which wife replies, 'I know *I* can't, so you will have to fix dinner.'

● Make up another example of a competitive symbiosis for the Parent position, ending with one of the parties backing down to Child.

Diagram the transactions that take place during the exchange.

What positions on the OK Corral would you say each party visits during the competition, and after one of them backs down?

Make up an example of a Child-competitive symbiosis, ending with one of the parties backing down and reluctantly taking the Parent role. Again diagram the transactions and analyse the OK-Corral positions.

Draw a transactional diagram for the exchange between Jim and the lecturer, in which Jim issued his symbiotic invitation and the lecturer accepted it.

What do you think might be important counterinjunctions and injunctions in Jim's script matrix? In the lecturer's? In Bill's and Betty's? ●

Second-order symbiosis

In some symbiotic relationships, there's a second symbiosis going on underneath the first. It takes the form shown in Figure 20.2. This kind of symbiosis is called a *second-order symbiosis* because it occurs within the second-order structure of the Child ego-state.

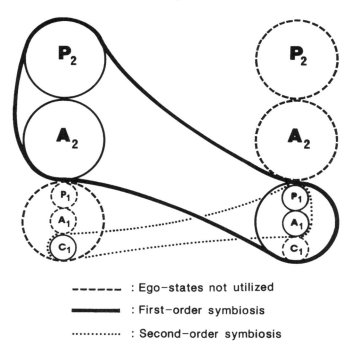

– – – – – – : Ego–states not utilized

━━━━━━ : First–order symbiosis

··············· : Second–order symbiosis

Figure 20.2 Second–order symbiosis

Relationships between couples like Bill and Betty often entail second-order symbiosis. On first impression, it seems clear that Bill is in the Parent-Adult role in their symbiosis, while Betty plays Child. He gets to be in control and to deal with practical problems. She gets to be controlled and express feelings. And on the level of first-order symbiosis, that is indeed what is going on. Bill is re-playing an early decision: 'The only way I can get by is to be in charge and in tight control of everybody, including myself.' Betty's decision was: 'My mission in life is to please others, especially men, and not to think about things.' The first-order symbiosis represents their joint efforts to get their needs met through these script decisions.

However, Bill has yet another need. It is even further below his awareness than the need to be in charge and in control, and it comes from an earlier stage of his development. That is the need for physical strokes and comfort. We show this as part of the content of Bill's C_1, the early Child in the Child.

The trouble for Bill is that in making his later script decisions, he shut out those early Child needs. So how is he to get them met now? The answer is that in choosing Betty as his symbiotic partner, he adeptly picked someone who would take up the complementary role in the second-order symbiosis.

Betty's mother, like Betty herself, had married a strong, silent man who was not keen to give physical strokes. When Betty was an infant, her father had not been around much. He had preferred to spend his time at work or out drinking with his friends. Mother had had no other grown-up to satisfy her own early Child needs for stroking and being looked after.

With her acute infant perception, Betty had decided without words: 'To keep Mother around and in good shape, I'd better look after her myself.' Using her own rudimentary Parent and Adult, P_1 and A_1, she became caretaker to her mother's Somatic Child. Now in grown-up symbiosis, she replays this pattern with Bill.

A symbiosis like this may be particularly difficult to break. Recall that stroking is a survival issue for the early Child. Thus in this example, if Betty makes to break out of the symbiosis, Bill in his Somatic Child may experience mortal terror. His Child belief is that he is about to lose his only source of physical strokes, and that means death.

At the same early Child level, Betty may perceive breaking the symbiosis as meaning the loss of Mother. To the infant, this also implies a death sentence.

It's likely that neither Bill nor Betty will allow this early Child terror into their awareness. Instead, they are likely to find rationalizations of why they should continue in their symbiotic relationship. If they do want to break out of that relationship, they may need script insight and therapeutic help.

Part VI

JUSTIFYING OUR SCRIPT BELIEFS

Rackets and Games

Chapter 21
RACKETS AND STAMPS

Here's an exercise to start this chapter. We suggest you do it before reading on. If you are working in a group, have the group leader or a volunteer lead the rest of the group through the scene, improvising on the instructions that follow.

● In this exercise, you will be asked to imagine a scene, and then to answer a few questions about it. There are no 'right' or 'wrong' answers.

Imagine that tomorrow is going to mark the beginning of a holiday period in your area, a time when all the shops will be shut for several days.

Imagine too that it's quite some time since you did any shopping. You are almost out of essential food and provisions. Looking at the time, you realize with relief that you've just got long enough to get down to the supermarket and get around it before it closes.

Mentally checking a list of the things you need to buy, you set off for the supermarket. Arriving there, you see a crowd of other shoppers on the same mission as yourself, stocking up before the holiday closing period begins.

Keeping an eye on the time, you go round the shelves collecting the items you want. As you finish, you note with satisfaction that there are still just a few minutes to go before the store closes. You'll have plenty of time to get through the checkout.

You get to the checkout desk. The clerk enters your purchases on the cash-till, and tells you the total cost.

You reach for your money. And you can't find it. You search again, and still it isn't there. You realize why: you have left it at home. In your haste, you have come to the supermarket without any money. You don't have a credit card or cheques either.

As a line of shoppers builds up behind you, you tell the clerk what's happened. You ask: 'Would it be OK for me to leave my name and address, take the goods away and come back to pay you after the holiday?' The clerk replies: 'No, I'm afraid that isn't possible.'

You don't have time now to go home and get your money before the store closes. So you won't get your goods. You'll have to go without them. And it will be several days before the shops open again.

As you realize this, *how do you feel?*

Register how you are feeling, and give a name to that emotion. Then come out of the imagined scene. ●

Keep note of the feeling you registered. Whenever people do this exercise, the emotions they report at the end have certain typical characteristics. We will list these below. Check whether each one applies to the emotion that you registered.

(1) Different people report different feelings. If you are working in a group, go around and ask each member to name the emotion he or she felt at the end of the scene. Have someone note these up as each person reports.

The scene itself was the same for everybody. But you'll discover that the people in the group report a whole range of different emotions. Typically, the list of different feelings may read: 'Angry at myself, panicky, embarrassed, angry at the clerk, sick, blank...' The bigger the group, the greater the range of different feelings that will be reported.

If you are working individually, you can test this by finding some willing friends who will go through the scene and report their feelings at the end.

(2) The feeling registered is one you experience in a wide range of different stress situations. For example, if I report at the end of this scene that I feel 'angry at myself', it's likely that I would also report feeling angry at myself in many other situations where I felt under stress. If you reported feeling 'panicky', then you would probably report that same bad feeling in different situations.

It's as if each of us has a 'favourite bad feeling' we bring up for all-purpose use when we perceive things getting tough. Some people have a choice of two or three bad feelings to use in this way. They may keep one for use at home, another for work, and so on.

(3) The feeling registered is one that was modelled or encouraged in your family, while other feelings were discouraged or prohibited. For instance, if you registered feeling 'angry at someone else', it's likely that this feeling was shown frequently by your parents and family members when you were a child. When you yourself showed it, you would get some kind of recognition for doing so.

There would be a whole range of other feelings that were seldom or never shown in your family. In this example, while it was acceptable to be angry in your family, it may not have been considered OK to be sad, scared or happy. If you showed any of these other feelings you'd find that you either got scolded for it, or – worse still for you as a child – just got ignored.

(4) The emotion you felt did nothing towards solving your problem. If I got angry and started shouting at the clerk, that would do nothing to get me the goods I'd wanted. Whether I felt panicky, sick, blank, angry at myself, or any of the other feelings people typically report, none of these

emotions would help me in the slightest to get my purchases out of that supermarket.

These characteristics are typical of the kind of emotion that TA calls a *racket feeling.*[1]

In the sections that follow we discuss the nature and function of racket feelings. They are important to understand, because they play a central role in the way people live out their scripts.

Definitions of 'racket' and 'racket feeling'

There has been a lot of confusion in the TA literature about the meaning of the terms 'racket' and 'racket feeling'. Some writers have used the two terms interchangeably.

In this book, we don't do this. We follow another school of thought that says there is a useful distinction to be made between rackets and racket feelings.

We define a *racket feeling* as *a familiar emotion, learned and encouraged in childhood, experienced in many different stress situations, and maladaptive as an adult means of problem-solving.*

We define a *racket* as *a set of scripty behaviours, employed outside awareness as a means of manipulating the environment, and entailing the person's experiencing a racket feeling.*

In other words, a racket is a process in which someone sets up to feel a racket feeling, and feels that feeling. The set-up is outside the person's conscious awareness. The individual is escalating the feeling rather than taking action to solve the problem.

For instance, in our imagined scene where I came away without my money, I had set up to feel the bad feeling I experienced at the end. I *could* have made sure I had the money with me, but I didn't. If you were to ask me why I didn't, I might answer: 'I just didn't think of it.'

The outcome of the events that the person has set up is seen as 'justifying' the racket feeling. Suppose that as I stood at the checkout desk, I felt furious at the clerk. You might ask me: 'How come you're angry at the clerk?' My answer might be: 'Well, I'm not going to get my goods, am I?'

Anger at others is my favoured racket feeling in stress situations. Five other people might well feel five different bad feelings in that same situation. And they'd all be likely, as I did, to assume that *their* favoured racket feeling was the 'natural' way to feel in those circumstances.

Do people always need to set up a racket in order to feel a racket feeling? No. We can also experience a racket feeling in response to independently occurring stress situations, ones that we have genuinely done nothing to set up. For example, imagine yourself making a journey on some form of public transport – plane, train or bus – with a time deadline to meet at your destination. Because of a mechanical fault, your journey is delayed. As you sit there watching the minutes tick away, how do you feel?

Chances are that I would feel angry at the transport company. You might feel panicky, another person feel sick, and so on.

Rackets and script

Realize first one universal connection between scripts and rackets: *any time you experience a racket feeling, you are in script.*

Why do racket feelings play such an important part in the mechanism of the script? The answer lies in the way children learn to use racket feelings as a means of getting needs met in their families.

We've seen that racket feelings are learned and encouraged in childhood. Every family has its own restricted range of permitted feelings, and another wider range of feelings that are discouraged or prohibited.

Sometimes the permitted feelings will differ according to whether the child is a boy or girl. Often, little boys are taught that it's OK to be angry and aggressive, but not to be scared or tearful. Little girls may learn that they are supposed to react to stress by crying or being sweet and bubbly, even though they may feel like showing anger.

So what happens, then, if the child does go ahead and show one of the prohibited feelings? Suppose for instance that the little boy gets scared, and shows it. Maybe he's being chased by the local bully. He comes running to Mother, shaking with fright and looking for her protection. Mother looks down her nose at him and says: 'Now, now! Be a brave soldier! Out you go and stand on your own two feet.' Then she gets on with the chores.

The child registers: 'If I get scared and show it, I don't get the results I want around here. I wanted protection and I got ignored instead.'

In his acute Little Professor, the boy casts around for ways he *can* get results in the way he wants. He is likely to test out a whole range of feelings day by day as responses to stress situations. He tries out sadness, cheerfulness, aggressiveness, confusion, blankness, and as many other different feelings as you can name. Suppose he discovers that aggressiveness gets the best response from Mother.

Now if the neighbourhood bully chases him, he fights back (and loses, because the bully is bigger than he is). Though he's hurting from the bruises, at least he gets approval from Mother: 'That's right. Big boys don't cry!'

He has discovered a feeling that 'gets him the results' he most wants: recognition from his parents. To get the strokes he wants, he needs to show aggression. For sure, he buys these strokes at the cost of hurting.

This sequence of events is likely to be repeated over and over again as the little boy continues to grow. With each repetition, he gradually comes to a further conclusion about feelings and their results. 'Except for aggressiveness, no other kinds of feeling seem to be any use around here. In fact, if I do show any other feelings, my parents take away their support, and that's dangerous. Therefore, I'd best not even let myself *feel* any feelings except aggressiveness.'

Now, each time he begins to feel scared or sad, he hides the feeling even from himself. Instead, he switches straight into getting aggressive.

Rackets and rubberbands

Suppose I was that little boy, and suppose I'm now standing at the checkout desk in the supermarket as the clerk refuses my request for credit.

As I experience the stress of this situation, I *rubberband* back to being a small child in a stressful situation of the past. For me, it's as if the clerk and indeed the whole world were threatening me, just as that neighbourhood bully used to threaten when I was little.

In an instant, I do what I learned to do as a child. I get aggressive. Facing up to the clerk, I yell: 'It's disgraceful! Are you trying to say you don't trust me?' The clerk shrugs.

Still fuming with anger, I march stiffly off out of the supermarket. For a few moments I feel a certain grim sense of satisfaction. I say to myself: 'Well, at least I told that clerk where to get off!' But at the same time, I know that all my shouting will not change the fact that I've had to leave my goods behind. I'm still burning up inside, and later that day I get acid indigestion.

My feeling reaction was not of the slightest use to me in solving my here-and-now problem. But outside of awareness, I had been pursuing a motive that was much more important to me than that. *I was attempting to manipulate the environment so as to gain the parental support I gained in childhood by experiencing and showing these racket feelings.* Mother in my head still says 'That's right!'

This is always the function of racket feelings in adulthood. Each time I experience a racket feeling, I am re-playing an outdated childhood strategy. In other words, I am in script.

By contrast, if I stay in the here and now, I'm going to feel what is appropriate to the present moment. The only way I can feel a racket is in fantasy to go to some other time or place.

The magic of the racket

Rackets are used as a magical way to try to get other people or things to change. I may think, 'If I stay angry long enough, you will do what I want,' or 'If I stay helpless long enough, you will do it for me,' or 'If I stay sad long enough, you will love me,' or 'If I stay scared long enough, you will take care of me.' Rackets are reinforced in childhood because they often work. The problem is when the person uses this strategy in adulthood rather than asking directly for what they want. It will sometimes work, but it is a very inefficient way of getting needs met; the person has to feel like a victim, and others feel manipulated by it.

The worst is when people try to use a racket to get someone or something in the past to change. That is not going to work, but some people magically try to do that, e.g., 'If I feel sad enough, long enough, my parents will love me when I was ten.'

Setting up rackets

In our example, I had set up the racket, the sequence of events that 'justified' me in experiencing my racket feeling. I had 'accidentally' forgotten to bring my money with me.

Now that we know the script function of racket feelings, we can see why I did so. I set up the racket *so that I could experience the racket feeling.* In my Child, I had been experiencing a need for strokes. So I had arranged to manipulate for those strokes in the way I had learned as a child. I had set up to feel the same feeling that 'got results' for me in my family.

In this way, racket theory gives us an entirely new perspective on why people get bad feelings. Let's return to our supermarket example. The everyday explanation of this would be: 'I went without the goods I needed, therefore I felt angry.'

But with a knowledge of rackets, we'd say instead: 'I wanted to justify feeling angry, therefore I set myself up to go without the goods I needed.'

Racket feelings and authentic feelings

We have explained how children learn that certain feelings are encouraged in their family, while others are discouraged or prohibited. When the child experiences any of the prohibited feelings, he makes a rapid switch into an alternative feeling that is permitted. He may not even allow himself to be aware of the prohibited feeling. When we experience racket feelings in adulthood, we go through the same process. In this way, a racket feeling is always a *substitute* for another feeling, one that was prohibited in our childhood.

To convey this quality of substitution, we refer to racket feelings as *inauthentic* feelings. By contrast, *authentic* feelings are those feelings we experience as young children, *before* we learn to censor them as being discouraged in the family.

This distinction between racket and authentic feelings was first suggested by Fanita English.[2] In her original work, she used the phrase 'real feelings' as a contrast to racket feelings. However, it's more usual nowadays to talk of 'authentic' rather than 'real' feelings. The point here is that when I am experiencing a racket feeling, that feeling is certainly 'real' as far as I am aware. When I started bawling out the clerk, I wasn't feigning anger: I was really angry. But my anger was a racket feeling, not an authentic feeling.

We often speak of a racket feeling as being used to *cover* an authentic feeling. Say for instance that a little girl learns: 'In my family, it's permitted for a girl to be sad, but never angry.' When in script as a grown-up, suppose she is in a situation where she might be about to get angry with somebody. For instance, suppose she is elbowed rudely by somebody on a crowded bus. The instant she begins to feel angry, she moves into her learned childhood pattern almost like a conditioned reflex. Instead of getting angry, she starts feeling sad and perhaps bursts into tears. She has *covered* her authentic anger with inauthentic racket sadness.

Some people not only cover authentic feelings with racket feelings, but also cover one racket with another racket. For example, Robert spent a lot of his early childhood feeling scared in case Mother might abandon him. Without words, he learned that if he showed anger every time he felt scared, he at least got some strokes from Mother. So while he was still an infant, he began covering fear with anger.

When he got a bit older, he discovered that for everybody in his family except small babies, there was a prohibition on showing any feelings at all. In order to fit in with family norms, you were supposed to keep a stiff upper lip and stay blank. Robert then decided: 'I'd better stop even feeling angry, because if I get angry I *will* be in danger of ending up outside the family.' So he joined in with the rest of the family, suppressed his anger just as he had his scare, and covered it with blankness.

Now suppose Robert, in adult life, gets into a situation where his uncensored feeling would be scare. Maybe he perceives that a partner in a relationship is making signals of rejection, and thus is threatening to leave Robert in the position he didn't want to be as a child – alone. The instant Robert begins to feel scared of this, he covers the scare with anger. Just as rapidly, he covers the anger with blankness. As far as he is aware, the blankness is his 'real' feeling. Were you to ask him how he feels, he'd reply: 'I don't feel much, really.'

Naming racket and authentic feelings

What are the authentic feelings, those emotions that we feel when we are not censoring? In TA it's usual to list four of them:

- *mad*
- *sad*
- *scared*
- *glad.*

The word 'mad' is used here in the American sense of 'angry', not the English sense of 'crazy'.

To these we would add various physical sensations that a child can feel, e.g. relaxed, hungry, full, tired, turned-on, disgusted, sleepy, etc.

In contrast to this short list of names for the authentic feelings, you could fill pages and pages with names that people give to their racket feelings. Perhaps you'd like to test this for yourself.

You could start with the inauthentic feelings that would usually be categorized as 'emotions': embarrassment, jealousy, depression, guilt, etc. Then you can add the vaguer terms that express how people feel about themselves when they are in script: lost, stuck, cornered, helpless, desperate, and so on.

Some racket names relate more obviously to thinking than to feeling: confused, blank, puzzled, etc.

Not all racket feelings would be categorized as 'bad' by the people who are experiencing them. Recall our example of the little girl who learned that she was supposed to be sweet and bubbly, even when she really felt angry. As a grown-up, she'll have a reputation of being 'everybody's ray of sunshine'. She may get a lot of strokes for her racket happiness, just as she did when she was a child. Other racket feelings that may be experienced as 'good' are triumphancy, aggressiveness, blamelessness, or euphoria. Nevertheless, all these feelings are inauthentic. They have been learned during childhood and are used in grown-up life as an attempt to manipulate support from the environment.

Another complication in naming feelings is this: the names given to the authentic feelings are *also* given to racket feelings. For instance, you can get authentic anger or racket anger, authentic sadness or racket sadness, and so on. Perhaps I learned as a child to cover anger with confusion, while you learned to cover anger with sadness. Your racket feeling happens to have the same name as one of the authentic feelings. Mine does not. But your inauthentic sadness and my confusion are both racket feelings.

Racket feelings, authentic feelings, and problem-solving

So if racket feelings aren't always experienced as 'bad', why is it important to distinguish between racket and authentic feelings?

The answer is: expression of authentic feelings is appropriate as a means of here-and-now problem-solving, while expression of racket feelings is not.

In other words, when we express an authentic feeling, we do something that helps finish the situation for us. When we express a racket feeling, we leave the situation unfinished.

George Thomson has explained the problem-solving function of three of the authentic feelings: fear, anger and sadness.[3] He points out that these feelings deal respectively with the future, the present, and the past.

When I feel authentic *fear* and act in some way to express that emotion, I am helping solve a problem that I foresee arising in *future*. For sure, that future may be very close. Suppose I'm crossing a road, having checked to see the way is clear. Suddenly, a car shoots out of a side road, being driven much too fast, and skids towards me. Galvanized by fear, I leap to one side. I have avoided the *future* event of being struck by the car.

Authentic *anger* is for solving problems in the *present*. Maybe I am waiting in line to be served in a shop. A woman tries to push ahead of me, shoving me to one side with her shopping-basket. Expressing my anger, I react appropriately to look after myself in the *present*. I push her back with equal force, and growl: 'I got here before you. Get to the end of the line, please.'

When I feel authentically *sad*, I am helping myself get over a painful event that has happened in the *past*. This will be some kind of loss, something or someone that I will never regain. By allowing myself to be openly sad, to cry for a while and talk out my loss, I free myself from that past pain. I finish the situation and say goodbye. Then I am ready to go on to whatever the present and future have to offer me.

George Thomson does not discuss the function of happiness. We'd suggest that authentic happiness signals: 'No change needed.' In this sense, happiness has a timeless quality. It means: 'What was happening in the past is OK to be happening now, and to keep on happening in future.' The expression of authentic happiness is to relax, feel comfortable, enjoy the present, and when satiated fall asleep.

In sharp contrast to this problem-solving function of authentic feelings, racket feelings never help finish the situation. You can check this from the many examples already given in this chapter. When I shouted at the clerk, I didn't help myself get my purchases home in the future. I didn't get any productive result in the present. And I didn't help myself say goodbye to the past possibility of getting my goods before the supermarket closed.

Any time you begin feeling fear, anger or sadness out of their appropriate time frame, *you know the emotion is a racket feeling.* For instance, some people go through life feeling angry about things that have happened in the past. But the past cannot be changed. Therefore, this anger is non-productive as a means of solving problems, i.e. it is a racket feeling. Check that the same applies to any of the other possible mis-matches between feelings and time frames.

● What would you say would be the authentic feeling that would have helped finish the situation for you in our opening example? Once you had realized you weren't going to get your purchases, would you authentically have felt angry, sad, scared or happy? Check whether each of these feelings would have helped you finish the situation. ●

Because rackets represent the re-playing of an outdated Child strategy, the expression of racket feelings in the here-and-now is bound to result in the same unsatisfactory outcome over and over again. While in script, the person may temporarily feel satisfied at having manipulated some strokes from the environment. But the underlying need, which would be addressed by expressing the authentic feeling, has still not been met. Thus the person is likely to *re-cycle* the entire pattern, playing it out anew in each stress situation. We shall meet this idea again when we look at the Racket System in a coming chapter.

Racketeering

Fanita English coined the word 'racketeering' to describe a way of transacting that people may use as a means of seeking strokes for their racket feelings.[4]

A racketeer invites others into exchanges in which he expresses a racket feeling and aims to extract strokes for that feeling from the other person. These transactions will go on as long as the other person is willing to keep dealing out strokes to the racketeer.

Fanita English suggests that racketeering can be of two types, both of which entail parallel transactions between Parent and Child. In Type I, the racketeer takes up the Child role initially. His life position is 'I'm not-OK, you're OK (ha ha)'. In Type II, he comes from Parent, with a life position of 'I'm OK (ha ha), you're not-OK'.

The Type I racketeer may sound sad and pathetic, a mode of racketeering that Fanita English labels Type Ia and calls 'Helpless'. For example, you might hear this sort of exchange:

Racketeer (C – P): 'I'm feeling down again today.'
Partner (P – C): 'Oh, dear, sorry to hear that.'
Racketeer: 'And the boss was getting at me again.'
Partner: 'Tut, tut, that's bad.'

Alternatively, the Child racketeer may come from a whiny, complaining position. This is Type Ib, 'Bratty'. Typically, the partner may respond with strokes from negative Controlling Parent instead of negative Nurturing Parent:

Racketeer: 'And you weren't much help, either.'
Partner: 'Huh! Can't you stand up for yourself?'
Racketeer: 'What do you expect me to do? He's the boss, isn't he?'
Partner: 'Well, why didn't you complain to the union?'

The Type II racketeer also has two possible modes of operating. In Type IIa, 'Helpful', he takes up a negative Nurturing Parent stance, aiming to extract strokes of gratitude from the other person in Child:

Racketeer (P – C): 'Sure you've had enough to eat?'

Partner (C – P): 'Ooh, yes, thanks.'

Racketeer: 'Come on, now, how about finishing this slice of pie?'

Partner: 'Well, honestly, it was great, but I'm full, thanks.'

'Bossy' describes the Type IIb racketeer, who initiates the transactions from negative Controlling Parent. He seeks apologetic Child strokes from his partner.

Racketeer: 'You're late again!'

Partner: 'Sorry!'

Racketeer: 'What do you mean, sorry? This is the fourth time this week...'

Though Fanita English does not say so, we would suggest that people can also racketeer Parent-to-Parent, on themes such as 'Ain't It Awful', or Child-to-Child with an escalation of racket feeling exchanges.

You'll see that racketeering is one kind of pastime, where the exchanges carry a charge of racket feelings. The parallel transactions will only cease when one of the participants withdraws or crosses a transaction. Often, the person initiating the cross will be the racketeer and not the partner. That's because habitual racketeers become adept at sensing when the other person is about to withdraw from the exchange. Rather than have his source of strokes run out in this way, the racketeer prefers to keep the initiative.

The frequent result is to transform the racketeering exchange into a *game*. When we look at games in a later chapter, we'll consider how this happens.

● Did you racketeer during the past week?

If so, were you Helpless or Bratty, Helpful or Bossy? Or did you test out several of these positions?

Do you want to keep on racketeering like this? If not, how will you get non-rackety strokes that will be acceptable in place of the strokes you got from racketeering?

Did you accept anyone else's invitation to be a partner to their racketeering? If so, which of the four modes were they in?

Do you want to keep on stroking their racket feelings? If not, how will you cross the transactions next time? ●

Stamps

When I experience a racket feeling, there are two things I can do with it. I can express it there and then. Or I can store it away for use later. When I do the latter, I am said to be saving a *stamp*.[5]

● In the past week, was there an occasion when you felt a racket feeling and saved it up instead of expressing it there and then?

If so, you saved a stamp. What was the name of the racket feeling written on this stamp? Was it a jealous, triumphant, angry, irritated, gloomy, helpless stamp...or what?

How big a collection do you have of this kind of feeling?

How long do you intend building up your collection?

When you decide to cash in your collection, what are you going to cash it in for? ●

The word 'stamp' is short for 'psychological trading stamp'. It refers to a practice popular with supermarkets in the 1960s, whereby customers were given stamps of different colours along with the goods they were buying. These trading stamps could be pasted in stamp books. When you'd saved up a certain number, you could cash the collection in for a prize.

Some people preferred to cash the stamps frequently in small lots, for small prizes. Others saved books and books full and finally cashed them in for a really big prize.

When people save up psychological trading stamps, they have the same kind of choice about cashing them. For instance, suppose I save anger stamps. At work, the boss criticizes me. I feel angry at him, but don't show it. I hang on to the stamp until I get home that night. Then I yell at my dog for getting under my feet. Here, I've only saved a single stamp, which I've cashed within the day.

The example illustrates another common feature of stamp-cashing: the person who eventually gets the collection dumped on them is frequently not the person who was the object of the racket feeling in the first place.

My workmate may also save up angry stamps. But suppose he prefers to make a much bigger collection before cashing them in. He may save up his anger against the boss for months and years. Then, collecting his mountain of angry-stamp books, he may march into the boss's office, bawl the boss out, and get fired.

Stamps and the script

Why do people save up stamps? Eric Berne suggested the answer. They do so because *by cashing in the stamps, they can move towards their script payoff.*

If a person's script is hamartic, he is likely to favour making big collections of stamps that he can then cash in for his heavy payoff. For instance, he may collect depression stamps for years and years, then finally cash them in for a suicide. Someone whose hamartic payoff is 'harming others' may stack up a huge collection of rage stamps, then use them to 'justify' homicide. On a lighter level but still as part of a losing script, a business executive might save harrassed stamps and cash them for a heart attack, ulcer or high blood pressure.

People with banal scripts will keep smaller collections of stamps and trade them in for lighter payoffs. A woman who saves 'misunderstood' stamps may cash them in every few months for a huge quarrel with her husband. Someone like my workmate, who collects anger stamps against authority figures, may trade them in for getting into disputes at work and occasionally getting fired.

There are varying opinions in TA on whether stamp collecting has any place in a winning script. Some writers have referred to 'gold stamps', meaning stamps that are saved up for a positive outcome. (They contrast these with 'brown stamps', the negative ones we have been talking about so far.) For instance, they suggest, a hard-working executive might save gold stamps for jobs well done, and cash them in for a well-deserved holiday.

We believe that stamp saving is not needed at all in a genuinely winning script. That hard-working executive doesn't need to justify his holiday, for 'jobs well done' or on any other grounds. He can go ahead and have his holiday just because he wants it.

● With this knowledge of the script function of stamps, review your own stamp collection and the payoff you may have in view when you cash it in. Do you still want this payoff?

If not, you can simply let your collection go. But before deciding to let it go, be sure that you genuinely want to let go of the expected payoff. Be clear that, if you do choose to let go of your stamp collection, you must also say a permanent goodbye to the payoff you had been planning.

Having thought about this, do you still want to let the stamps go?

If your answer is 'yes', then choose a way in which you will dispose of the stamps permanently. Some people throw them on a fire. Others flush them down the toilet. Still others drop them in a fast-flowing river and watch them being carried away to sea. Choose your own way. Whatever you choose, it must be a way that will make it impossible for you ever to get the stamps back.

Once you have decided on your means of disposal, get comfortable and close your eyes. Visualize yourself holding your stamp collection. See how many books or bags of stamps there are. Note their colours. See written across them the name of the racket feeling you have been saving up. If you have been saving the stamps against a particular person or group of people, see their name also written on the stamps.

Are you ready to let the stamps go? Then go ahead and make your disposal in whatever way you have decided. Throw them on the fire and watch till they have disappeared in smoke. Or flush them down the toilet, maybe flushing several times to make sure they've all gone down. If you throw them in a river, watch them until the last stamp has been carried away out of your sight.

In imagination, now look at your hands and confirm that they are empty of the stamps you had been carrying.

Now visualize that you turn around and look up. You'll see someone or something very pleasant that you had not seen before.

Say hello to that pleasant someone or something. That's where you'll get the good strokes that will mean you don't feel the need to save stamps in future.

Welcome these strokes. Feel the relief of not carrying the stamp collection around any longer. Then come out of the exercise. ●

Chapter 22
THE RACKET SYSTEM

The Racket System is a model that explains the nature of life-scripts and shows how people may maintain their script throughout life. It was devised by Richard Erskine and Marilyn Zalcman.[1]

In this chapter, the diagrammatic presentation of the Racket System, and the factual explanations of the diagram's meaning, are drawn directly from Erskine and Zalcman's article 'The Racket System: a model for racket analysis', for which they won the Eric Berne Memorial Scientific Award. The case illustrations and supporting interpretations have been supplied by the present authors.

The Racket System is defined as *a self-reinforcing, distorted system of feelings, thoughts and actions maintained by script-bound individuals.* It has three inter-related and interdependent components: the *Script Beliefs and Feelings,* the *Rackety Displays* and the *Reinforcing Memories.* It is shown diagrammatically in Figure 22.1.

Script Beliefs and Feelings

When I am in script, I will be replaying outdated beliefs about *myself, other people* and the *quality of life.*

Erskine and Zalcman suggest that script decisions are adopted in childhood as a means of 'explaining away' unfinished feelings. When under stress in grown-up life, I may re-run this infant strategy. To defend against experiencing the feeling, I 'explain it away' by reviving those childhood conclusions and experiencing them as being true in the present. These then constitute my Script Beliefs.

Erskine and Zalcman picture the Script Beliefs and Feelings, taken in total, as representing a *double contamination* of the Adult. If you wish to check your understanding of this, refer back to Chapter 6.

The Script Beliefs under each heading are divided into *Core Script Beliefs* and *Supporting Script Beliefs.*

Core Script Beliefs

The Core Script Beliefs correspond to the child's earliest and most fundamental script decisions. For every infant, there are times when the expression of uncensored feelings fails to get the infant's needs met. We saw in the previous chapter how the child then tests out a range of substitute feelings until she discovers those that do 'get results' in terms of

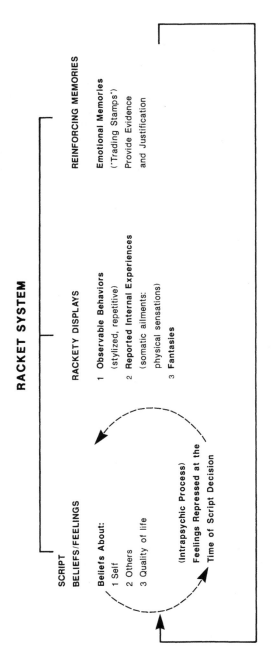

Figure 22.1 The Racket System

parental attention. These substitute feelings are adopted as racket feelings, and the original uncensored feeling is suppressed.

Yet because the original feeling has not been responded to, the infant's emotional experience is left unfinished. In an attempt to make sense of this, she comes to conclusions about herself, others and the world. These form the Core Script Beliefs. They rest on the kind of concrete and magical thinking of which young children are capable.

Let's take the example of a client whom we will call David. In his late twenties, David had been through several living-in relationships with women. Each time, the woman had walked out on David after a year or so. He himself recognized he had invited this outcome, by picking fights with his girlfriends, getting jealous, and acting in a touchy, aggressive manner. Now David was in yet another relationship, with a woman he loved and valued. He was scared he was going to break up that relationship in the same old way. Though he was aware of his own aggressiveness and jealousy, he didn't feel he was able to control himself when he began feeling these emotions. Recently he had struck his girlfriend, and she was threatening to leave him. At this point, he came to therapy.

A Racket System analysis of this problem takes us right back to David's infancy. In the earliest months of his life, David enjoyed the intimate physical closeness that exists between a very small baby and his mother. But when David got a little older, just after his first birthday, Mother began feeling that he was not any longer just the cuddlesome bundle he had been when he was smaller. He was more mobile now, and often got grubby. He drooled, and when he made messes he got smelly. Though she was not aware of it, Mother reacted by pushing David away physically.

With his acute infant awareness, David picked up Mother's signals of rejection. He felt a sense of shock and disorientation: what had gone wrong with the world? Worst of all, was Mother going to leave him quite alone? Contemplating that possibility, David felt sheer terror and abject hurt. Yet still, each time he reached out for Mother to give him comfort, she seemed to reject him yet again. Expressing his scare and hurt, David did not get his needs met.

Unable to comprehend the factual reasons for Mother's withdrawal, David 'made sense of' his own unfinished feelings by concluding: 'I'm unlovable. There's something wrong with me.' Thus he formed a Core Script Belief about himself.

In line with this, he also adopted the Core Script Beliefs: 'Other people (especially important women) reject me. The world is a scary, lonesome, unpredictable place.'

Concluding that his expression of hurt and anger was not going to get his needs met, David gave up after a while and adopted a second-best strategy. He discovered that if he expressed anger, he at least got some attention from Mother. By flying into a tantrum, or by grizzling, he could at least get her to shout or scowl at him. Though this negative attention was painful, it was better than nothing at all. David decided: 'The best way for me to get my needs met is to act angry.' He had learned to cover his authentic feelings of scare and hurt with racket anger, and in so doing had laid the foundation for his Rackety Display.

Supporting Script Beliefs

Once the infant has arrived at his Core Beliefs, he begins to interpret his experience of reality in accord with these beliefs. They influence what experiences he attends to, the meaning he attaches to these experiences, and whether he regards them as significant. In this way, he begins to add Supporting Script Beliefs that re-affirm and elaborate upon the Core Script Beliefs.

David had a brother who was a couple of years older than himself. Because of the age difference, he was naturally bigger than David, as well as being more advanced in thinking ability. With the reasoning power of a toddler, David came to some further conclusions. 'Now I think I know what it is that is so wrong with me. It's that I'm not big enough or smart enough. I can tell this because my brother, who *is* big and smart, gets all the attention.'

Thus David had begun to build up some of his Supporting Script Beliefs. 'I am stupid. I'm physically weak and too small. My needs are not important. Others are bigger and smarter than I am. Because of this, they are more important than me and they get all the attention, especially from important women. Life is very, very unfair.'

Recycling Script Beliefs and Feelings

Now David is an adult. At moments of stress, he may go into script. As we've seen, this is especially likely if the here-and-now situation somehow *resembles* a stress situation in childhood – if there is a *rubberband.*

At such times, David re-experiences the feelings and beliefs of his early childhood. Suppose he perceives his girlfriend as 'pushing him off' in their relationship. Unknowingly, he responds as he did when Mother pushed him away as an infant. Below the level of awareness, he begins experiencing hurt and terror.

As he does so, he replays his Script Beliefs. He 'explains' the rejection he has perceived by saying to himself internally, outside of awareness: 'I'm unlovable, because there's something fundamentally wrong with me. This important woman wants to reject me utterly. If she does, I'll be left all alone.'

Each time David makes these statements to himself, he 'justifies' his feelings of scare and hurt. And each time he re-experiences these feelings, he re-states the Script Beliefs in order to 'explain' to himself how he feels. In this way, the Script Beliefs and Feelings are continually *recycled*. This is illustrated by the dotted arrows on Figure 22.1. Erskine and Zalcman stress that this process goes on *intrapsychically* – that is, inside the person's own head. Because David already has an internal scripty 'explanation' of what he has perceived as a rejection, he does not make his Script Beliefs available for updating against here-and-now reality. On the contrary: every time he repeats this recycling process, he reinforces his perception that reality has 'confirmed' the Script Beliefs.

Rackety Displays

The Rackety Displays consist of all the overt and internal behaviours that are manifestations of the Script Beliefs and Feelings. They include observable behaviours, reported internal experiences and fantasies.

Observable behaviours

The observable behaviours consist of the displays of emotion, words, tones, gestures and body movements that the person makes in response to the intrapsychic process. These displays are repetitive and stylized because they reproduce the scripty behaviours that the child learned to use in a wide range of situations as a way of 'getting results' in his or her family.

The Rackety Displays may entail behaviours that are in accord with the Script Beliefs or that defend against them. For example, David, who concluded in childhood 'I am stupid', acts confused and stupid when re-playing this Script Belief as an adult. Someone else who reached the same childhood conclusion might defend against it by working long hours at studies, getting high grades at school and college then going compulsively through one professional qualification after another.

David's Rackety Displays of aggression towards his girlfriend arise from his early conclusion: 'The way for me to get my needs met is to get angry whenever I start feeling hurt or scared.' When his girlfriend behaves in any way that he perceives as a slight or rejection, he begins re-playing his Core Script Beliefs and the feelings of terror and hurt that go with them. But, just as he learned to do as an infant, he instantly covers those emotions with anger. In the manner of a 'conditioned reflex', he becomes angry and aggressive. He may start a furious argument with his girlfriend, shout at her or push her about. Or he may choke back his anger, and storm out of the house to walk the streets fuming with rage.

This behaviour gives David's girlfriend no way of knowing that his authentic emotions are hurt, scare and a longing for closeness. Indeed, David himself has suppressed these feelings from awareness. He comes across instead as a touchy, physically aggressive individual. In the history of David's relationships, the end-result has been that his girlfriends have eventually walked out on him. Each time, David has used this response to 'justify' his Script Beliefs 'I'm unlovable, women reject me, and I get left on my own.'

Reported internal experiences

We have seen that the infant adopts the Script Beliefs in an attempt to make sense of an unfinished emotional experience, and thus finish that experience as best he can. In addition to this *cognitive* process, the person may go through a similar sequence *somatically* – in terms of what he does in his body. In order to divert energy away from his unfinished need, he may use that energy to set up some kind of held physical tension or discomfort.

We gave an example of this in an earlier chapter. You'll recall the infant who repeatedly reaches out for Mother but gets no response. So after a while he tenses up his shoulders to stop himself from reaching out. Though this is uncomfortable, it's not so distressing as it would be to keep on reaching out and facing Mother's apparent rejection. He then suppresses both his awareness of his original need and his awareness of holding tension in his shoulders. As a grown-up he is likely to experience aches and pains in his shoulders, neck and upper back. This is true for David in our case example.

People have a whole range of tensions, discomforts and somatic ailments that are responses to the Script Beliefs they hold. They may not be apparent in observable behaviour, but can be reported by the person. Sometimes, muscular tensions may have been so thoroughly suppressed that they do not come into the person's awareness except under massage.

Fantasies

Even when nobody is actually behaving in accordance with a person's Script Beliefs, the person may go ahead and fantasize such behaviour. The imagined behaviour may be his own or someone else's.

For instance, David sometimes fantasizes being punished or imprisoned for having committed a physical assault on a girlfriend.

He frequently imagines that people are belittling him behind his back, dwelling on a whole range of things that they find wrong with him. Sometimes his fantasy is a grandiose picture of 'the best that could happen': he imagines having met the perfect girlfriend, who will accept him one hundred per cent and will never behave in a way that he could interpret as a rejection.

Reinforcing Memories

When in script, the individual consults a collection of memories that reinforce the Script Beliefs. Each of these remembered occurrences will be one in which the person re-cycled Script Beliefs and Feelings. As she did so, she would engage in the accompanying Rackety Display, either by experiencing a racket feeling or engaging in any of the other external and internal behaviours that typify her own Racket System. As the event is remembered, the racket feeling or other rackety manifestation is recalled along with it. In other words, each Reinforcing Memory is accompanied by a *stamp*.

The events remembered may be other people's responses to the individual's Rackety Displays, as when successive girlfriends have abandoned David in response to his aggressive behaviour. They may also include responses that the individual has interpreted internally as confirming the Script Beliefs, even though in reality they were neutral or even contrary to these beliefs. For example, a girl might invite David to a party. Internally he might tell himself: 'She didn't really mean it. She was only saying it to be nice to me.' Making this interpretation, he might feel angry at yet another 'rejection'. Thus he would notch up another 'confirmation' of his Script Beliefs, and collect another Reinforcing Memory with its associated trading stamp.

There are some events that not even the most ingenious Little Professor can construe as fitting the Script Beliefs. But in that case, the individual may adopt another strategy: to selectively forget such events. For instance, there have been occasions when a woman has openly told David she values him just for himself, and would love to stay close to him. But while in script, he blanks those memories out of his recollection.

We have seen also that the individual may construct fantasies of scenes that fit the Script Beliefs. Memories of these fantasies serve as Reinforcing Memories just as effectively as do memories of actual events. Each time David makes mental pictures of people talking about him behind his back because of whatever is 'wrong with him', he adds another Reinforcing Memory to his stock.

Here again, we see how the Racket System is self-reinforcing. The Reinforcing Memories serve as *feedback* to the Script Beliefs. This is shown by the solid arrow on Figure 22.1.

Each time a Reinforcing Memory is recalled, the person replays a Script Belief, which itself is strengthened by the Reinforcing Memory. As the Script Belief is replayed, the accompanying Racket feeling is stimulated, and the process of intrapsychic 'recycling' is set in motion once more.

As this takes place, the person engages in Rackety Displays. These may include observable behaviours, internal experiences, fantasies, or a combination of the three. In turn, the outcome of the Rackety Display enables the person to collect more Reinforcing Memories, with their accompanying emotional stamps.

The Racket System is a *closed* system. That is to say: so long as the individual remains in script, cycling round and round the feedback loops in the Racket System, there is no element within that system that will show her a 'way out'. Luckily, there is an upside to this apparently gloomy picture. When we realize a system is closed, we know that the only way to achieve change is to break right out of that system. Later in this chapter, we'll discuss ways in which you can break out of your own Racket System if you wish to do that. An important first step, however, is to compile the detail of the existing content of your Racket System. That is the objective of the exercise that follows.

● COMPILING YOUR OWN RACKET SYSTEM

Take a big sheet of paper and draw out a replica of Figure 22.1. Leave plenty of space below each sub-heading in each of the three columns. On this blank diagram, you can begin to fill in the content of your own Racket System.[2]

If you want to proceed with the exercise, think of a recent situation that was unsatisfactory or painful for you and in which you finished up feeling bad. You need not re-experience the bad feeling now if you do not want to.

Imagining yourself back in that situation, fill in the details of the Racket System as they applied to you. Work quickly and intuitively.

To get to the Script Beliefs, a good way is to ask yourself: 'In that situation, *what was I saying in my head* about myself? About the other people concerned? About the quality of life and the world in general?'

How do you enter up the 'Feelings repressed at the time of script decision'? By the very fact that these feelings are being repressed while you are in the Racket System, you will *not* have been clearly aware of them during the scene you are analysing. However, there are various clues you can use. Sometimes, you may have experienced a brief flash of the authentic feeling before you went into the racket feeling. For instance, if your racket feeling in the scene was irritation, you may have felt scared for a split second beforehand. Another way is to ask yourself: 'If I were an infant and had no concept of censoring my feelings, how would I have felt in this situation? Would I have felt rage? Desolate sadness? Terror? Ecstasy?' If in doubt, guess. As a final check, look back at the previous chapter's section on 'Racket feelings, authentic feelings and problem-solving'. Which of the authentic feelings would have been appropriate to finish this situation for you?

Now move to the column on Rackety Displays. To list your observable behaviours, imagine you are seeing the scene on a video, with yourself in it. Note your words, tones, gestures, postures and facial expressions. What rackety emotion are you expressing? Check this against your memory of the racket feeling you were experiencing during the scene.

Under 'reported internal experiences', note any tensions or discomforts anywhere in your body. Did you have a headache? Churning stomach? Pain in the neck? Bear in mind that 'no sensation' is one kind of sensation. Thinking back, were there any parts of your body that you were blanking out of your awareness?

Enter any fantasies that you were experiencing. A good way here is to imagine yourself back in the scene, then ask yourself: 'What is the *very worst* thing I feel could happen here?' Put down whatever you first bring to mind in response, no matter how fanciful it may seem. Next, ask yourself: 'What is the *very best* thing I feel could happen here?' *This fantasy also is part of the Racket System*, so note it down in the same way.

Finally, go to the column for Reinforcing Memories. Letting your memory run free, note down your recollections of past situations similar to the scene you are analysing. These may be from the recent past or from longer ago. In all of them, you will recall experiencing the same racket feeling, the same physical discomfort or tension, etc., which you have noted above under 'Rackety Displays'.

You may find it interesting to check your Racket System details against the script matrix you compiled for yourself in an earlier exercise. How much do they have in common? You can use each of them to refine and revise the other. ●

Breaking out of the Racket System

As well as being a tool for analysis, the Racket System is an instrument for change. Erskine and Zalcman say:

'Any therapeutic intervention which interrupts the flow in the Racket System will be an effective step in the person's changing their Racket System and therefore their script.'

In other words, you can step in at *any* point in the Racket System and make a change at that point that begins to move you out of script. When you effect that change, you break the old feedback loops. Thus further change becomes easier. The process is still self-reinforcing, but now you are reinforcing movement out of script instead of staying stuck in script.

You don't need to stop at just one point of intervention. If you want, you can break the flow of the Racket System at several different points. The more of these you change, the greater your movement out of script.

In their article, Erskine and Zalcman describe various specific interventions that therapists can use to interrupt the Racket System. You can use a similar approach in self-therapy. If you want to use the Racket System in this way, here is an exercise to give you a starting framework. You can add to it and modify it in whatever creative ways you like.[2]

● Take a big sheet of paper like the one on which you drew out your Racket System. On it, you are going to draw a diagram that looks like a Racket System, but is actually its *positive* counterpart. If you like, you can call this new diagram 'The Autonomy System'.

Once again, draw up three columns. Head the left-hand column 'Updated Beliefs and Feelings'. The middle column gets the title 'Autonomous Displays', and the third column has the same title as on the Racket System, 'Reinforcing Memories'.

Under 'Updated Beliefs and Feelings', enter sub-headings for beliefs about self, others and the quality of life, as on the Racket System.

Think back once more to the scene you recalled when compiling your Racket System. Start with 'beliefs about self'. What is the positive reality about yourself that you will now enter as your updated belief?

For example, suppose David were to do this exercise. He might enter under this heading: 'I am thoroughly lovable, and I'm every bit good enough just as I am.'

Here and throughout, it's important to use *positive wording* of this kind. Avoid negative words like *not, stop, lose, without*. If your first version of the entry has any such words in it, take time to re-phrase so that you say it in positive words only. In the example for David, his Script Belief was 'There's something wrong with me.' Instead of changing this to 'There's nothing wrong with me,' he would change it to a positive statement such as 'I'm every bit good enough.'

Go on and update your beliefs about others and the quality of life in the same way, using positive words. Watch out for grandiosity, which would still be part of your Racket System. But if in doubt, err on the side of optimism.

At the foot of the left-hand column, where you entered up 'Repressed feelings' in your Racket System, now write the heading 'Authentic feelings expressed'. Write in the same authentic feelings as you entered in your Racket System. Imagining yourself back in the scene, visualize how you could have expressed your authentic feeling in a safe way that would have finished the situation for you.

Go next to the middle column, 'Autonomous Displays'. Once again, see the scene with yourself in it as on a video. But this time re-run it so that you are behaving in a positive way, out of script and feeling an authentic emotion instead of a racket. Enter up under 'observable behaviours' the words, gestures, etc. which you see and hear yourself using in this updated version.

In the same way, complete 'reported internal experiences' for the revised scene. In place of discomforts, what comforts do you feel? Do you become aware of any tensions you had not been aware of before? If so, do you choose to relax these tensions? What happens when you do?

In the Autonomy System, you do not enter 'fantasies'. As we saw, grandiose fantasies of 'the very best' *and* 'the very worst' outcomes are both part of the Racket System. Instead, now enter here 'Plans and positive visualizations.' This is a heading to complete at leisure. It refers to the Adult life-planning you can do to ensure that future situations are run in the positive way you are now constructing, instead of the rackety way you analysed in your Racket System. In place of fantasies, you can employ creative visualization techniques to empower and advance your life plans.

Finally, complete the column for Reinforcing Memories. It's almost certain that you will be able to recall *some* past instances in your life of positive situations that resemble the re-run situation you are now compiling. Maybe, when you think of it, you will be able to recall many.

And what if you really can't recall any? Just make some up. Recalling made-up positive situations is every bit as effective as recalling actual ones.

Now you have a starting version of your Autonomy System. As with the Racket System, you can revise and refine it as time goes on.

Imagine the completed diagram for your Racket System held a few inches above the diagram for your Autonomy System. In future, you can make a trap-door at any point in the Racket System, and step down through it to land at the corresponding point in the Autonomy System. From that point, you will go with the flow of the Autonomy System, instead of going round the rackety feedback loops that you went round in the past.

Maybe you will make yourself several trap-doors. The more you have, the easier you will find it to step out of your Racket System and into autonomy. And each time you do make this step, it will become even easier to make in future. ●

Chapter 23
GAMES AND GAME ANALYSIS

Have you ever had an interaction in which you and the other person both ended up feeling bad, and afterwards you said to yourself something like:

'Why does this keep on happening to me?'

'How on earth did *that* happen again?'

'I thought he/she was different from the others, but...'

Did you feel surprised at the painful way things had turned out – yet, at the same time, realize that the same sort of thing had happened to you before?

If you have had an interaction like this, it's most likely that in TA language you were involved in a *game*.[1]

Just like a game of football or a game of chess, a psychological game is played according to predetermined rules. It was Eric Berne who first drew attention to this predictable structure of games, and suggested ways in which they could be analysed.

In this chapter, we look at methods of game analysis devised by Berne and other TA writers.

Examples of games

Here are two examples of how people play games.

Example 1: Jack meets Jean. They fall in love and decide to live together. All goes well early on. But as the months go by, Jack begins giving his partner a hard time. He ignores her wants and feelings. He shouts at her, sometimes pushes her about. He gets drunk and comes home late. He spends Jean's money and 'forgets' to pay her back.

Jean stays with him despite his ill-treatment. The more aggressive he becomes, the more she makes allowances for his behaviour.

This goes on for almost three years. Then, without warning, Jean leaves Jack for another man. Jack comes home to find a note on the kitchen table saying she has gone for good.

Jack is dumbfounded. He says to himself, 'How on earth did this happen to me?' He traces Jean, pleads unsuccessfully with her to come back. The more he begs her, the more harshly she rejects him, and the worse he feels. Jack spends a long time feeling depressed, abandoned and worthless. He tries to work out what is wrong with him: 'What has this other man got that I haven't got?'

The strange thing is that all this has happened to Jack before. He has been through two relationships, and two rejections, that followed the same pattern. Each time he has said to himself, 'Never again.' But it does happen again, and each time Jack feels surprised and rejected.

Jack is playing the game called *Kick Me*.

Jean also has been through this all before. She has had several other relationships with men before meeting Jack. Somehow, she seems to pick men who are good to her when they first know her, but who soon start ill-treating her as Jack did. Each time, she has put up with the man's behaviour, acting the 'little woman' – for a while. Each time too, she has eventually had a sudden change of mind and has rejected the man abruptly. When she does so, she feels blameless and somehow triumphant. She says to herself: 'I thought so. Men are all the same.' Nevertheless, after a while she starts a relationship with somebody new, and the whole sequence is played through again.

Jean's game is *Now I've Got You, Son of a Bitch* – known for short as *NIGYSOB*.

Example 2: Molly gets a visit from her son Dave. He's a college student in late teenage, and has been living in student lodgings in a nearby city. Today, he looks dejected.

Dave says: 'I'm afraid something awful has happened. My landlord has thrown me out, so I've nowhere to live. I don't know what to do.'

'Oh, dear, that's bad,' says Molly, with a worried frown. 'What can I do to help?'

'I don't know,' says Dave gloomily.

'I'll tell you what,' says Molly. 'Why don't you and I look through the evening paper and find a room for you to rent somewhere in town?'

'That's the trouble,' says Dave, looking even more downcast. 'I don't think I could afford the rent for a room in this neighbourhood.'

'Well, you know your Dad and I are always ready to help you with that.'

'Thanks a lot for offering', says Dave. 'But honestly, that would just feel to me like I was living on your charity.'

'Ah. Well, how's about I fix you up a bed right here at home?'

'Thanks,' says Dave, 'but really I don't think I could put up with being back here among the family when I'm feeling like this. Besides, I think the commuting would be a problem.'

A silence falls as Molly racks her brain for more ideas. She can't think of any.

Dave heaves a long sigh, gets up and makes to leave. 'Well, thanks anyway for trying to help,' he says glumly as he disappears through the door.

Molly asks herself 'What on earth happened?' She feels first astonished, then inadequate and depressed. She tells herself she is no good as a mother.

Meantime, Dave is walking down the street feeling indignant and angry at Molly. He says to himself: 'Didn't think she was going to be able to help me, and she hasn't!'

Both for Molly and for Dave, this scene is a replay of many others that have happened in the past. Molly quite often gets into this kind of interaction. She offers help and advice to people then feels bad when they don't accept it. Dave is equally familiar with the receiving end. He somehow ends up again and again rejecting the help that people offer him, while feeling angry at being let down by the helper.

Molly and Dave are playing a pair of games that very often go together. Molly's game is *Why Don't You...?*. Dave plays *Yes, But...* [2]

Typical features of games

From these examples, we can pick out some features that are typical of games.

(1) *Games are repetitive.* Each person plays her favourite game through time and time again. The other players and the circumstances may change, but the pattern of the game remains the same.

(2) *Games are played without Adult awareness.* Despite the fact that people repeat games over and over, they go through each replay of their game without being aware they are doing it. It's not until the closing stages of the game that the player may ask himself: 'How did *that* happen again?' Even at that point, people usually don't realize that they themselves have helped set up the game.

(3) *Games always end up with the players experiencing racket feelings.*

(4) *Games entail an exchange of ulterior transactions between the players.* In every game, there is something different happening at the psychological level from what seems to be happening at the social level. We know this from the way people repeat their games again and again, finding others whose games interlock with their own. When Dave comes for help and Molly offers it, they both believe that is their real purpose. But the outcome of their interaction shows that their unaware motivations were very different. At the psychological level, they were sending each other 'secret messages' which declared their true intentions. Molly was setting out to offer help that was not going to be accepted. Dave had come to ask for her help and then not take it.

(5) *Games always include a moment of surprise or confusion.* At this point, the player has the sensation that something unexpected has happened. Somehow, people seem to have changed roles. This was what Jack experienced when he discovered Jean had left him. Jean, for her part, left because she had quite suddenly changed her mind about Jack.

● Think of a painful interaction in your own recent experience that fits this description of a game.

Take a pencil and paper and note down what the situation was. Check that it had the five features we have given as being typical of games.

Note too how you felt at the end of it. Is this a familiar feeling of yours? •

Sweatshirts

It's uncanny how people manage to seek out others who will play games that interlock with their own games. Jack consistently finds women who will leave him for someone else. Molly picks out people who will ask for her help and then not take it.

It's as if each person were wearing a *sweatshirt* with her game invitations printed on it. The sweatshirt has a motto on the front which is the one we consciously want the world to see. On the back is the psychological-level 'secret message'. The message on the back is the one that actually determines whom we pick for our relationships.

We can imagine that on the front of Jean's sweatshirt there's a motto something like: 'I'll be sweet and longsuffering.' On the back her motto reads: 'But just wait till I get you!'

• What do you think are the mottoes on the front and back of Jack's sweatshirt? Of Molly's?

Go back to your own personal game example. What do you imagine was the motto on the front of your sweatshirt? On the back?

What do you think were the front and back messages on the sweatshirts of any others you related to in that situation?

If you are working in a group, get into a subgroup with two or three other people. Each member of the small group uses intuition to jot down the front and back sweatshirt messages of the other members. Then share with each other what you wrote down.

Don't worry if the other people in the small group are not well known to you. It's usual for us anyway to read sweatshirt messages from first impressions.

If you want, you can repeat the exercise with others you know well. You may find out some interesting things about yourself by comparing the different mottoes that different people read on your sweatshirt. •

Different degrees of games

Games can be played at different degrees of intensity.[3]

A *first-degree game* has an outcome that the player is willing to share with her social circle. In the game examples at the beginning of this chapter, all the players were playing at a first-degree level. You can guess that while Molly is unloading her feelings of self-doubt on one of her friends, Dave will be grumbling to *his* friends about how useless she is. The friends will regard this as quite acceptable behaviour. In fact, first-degree games usually make up a big proportion of the time-structuring at parties and social gatherings.

Games played at a *second-degree* level bring heavier outcomes, of a kind that the player would rather not make public in her social circle. For instance, suppose Dave had not just grumbled, but had gone off back to the city, broken off all contact with her and ended up living on the street? Molly might then have experienced deep depression. She'd certainly have been unlikely to talk casually to her friends about what had occurred.

A *third-degree* game, in Berne's words, '...is one which is played for keeps, and which ends in the surgery, the courtroom or the morgue.' If Jack and Jean had been playing at this grim intensity, Jack might have physically maltreated Jean. Jean in turn might have saved up her anger until one day she picked up the kitchen knife and stabbed him with it.

Formula G

Berne discovered that every game goes through a sequence of six stages.[4] He named them as follows:

Con + Gimmick = Response —> Switch —> Crossup —> Payoff

or just using their initials:

C + G = R —> S —> X —> P

He called this sequence *Formula G*.

Let's apply Formula G to the games played between Molly and Dave. He opens by telling her his landlord has thrown him out. Under this so-cial-level message lies his *Con*. It is delivered non-verbally, and implies that he is helpless but also secretly conveys: 'But when you try to help me, I'm not going to be helped, ha ha!'

As Molly buys into the game set-up, she signals her willingness to play by revealing her *Gimmick*. Berne used this word to describe a scripty 'weak spot' that leads someone to buy into someone else's Con. For Molly, it's a Parent message in her head that says 'You *have* to help someone who is in such bad shape!'

Listening to this message internally, she responds to Dave on the psy-chological level: 'OK, I'm going to try to help you, but we both know that in the end you aren't going to let yourself be helped.' At the social level, she covers this by saying 'What can I do to help?'

The *Response* stage of a game consists of a series of transactions.

They may only last for a second or two or may go on for hours, days or years. In this case, Molly offers several pieces of advice to Dave. He counters with justifications of why each one won't work. At social level, these transactions seem like straightforward exchanges of information. But at psychological level, they repeat the Con-Gimmick exchange that opened the game.

The *Switch* is pulled when Molly runs out of suggestions and Dave says 'Thanks for trying to help.'

At the next instant, Molly feels as though she had been taken by surprise. This moment of confusion is the *Crossup*. Dave has a similar experience.

Straight away, both players collect their *Payoff* of racket feelings. Molly feels depressed and inadequate. Dave feels righteously indignant.

● What were the stages of Formula G in the interlocking games played by Jack and Jean?

Identify the stages of Formula G in your own personal example of a game. What were the psychological-level messages exchanged at each stage? ●

The Drama Triangle

Steve Karpman devised a simple yet powerful diagram for analysing games, the *Drama Triangle* (Figure 23.1).[5] He suggests that whenever people play games, they are stepping into one of three scripty roles: *Persecutor, Rescuer or Victim.*

A *Persecutor* is someone who puts other people down and belittles them. The Persecutor views others as being one-down and not-OK.

A *Rescuer*, too, sees others as being not-OK and one-down. But the Rescuer responds by offering help from a one-up position. She believes: 'I have to help all these others because they're not good enough to help themselves.'

To a *Victim*, it is himself who is one-down and not-OK. Sometimes the Victim will seek a Persecutor to put him down and push him around. Or the Victim may be in search of a Rescuer, who will offer help and confirm the Victim's belief 'I can't cope on my own.'

Every one of the Drama Triangle roles entails a *discount*. Both the Persecutor and Rescuer discount others. The Persecutor discounts others' value and dignity. Extreme Persecutors may discount other people's right to life and physical health. The Rescuer discounts others' abilities to think for themselves and act on their own initiative.

A Victim discounts herself. If she is seeking a Persecutor, then she agrees with the Persecutor's discounts and views herself as someone worthy to be rejected and belittled. The Victim seeking a Rescuer will believe that she needs the Rescuer's help in order to think straight, act or make decisions.

● Take one minute to write down all the words you can think of that might be applied to a Persecutor.

Do the same for a Rescuer and for a Victim. ●

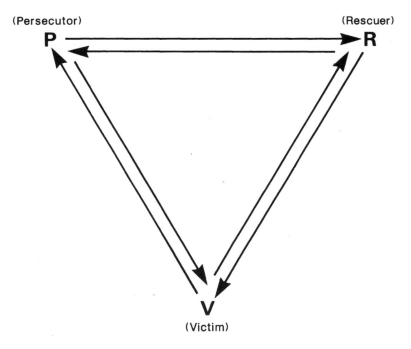

(Persecutor)   (Rescuer)

P ⟶ **R**

(Victim)

Figure 23.1 The Drama Triangle

All three Drama Triangle roles are *inauthentic*. When people are in one of these roles, they are responding to the past rather than to the here-and-now. They are using old, scripty strategies they decided upon as children or took on board from their parents. To signal the inauthenticity of the Triangle roles, the words Persecutor, Rescuer and Victim are spelled with initial capitals. If we spell the words beginning with small letters, we mean real-life persecutors, rescuers or victims.

● Can you think of a real-life persecutor who would not also be a Persecutor?

What would be examples of the difference between an authentic rescuer and a person playing the role of Rescuer?

Would you say it is possible for anyone to be a victim without also being a Victim? ●

Usually, someone who is playing a game will start at one of the positions and then will switch to another. This switch in Drama Triangle positions takes place at the moment of the Switch in Formula G.

In the Kick Me game played by Jack, he began in the Persecutor position and stayed there through the Response stage of his game. When the Switch was pulled, Jack switched to Victim.

● What Drama Triangle switches were made by Jean in her NIGYSOB game? By Molly and Dave in their game interaction?

What Drama Triangle switches did you make in your own personal game example? ●

Transactional analysis of games

Another way to analyse games is to use a transactional diagram. This is specially useful in bringing out the ulterior transactions between the players.

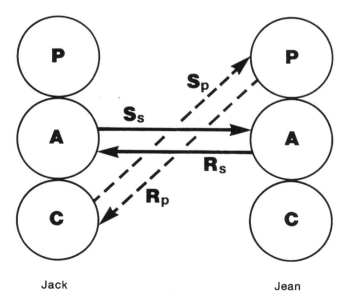

Jack   Jean

Figure 23.2 Example of Berne's transactional game diagram

Berne's transactional game diagram

Figure 23.2 shows Eric Berne's version of the transactional game diagram.[6] It describes the opening exchanges between Jack and Jean.

Jack *(social level, S_s):* 'I'd like to get to know you better.'

Jean *(social level, R_s):* 'Yes, I'd like that too.'

Jack *(psychological level, S_p):* 'Kick Me, please!'

Jean *(psychological level, R_p):* 'I'll Get You, You S.O.B.!'

The ulterior 'secret messages' of S_p and R_p stay outside the awareness of each player until they are revealed at the moment of the Switch.

The Goulding-Kupfer diagram

Bob Goulding and David Kupfer developed a different version of the transactional game diagram (Figure 23.3).[7] For them, games have five required features.

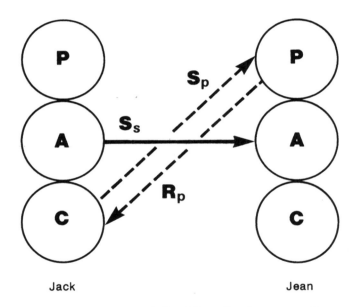

Jack   Jean

Figure 23.3 Example of Goulding–Kupfer game diagram

(1) First comes the social-level 'opener' of the game (S_s). Goulding and Kupfer call it the 'ostensible straight stimulus'. In this case, Jack says: 'I'd like to get to know you better.'

(2) The second element of the game is the simultaneous psychological-level message (S_p) that is the game's Con. It is called the 'secret mes-

sage', and includes a scripty statement about the self. Jack's 'secret message' is 'I deserve to be rejected, and I'm going to test you out till I prove it. Kick Me, please!'

(3) As always, the outcome is determined at the psychological level. Jean reads Jack's 'Kick Me' message and responds accordingly, by stringing him along for a while and then rejecting him. In the Goulding-Kupfer sequence, this is the 'response to the secret message'.

(4) Both players end up experiencing racket feelings, the 'bad-feeling payoff'.

(5) The entire series of ulterior transactions stays outside the Adult awareness of the players.

The Gouldings point out that if anyone has enough investment in getting into his favourite game, he can twist the actual responses he is getting from the other person so as to read the game response into them. Thus he can take his racket payoff even if the other person's responses were not gamey.

For instance, suppose Jean had steadfastly refused to reject Jack despite all his pushing. He might redefine her response by saying to himself: 'She's only pretending to want me around. I *know* she really wants rid of me, and she's probably going round with someone else in secret.' In this way he might manufacture the discount he had been expecting and go ahead to take his bad-feeling payoff anyway.

● Use Berne's transactional game diagram and the Goulding-Kupfer diagram to analyse the games played by Molly and Dave.

Use them to analyse your own personal game example. ●

The Game Plan

John James has developed a set of questions that give us another way of understanding the progress of a game. He calls it the *Game Plan*.[8]

The following exercise uses a variation of the Game Plan that includes two additional 'mystery questions'. It was devised by Laurence Collinson.

You can use the Game Plan questions to analyse the personal game example you have already noted. Or, if you like, use it to examine a different gamey situation that you recognize in your life.

● Take a pencil and paper and note down the answers to the following questions, as they apply to your chosen example. It's a good idea if you find someone else to share your ideas with as you complete the Game Plan questions.

The 'mystery questions' are printed at the end of this chapter. *Do not look at them until you have answered all the other Game Plan questions.* Then add the answers to the two 'mystery questions'.

1. What keeps happening to me over and over again?
2. How does it start?
3. What happens next?
4. (Mystery question)
5. And then?
6. (Mystery question)
7. How does it end?
8a. How do I feel?
8b. How do I think the other person feels? ●

Interpretation

The sequence of answers to the Game Plan questions should show you the Drama Triangle switches and Formula G stages in the game.

The feelings you listed at Questions 8a *and* 8b are *both* likely to be racket feelings of yours. It may be that you recognize the feeling at 8a as being familiar, but are surprised to think that the one named at 8b is also your own racket. If this is true of you, check with someone who knows you well.

The answers to the two 'mystery questions' are the psychological-level messages of the transactional game diagram. However, Laurence Collinson suggests that *both these statements are also likely to be messages your parents conveyed to you while you were a young child.* Check whether this is true for you.

A second possibility is that one or both of the 'mystery question' answers may be a message which *you* conveyed to your parents when you were very young.

Keep your Game Plan answers. You can use them again as you read the following two chapters.

Definitions of games

There's disagreement among TA writers about the proper definition of a game.[9] Perhaps this is because Berne himself defined games differently at different stages of his thinking.

In his last book, *What Do You Say After You Say Hello*, Berne spells out Formula G and explains the six stages as we have done above. Then he adds:

'Whatever fits this formula is a game, and whatever does not fit it is not a game.'

As a definition, this couldn't be clearer. Yet in an earlier book, *Principles of Group Treatment*, Berne had defined a game in different words:

'A game is a series of ulterior transactions with a gimmick, leading to a usually well-concealed but well-defined payoff.'

You'll see the crucial difference between the two definitions. The later version, in *What Do You Say...*, refers to the *Switch* and *Crossup* as essential features of a game. The earlier definition does not.

In fact, it wasn't until quite late on in his development of game theory that Berne introduced the idea of the Switch. It appears first in *Sex in Human Loving*. In the earlier *Games People Play*, he used a definition similar to the one in *Principles of Group Treatment*, making no reference to the Switch or Crossup.

Since Berne, some writers have used definitions that follow his earlier version. In various different words, they have defined a 'game' as any sequence of ulterior transactions that ends up with the parties feeling bad (experiencing racket feelings).

We prefer to follow the alternative school of thought, and use Berne's later definition. We define as 'games' only those sequences that follow all the stages of Formula G, *including* the 'switch of roles' and 'moment of confusion' represented by the Switch and Crossup.

Why? Because Berne's earlier definition, without the Switch, is already described in modern TA by another concept: *racketeering*. And there's a clear distinction between the process of racketeering and the process of a game, in a way which Fanita English has described. Racketeers resemble game-players in that they exchange ulterior messages, taking racket-feeling payoffs at the same time. But in racketeering, no Switch is pulled. The parties may keep on racketeering as long as they both want or have energy to, and then simply stop or do something different.

It's only if one of the parties does pull a Switch that the racketeering exchange is transformed into a game. (In the coming chapter, we'll say more about why people may do this).

We think that this distinction between racketeering and game-playing is a useful one to make. It gives us practical help in understanding how people get into painful exchanges and how they can get out of them. Therefore, it's useful also to have two distinct definitions, so that we can always make it clear which of the two concepts we're talking about.

Suppose you want to define a 'game' to somebody who doesn't know the technical language of Berne's Formula G? You can use this way of saying it, suggested by Vann Joines:

'A game is the process of doing something with an ulterior motive that:

(1) is outside of Adult awareness;

(2) does not become explicit until the participants switch the way they are behaving; and

(3) results in everyone feeling confused, misunderstood, and wanting to blame the other person.'

The 'mystery questions'

Mystery question 4: What is my secret message to the other person?
Mystery question 6: What is the other person's secret message to me?

Chapter 24
WHY PEOPLE PLAY GAMES

Games are no fun. So why do we play them?

TA writers have suggested several answers to this question.[1] They all agree on one point. That is: in playing games, we are following outdated strategies. Game-playing was one of the devices we adopted as young children to get what we wanted from the world. Games satisfy all of the basic psychological hungers. They provide intense strokes, they structure time in a dramatic and exciting way, and they confirm our basic existential life position. The only problem is that they involve negative outcomes. In adult life we have other, more effective options that provide positive ways of meeting those hungers.

Games, stamps and script payoff

Above all, people play games to further their life script.

Eric Berne suggested the sequence by which we achieve this. At the payoff of every game, the player experiences a *racket feeling*. Each time he does this, he can store the feeling away as a *stamp*.

You learned the rest of the story in Chapter 21. When the game-player has built up a big enough collection of stamps, he feels 'justified' in cashing it in for whatever negative *script payoff* he decided upon as a child.

Thus each person chooses her games to yield the kind of stamps that will advance her towards the script ending she has decided upon. As usual with scripts, the script story may be played through in miniature many times during the player's life.

Consider Jean's NIGYSOB game. Each time she plays it, she collects anger stamps and then cashes them in for a rejection of the other person. Her long-run script payoff is to end up old and alone, having rejected all the men she has known.

People choose the degree of their games to suit the degree of their script payoff. Suppose Jean's script were hamartic instead of banal. She would likely play her NIGYSOB at third degree. The men she chose would batter her physically instead of with words. At the game switch, she in turn would cash her anger stamps by harming the man physically. Her script payoff would be homicide or seriously harming others.

● Look back at your own game example. What feeling stamp did you save?

How might you have been saving up these stamps for a negative script payoff? ●

Reinforcing script beliefs

You know that the child views her early decisions as being the only way to get by and survive. So it is not surprising that when we are in script as grown-ups, we want to confirm time and time again that our script beliefs about self, others and the world are 'true'. Each time we play a game, we use the payoff to reinforce those script beliefs.

For example, when Molly was an infant she decided non-verbally that her job in life was to help others, but that she could never help them well enough. Each time she plays out her Why Don't You...? game, she ends up repeating this decision in her head. In the language of the Racket System, she stacks up another Reinforcing Memory to further her Script Beliefs about self, others and the quality of life.

Games and life position

We can also use games to 'confirm' our basic life position. (To review this concept, see Chapter 12). For instance, people like Jack who play Kick Me are reinforcing a life position of 'I'm not-OK, you're OK'. This position 'justifies' the player in getting-away-from others. A NIGYSOB player such as Jean believes she is confirming 'I'm OK, you're not-OK' each time she reaches her Persecutor payoff, and thereby 'justifies' her strategy of getting-rid-of other people.

If a person's position is down in the lower-left quadrant of the OK Corral, at 'I'm not-OK, you're not-OK', she will most likely use her games to 'justify' getting-nowhere-with people. For example, this is where Molly ends up each time she plays out her game of Why Don't You...?

● In your own game example, what script beliefs about self, others and the world might you have been reinforcing at the payoff?

Which of the life positions do these beliefs fit?

Does that check with the basic life position you saw yourself in when you were learning about the OK Corral? ●

Games, symbiosis and the frame of reference

The Schiffs suggest that games result from unresolved symbiotic relationships, in which each player discounts both himself and the other.[2] The players maintain grandiose beliefs in order to 'justify' the symbiosis, such as 'I can't do anything' (Child) or 'I only live for you, dear!' (Parent). Thus every game is either an attempt to maintain an unhealthy symbiosis,

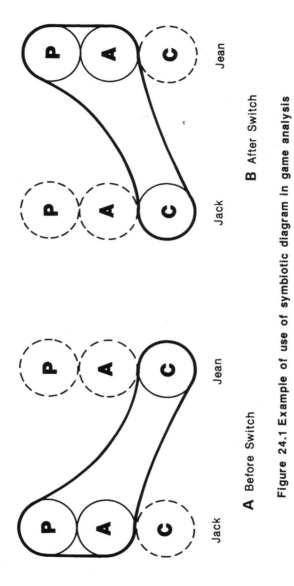

A Before Switch   **B** After Switch

Figure 24.1 Example of use of symbiotic diagram in game analysis

or an angry reaction against that symbiosis.

We can draw a symbiotic diagram to analyse the interlocking games that Jack and Jean are playing (Figure 24.1). In Figure 24.1a, we see their initial symbiotic positions. Jack takes the Parental role, while Jean plays Child. In line with the standard way of drawing the symbiotic diagram, we show Jack also taking on ownership of the Adult ego-state. However, when the partners are playing through the early stages of their respective games, neither is aware of what is going on. You could therefore imagine re-drawing the diagram to show the Adult out of commission for both Jack and Jean.

At the Switch, the symbiotic positions are switched also. Now Jack takes on the role of hurt Child. Jean switches into rejecting Parent. This gives the closing symbiotic picture shown in Figure 24.1b.

Without knowing it, Jack has been replaying his childhood symbiosis with his mother. When he was an infant, he picked up non-verbally that his mother was rejecting him. Without words, Jack decided: 'It seems I only get attention from Mother when she does something to reject me. Otherwise, I might get no attention at all. So I'd better set up to keep the rejections coming.' He had soon worked out a range of strategies to get this result. Sometimes he would whine and grizzle, on and on. At other times he would fly into a tantrum. Either way, Mother eventually got angry with him. When she did, she would shout at Jack or even slap him. This kind of attention hurt. But it was better than no attention at all.

As a grown-up, Jack still follows the same infant strategy outside of awareness. He seeks out women who are likely to reject him from a Parental position. If the rejection is slow in coming, he helps it along by Persecuting the woman, in the same way as he Persecuted his mother when he was fifteen months old.

Jean, too, has been replaying a childhood symbiosis. As an infant and a toddler, she had enjoyed getting lots of playful strokes from her father. But there came a time when Jean became not just a baby, but a feminine little girl. In his Child, Father began feeling uncomfortable at his own sexual response to her. Without awareness, he withdrew from Jean physically.

Jean felt betrayed and hurt. To blank out the pain, she covered her hurt with anger, and decided she'd feel less uncomfortable if she became the one who did the rejecting. She got into her Parent to put down her father's Child. As a grown-up woman, she unknowingly acts out this same decision. She 'puts Father's face' on men she relates to, and rejects them while once again feeling her childhood anger.

● Draw the symbiotic diagrams for the games played by Molly and Dave.

Find what symbiotic position you took up at the beginning of the game in your own personal example, and what position you moved into at the Switch. Do you identify what childhood symbiosis you were re-playing or reacting against? ●

When people use games to replay a childhood symbiosis, they 'justify' and maintain the problem that is being discounted. In so doing, they defend their frame of reference.

Thus games are played in order to 'justify' what the players are already feeling and believing (their racket feelings and life position) and to shift the responsibility on to someone or something else. Each time a person does this, he reinforces and furthers his script.

Games and strokes

You know that the Child needs strokes for survival. Every child gets scared at times that the supply of strokes may run out. To guard against this, she develops a repertoire of manipulations to keep the strokes coming.

Games are a reliable way of getting a supply of intense strokes. The strokes exchanged in the opening stages of the game may be positive or negative, depending on the game. At the switch, each player gets or gives intense negative strokes. Whether positive or negative, every stroke exchanged during a game entails a discount.

Games, strokes and racketeering

Fanita English suggests that people begin seeking game strokes when their strokes from *racketeering* are in danger of running out.[3] Perhaps I may have been getting into a Helpless role with you, while you have been acting Helpful. I may tell you all the bad things people have been doing to me that day, while you offer Rescuing sympathy. For a while, we exchange these racketeering strokes.

Then you get tired of the exchange and signal that you want to move on. Feeling scare in my Child, I may respond by pulling a NIGYSOB game switch, saying something like 'Huh! I always thought you were somebody I could rely on, but now I see I was wrong.' Outside of my awareness, I'm hoping you will come back with a Kick Me and keep the supply of strokes coming.

Whenever people get into games to manipulate for strokes, they are discounting reality. They are ignoring the many grown-up options they have to get strokes in positive ways.

● What strokes were you getting and giving at each stage of your own game example?

Did you get into the game when racketeering strokes were in danger of running out? ●

267

Berne's 'six advantages'

In *Games People Play*, Eric Berne listed 'six advantages' of game-playing.[4] Nowadays, they are not often referred to in practical TA work. Each can be understood more simply in terms of other TA ideas. Let's review them briefly. For illustration, say I am a Kick Me player.

(1) Internal psychological advantage. By playing games, I maintain the stability of my set of script beliefs. Each time I play Kick Me, I reinforce my belief that I need to be rejected in order to get attention.

(2) External psychological advantage. I avoid situations that would challenge my frame of reference. Thus I avoid the anxiety I would feel at the challenge. By playing Kick Me, I avoid facing up to the question: 'What would happen if I did ask others for straight positive strokes?'

(3) Internal social advantage. In Berne's words, games 'offer a framework for pseudo-intimate socializing indoors or in privacy.' Part of my Kick Me game may be long, agonizing 'heart-to-heart' exchanges with my gaming partner. We feel as though we are being open with each other. In reality, this is not intimacy. Beneath the social-level messages are the ulteriors that confirm that we are in a game.

(4) External social advantage. Gaming gives us a theme for gossiping in our wider social circle. When I am in the bar with a crowd of other male Kick Me players, we may pastime or racketeer on the theme 'Ain't Women Awful?'.

(5) Biological advantage. This refers to the game's yield of strokes. Kick Me yields mainly negatives. As a child, I decided that since positive strokes seemed hard to come by, I had better set up reliable ways of getting kicks in order to survive. Also, each time I replay the game, I am satisfying structure-hunger as well as stroke-hunger.

(6) Existential advantage. This is the function of the game in 'confirming' the life position. Kick Me is played from a position of 'I'm not-OK, you're OK'. Each time I take a gamey kick, I reinforce this position.

● What are the 'six advantages' of Jean's NIGYSOB game?
What were the 'six advantages' in your own game example? ●

Positive payoffs of games

John James has developed the idea that games have real advantages as well as scripty ones. He points out that every game brings a *positive payoff* as well as its negative payoff.[5]

A game represents the child's best strategy for getting something from the world. When we play games in adulthood, we are attempting to meet a genuine Child need. It's just that the means of satisfying that need are outdated and manipulative.

James suggests that the positive payoff comes *after* the negative payoff in the Game Formula. For instance, what's the positive Child need that I am satisfying by playing my Kick Me game? It's that each time I play the game, after I have collected my bad-feeling payoff, I say to myself in Child: 'Phew! Thank goodness for a bit of time and space for myself!'

Other Kick Me players may gain different positive payoffs from mine. The positive payoff is unique to each game player. But, says John James, it is always there to be found.

● What positive payoffs might Molly and Dave have been seeking when they got into their Why Don't You? – Yes, But exchange?

What positive payoff did you get at the close of your own game example? You may realize the answer immediately, or it may take you some time and thought. ●

Chapter 25
HOW TO DEAL WITH GAMES

You have already taken the most important steps in defusing game-playing. You have learned what games are and how they can be analysed. You know the covert motives people have in playing games.

In this chapter, we outline a 'tool-kit' of practical ways to counter games.

Need we name the game?

In his best-selling *Games People Play*, Eric Berne fascinated his readers by giving catchy names to the games he listed.[1] Others followed Berne's lead, and game-naming became a fashion in TA that lasted for some years. Literally hundreds of games were 'discovered', each with its own name.

With over forty years' hindsight, we can see now that only a few of these represented genuine additions to our understanding of games. Many of the suggested names turn out to describe interactions that are not games at all, according to the definitions we met in Chapter 23. In particular, many do not have a Switch, and so can be more consistently classified as pastimes or racketeering. This is the case with many of the 'games' listed in *Games People Play*.

When we eliminate these non-games, we discover that the remaining games can be classified into a relatively small number of basic patterns. Each of these patterns can be represented by one well-known game title. All the other names represent variations on these, and the variation is in *content* rather than *process* – in the details of *what* goes on during the game rather than *how* the game is being played. Games fall into three basic categories: (1) Those that involve finding fault with others, (2) Those that involve inviting others to find fault with me, and (3) Those that involve getting nowhere.

Most TA practitioners nowadays prefer to economize on the number of game names they use. We favour this approach. We think you can best develop an understanding of games by concentrating on the general patterns that define *how* games are played. This also allows you to work out general principles for countering games, instead of having to develop a separate 'antithesis' specific to the content of each game, as Berne did.

Some familiar games

In this section we list some of the most commonly-used game names. They are classified according to the shift in Drama Triangle positions that the player makes at the moment of the Switch.[2]

Persecutor-to-Victim switch

This is typified by *Kick Me*, which we have already illustrated by examples.

Cops and Robbers is a version of the same game played in a legal setting. Here, the player opens by seeking to Persecute the forces of law and order. But eventually he sets up to get caught, thus finishing up as Victim.

In *Blemish*, the player finds fault with others, criticizing their appearance, work, dress, etc. He may keep this up indefinitely as a theme for racketeering, without necessarily pulling a game Switch. However, the blemisher may eventually get himself rejected by those he has been criticizing, or set up to be 'accidentally' overheard as he dwells on someone's faults behind their back. Then he makes the move from Persecutor to Victim on the Drama Triangle, converting his racketeering into a game.

The player of *If It Weren't For You* is always moaning to others about how they prevent her from doing something she wants. For instance, a mother may tell her children: 'If it weren't for you, I could be away travelling in foreign countries.' Now suppose something happens to interrupt her racketeering on this theme. Maybe she inherits a sum of money large enough to pay for child care. Or her children simply get old enough not to need her around. Do you think she then goes on those foreign travels? No. She discovers she's too scared to leave her own country. In so doing, she makes a Switch to the Victim position.

Victim-to-Persecutor switch

This pattern is exemplified by *Now I've Got You, Son of a Bitch (NIGYSOB)*. You'll recall this as the game played by Jean in one of our opening examples. In this and all its variations, the player gives some sort of 'come-on' from a Victim position. When the gaming partner takes the bait, the player delivers a Persecuting kick.

In *Yes, But...*, the player starts by asking for advice while fending off all the suggestions that are given. The Switch comes when the advice-giver runs out of suggestions and the Yes, But... player deals out a rejection of the helper. You'll remember how Dave played this in our example.

Rapo is the sexual version of NIGYSOB. Here, the player signals a sexual come-on. When the gaming partner responds with a sexual advance, the Rapo player comes back with an indignant rejection. The Rapo player wears a sweatshirt that says on the front: 'I'm available!' On the back it reads: 'But not to *you*, ha ha!' First-degree Rapo is a common source of game strokes at parties, and has a mild sexual rebuff as its outcome. Second-degree Rapo involves enough embarrassment that the players prefer to keep it hidden and may involve a face slap or public scene. At third degree, the Rapo player may wait until there has been physical sexual contact, then pull the Switch by crying 'Rape!'.

There are several games of the NIGYSOB pattern in which the initial Victim position is taken up as a racketeering stance, and the Switch is usually not pulled unless that stance is confronted. Players of *Stupid* and *Poor Me* begin by racketeering from postures of 'I can't think' and 'I can't help myself' respectively. They may be content to stay in this Victim position for as long as the strokes keep coming. However, if someone confronts these players with demands to think or do things for themselves, they may pull the Switch by becoming angry or accusing: 'Huh! Should have known better than to think I'd get any help from *you*!'

Wooden Leg is a variation of Poor Me, with a sweatshirt motto that runs: 'What can you expect from someone who...had a mother like mine / is an alcoholic like me / was brought up in the inner city / (supply any other excuse).'

The player of *Do Me Something* seeks covertly to manipulate other people into thinking or acting for him. For example, a student who is asked a question in class may sit dumbly, chewing his pencil and waiting for the lecturer to supply the answer. As long as the hoped-for assistance is produced, the player may stay in the position of helpless Victim. But later, he may pull the Switch and collect a further harvest of game strokes by accusing the helper of giving bad advice. For example, that same student might go to the principal after the examination and complain that he'd scored a low mark because the lecturer had been unclear in his teaching. This end-of-game stance has sometimes been given a different game name, *See What You Made Me Do*.

Rescuer-to-Victim switch

The prototype game here is *I'm Only Trying To Help You*. This title can be used for any game in which someone begins by offering 'help' from a Rescuing position, then switches to Victim when the person they are 'helping' either rejects the help, goes ahead and gets into a mess anyway, or signals that the help offered has not been good enough. The would-be 'helper' then collects a payoff of inadequacy stamps.

The game Molly was playing in our opening example, *Why Don't You...?*, is a variation on this theme that involves the giving of advice which is rejected by the gaming partner.

Rescuer-to-Persecutor switch

See How Hard I've Tried begins like I'm Only Trying To Help You, with the 'helper' in the Rescuer role. But at the Switch, the one-time Rescuer changes to an accusing Persecutor instead of a woeful Victim. For instance, imagine a woman who has acted the 'smother-mother' to her son right through his childhood. Now he's a rebellious teenager and has just announced he intends to leave home. Pulling her game Switch, the mother screams: 'After all I've done for you! I hope you get just what you deserve! I'm washing my hands of you, do you hear?'

Using Options

In Chapter 7, you learned about Options. If you have practised them, you will be skilled in their use by now. This skill, combined with a knowledge of game analysis, gives you an effective armoury for countering games.

Options can be used to break the flow of a game at *any* stage in the Game Formula. If you realize that you yourself are part-way through a game of your own, you can take your Option of shifting out of a negative and into a positive functional ego-state. If someone else has invited you into their game, use Options to come back with a response that cuts across their expectations of what you are 'supposed' to do at that stage of the game.

We suggest you use only positive ego-state Options. Rather than engage in a dance around the Drama Triangle with the other person, step off the Triangle altogether.

You cannot *make* anyone else stop playing games. Nor can you stop them trying to hook you into a game. But by using Options, you can stay out of game-playing yourself, or get back out of it if you find that you have already got in. And you maximize the chance that you will also invite the other person out of their game, if this aim matters to you.

Catching the 'opening Con'

Bob and Mary Goulding have stressed the importance of catching the game right at the beginning, at the 'opening Con'.[3] If you immediately come back with an Option to confront this, you're likely to forestall the rest of the game.

This calls for skill in 'thinking Martian'. You need to pick up the ulterior message that forms the Con, and cut across that instead of responding to the social level.

You can use a cross from straight Adult. For example, consider the start of the game between Molly and Dave. When he came out with his request for assistance, Molly might have responded: 'You sound like you have a problem. What do you want to do about it?' With this question, she would address the covert agenda directly. If Dave were to redefine in a further attempt to hook her into his game, she could simply repeat the same cross until he either gave an Adult answer or gave up and left. In the latter case, he might take his own game payoff anyway. But Molly would have avoided taking a payoff for herself.

If it fits the setting, a specially effective way of cutting across the opening Con is to come back with an exaggerated, 'over-the-top' response from either Child or Parent. For instance, Molly might have greeted Dave's opening moan by slithering down in her chair until she ended up sitting on the floor, groaning: 'Oh, *dear*! You are in bad shape again, aren't you?' When a client told Bob Goulding that she had come into therapy to 'work on' a problem, Bob's frequent response was to assume an expression of pained boredom, and drone: 'Work on, and work on, and work on...' Responses like these cross the opening Con at psychological level, conveying: 'I've seen through your game, so let's have some fun instead.'

Confronting the game discounts

The opening Con in a game always entails a discount. There are further discounts at each stage of the game. Therefore, the skill of detecting discounts helps you identify game invitations and defuse them with Options.

If you accept the discount offered in the Con, you will have exposed your Gimmick and the game will be under way. Thus the way to defuse the game is to confront the other person's discount. This, of course, means that you yourself need to stay out of discounting.

Refusing the negative payoff

What if you miss the opening Con, get into the game, and become aware of it only at the Switch? All isn't lost. You can still refuse to take your bad-feeling payoff. Better still, you can give yourself a good-feeling payoff instead.

For instance, suppose I'm attending a lecture given by a well-known speaker. When the time comes for discussion, I put up a spirited attack on his ideas. In fact, though I'm not aware of it yet, I've started Persecuting him. When I'm through, the lecturer smiles quietly and demolishes my critique with one well-chosen sentence. The audience laughs.

At this point, my script calls for me to hit the Switch of my Kick Me game. I'm 'supposed' to feel rejected and useless. Instead of that, I step out of script. I tell myself: 'Interesting! I've just identified that I've been setting up Kick Me for the past three minutes. How clever I am to have realized that!' I award myself a bundle of good feelings for my own cleverness in spotting the game.

Note that I don't congratulate myself for having got into the game. I congratulate myself for being clever enough to realize I've got into it.

The interesting thing is that if you use this technique consistently, you will find you play the game less often and less intensely as time goes on. And this is no surprise, given the role games play in relation to the script. Each time I refuse the bad-feeling payoff of a game and give myself a good-feeling payoff instead, I throw away a negative stamp. I collect a positive Reinforcing Memory in place of the negative one called for in the game. Thus, I help defuse my Script Beliefs and reduce the intensity of my Rackety Displays, of which the game itself is one.

Going straight to the positive payoff

A similar technique is suggested by John James.[4] You'll recall his idea that every game has a positive payoff as well as a negative one. When you identify a particular game as one you have often played, you can work out what authentic Child need you have been meeting in the past by doing so. Then you can find ways of satisfying that need in straight instead of scripty ways.

For instance, suppose the positive payoff of my Kick Me game is to get time and space for myself. Knowing this, I can use my grown-up options to get these benefits without getting kicked first. I may begin taking ten minutes' quiet time for myself each morning and afternoon, or block out time in my schedule to go for walks alone in the country. As I do so, I meet my Child needs in a straight way. As a result I'm likely to find myself playing Kick Me less and less often. Furthermore, when I do play the game, I will most likely play it at a lesser degree than I did previously.

Moving to intimacy at the Switch

Once you have become accustomed to tracking the successive stages of a game, you will find it particularly easy to recognize the Switch. You will realize that you and the other person seem to have switched roles in some way, and you will almost simultaneously recognize the moment of confusion that constitutes the Crossup.

At this point you have yet another strategy for stepping out of the game. When a person remains in script at the moment of the Switch and Crossup, he believes his *only* option is to move to the Payoff. But with Adult awareness you can take a different route. Instead of moving into racket feelings, you can be open with the other person about your authentic feelings and wants. Thus you invite intimacy in place of the game Payoff.

For instance, imagine I had played my Kick Me game through in a relationship, and that I had just arrived at the Switch in the game. I might say to the other person: 'I've just realized what I've been setting up – to push you away until you reject me. Now I'm scared you're going to leave me, and I really want you to stay close to me.'

By this open statement, I cannot *make* the other person stay with me. I cannot even *make* her move out of her own game if she is invested in staying in it. But I *invite* her to respond with her own authentic feelings and wants. If she does, we may move back into the relationship with feelings of happiness and relief. Alternatively, we may decide to part anyway, though for straight rather than gamey reasons. If we make the latter decision, both of us may have to face up to a period of sadness at our loss. As always, intimacy is less predictable than game-playing, and we may or may not experience it as more comfortable.

Replacing game strokes

Game-playing is seen by the Child as a reliable way of getting strokes. So what may happen when, for good Adult reasons, you reduce your game-playing?

Outside of awareness in Child, you may feel panic and ask yourself: 'What's happening to my stroke supply?' Recall that to the Child, loss of strokes means a threat to survival.

Thus without knowing it, you may begin using Little Professor strategies to regain the lost strokes. Perhaps you find other ways of playing the same old games. Or you start playing different games with the same Drama Triangle switch. Or you 'forget' to confront discounts.

Superficially, these actions might be interpreted as 'self-sabotage'. As far as the early Child is concerned, their purpose is just the opposite. The motive is to maintain the supply of strokes, hence ensure survival.

For this reason, it's important that you not merely set out to 'stop playing games'. You also need to find a way of *replacing* the yield of strokes that you previously got from game-playing.

Stan Woollams has drawn attention to an additional catch here.[5] Game strokes are plentiful and intense. By contrast, the strokes we can get from game-free living are relatively mild, and sometimes may not be in such reliable supply. For sure, these new strokes are straight ones instead of involving discounts. But as we know, the stroke-hungry Child is more concerned with quantity than quality.

There's no way around this, other than to take time to convince yourself in Child that the new stroke supply is acceptable and is going to last. During this transition period, it may be a good idea to set up extra sources of strokes that you can draw on to tide you over. This is one way in which the support of a group can help personal change.

In the longer term, you will become accustomed in Child to this new and less intense stroke input. Game-freedom may entail the loss of some familiar sources of excitement. But it allows us to use grown-up options that we denied ourselves through game-playing. And by moving out of games, we make it easier to move into the authentic closeness of intimacy.

● Look back at the game example that you analysed by means of the Game Plan (Chapter 23).

Do you identify it with one of the named games given above? Check this against the switch in Drama Triangle positions you made at the Switch in the game.

Refer to the various techniques for countering games that you have learned in this chapter. Apply each of them to your game example. You will end up with a list of ways to disarm this game in the future.

If you want to apply these techniques, decide first how you are going to get strokes to replace those you will lose when you move out of the game. Set up this alternative stroke supply.

Then go ahead and begin countering the game. Choose one technique and use it consistently for a week. Then test out others in the same way. If you are working in a group, report back on your successes. ●

Part VII
CHANGING

TA in Practice

Chapter 26
CONTRACTS FOR CHANGE

It is outside the scope of this book to give detailed guidance on the professional uses of TA. Our aim in this final Part is to present you with a brief overview of the ways in which TA is used to promote change.

We begin in this chapter by looking at one of the central features of TA practice: the use of contracts.[1]

Berne defined a *contract* as *an explicit bilateral commitment to a well-defined course of action.* We also like James and Jongeward's definition: *'A contract is an Adult commitment to one's self and/or someone else to make a change.'*

Contracts specify:
- who both parties are;
- what it is they are going to do together;
- how long this will take;
- what the goal or outcome of that process will be;
- how they will know when they have got there; and
- how that will be beneficial and/or pleasing to the client.

TA practitioners distinguish two different kinds of contract: the *administrative* or *business contract* and the *clinical* or *treatment contract*.

The business contract is an agreement between the practitioner and client about the details of payment and administrative arrangements for their work together.

In the treatment contract, the client sets out clearly what changes he wants to make, and specifies what he is willing to do to help bring about these changes. The practitioner says whether she is willing to work with the client in the achievement of his desired changes, and states what her input to this process will be.

Steiner's 'four requirements'

Claude Steiner has set out four requirements for sound contract-making. They were derived from the practice of contract-making in legal settings.

(1) Mutual consent. This means that both parties must agree to the contract. The practitioner does not impose business arrangements nor treatment goals on the client. Nor can the client impose them on the practitioner. Instead, the contract is arrived at by negotiation between the two parties.

(2) Valid consideration. In legal language, a 'consideration' means

some form of recompense given in return for someone's time or work. In TA settings, the consideration will usually be in the form of money paid by the client to the practitioner. Sometimes the parties may contract for the consideration to be made in kind. For example, the client might agree to do a certain number of hours' work for the practitioner in return for each hour of treatment. Whatever the details, the nature of the consideration must be explicit and be agreed by both parties to the contract.

(3) Competency. Both the practitioner and the client must be competent to carry out what has been agreed upon in the contract. For the practitioner, this means having the specific professional skills needed to facilitate the client in his desired change. The client must be able to understand the contract and have the physical and mental resources to carry it through. This implies that, for example, a severely brain-damaged person might not be able to enter competently into a treatment contract. Nor can a competent contract be made by anyone who is under the influence of alcohol or mind-altering drugs.

(4) Lawful object. The goals and conditions of the contract must be in conformity with the law. For the practitioner, 'lawful object' also implies adherence to ethical principles laid down by the professional body to which she belongs.

Why use contracts?

First and foremost, the emphasis on contracts in TA practice arises from the philosophical assumption *'People are OK'.* The practitioner and client relate to each other as equals. Hence they share responsibility for the change the client wants to make.

This follows from the belief that everyone has the capacity to think and is ultimately responsible for her own life. She is the one who will live with the consequences of what she decides. Therefore it is up to the client, not the practitioner, to decide what she wants for her life. The practitioner's job is to point out everything that seems dysfunctional.

If this sharing of responsibility is to be meaningful, both parties need to be clear about the nature of the change that is desired and the contribution each will make to its achievement.

Contracts and the covert agenda

You know that in any relationship, the parties may exchange ulterior messages. This is especially likely to be true in situations where personal or organizational change is being sought, since such changes usually mean a challenge to someone's frame of reference. Both practitioner and client are likely to come into their working relationship with a *covert agenda* as well as their social-level agenda. One important function of a contract is *to make the covert agenda explicit.* By exposing ulterior messages, clear contract-making cuts through psychological games and helps both the client and the practitioner to stay off the Drama Triangle.

The practitioner has her own frame of reference, and it will be different from that of the client. Therefore she will come into their relationship bringing her own internal definitions of what kinds of change are 'good' for people. Without a contract, it would be tempting for her to assume that her client's definitions were the same as her own. Further, because the definitions in her frame of reference might not be fully in her awareness, she might not be fully aware that she *was* making assumptions about the 'proper' goals for her client to pursue.

In this situation, it is likely that the practitioner would move into a Drama Triangle role. She might begin 'railroading' the client in a particular direction, thus playing Persecutor to the client's Victim. In Bob Goulding's words, working without a contract may mean that a therapist becomes *the rapist*.

Alternatively, the practitioner might say internally: 'This client obviously needs to make such-and-such a change. He hasn't made it yet. Therefore, he's in a sorry plight and can't get by without my help.' With this, she would step into the Rescuer role.

The client also is likely to have a covert as well as an overt agenda. By coming to the practitioner, he has declared on social level that there is some change he wants to make. (In some cases, he comes because there's a change that other people want him to make.) But he hasn't yet made the change. This may be because he genuinely doesn't know how. Or it may be that he does know how, but is defending on a covert level against making the change. In the latter case, he will be giving the practitioner ulterior messages like: 'I've come to change, but I'm helpless to do it,' or 'I've come to change, but you can't make me.'

If the covert agenda goes ahead on both sides, practitioner and client will take up complementary roles on the Drama Triangle, opening the way for racketeering and games.

One function of the contract is to forestall this. In *negotiating* clear objectives and methods of change, practitioner and client are forced to compare frames of reference. This process helps bring the covert agenda into Adult awareness, so that both parties can assess it against reality. Since neither the practitioner nor the client is perfect, it is unlikely that either will bring his full hidden agenda to light at the initial negotiation. Instead, the contract may have to be reviewed and if necessary renegotiated many times during the process of change.

Contracts and goal-orientation

Most clients come to the practitioner bringing a *problem* they want to tackle. One of the purposes of contract-making is to shift the focus of attention away from the problem, and centre instead on the *goal of change.*

In the process of making a contract, both client and practitioner must necessarily construct a mental picture of the desired outcome of their work together. When they orient themselves to a clear goal in this way, they automatically mobilize the personal resources they need to achieve that outcome. This is the principle behind all systems of 'creative visualization'.

By contrast, if practitioner and client had given their attention mainly to 'the problem', they would have had to construct a mental picture of that problem. Without intending to, they would have been engaging in negative visualization, directing their resources to examining the problem rather than solving it.

There is still another advantage in agreeing a clearly-stated contract: it gives both parties a way of knowing when their work together has been completed. It also allows them to assess the progress they are making along the way. Thus the use of contracts prevents the situation where treatment might drag on interminably, with the client and practitioner spending months and years 'working on' the client's problems.

Making an effective contract

Here in summary are the main features that TA practitioners would look for in an effective contract. Rather than just stating these in the abstract, we invite you to put them into practice on a desired change of your own. As James and Jongeward point out, you can make a contract for change with yourself as well as with a therapist.

The *Contract Checklist* exercise that follows has been developed by one of the present authors (IS)[2]. You need writing materials and plenty of paper (or your word processor), and time to work.

You'll see that the exercise consists of a sequence of numbered steps. The commentary that follows each step is designed to lead you to the *next* step in the sequence. Step 1 simply asks you to write down a personal change you want to make, using whatever wording occurs to you. The commentary following step 1 describes why the wording of an effective contract needs to be positive rather than negative. Then at step 2, you are invited to find that positive wording for your desired change. The same structure is used throughout the exercise.

● 1. Decide on a personal change you want to make. Write it down, using whatever words you bring to mind. ●

A contract goal must be *phrased in positive words*. Often, the initial wording of a goal will contain negatives. For example, the person may want to *stop* smoking or *control* drinking, to *lose* weight, or *not* to be scared of authority figures. Such 'stop contracts' and 'not contracts' never work in the long term. Partly, this is because of the way in which the contract goal acts as a visualization. You cannot visualize 'not something'. (If you doubt this, go ahead and visualize 'not a red elephant'.) When you try to do so, you automatically make a mental picture of whatever follows the 'not', or any other negative word. For instance, if a person takes on a contract to 'stop smoking', she cannot address that contract without continually visualizing the problem activity she is setting out to stop.

There's also a good reason in TA theory for the ineffectiveness of 'stop contracts'. Remember that all scripty behaviour represents the Child's best strategy for surviving, getting strokes and getting needs met. So what happens if you simply contract to 'stop doing' that scripty behaviour? At the very least, you have failed to give yourself in Child any clear directive on what you *are* going to do instead; you have simply added one more to the endless list of 'don'ts' and 'stops' you got from your parents when you were young. At worst, you may be contracting to give up a behaviour which in Child you have been perceiving as essential to your survival.

To get to an effective contract, you must specify the *positive* that will provide you in Child with a clear directive to action. It must provide a new option for surviving and getting needs met that is at least as good as the old scripty option.

● 2. If your stated want contains any negative words, re-phrase it to contain only positives. Your re-phrased statement will say what positive you are going to use to *replace* the negative. ●

The goal must be *specific and observable*. Both you and other people must be able to tell clearly whether you have achieved the goal. Beware of *over-generalized* goals and of *comparatives*. Often, people will start with global goals like: 'I want to be a warm, outgoing person' or 'I want to get closer to others.' To take a contract like this would be to buy into endless 'working on', since the stated goals are not specific enough to let anyone know whether they have been achieved.

● 3. How will you and others know when your desired change has been achieved? State your answer with full detail of what you and others will be able to *see* and *hear* you doing differently. If your goal concerns the way you relate to other people, specify *which people, by name*. ●

The contract must be for a goal that is *achievable*, given your present situation and resources. Generally speaking, we deem 'achievable' anything that is physically possible. Note that this condition implies that you can only contract for a change you want to make in *yourself*. It is not physically possible to 'make' anyone else change.

● 4. Check whether your desired change is possible for you. As a check question, ask: has at least one other person in the world achieved it? If so, list it as being possible. (Be sure to specify fully, however, what the 'it' entails). ●

The change you are aiming for must be *safe.* Use Adult appraisal, and consider physical and legal safety as well as social appropriateness. Consider the future as well as the present.

● 5. Check: Is this desired change safe for you? ●

The contract must be made *from Adult,* preferably with the co-operation of the Child. In other words, the contract goal must be appropriate to your grown-up situation and abilities, and should help satisfy your authentic Child needs rather than denying them. (Note, however, that it may sometimes be necessary to contract for a goal to which the Child may at first bitterly object – like, for example, changing from 'junk food' to healthy food – in order to achieve a *longer-term* outcome that is genuinely in the Child's interest, in this case improved health and a longer life).

● 6. Check: how much do you want this change for *you*, rather than to please others, get someone's approval, or rebel against someone? The 'others' and 'someone' may be people from your past or your present. If you discover you are pleasing, seeking approval or rebelling, you can pursue with this further check: 'I want this change to please / get approval from / rebel against ... [*complete the sentence by listing people by name*].' Note that any wanted change may be *partly* aimed at pleasing, getting approval or rebelling, and *partly* be for you. Now that you are clear on the extent to which you're pleasing, getting approval or rebelling, do you still want the change? ●

Achieving your goal *will always involve some cost.* This may be in terms of time, money, commitment, upheaval, saying goodbye, or facing the scare of change.

● 7. Check: what will this change cost you to achieve? Now that you have worked out the cost, do you still want the change? ●

Do you want to achieve the contract goal everywhere, all the time and with everyone? If not, what are the limitations you want to apply as to where, when and with whom you will carry out the contract? (This is the *context* of the contract).

● 8. Check: Where, when and with whom am I going to carry out this contract? Where, when and with whom am I *not* going to carry out this contract? ●

The remaining steps of the checklist concern a *commitment to specific action.*

● 9. Write down at least five things you will *need to do* to achieve your contract goal. Again be specific in stating actions that you and others will be able to see and hear you taking. If these actions involve people, say *which* people by name. ●

● 10. Now, from the list of things you need to do, select and write down *one* thing you *will* do in the coming week. Then go ahead and do it. ●

Chapter 27
AIMS OF CHANGE IN TA

You saw in the previous chapter how specific contract goals are negotiated between the TA practitioner and the client. But what end-product are they to aim for in the change process? How will client and practitioner know when their work together is complete?

Autonomy

Eric Berne's suggested ideal was *autonomy*.[1] He never offered a definition of the word, but he described autonomy as being 'manifested by the release or recovery of three capacities: *awareness, spontaneity* and *intimacy.*'

Awareness

Awareness is the capacity to see, hear, feel, taste and smell things as pure sensual impressions, in the way a new-born infant does. The aware person does not interpret nor filter his experience of the world to fit Parental definitions. He is in contact with his own bodily sensations as well as with external stimuli.

As we grow up, most of us are systematically trained to deaden our awareness. We learn instead to devote energy to naming things and criticizing our own or other people's performance. For instance, suppose I am at a concert. As the musicians play, I may be engaged in an internal monologue: 'This was written in 1856, wasn't it? Hm, the tempo is a bit too fast. I wonder when this is going to finish? I must get an early night, lot of work to do tomorrow...'

If I let myself become aware, I switch off this voice in my head. I simply experience the sound of the music and my own bodily responses to it.

Spontaneity

Spontaneity means the capacity to choose from a full range of options in feeling, thinking and behaving. Just as the aware person experiences the world, so the spontaneous person responds to the world: directly, without blanking out portions of reality or re-interpreting it to fit Parental definitions.

Spontaneity implies that the person can respond freely from any of her ego-states. She can think, feel or behave as her grown-up self, using her

Adult ego-state. If she wants to, she can go into Child and get back in touch with the creativity, intuitive power and intensity of feeling she possessed in her own childhood. Or she may respond from Parent, re-playing the thoughts, feelings and behaviour she learned from her parents and parent-figures. Whatever ego-state she uses, she will choose her response freely to suit the present situation, not to comply with outdated Parental commands.

Intimacy

You learned in Chapter 9 that intimacy means an open sharing of feelings and wants between you and another person. The feelings expressed are authentic, so intimacy excludes the possibility of racketeering or game-playing. When a person is in intimacy he is likely to move into Free Child, having first assured a safe setting for this through Adult contract-making and Parental protection.

Becoming free from the script

Though Berne didn't say so explicitly, he implied that autonomy was the same thing as *freedom from the script*. Most TA writers since Berne have also equated these two ideas. Thus we can suggest a definition of autonomy: *behaviour, thinking or feeling that is a response to here-and-now reality, rather than a response to script beliefs.*

You may ask: 'But isn't the Adult ego-state defined as the set of behaviours, thoughts and feelings that are a direct response to the here-and-now? So does being autonomous mean being in Adult all the time?'

The answer is 'No.' We have already seen how the spontaneous person may sometimes *choose* to respond to the here-and-now by moving into Child or Parent ego-states. In autonomy, this *choice* is itself made freely in response to the present situation. By contrast, when a person is in script she will make her ego-state shifts in response to her own self-limiting childhood decisions about the world, her script beliefs.

Though autonomy doesn't mean being in constant Adult, it does imply processing all incoming data about the world through your Adult ego-state, then maintaining Adult awareness as you choose which ego-state to respond from. Like any other new skill, this may feel awkward at first. Autonomy always offers more options than does the script. Intimacy may well seem less comfortable initially than game-playing or racketeering, because intimacy is less predictable. However, autonomous ego-state choice becomes easier with practice. It can become so swift and natural that it's almost as though the person's Adult ego-state had positive Child and positive Parent qualities integrated into it.[2] Another way of thinking about autonomy is that it involves Child experiences and Parent information that have Adult perceptions integrated with them.

Problem-solving

In Schiffian terms, we can say that the autonomous person engages in *problem-solving* instead of *passivity*. Here, 'problem-solving' doesn't only imply *thinking* to work out the solution to the problem; it means also taking effective *action* to bring that solution about. As we saw in Chapter 21, the expression of authentic *feelings* also serves a problem-solving function.

When someone is problem-solving, he is accurately perceiving and responding to reality. Thus he is neither discounting nor redefining. And this in turn means he is script-free.

For TA work in organizational, educational or other settings outside therapy, it can be particularly appropriate to set 'effective problem-solving' as the goal for change, rather than 'autonomy' or 'being script-free'. In these settings, discounting and unsolved problems may often arise because people are *misinformed*, rather than because they are in script. Thus the practitioner needs to focus attention not on script-work, but on information exchange and the development of effective ways for people to act on that information.

Views of 'cure'

Another of Berne's enthusiasms was his emphasis on *cure*. He stressed time and again that the TA practitioner's job was to 'cure the patient', not merely to help him 'make progress'.[3]

In his book *Principles of Group Treatment*, Berne uses the metaphor of 'frogs and princes' to underline his own concept of cure. He suggests that 'cure' means casting off the frog skin and resuming the interrupted development as prince or princess, whereas 'making progress' means becoming a more comfortable frog. In *What Do You Say After You Say Hello?*, he describes cure as breaking out of the script entirely and 'putting a new show on the road'.

Some years ago, the *TA Journal* produced a symposium issue in which various TA writers gave their own interpretations of 'cure'.[4] There were almost as many differing views as there were contributors. Here are just a few of the ideas that emerge from that discussion.

Some writers take the down-to-earth view that 'cure' can best be defined in terms of *contract completion*. Rather than have any global goal for change, the practitioner and client simply work together until the client has completed as many mutually agreed contract goals as she wants.

More widely held is the view that, in therapy applications at least, 'cure' must entail some kind of movement out of script. Such *script cure* can be *behavioural, affective* or *cognitive*, or a combination of the three. In other words, someone who moves out of script can do so by acting, feeling or thinking in new ways.

Several writers suggest a fourth dimension to script change: *somatic cure*. This means that the person moving out of script will change the ways she uses and experiences her body. For instance, she may release chronic tensions or be relieved of psychosomatic ailments.

Cure: progressively learning new choices

No matter how you define 'script cure', it is seldom a once-for-all event. Much more often, cure is a matter of progressively learning to exercise new choices.

Whenever anyone makes a significant change in their script, they usually experience a natural 'high' for a few weeks or months. Then after a while they often go back to experiment with the old behaviour. It's as though a part of them wants to see if there are any goodies left in that old behaviour. The difference is that they recognize where they are and don't stay there as long. The old behaviour is no longer as satisfying as it used to be and they have new options, so they move out sooner. Pretty soon it no longer has any appeal and they skip it altogether.

Perhaps this process is best summarized by the following poem:[5]

Autobiography in Five Short Chapters

by Portia Nelson

I

I walk down the street.
   There is a deep hole in the sidewalk.
   I fall in
   I am lost...I am helpless
   It isn't my fault.
It takes forever to find a way out.

II

I walk down the same street.
   There is a deep hole in the sidewalk.
   I pretend I don't see it
   I fall in again
I can't believe I am in the same place.
   But, it isn't my fault.
It still takes a long time to get out.

III

I walk down the same street.
>There is a deep hole in the sidewalk.
>I see it is there
>I still fall in...it's a habit
My eyes are open.
I know where I am.
>It is my fault.
I get out immediately.

IV

I walk down the same street.
>There is a deep hole in the sidewalk.
>I walk around it.

V

I walk down another street.

Chapter 28
TA THERAPY AND COUNSELLING

Therapy and *counselling* are processes designed to help people achieve personal change. In this chapter, we look at the nature and techniques of therapy and counselling in TA practice.

'Therapy' or 'counselling'?

How should we define the differences between the activity called 'therapy' (or more fully, 'psychotherapy') and that called 'counselling'? Within the helping professions, there's a wide range of views on this question. Some professionals take the view that there is no significant difference between the two activities, or that the overlap between one and the other is so large that it's pointless to use two different words to describe them.

In TA's framework for professional accreditation, however, therapy and counselling are regarded as clearly separate fields of application (see Appendix E). A TA qualification in one does not imply any qualification in the other.

The Training and Certification Council (T&CC), which oversees training and accreditation for the ITAA, has suggested descriptions to explain the differences between these two fields.[1] They describe *psychotherapy* as follows:

> 'The Psychotherapy field of specialization is for practitioners who aim to facilitate the client's capacity for self-actualization, healing and change. The psychotherapeutic process enables the client to recognize and change archaic, self-limiting patterns – "to deal with the pain of the past in the present so that they are free to live their lives in the future". The aim is for clients to understand themselves and their relationships and create options to live their lives in an aware, creative, spontaneous way and open to intimacy.'

And here is the description that the T&CC suggest for *counselling:*

> 'TA Counselling is a professional activity within a contractual relationship. The counselling process enables clients or client systems to develop awareness, options and skills for problem management and personal development in daily life through the enhancement of their

strengths, resources and functioning. Its aim is to increase autonomy in relation to their social, professional and cultural environment. The field of counselling is chosen by those professionals who work in the socio/psychological and cultural fields of practice. Some examples amongst others are: social welfare, health care, pastoral work, prevention, mediation, process facilitation, multicultural work and humanitarian activities.'

While these two descriptions bring out some clear differences between therapy and counselling, they also confirm that there is an overlap between the two. In TA practice, therapy as well as counselling is 'a professional activity within a contractual relationship'. There can be few counsellors who would deny that part of their job is to help clients 'understand themselves and their relationships'. Likewise, there can be few therapists who do not seek to help their clients 'develop awareness, options and skills for problem management'.

One basic difference that is often suggested is that psychotherapy works with individuals in regressed states (that is, in their Child ego-states) in order to help them work through archaic emotional issues. Counselling, on the other hand, usually works with people in the here and now to help them problem-solve current issues in their lives.

However, the core framework of TA theory and contractual practice that we are going to discuss in this chapter is the same in TA psychotherapy as it is in TA counselling. For that reason, in the remainder of this chapter, we shall use the word 'therapy' as a shorthand for 'therapy and counselling'. Our purpose in doing so is simply to avoid unnecessary repetition, not to discount the differences between the two fields.

Self-therapy

If you have read this book and worked through the exercises, you have already done a great deal of *self-therapy*. You have examined the typical patterns of your own behaviour, feelings and thinking. To help understand these, you have learned to use the many analytical devices that TA offers. You have recognized the outdated Child strategies that you now realize are not the most effective options for you as a grown-up, and you have tested active ways of replacing these with new and more successful options.

Some TA writers have given special attention to developing ways in which TA can be used in self-therapy. Notable among these is Muriel James. She won the Eric Berne Memorial Scientific Award for her work on *self-reparenting*.[2] This is a system by which the person can build a 'new Parent', providing positive new messages to overcome the negative, restrictive messages that may have been given by the actual parents. It employs a combination of techniques, including questionnaires, contract-making, fantasy and visualization, and behavioural change assignments.

In a sense, all therapy is self-therapy. TA recognizes that everyone is responsible for his own behaviour, thoughts and feelings. Just as nobody can make you feel, so nobody can make you change. The only person who can change you is you.

Why therapy?

So, given that people are responsible for their own change, what is the point of working with a therapist?

One way to answer this question is in terms of *discounting* and the *frame of reference*. We all have some investment in blanking out aspects of reality that would threaten the picture of the world we put together in childhood. Any time I get into script in adulthood, I will be discounting to defend my frame of reference. If I am to solve problems and change effectively, I need to become aware of the aspects of reality I have been discounting.

But that's where the catch comes. By the very fact that I am discounting them, these features of reality are 'blind spots' for me. I *may* be able to detect and correct my discounting by my own Adult effort. TA's armoury of analytical tools can help me greatly in this.

However, there are likely to be some parts of my frame of reference that I see in Child as being particularly important to my survival. These I will defend with especial energy. I will do this outside of awareness, by maintaining blind spots on any perceptions of reality that would confront these crucial discounts. In order to change in these areas, I need input from someone else who does not have the same blind spots.

Friends and family members are not likely to be the best source of this input. Families typically have blind spots that all the members of the family are brought up to share. I am also likely to select my friends, and my spouse or partner, because they have blind spots in common with my own. One purpose of working with a therapist, or of joining a therapy group, is that it gives me a source of feedback that is not subject to my own blind spots.

If I go on to use this feedback and begin altering my frame of reference, I am likely to begin feeling scared in Child. To see me through the change, I may need support and protection. I may also benefit from further confrontation as I employ all kinds of diverting tactics outside of my awareness as ways of defending against change. I will find it easier to make the change, and establish it as permanent, if I get strokes and encouragement from others. All of these benefits I can get from working with a therapist or group.

Who can benefit from therapy?

There's a TA saying: 'You don't need to be sick in order to get better.' You do not have to be disabled, disadvantaged or disturbed to get benefit from therapy. In fact, you do not even need to 'have problems'. You can be a well-functioning, fulfilled person, and enter therapy simply to get even more of what you want from life. Nobody is one hundred per cent script-free, no matter how lucky they were with their parents. For most of us, there are some areas of life where we have been setting up problems for ourselves by getting into script. If so, we may find it worth the time, money and commitment involved in going into therapy to resolve these script issues.

This said, TA therapy may also be sought by anyone who is experiencing personal problems, ranging from temporary relationship or work difficulties to severe mental disturbance. Treatment of the more serious disorders requires an appropriate setting, sometimes with psychiatric support.

Characteristics of TA therapy

If you decide to go into TA therapy, your first step is to find a qualified therapist and contract to attend for a certain number of sessions. These may be individual consultations, or you may become a member of a group. TA was originated by Berne as a method of group therapy, and most TA therapists still favour group treatment as the setting of choice.

In earlier chapters, you have already learned the main characteristics of TA therapy. Let's review these.

The practice of therapy in TA is founded upon a coherent *theoretical framework*, which you have learned in this book. You know that the main building-blocks of this theory are the *ego-state model* and the concept of *life-script*.

Personal change is seen in terms of a *decisional model*. In Part IV, you met TA's account of how each of us decides in childhood upon script patterns of behaving, thinking and feeling. A premise of all TA therapy is that that these early decisions can be changed.

You learned in Chapter 26 how TA treatment is based on a *contractual method*. The client and therapist take *joint responsibility* for achieving contract goals. These goals are chosen to promote movement out of script and into *autonomy*, in the way described in Chapter 27.

The therapeutic relationship in TA rests on the assumption that *people are OK*. The client and therapist are viewed as being on a level with each other, neither one-up nor one-down.

Open communication is fostered. Therapist and client speak a common language, using the simple words you have met in this book. The client is encouraged to learn about TA. Therapists will often ask their clients to attend introductory courses or read books on TA such as this one. If the therapist takes case notes, these are open to the client's inspection. In all these ways, the client is empowered to take an active and informed part in the treatment process.

An additional feature of TA therapy is that it is oriented to *change*, rather than simply to the achievement of insight. Certainly, TA lays stress on understanding the nature and sources of problems. But this understanding is never viewed as an end in itself. Instead, it is a tool to use in the active process of change. The change itself consists in making a decision to act differently, then going ahead and doing so.

With this orientation, TA practitioners have never attached value to long-drawn-out therapy for its own sake. It's not expected that a client must necessarily take months and years of on-going work to achieve insight before he can change. Berne underlined this in a famous recommendation to clients: 'Get well first, and we'll analyse it later if you still want to.'

At the same time, TA is not solely a 'brief-therapy' approach. For the resolution of some problems, a long-term relationship needs to be set up between client and therapist, and this also can be done within a TA framework.

Three schools of TA

It's usual to distinguish three main '*schools*' within TA. Each of these has its own distinctive theoretical emphasis and its preferred range of therapeutic techniques. These three schools – the classical, redecision and Cathexis – trace their origins back to the earliest years of TA, and had become clearly distinct from one another by the 1970s.[3] Because of this long ancestry, these three styles of TA are often known as 'traditional schools'.

TA has of course continued to develop since these three traditional schools were first described. Today there are several other well-recognized approaches to TA that are widely agreed to fall outside the boundaries of any of the three schools. One of these newer arrivals – the relational approach – began to emerge in the late 1990s and has since attracted particular attention. We shall describe it below.

Few individual TA therapists nowadays belong exclusively to any one of the three 'schools'. In fact, in order to gain professional accreditation, the therapist must demonstrate the ability to draw freely on the thinking and techniques of all current TA schools and approaches. The following 'thumbnail sketches' bring out the central features of each traditional school, deliberately making them seem more sharply distinct than they really are.

The classical school

The classical school is so called because it follows most closely the approach to treatment developed in TA's early days by Berne and his associates. Classical practitioners use a whole range of analytical models to facilitate Adult understanding and at the same time 'hook' Child motivation. You learned many of these devices in the earlier chapters of this book: the Drama Triangle, the egogram, the stroking profile, Options, etc.

Thus in the classical approach, the first step is for the client to develop understanding of how he has been setting up problems. He then contracts to make behavioural changes that will mark movements out of his old scripty patterns and into autonomy. It is recognized that as the client changes his behaviour, he is likely also to begin feeling differently, but encouragement to express feelings is not itself a central focus of classical TA.

Group treatment is strongly favoured by the classical school. The *group process* is viewed as centrally important. This means that the client's interactions with other group members are assumed to be a re-play of the problem the client has brought to therapy, which in turn is a re-play of problem situations left unresolved in childhood. The therapist's role is to allow the group process to develop, then feed in interventions that help the group members become aware of the games, racketeering and other scripty patterns they have been exhibiting in their relationships with other members and with the therapist.

In the view of the classical school, an important function of the therapist is to give the client new Parental messages. Pat Crossman and Claude Steiner have suggested 'three P's' that the therapist must provide in order to do this effectively: *permission, protection* and *potency.*[4]

In giving *permission*, the therapist gives the client messages that actively contradict injunctions or negative counterinjunctions in the script. These may be delivered verbally, as for example: 'It's OK for you to feel what you feel! – because everyone is entitled to feel their feelings,' or 'Stop working so hard! – because you are likely to affect your health.' They are a combination of a Parent directive followed by Adult information. This is called the '*Permission Transaction.*' Permissions may also be modelled by the therapist.

If he is to accept the therapist's permission, the client in Child must perceive the therapist in Parent as being more powerful – having greater *potency* – than the actual parent from whom the original negative messages came. The client must also see the therapist as being able to provide *protection* against the disastrous consequences he fears may result from disobeying his parents' negative commands.

The redecision school

Bob and Mary Goulding are the originators of a therapeutic approach that combines the theory of TA with the techniques of gestalt therapy, developed by Frederick (Fritz) Perls. The Gouldings point out that early decisions are made from a feeling rather than a thinking position. Therefore, in order to move out of script, the person must re-contact the Child feelings he experienced at the time of the early decision, finish the business by expressing those feelings, and change the early decision for a new and more appropriate *redecision*. This may be accomplished through fantasy or dreamwork, or by 'early scene work', in which the client tracks back in recollection to an early traumatic scene and re-experiences it.

Bob and Mary Goulding follow Perls in believing that when someone is 'stuck' with a problem, this indicates that two parts of their personality are pushing in opposite directions with equal force. The net result is that the person is using a great deal of energy, but getting nowhere. This situation is called an *impasse*. The Gouldings elaborated Perls' theory by picturing impasses as occurring between different ego-states. In therapy, impasse resolution is usually carried out using the gestalt technique known as 'two-chair work'. The client imagines the conflicting parts of himself in different chairs, 'becomes' each part in turn, and carries on a dialogue with the object of resolving the conflict. During this process, suppressed Child feelings may often be brought to the surface.

Even more than TA practitioners generally, redecision therapists emphasize personal responsibility. In redecision work, the therapeutic contract is not viewed as a two-sided agreement between client and therapist; it is a commitment made by the client to himself, with the therapist as witness. The therapist does not 'give the client permissions'. The client *takes* permission to behave and feel in new ways, with the therapist acting as a positive model. Likewise, *potency* is seen as a resource that the client already has, rather than being provided by the therapist.

Redecision therapists frequently work with groups, but they do not focus on group process. Instead, therapy is done one-to-one, with the rest of the group acting as witnesses and providing positive strokes to encourage and reinforce change.

While the expression of feeling is central to redecision work, therapists in this school stress that it is also important for the client to understand what is going on. Typically, the feeling work will be followed immediately by an 'Adult de-brief'. Equally important is for the client to make a contract for behavioural change to practise and consolidate his new decisions.

The Cathexis school

In Part V, we met the important contributions to TA theory made by the Cathexis school. The Schiffs originally founded the Cathexis Institute as a centre for the treatment of psychotic clients. They used an approach which they called *reparenting*. It is based on the premise that 'craziness' is the result of destructive, inconsistent Parental messages. In treatment, the client is first helped to get into an OK place in his Adult in relationship with the therapist, who contracts with him to support him in his regression. Then he is encouraged to regress to early infancy to a time before he experienced a problem. The Schiffs state that this fundamental degree of regression is achievable only by psychotic clients. The client may also be asked to *decathect* his 'crazy Parent' ego-state, i.e. to withdraw all energy from it – another process, say the Schiffs, that is only possible for psychotic clients.

The client is then literally given the chance to re-do his growing up, this time with the therapist providing positive and consistent Parent input. Luckily, this second time of growing up proceeds much more quickly than the first time around. Even so, reparenting means that the fully-grown 'infant' will be heavily dependent for some time on his new 'mother' and 'father'. This style of treatment, then, requires a secure setting and a high degree of commitment on the part of the therapist, as well as psychiatric back-up. In the early days of Cathexis, the Schiffs legally adopted their 'children', so that there is now a widespread 'Schiff family'. Among them are counted some of the most respected theorists, therapists and teachers in present-day TA.

The Schiffian method has also proven effective in therapy with non-psychotic clients. The emphasis here is on the consistent confronting of discounts and redefinitions. Instead of being passive, people are urged to think and act in order to solve problems. The intense therapeutic commitment of reparenting is not appropriate in work with non-psychotic clients. However, the Schiffian therapist may enter into a *parenting* contract with such clients. The therapist contracts to be consistently available to the client, within specified time boundaries, and serve as a 'replacement parent', giving the client new and positive Parental definitions in place of the restrictive messages that may have been received from the actual parents.

When Schiffian therapy is done in groups, the group is seen as providing a *reactive environment* from a caring position. This means that all the members of the group, including the therapist, are expected to respond actively to the actions of other members. If you do something in the group that I don't like, I am expected to tell you: 'I don't like what you just did. I want you to do (x) instead.' If anyone in the group gets into passive behaviour or discounting, the other group members are expected to confront this immediately, and call for active problem-solving. Here, 'confronting' does not mean Persecuting. It implies a straight demand on the other person, made from an I+U+ position. The person who makes the confrontation does so with the genuine motive of looking after herself *and* of helping the other person. Shea Schiff has used the phrase 'caring confrontation' to convey this idea.

The relational approach

The ideas of the relational approach have largely been articulated in the writing of Helena Hargaden and Charlotte Sills, who were awarded the Eric Berne Memorial Award in 2007 for this work.[5]

In line with the name given to this approach, its practitioners start from the proposition that the relationship between therapist and client is the most important factor in promoting personal change. There is, of course, a relationship between client and therapist in *all* the approaches to TA therapy, always based on the core principle that 'everyone is OK'. The relational approach, however, lays especial stress on the idea that unconscious processes are continually at play in the therapeutic relationship. The task of the relational therapist is to remain open to her own responses to the client as the unconscious dialogue between them develops. Moment by moment, client and therapist are seen as *co-creating* whatever happens in the process of the therapy. The therapist, as well as the client, is likely to undergo change as therapy progresses.

Congruently with this approach, relational practitioners downplay the highly specific contracts that typify the three traditional schools of TA. The contract is seen as emerging from one moment to the next, along with all the other content of the therapy session.

Relational therapists also minimize the use of explicit 'techniques' to promote change – here again, marking off a distinct difference between the relational style and the more traditional approaches in TA. In relational work it is assumed that therapeutic change occurs principally at an unconscious level, and will materialize of itself as the unconscious issues arising in the relationship are worked out between client and therapist.

Because of the close focus on the unique interpersonal relationship between therapist and client, relational TA usually employs one-to-one therapy rather than group sessions.

The model of ego-states is central to the theory of relational TA, as it is to the theory of all TA approaches. In accord with the emphasis that relational therapists place on early developmental issues, their preferred version of the model is drawn up to portray how the 'self', the infant's sense of identity, develops through the interaction between the infant and the caregiver. This is in line with the relational presupposition that the crux of change lies in the emerging relationship between client and therapist.

In some ways, the theory and practice of the relational approach resemble those of traditional psychoanalysis. This similarity is recognized and welcomed by many relational practitioners. It is reflected in the fact that relational writers often choose to describe their work in formal psychoanalytic language, rather than in the colloquial language preferred by Eric Berne.

Beyond the 'three schools'

Several other major developments in today's TA, all of them already described in this book, also lie outside the boundaries of any of the 'three schools'. Examples are Erskine and Zalcman's Racket System, Kahler's work on drivers, and the studies of personality adaptations by Ware, Kahler and Joines. Each of these theoretical models has generated its own distinctive therapeutic approach.

One of TA's most positive features has been its ability to incorporate ideas and techniques from other therapies. These have proven readily compatible with the theoretical foundations of TA. The result is that the modern-day TA therapist possesses a large, adaptable 'tool-kit' of techniques she can draw upon according to the client's needs. Most TA practitioners have also trained in other modalities, and bring these into their TA work. We have already spoken of the TA-gestalt combination used in redecision therapy. TA therapists may also use concepts and techniques drawn from psychoanalytic and brief-therapy approaches, bioenergetics, neuro-linguistic programming, systems theory, visualization and self-image modification techniques, Ericksonian therapy, behavioural psychology, developmental theory, and numerous other fields, according to the practitioner's background and interests. Always, the ego-state model and the theory of life-script act as organizing principles, guiding the use of these varied techniques within a TA framework.

Chapter 29
TA IN EDUCATION AND ORGANIZATIONS

From the earliest days of Eric Berne's development of TA, he regarded it as 'a theory of social action' rather than simply a theory of therapy or counselling. He saw that TA could be used in diverse fields of activity as a method of working with individuals or groups. TA can enhance effectiveness in almost any human endeavour where people are dealing with other people.

TA is employed in a great diversity of educational and organizational settings. The theory and practice of TA can be useful to teachers, trainers, students, educational and management consultants, coaches, managers, employees, parents and children. Each of these applications has its own individual characteristics and needs. In this chapter, we give only a brief overview of these uses of TA. The list of References for this chapter will give you a guide to the literature in this field.

Some current writers use the term *developmental TA* as a cover-all name for the entire wide range of applications we have just described.[1] In this chapter we shall stay with the more traditional terms 'educational and organizational', since these are still the titles that are used by the international TA associations in accrediting practitioners.

Main features of educational and organizational applications

The basic theory of TA is the same for educational and organizational (EO) work as for therapy and counselling, but there are differences in approach and in techniques.[2] The training and accreditation of TA practitioners takes account of these differences (see Appendix E).

In therapy and counselling, the *contract* is usually two-handed, being negotiated between the therapist and the individual client. By contrast, contracts in EO settings are most often multi-handed. The business contract will be negotiated between the practitioner and the sponsoring agency, for the benefit of the members of the agency. For example, a business firm may hire a TA trainer to work with their employees. It is then the task of the trainer to negotiate treatment contracts with *all* the parties involved: in this case, the paying agency, and the individuals or groups with whom the practitioner is actually working.

This implies that the practitioner must be particularly careful to negotiate clear, above-board contract procedures, in order to avoid multi-handed game-playing. For example, a business firm may assign employees to a TA training course even though the employees themselves have no initial motivation to attend. Unless this starting-point is made overt in the contract negotiations between the firm, the trainer and the group members, there are immediate possibilities for some or all of the parties to take up Drama Triangle roles, with subsequent game switches.

In organizational work, the TA practitioner typically operates as a facilitator, trainer or coach. The practitioner in educational TA may typically be a teacher, headteacher or a specialist in areas such as behaviour support and SEN (special educational needs).

The EO practitioner will usually invite his clients to address what is going on at the *social level*, rather than the *psychological level*. Needless to say, the practitioner himself needs to be keenly aware of the 'Martian' messages that underlie what is happening at social level, and will base his treatment strategies on them. It would not be possible to do effective TA otherwise. However, in many EO work settings it may not be appropriate for him to bring these psychological-level messages explicitly to his clients' awareness.

In EO work, then, the practitioner will most often focus on how the individual or group can most effectively solve problems by thinking and acting in the present, rather than exploring what past business a person may need to finish. When ego-state diagnosis is used, it will tend to be behavioural and social, rather than historical or phenomenological. The practitioner may teach his group members the concept of life-script, as a way of explaining why people may act in ways that appear self-defeating or painful. But individual script analysis will seldom be used.

That having been said, any work that entails personal or organizational change – even if conducted at social level – always has the potential to impact the individual's script. For that reason, the EO practitioner needs to be highly skilled in establishing contracts and managing boundaries so as to provide the *protection* that is required to ensure that script changes are made safely.

In the sections that follow, we review some of the ways in which TA concepts can be applied in organizational and educational settings.

Organizational applications [3]

The Training and Certification Council (T&CC) describe the *organizational* field of TA as follows:

'The Organizations field of specialization is for practitioners who work in or for organizations, taking into account organizational frames of reference and contexts as well as the organization's development. Their work is aimed at the development, growth and increased effectiveness of people working within organizations. Transactional Analysis is a powerful tool in the hands of organizational development specialists. Through presenting the basic concepts of transactional analysis and using it as the basic theory to undergird the objectives of their clients, organizational development specialists build a common strategy with which to address the particular needs of organizations and to build a functional relationship, as well as eliminate dysfunctional organizational behaviours.'

Objectives of change in organizational TA

In organizational TA – as in TA therapy and counselling – the fundamental goal of change is *autonomy*. Julie Hay, organizational TA practitioner and trainer, writes: 'We [in organizational TA] contract that our intention is that people within an organization will become more autonomous, more here-and-now – and in that way the organization gains psychologically healthier employees'.[4]

Ego-states

Organizations do not themselves have ego-states, but they do have elements that function in an analogous way. They have patterns of beliefs, etiquette and rules that correspond to the Parent ego-state. They have technologies and problem-solving strategies that are analogous to the Adult. And they have patterns of behaviour and feelings that parallel the Child ego-state. The organizational analyst can examine the amount of energy that the organization devotes to each of these three elements, in the same way as the therapist examines the distribution of cathexis among a person's ego-states.

On a more obvious level, communication and interactions between individuals in an organization can be enhanced by knowledge of the ego-state model. Managers, for instance, may realize they are taking up a negative Parental stance, while their employees respond from a negative Adapted Child by being rebellious or overly compliant. To improve effectiveness, both managers and employees might take action to raise their use of Adult. Free Child, hence job satisfaction, might be encouraged by such means as making the workplace brighter and more comfortable.

Transactions, strokes, time structuring

The analysis of *transactions* has been widely applied in training personnel who are in direct contact with the public, e.g. receptionists and booking clerks. They learn how to keep the flow of communication smooth and comfortable by maintaining parallel transactions, or how to thwart a potential Parent-Child argument by crossing a transaction.

The analysis of *stroking* patterns has obvious application in enhancing job motivation. Managers may need to learn to give positive strokes for jobs done well, rather than giving only negatives for jobs done badly. The principle of 'different strokes for different folks' applies: while you may get your greatest satisfaction from the praise of respected superiors, I may prefer to get my strokes through the offer of a bigger wage-packet or longer holidays.

When *time structuring* at meetings is examined, it may sometimes turn out that these gatherings consist of much pastiming and little activity. As for *games*, they probably account for the greatest waste of time and human resources in organizations. Game playing rises in organizations where stress levels are high, for example when individuals feel bored, not recognized or not sufficiently challenged within the organization. Changing stroking patterns and increasing the opportunities for positive challenge can do wonders to reduce game-playing and open the way to enhanced creativity and teamwork. TA procedures of *contract-making* can also help direct organizational energy into constructive action rather than the pursuit of hidden agendas.

Confronting passivity

Schiffian concepts have proven widely useful in organizational applications. The *Discount Matrix* provides a means of systematic problem-solving. It is particularly useful in situations where information and instructions are 'passed down the line', with the accompanying tendency for details to get lost or distorted on the way. An awareness of verbal discounts, tangential and blocking transactions can enhance communication and improve the effectiveness of meetings.

Personality adaptations [5]

A knowledge of personality adaptations gives the organizational practitioner or manager a valuable aid to recruitment and team-building. Each team member can be allocated to a position where the main strengths of her or his personality style are brought into play. An understanding of personality adaptations means also that each individual's typical failure patterns can be forestalled and their success patterns encouraged.

TA in education [6]

Here is the description that the Training and Certification Council suggests for the *educational* field of application in TA:

'The Education field of specialization is for practitioners who work in the area of learning and study in pre-school, school, university and post-university contexts or for the support of child, adolescent and adult learners within the family, the institution or society. The work may be applied to the development of teaching teams and institutions. The aim is to further personal and professional growth, both scholastic and social. TA can be used as a practical educational psychology that offers a way of transforming educational philosophy and principles into everyday practice. Educational TA is both preventive and restorative. The aim is to increase personal autonomy, to support people in developing their own personal and professional philosophies and to enable optimum psychological health and growth.'

Objectives of change in educational TA

Autonomy implies clear thinking and effective problem-solving. The educator aims to help her students develop these abilities. Therefore, autonomy as an overall goal is as relevant in educational settings as it is in all the other fields of TA. Trudi Newton, educational practitioner and trainer, expresses the philosophy of educational TA as follows:

'...real education is much more than teaching children in school; it is a continuing, observable, communal process that everyone can choose to be aware of and decide to engage in. Berne recognized this. He was one of the first psychiatrists to begin from the visible evidence of people's observable behaviour, to read from that what they believe about themselves and others, and to teach them to do that for themselves. Those beliefs are formed by education in its broadest sense, that is, by the way a society talks to itself. TA is a great tool for analysing and exploring this social phenomenon because to this day transactional analysis has maintained this "out there" quality. ... We in transactional analysis still have an exciting story to tell, and we are all storytellers engaged in interpreting the world through metaphor and creativity.'[7]

By the nature of educational settings, it is especially likely that the students may 'put a face on' the teacher, and that she in turn may buy into these replays of the past by taking on a Parental role. The educational transactional analyst uses her knowledge of TA models to help avoid this gamey situation. Instead, she invites an OK-OK relationship with her students or trainees.

TA theories of child development can guide the educator in dealing effectively with young people at various developmental stages. The work of the TA educator and writer Jean Illsley Clarke, in particular, is seen by many practitioners as being central to the current theory and practice of educational TA.[8]

Ego-states

The basic ego-state model is readily understood by children from early school age on. TA's simple language helps in this learning. By examining the content and motivations in all three of their ego-states, students become better able to learn with a clear knowledge of their own intentions and desires. Learning experiences themselves are most likely to be effective if they appeal to all three ego-states. It is especially important to recognize that the Free Child is the source of creativity and energy in the personality and needs to be included in the learning process.

The educator himself needs to have free access to all his ego-states. For much of the time, he will be demonstrating Adult problem-solving. Often he will need to set firm boundaries from positive Controlling Parent, or to show caring from positive Nurturing Parent. He can get into Child to model spontaneity, intuitive ability, creativity and the enjoyment of learning.

Transactions, strokes, time structuring

The analysis of transactions is useful in keeping communication between teachers and students clear, productive and free of hidden agendas. Using *Options* can help both teachers and students to break out of 'locked' Parent-Child interactions.

Attention to patterns of *stroking* and *time structuring* is relevant to education in much the same way as to organizational work. The classroom and lecture-hall are especially rich breeding-grounds for *games* and *racketeering*. Students may play games such as Stupid, You Can't Make Me, or Do Me Something (with its potential Switch into See What You Made Me Do). Teachers can play See How Hard I've Tried, I'm Only Trying To Help You, Why Don't You..., or Blemish. A knowledge of game analysis enables students and teachers to create an environment in which learning is enhanced while games and racketeering are kept to a minimum.

The use of *contract-making* helps educators and learners to reach clear, overt agreement about what they are each there to do and how best they can do it.

Confronting passivity

In educational settings, it is especially likely that people may be expecting *symbiosis*. This expectation may even be overt in some cultures, where teachers are traditionally pictured as playing the Parent and Adult role while the student plays Child. Current approaches to education agree with TA in viewing this as a discount of the abilities of both parties.

A knowledge of Schiffian concepts helps teachers and students to stay out of symbiosis and make full use of all their ego-states. Educators can learn to recognize the four *passive behaviours* and confront them instead of buying into games. If the institutional setting makes it possible, tutorial groups and classes may be set up to provide a reactive environment where teachers and students take mutual responsibility to promote clear thinking and active problem-solving.

Personality adaptations

A knowledge of personality adaptations helps educators to make and maintain effective rapport with their students or trainees. In educational as in organizational work, each individual's likely failure patterns can be forestalled and their success patterns encouraged. The Ware Sequence is itself a model of learning styles. When communicating with individual students, the educator can use each student's appropriate contact area; when presenting to groups, the teacher or trainer can ensure that her teaching methods address all three areas in approximately equal measure.

Chapter 30
HOW TA HAS DEVELOPED

At press date for this book's second edition, it is 55 years since Eric Berne delivered the first professional paper to bear the title 'Transactional Analysis'. TA as a recognized discipline thus traces its origins back more than half a century.

Of those 55 years, over three-quarters have gone by since Berne's early death in 1970. During the whole of that time, TA has continued to expand and develop. While Berne is universally recognized as the founder of the discipline, other path-breaking writers and practitioners have built upon his ideas and contributed new ideas of their own. TA today is the work of many hands.

In this chapter, we first trace Eric Berne's life and the origins of his thinking in the 1950s and earlier. The decade following that 1957 paper saw a phase of early development, in the fertile minds of a handful of TA professionals centred on America's West Coast. The publication of Berne's best-selling *Games People Play*, in 1964, catapulted TA into the public eye and marked the beginning of a period of mass popularity that reached its peak in the mid-1970s. At the same time, in the ten years or so following Berne's death, TA professionals were continuing to make important contributions to both theory and practice.

The years from the 1980s until the present have seen a period of consolidation and expansion. Theory and practice have been further refined and developed. Perhaps the most striking feature of all has been the worldwide spread of interest and professional activity in TA. From its 1950s origins in a small seminar group on the West Coast of the USA, TA has expanded so that there are now active TA associations in 52 countries throughout the world. The TA community today is truly international.

Eric Berne and the origins of TA

Eric Berne[1] was born Eric Lennard Bernstein in Montreal in 1910. His father was a general practitioner and his mother a professional writer. His early years were happy, and he especially enjoyed accompanying his father on his medical rounds. Then, when Eric was only nine, his father died. His loss affected the little boy deeply, and this may have been a major influence in Berne's later development.

Encouraged by his ambitious mother, Berne went on to enter medical school, and qualified as a doctor in 1935. Shortly afterwards he moved to America and began psychiatric residency. He became an American citizen and changed his name to Eric Berne.

In 1941 he began training as a psychoanalyst, becoming an analysand of Paul Federn. This was interrupted by the outbreak of World War II, and Berne joined the Army Medical Corps in 1943 as a psychiatrist. During this period of service, he began practising group therapy. He had already started compiling critical notes on psychiatry and psychoanalysis which were to form the basis for his later writings.

Following his release from the Army in 1946, Berne resumed his psychoanalytic training, this time under Erik Erikson. He began the regime of hard work that marked the rest of his life, combining a private practice with several official appointments and a crowded schedule of writing commitments. His first book, *The Mind in Action*, was published in 1947; it was to be revised in 1957 as *A Layman's Guide to Psychiatry and Psychoanalysis.*[2]

In 1949, Berne published the first of six professional journal articles concerning the nature of intuition. Appearing from that year until 1958, these were to present the emerging ideas on which Berne founded his development of TA.

All this time, Berne had continued training in psychoanalysis. In 1956 he applied for membership of his professional psychoanalytic institute, but was turned down. No one really knows why. Some have speculated that it was because he was too much of a maverick, doing things his own way.

Spurred on by this rejection, Berne resolved to go ahead by himself and construct a new approach to psychotherapy. By the end of that year, he had completed two more in his series of papers on intuition, in which he first presented his concept of Parent, Adult and Child ego-states and used the term 'structural analysis'. These articles were published in 1957. Berne went on to write a further paper, which he presented to the American Group Psychotherapy Association in November 1957. It was entitled 'Transactional Analysis: A New and Effective Method of Group Therapy'.

In this article, which appeared in print the following year, Berne restated his concepts of Parent, Adult and Child ego-states, and introduced the notions of games and script. Thus the basic framework of TA theory was already complete.

What kind of man was Berne? At the recent Centennial Conference in Montreal, Canada (August 2010), his children said he was a very loving and involved father. Different people who knew him have different memories of his complex personality. Some say he was genial, supportive, fun-loving. Others recall him as sharp-tongued, competitive and personally distant.[3] What is certain is that he was a clear thinker, and demanded clear thinking in others. This quality has come down to us in the coherent structure of TA theory.

Throughout his career, Berne kept up a keen interest in the function of intuition. As well as providing the impetus to Berne's original formulation of TA concepts, this focus on intuition was reflected in the emphasis he placed on 'thinking Martian': understanding covert as well as overt messages.

Berne was an individualist, even a rebel. We can only guess whether his rejection by the psychoanalytic establishment was genuinely the spur for his development of TA. But he did succeed in originating a method of psychotherapy that 'broke the rules' of the establishment, as Berne saw them at the time. His ideal was to cure people quickly, rather than having them 'make progress' during years of therapy. He determined that TA should speak the language of the layman, instead of cloaking itself in Latin and Greek, so that client and therapist could more readily co-operate in the process of cure.

Paradoxically, some of Berne's most deeply felt ideals sprang directly from a medical background. Perhaps this reflected not only his own medical training, but also his memories of a happy childhood spent with his father. When Berne wrote *Transactional Analysis in Psychotherapy*, he gave it a Latin dedication: 'To the memory of my father David, Doctor of Medicine and Master of Surgery, and doctor to the poor'.

To Berne, the effective therapist had to be a 'real doctor'. Berne was not suggesting that only medically qualified persons should become therapists. On the contrary, he meant that *any* therapist had to accept the responsibilities expected of a medical doctor. The 'real doctor', said Berne, is always oriented first and foremost towards curing his patients. He must plan his treatment so that at each phase he knows what he is doing and why he is doing it. These qualities are still demanded today in the accreditation of TA practitioners.

The early years

Since the early 1950s, Berne and his associates had been holding regular clinical seminars.[4] In 1958 they formed the San Francisco Social Psychiatry Seminars (SFSPS), meeting each Tuesday at Berne's home.

In those early years, the San Francisco seminars provided a fertile breeding-ground for the emerging ideas of TA. Berne's *Transactional Analysis in Psychotherapy*, the first book entirely devoted to TA, appeared in 1961. It was followed in 1963 by *The Structure and Dynamics of Organizations and Groups*. The *Transactional Analysis Bulletin* began publication in January 1962, with Berne as Editor.

The membership of the SFSPS included many who are now well-known figures in the 'Classical school' of TA, such as Claude Steiner,

Jack Dusay and Steve Karpman.

Also among the participants in the early seminar meetings was Jacqui Lee Schiff. In addition, Bob Goulding entered clinical supervision with Berne in the early 1960s. Thus were sown the seeds of development of the other two main 'schools' of current TA, which we described in Chapter 28.

In 1964, Berne and his colleagues decided to form the International Transactional Analysis Association (ITAA) in recognition of the fact that TA was now being practised by a growing number of professionals outside the USA. At the same time, the name of the San Francisco seminar was changed to the San Francisco Transactional Analysis Seminar (SFTAS).

The impact of *Games People Play*

The year 1964 also saw what was to be a landmark in TA's history: the publication of *Games People Play*. Berne had intended the book to be a reader for a relatively small circle of professionals. Instead, it became a best-seller. As its sales boomed worldwide, so the language and ideas of TA caught the imagination of a mass audience. Berne's book was serialized in mass-circulation magazines, chosen as Book of the Month, and eventually translated into fifteen languages. Berne became a public figure. TA terms like 'game', 'stroke' and 'OK' passed into everyday conversation, with or without an understanding of their original meaning. In this way, *Games People Play* carried Berne and his system of TA into the public eye in a manner quite unique in the history of psychotherapy. Millions of people, literally, got to hear of Berne and TA. Their knowledge of TA came either from reading *Games People Play* or from versions of it summarized in the media. The mass interest in TA that was sparked off at that time was to last well into the following decade.

But *Games People Play* had not been written for a mass audience. Its account of the general theory of TA was deliberately sketchy; Berne had originally expected his professional readers to have read his earlier work or to refer back to it for a fuller understanding. Thus what came through now to the general reader was the catchy language of 'game names' and the other plain-language terms that Berne used, without the depth of the theory that underlay these deliberately chosen colloquial titles. This oversimplification of theory was compounded still further in popular media coverage of TA, again based on a superficial reading of *Games People Play*.

One of the main casualties of this process was the ego-state model itself. In place of Berne's original version of the model, in which Parent and Child are both echoes of the past and only Adult is fully based in the present, most popular media stories featured the grossly oversimplified version that we described briefly in Chapter 2 – the one that says: 'Parent is values, oughts and shoulds, Adult is thinking, and Child is feelings.' Since the entire structure of TA theory is based on the ego-state model, this trivialization of the model made the whole of TA appear trivial.Tom Harris' best-selling book *I'm OK, You're OK,* published in 1967, unwittingly furthered that trend, because its account of 'TA theory' was based upon the 'values-thoughts-feelings' model.

The net result was that 'TA' became known to a huge audience worldwide – but in a version that was misrepresented and over-simplified. It was to be one of the main tasks for TA professionals, over the following two decades, to correct this distorted image and restore TA to its proper place as an established and respected approach in psychotherapy, counselling and the other helping professions.

Professionalism and the beginnings of international expansion

The commercial success of *Games People Play* did not produce an immediate explosion in the number of professionals using TA. The 1965 membership roll of ITAA contained a mere 279 names. However, these small numbers of practitioners continued a steady development of TA theory and practice. In 1965 the Schiffs, now based in the Eastern USA, began their work with psychotic clients. Berne's *Principles of Group Treatment* was published in 1966, and the same year saw the appearance of Steiner's seminal article on 'Script and Counterscript' in the *TA Bulletin*.

Active interest in TA outside the USA was already well under way. As early as 1964, a TA approach to group interaction was being taught in adult-education settings by Professor John Allaway of the University of Leicester, England.[5] However, the ITAA's 1965 membership roll still contained only a handful of names from outside the US

In 1968, the membership of ITAA had grown to more than 500, and Steve Karpman's Drama Triangle made its first public appearance in a *TA Bulletin* article.

All the while, Berne continued with his unremitting routine of hard work. By June 1970, he had completed the manuscripts of two books, *Sex in Human Loving* and *What Do You Say After You Say Hello?*. But he was never to see them in print. Late in June he suffered a heart attack and was rushed to hospital. Thought at first to be recovering, he had a second attack and died on July 15, 1970.

The 1970s: years of mass popularity and professional innovation

With hindsight, we can see two separate 'threads' in TA's history that ran through the 1970s and extended into the early 1980s. One was the expansion, peaking and subsequent contraction in the mass popularity of TA. The other was the continuing strength in the creative energy of TA professionals, who achieved innovations in theory and practice that still form the core of today's transactional analysis.

Berne's two final books, *Sex in Human Loving* and *What Do You Say After You Say Hello?,* were published posthumously in 1970 and 1972 respectively. In 1971, Muriel James and Dorothy Jongeward's best-selling *Born To Win* brought Berne's ideas together with the gestalt approach of Fritz Perls. (Unlike Tom Harris, James and Jongeward based their presentation of TA theory upon Eric Berne's original time-based definitions of ego-states.)

Thus the snowball of mass popularity continued to roll. ITAA's membership, which numbered around 1,000 in 1971, grew to over 5,000 by 1973. It continued to rise until it reached a peak of almost 11,000 in 1976.[6] As the worldwide surge of interest in TA got under way, non-US numbers grew with the rest, until in 1976 there were some 2,000 members from outside the US on the ITAA membership register.

To cater to the expanding interest in TA in European countries, the European Association for Transactional Analysis (EATA) was founded in 1974, and had its first congress in 1975. This was followed in 1976 by the first Pan-American Congress.

Meantime, all three 'schools' of TA were busy with further advances in theory and practice. The first issue of the *Transactional Analysis Journal*, in January 1971, was a memorial volume in honour of Berne. In that same issue, Aaron and Jacqui Schiff published their pathbreaking article on 'Passivity', and Steve Karpman presented his concept of 'Options'. Jack Dusay's original article on 'Egograms' appeared in the *TA Journal* in 1972. In the same year, Bob and Mary Goulding published the article which presented their ideas on redecision and injunctions, and the Schiffs founded the Cathexis Institute.

Taibi Kahler's work on drivers, first presented in a 1974 *TA Journal* article, represented a major new departure for TA. Kahler's ideas fell outside the framework of any of the main 'schools'. And though his work is firmly rooted in basic TA theory, it introduces some crucial concepts that Berne had never heard of by the time of his death in 1970.

If TA was conceived in Berne's early studies of intuition, and born with the presentation of his 1957 paper, it came of age in 1978. By that year the membership of the ITAA had fallen back to 8,000. The number continued to decline, though at a decreasing rate, for the rest of the decade.

The novelty value of TA as a media item had worn off, as it was bound to do. Yet this decline in popular interest is only a part of TA's history, and perhaps a rather unimportant part. More to the point is that TA by the late 1970s was finding maturity as a discipline, and regaining international acceptance as a professional approach. In this regard, it can have been no bad thing for TA to have lost the 'pop psychology' image it had acquired in some people's minds during the years of rapid expansion.

Two books appeared in 1977 which in many ways symbolized this change. Both were symposium volumes, aimed principally at a professional audience. *Transactional Analysis After Eric Berne*, edited by Graham Barnes, documented the major growth and developments in TA theory and practice that had taken place since Berne's death. Muriel James was editor of *Techniques in Transactional Analysis for Psychotherapists and Counselors*, focusing principally on the practical applications of TA in psychotherapy and counselling.

TA writers continued to add to the depth and breadth of TA thinking. To give just a few examples of the landmark advances that were made: 1975 saw the publication of the *Cathexis Reader,* the 'bible' for the theory and practice of the Cathexis school. The two source-books by Bob and Mary Goulding on redecision therapy, *The Power is in the Patient* and *Changing Lives Through Redecision Therapy,* appeared in 1978 and 1979 respectively. Richard Erskine and Marilyn Zalcman's Racket System was first presented in a 1979 *TA Journal* article.

Taibi Kahler, building on his earlier work on drivers, continued to develop the wide-ranging model of personality and communication that he titled his Process Model. He showed how it could be used effectively in the fields of management and communication as well as in counselling and psychotherapy. The concept of personality adaptations, which came to be incorporated in the Process Model, was developed by Kahler and by Paul Ware. These two professionals worked first separately, then subsequently together, with Ware publishing his definitive article on personality adaptations in 1983.

1980s to the present: international expansion and consolidation

It's interesting to think how the development of TA may have resembled the typical development of a person, from infancy to adulthood. In the first few months and years of a young child's life, developmental stages go past very quickly, and the change from one stage to the next is clear and striking. In later childhood and teenage, the person is still growing and developing, but change is not so radical as it was in infancy. Once having moved out of childhood and into adult life, the person continues to develop. But the tasks of that development are different from those of childhood, and the pace of change is slower. That said, as the grown-up person faces the challenges and realities of life, she gains a degree of maturity and experience that she did not have earlier. It is that third stage of TA's development that we explore in this closing section of the chapter.

TA theory: reconstruction, consolidation and diversity

In the long period from the 1980s to the present, TA theorists have been as busy and productive as ever. However, progress in TA theory has changed its style and direction. Instead of the single-minded drive to 'advance' that characterized the earlier development of the discipline, theory in this later period has tended to 'spread outwards'. What we mean is that writers have taken the existing, well-tried framework of theory that had been laid down by the early 1980s and have shown how it can be applied in detail to particular situations and client groups. Alongside this trend, other writers have taken existing core theory and reconsidered, reconstructed or extended it.

In this connection it is interesting to take a look at the topics for which the Eric Berne Memorial Award was given in the years from the mid-1980s onwards (see Appendix C). The first thing we notice is that in the nine years from 1985 through 1993, there were no fewer than eight years in which the EBMA was not awarded. It's almost as though TA theory 'paused' during these years before taking off in its new direction. The one article for which the Award was given during this time – to Carlo Moiso in 1987, for work published two years earlier – was a reformulation of the role of transference in TA, based on Vann Joines' earlier work on the different types of projection in games, and applied to a specific client group (narcissistic / borderline).

The three joint Awards in 1994 were all for advances in the application of TA to specific areas of therapeutic technique, including Joines' integration of personality adaptation theory with redecision therapy, developmental theory, and traditional diagnosis. In the years from then until the present, the EBMA has reflected the 'outward spread', the increased diversity, that we have already noted. The Award has been given, for example, for works on the application of TA in parent education, studies of social power, and the understanding of family systems. Another line of diversification has been in the integration of TA with other modalities and philosophies, such as self-psychology, narrative theory and constructionism.

There are two significant 'threads' of discourse that do run through the EBMA list from 1987 to the present. One is the study of transference and unconscious communication in TA; the other is the restoration of the original ego-state model. The first of these 'threads' began with the Award to Moiso in 1987. From then on it can be traced through the Awards to Erskine and Trautmann (in 1998, for their 1991 paper on transference), to Novellino (in 2003) and to Hargaden and Sills (in 2007). This line of thought, together with some of the work on constructionism and on early ego-state development, can be seen as the main source of the relational approach in TA, which we described in Chapter 28.

Turning now to the ego-state model: in what sense did it need to be 'restored'? The answer is that during the heady days of the 1970s, the over-simplified 'values-thoughts-feelings' model had gained wide currency. It had even crept into some professional writing on TA. Its intuitive 'simplicity' had made it popular in many general textbooks and training courses. We have already spelt out the unfortunate consequences of this for the credibility of TA theory.

Prominent among the writers who opened a critique of the over-simplified model and called for restoration of Berne's original version were Erskine and Trautmann, writing in the *TA Journal* in 1981 and again in 1988. This was part of the work for which they gained the 1998 EBMA. Another clearly-stated argument in favour of Berne's original model was presented in an article by Hohmuth and Gormly that appeared in the *TAJ* in 1982 (though this work did not earn its writers the EBMA).[7]

When we (authors) wrote the first edition of *TA Today*, published in 1987, our main purpose was to offer a basic textbook on TA that was founded 'from the ground up' on Berne's original time-based model of ego-states, rather than on some simplified version. Thanks to these combined efforts, Berne's original model has by now been firmly restored to its place at the heart of TA theory.

Some further elaborations of the ego-state model, focusing particularly on developmental aspects, have also figured in the EBMA list since the 1980s. Awards in this area have been given for articles by Blackstone (in 1995) and Cornell (in 2010). Work in this field, along with the material on transference, feeds into the current interest in the relational approach in TA.

International expansion and the role of the ITAA

The international spread of interest in TA, which had already begun in the 1970s, has continued unabated from the 1980s to the present. First to emerge was a strong rise in the use of TA in the countries of Western Europe. Then in 1989, sweeping political changes in Eastern Europe – symbolized by the fall of the Berlin Wall and a new climate of 'openness' – cleared the way for a new upsurge of enthusiastic activity in TA in the previous Soviet-bloc countries. By 1991, the membership of EATA had risen to over 4,000. A relatively large proportion of these were professionals.

Meantime in 1987, a group of ITAA visitors had given the first 'TA 101' basic course in the People's Republic of China.[8] Existing TA associations in Latin America, Japan, India and Australasia continued to expand.

This expansion in international interest faced the ITAA with a challenging situation. Despite its 'International' label, the ITAA had in the first years of its life been essentially a US organization, though with a substantial non-US membership. Now, almost 'despite itself', the ITAA was becoming truly international. TA professionals within the US had already responded to this changing situation when in 1982 they had founded the USA TA Association (USATAA).

The problem for the ITAA was that with the rising membership of national and regional TA associations throughout the world, its own membership roll was continually being eroded, while at the same time the tasks it was asked to perform on an international scale were continually expanding. Its first response, in the late 1980s, was to undertake an assertive programme of affiliation. EATA became affiliated to ITAA in 1989, and this was closely followed by the affiliation of the TA associations in Canada and India. This gave a welcome boost to ITAA's total membership numbers, which rose to some 7,000 in 1991. However, this number included the 4,000 or so members of EATA, confirming that the centre of global activity in TA had swung decisively away from the US and into Europe.

As it turned out, the affiliation programme did not hold. For various reasons of governance and finance, EATA and the other affiliated associations later chose to de-affiliate from ITAA. Thus the problem that we have just described for ITAA in the late 1990s is even more pressing today. The membership has declined from 6715 in 1995 to 1169 in 2010. We (the authors) believe that a thriving ITAA is a great asset to TA worldwide, and we think that most transactional analysts share this view. At press date for our second edition, ITAA has developed a new vision as a 'worldwide professional network for the development of transactional analysis theory and practice' and is in the process of creating a new structure to implement that vision in order to remain viable.[9]

If we turn from the problems of ITAA and look instead at the overall number of people around the world who belong to TA associations, a much rosier picture emerges. EATA alone has a current membership of over 7,500 members.[10] Add to that the numbers of people belonging to TA associations outside Europe, and the worldwide total must at least come close to the figure of some 11,000 ITAA members that marked the peak of mass popularity of TA in 1976. And, though we have no definite statistics to support it, our belief is that today's membership figures contain a much higher proportion of professional users of TA than did that earlier figure from 1976.

Professional and academic recognition

Earlier in the chapter we drew attention to the damage that was done to TA's professional image by the over-simplified versions that circulated in the media during the period of mass popularity in the decade from the late 1960s. We said that TA professionals had the task of correcting the distorted image of the discipline which had arisen during that period. At the time of this book's first edition in 1987, this corrective task seemed still very much 'work in progress'; in fact, one of our purposes in writing the book was to contribute to the project.

Now, 25 years on, it is fair to say that the task has been completed – or, at least, completed in so far as any approach to personal change can ever claim 'complete acceptance' in the professional community. In fact, the task was probably completed to all intents and purposes about ten years ago, by the early years of the 21st century. In the professional literature, TA now stands on an equal footing with other established modalities in countries other than the US. It is featured in compendium volumes and book series produced by internationally respected publishing houses in the fields of psychotherapy, counselling, education and organizational work.

Many TA training courses have gained university validation for academic awards ranging from postgraduate diploma through Bachelors' and Masters' degrees, and in some cases to Doctorate level. In some countries, TA training forms an integral part of university degree courses.

The past 25 years have seen an increasing trend for psychotherapy and counselling to be subjected to regulation, whether by governments or by professional bodies. The outcome for TA has differed from one country to another. The European Association for Psychotherapy (EAP) recognizes TA as an established modality, as do the UK Council for Psychotherapy and the British Association for Counselling and Psychotherapy.

The Centenary Conference

In August 2010, the major TA associations came together to organize a conference to commemorate the 100th anniversary of the birth of Eric Berne. The event was held in Montreal, Berne's birthplace. Your authors had the honour of being invited to give the opening keynote speech.[11] After the conference, one delegate wrote:

'Can you imagine the buzz created by 267 participants from 31 different countries who came together with a shared sense of purpose and vision encompassing different languages, cultures, orientation, and approaches to transactional analysis theory and practice?'

One hundred years after the birth of its founder, TA remains a vital, ever-developing discipline, with its use expanding worldwide.

APPENDICES

Appendix A
BOOKS BY ERIC BERNE

For a complete bibliography of Berne's writings, see:
www.itaa-net.org/ta/BerneBibliography.htm. (*Note:* after March 2012, this web reference is likely to be shifted to the new ITAA web site, *www.itaaworld.org.*)

Following are the books written by Berne during his lifetime, together with two posthumous collections of his selected writings.

Berne, E., *A layman's guide to psychiatry and psychoanalysis.* New York: Simon and Schuster, 1957; third edition published 1968. *Other editions:* New York: Grove Press, 1957; *and* Harmondsworth: Penguin, 1971.

A revision of *The mind in action*, originally published in 1947. The 1967 edition of *A layman's guide* introduced a chapter on transactional analysis, contributed by John Dusay.

Berne, E., *Transactional analysis in psychotherapy.* New York: Grove Press, 1961, 1966.

The first book to deal wholly with TA. It contains Berne's original, and still definitive, formulation of the ego-state model, together with expanded statements of the other elements of basic theory introduced in his earlier journal papers.

Berne, E., *The structure and dynamics of organizations and groups.* Philadelphia: J.B. Lippincott Co., 1963. *Other editions:* New York: Grove Press, 1966; *and* New York: Ballantine, 1973.

The book's content is described by its title. Includes some TA concepts, e.g. analysis of transactions and games.

Berne, E., *Games people play.* New York: Grove Press, 1964. *Other editions include:* Harmondsworth: Penguin, 1968.

The world-famous best-seller which presents the ideas on game analysis that Berne had developed by the early 1960s. (He revised this theory in successive later books – see *TA Today*, Chapter 23.) Also contains a compendium of the games that had been named up to that time.

Berne, E., *Principles of group treatment.* New York: Oxford University Press, 1966. *Other editions:* New York: Grove Press, 1966.

A text on the theory and practice of group treatment in clinical settings, including the application of TA in this field.

Berne, E., *Sex in human loving.* New York: Simon and Schuster, 1970. *Other editions:* Harmondsworth: Penguin, 1973.
An exploration of sex in personal relationships, analysed in a TA framework.

Berne, E., *What do you say after you say hello?* New York: Grove Press, 1972. *Other editions:* London: Corgi, 1975.
An extended statement of the theory of script as developed by Berne and his associates up to the late 1970s, with applications to therapy. Berne was still working on this book at the time of his death, and it was published posthumously.

Steiner, C., and Kerr, C. (eds), *Beyond games and scripts.* New York: Ballantine Books, 1976.
A selection of Berne's writings on all aspects of transactional analysis.

McCormick, P. (ed.), *Intuition and ego states.* New York: Harper and Row, 1977.
A compilation of the papers Berne published in professional journals from 1949 to 1962 on various topics connected with intuition. They include his first statements on the basic theory of TA.

Appendix B
OTHER KEY BOOKS ON TA

In selecting the 'key books' named in this Appendix, we do *not* intend any adverse comment on the quality of the many other books currently available on TA. The books we cite here have been chosen on two criteria. They are either compendium volumes, which give a broad overview of TA theory and practice; or widely-accepted statements of the position of one of the three 'TA schools' and more recent approaches. In both these senses, they are 'keys' to further reading and study in TA.

To give a sense of historical development, we have listed the titles under each sub-heading in date order, rather than in alphabetical order by author.

We do not give any indication whether a book is currently in print, since this information may change at short notice with individual publishers' decisions.

Texts and compendium volumes

James, M., and Jongeward, D., *Born to win: transactional analysis with gestalt experiments.* Reading: Addison-Wesley, 1971. *Other editions include:* New York: Signet, 1978.

The 1971 best-seller, still a sound introduction to TA basics. Notable for its use of gestalt exercises to aid learning and self-knowledge.

Barnes, G. (ed.), *Transactional analysis after Eric Berne: teachings and practices of three TA schools.* New York: Harper's College Press, 1977.

Its 22 papers are centred mainly on the discussion of post-Bernian developments in theory, though practice is also well covered. Explores the nature and development of the three main 'schools' of TA as they existed in the late 1970s.

James, M. (ed.), *Techniques in transactional analysis for psychotherapists and counselors.* Reading: Addison-Wesley, 1977.

A symposium of 43 papers, with Muriel James contributing as well as editing. As the title indicates, the book is focused primarily on the techniques of TA, but theory is also examined, and there is a section examining the relationships between TA and other therapies.

Stern, E. (ed.), *TA: the state of the art.* Dordrecht: Foris Publications, 1984.

With 23 papers, contributed mainly by European practitioners, this book gives a view of the 'cutting edge' of theory and practice in TA as it existed in the mid-1980s.

Stewart, I., *Eric Berne.* London: Sage, 1992.

A detailed description and evaluation of Eric Berne's contributions to the theory and practice of psychotherapy. This book is part of Sage's series *Key Figures in Counselling and Psychotherapy.*

Stewart, I., *Developing transactional analysis counselling.* London: Sage, 1996.

A practical handbook for trainee and practising TA counsellors and therapists, giving 30 'helpful hints' for facilitating effective personal change.

Tilney, T., *Dictionary of transactional analysis.* London: Whurr, 1998.

As the title implies, Tony Tilney has compiled the first complete dictionary of theoretical and practical terms used in TA.

James, M., *Perspectives in transactional analysis.* San Francisco: TA Press, 1998.

This book is a collection of the articles and book chapters on TA written by Muriel James – one of Eric Berne's colleagues in the original San Francisco Seminars – from 1968 until the late 1990s. James' writing covers a wide range of aspects within the discipline.

Tudor, K. (ed.), *Transactional approaches to brief therapy.* London: Sage, 2001.

Shows how TA can most effectively be applied in settings where psychotherapy or counselling must be restricted to relatively few sessions.

Stewart, I., *Transactional analysis counselling in action.* London: Sage (3rd edn), 2007. (*Note:* the 4th edition of this title is due for publication in Spring 2013).

Aimed at trainees and practising counsellors and therapists in TA, this book describes the systematic process of TA treatment, through diagnosis and treatment planning to contract-making and the implementation of the planned treatment sequence.

Erskine, R. (ed.), *Life scripts: a transactional analysis of unconscious relational patterns.* London: Karnac, 2010.

A symposium volume of thirteen papers on the subject of life script, aimed at the more advanced reader.

Widdowson, M., *Transactional analysis: 100 key points and techniques.* London and New York: Routledge, 2010.
   True to its title, this book presents 100 concisely-phrased points of guidance on both the theory and the practice of TA. It is aimed at qualified practitioners and advanced trainees.

Classical school

Steiner, C., *Scripts people live: transactional analysis of life scripts.* New York: Grove Press, 1974.
   A thorough discussion of the theory and implications of life-script. Ranks alongside Berne's work as an essential source-book on the subject.

Dusay, J., *Egograms.* New York: Harper and Row, 1977. *Other editions:* New York: Bantam, 1980.
   A readable presentation of Dusay's egogram concept, plus the functional ego-state model and other aspects of classical TA.

Redecision school

Goulding, R., and Goulding, M., *The power is in the patient.* San Francisco: TA Press, 1978.

Goulding, M., and Goulding, R., *Changing lives through redecision therapy.* New York: Brunner/Mazel, 1979.
   These two books by the Gouldings describe both the theory and the practice of their redecision work. The latter volume is a compilation of papers originally published by them in journals and professional volumes.

Kadis, L. (ed.), *Redecision therapy: expanded perspectives.* Watsonville: Western Institute for Group and Family Therapy, 1985.
   A compendium volume covering a wide range of topics on the theory and practice of redecision therapy.

Cathexis school

Schiff, J., *et al., The Cathexis reader: transactional analysis treatment of psychosis.* New York: Harper and Row, 1975.
   A full statement of Schiffian theory, incorporating material originally published in the *TA Journal.*

Relational approach

Hargaden, H., and Sills, C., *Transactional analysis: a relational perspective.* London: Routledge, 2002.

This book is seen by many as the seminal volume on the theory, principles and practice of the relational approach.

Cornell, W., and Hargaden, H. (eds), *From transactions to relations: the emergence of a relational tradition in transactional analysis.* Chadlington: Haddon Press, 2005.

A compendium volume for more advanced readers, this is a good key to the relational approach in TA.

Personality adaptations

Joines, V., *Joines personality adaptation questionnaire administration, scoring and interpretive kit (JPAQ).* Chapel Hill, NC: Southeast Institute, 2002. (Or on-line at:)
www.seinstitute.com/books_videos_.html

Joines, V., and Stewart, I., *Personality adaptations: a new guide to human understanding in psychotherapy and counselling.* Nottingham and Chapel Hill: Lifespace, 2002.

A practical guide to understanding personality, based on TA concepts. Describes a research-based model of six personality adaptations, showing how to diagnose and work with each type to help them achieve lasting personal change. Gives annotated transcripts of psychotherapy with each personality type.

Kahler, T., *The process therapy model.* Little Rock: Taibi Kahler Associates, 2008.

Taibi Kahler, the originator of the Process Therapy Model, gives his latest thinking on the subject. Stresses the concept of *phasing,* by which the individual acquires the repertoire of additional personality type(s), and reviews the therapeutic approach to drivers and process scripts.

TA in education

Illsley Clarke, J., and Dawson, C., *Growing up again.* Center City: Hazelden, 1998.

Written as guidance for parents on providing children with the structure and nurture critical to healthy development, this is also a useful resource for anyone working with children, young people, families and schools.

Napper, R., and Newton, T., *Tactics: transactional analysis concepts for trainers, teachers and tutors*. Ipswich: TA Resources, 2000.
  A practical guide for professionals whose job is to enable others to learn, this book explores relationships in the learning process through a framework of transactional analysis.

Barrow, G., Bradshaw, E., and Newton, T. *Improving behaviour and raising self-esteem in the classroom*. Abingdon: David Fulton, 2001.
  Both an overview of how using TA can impact on school culture and build creative classroom relationships and a resource offering support and guidance to teachers in dealing with issues of behaviour.

Hay, J., *Transactional analysis for trainers*. Hertford: Sherwood Publishing (2nd edn), 2009.
  Distils the broad range of TA concepts into accessible frameworks and provides guidance and suggested activities for those wishing to teach personal and professional effectiveness.

Organizational TA

Mohr, G., and Steinert, T. (eds), *Growth and change for organizations*. Bonn: Kulturpolitische Gesellschaft, 2006.
  TA authors from around the world look at patterns of thinking, feeling and behaviour in organizations, methods of diagnosis and intervention on a personal and system level, and TA perspectives related to economies and societies.

Hay, J., *Transactional analysis for trainers*. Hertford: Sherwood Publishing (2nd edn), 2009. (*Op. cit.,* see note above)

Hay, J., *Working it out at work: understanding attitudes and building relationships*. Hertford: Sherwood Publishing (2nd edn), 2009.
  Converts models used by psychotherapists into terms that can be easily understood and applies them specifically to what happens at work. Uses numerous examples to show how to increase self-awareness and interpret the dynamics between people.

De Graaf, A., and Kunst, K., *Einstein and the art of sailing: a new perspective on the role of leadership*. Hertford: Sherwood Publishing, 2010.
  Uses Einstein as the personification of a brilliant interrogator, in order to invite readers to consider the central questions surrounding modern leadership and to reflect on the personal characteristics which will make

them good managers.

Mountain, A., and Davidson, C., *Working together: organizational transactional analysis and business performance.* Farnham and Burlington: Gower, 2011.
Applies current TA theory and practice to the workplace, showing how TA can help in communication, decision-making and business performance.

Hay, J., *Donkey bridges for developmental TA: making transactional analysis accessible and memorable.* Hertford: Sherwood Publishing (2nd edn), 2012.
Intended for those who already have some professional knowledge of TA, this book presents numerous ways of presenting TA constructs so that they are easy to comprehend and, most importantly, are focused on health rather than pathology.

Appendix C
WINNERS OF THE ERIC BERNE MEMORIAL AWARDS

The Eric Berne Memorial Scientific Award was established in 1971 to honour and perpetuate the memory of Eric Berne's scientific contributions. It was to be given annually to the originator of a new scientific concept in TA. Adjudication was by the Editorial Board of ITAA.

In 1990, the ITAA Board of Trustees decided to change the title and scope of the Award. It is now known as the Eric Berne Memorial Award in Transactional Analysis. The Award is given annually for published contributions to TA theory or practice, or for the integration or comparison of TA theory or practice with other therapeutic modalities. The winner(s) of the Award are chosen by a committee appointed by the ITAA Board of Trustees.

Following is a chronological list of winners of the Award for the years 1971-2011, together with references to the works for which they received their awards. This listing has been extracted from the Training and Certification Council web site at:

http://ta-trainingandcertification.net/exam_handbook_pdfs/Section4.pdf.

On the T&CC web site, some of the entries for the Awards are accompanied by a substantial list of citations of the sources (articles or books) for which that Award has been given. In the present list we give only the first two citations at each entry. Additional entries are signalled as, e.g., *[Two further citations]*. Full detail of citations can be found at the T&CC web link given above.

Numbers in brackets in *italic type* following each reference indicate the chapter of *TA Today* in which the topic is covered.

1971: Claude Steiner, SCRIPT MATRIX. Steiner, C., 'Script and counterscript'. *Transactional Analysis Bulletin, 5,* 18, 1966, 133-35. *(13)*

1972: Stephen Karpman, DRAMA TRIANGLE. Karpman, S., 'Fairy tales and script drama analysis'. *TAB, 7,* 26, 1968, 39-43. *(23)*

1973: John Dusay, EGOGRAMS. Dusay, J., 'Egograms and the constancy hypothesis'. *Transactional Analysis Journal, 2,* 3, 1972, 37-42. *(3)*

1974: Aaron Schiff and Jacqui Schiff, PASSIVITY AND THE FOUR DISCOUNTS. Schiff, A., and Schiff, J., 'Passivity'. *TAJ, 1,* 1,

1971, 71-8. *(17)*

1975: Robert Goulding and Mary Goulding, REDECISION AND TWELVE INJUNCTIONS. Goulding, R., and Goulding, M., 'New directions in transactional analysis'. In Sager and Kaplan (eds.), *Progress in group and family therapy.* New York: Brunner/Mazel, 1972, 105-34; *and* 'Injunctions, decisions and redecisions'. *TAJ, 6,* 1, 1976, 41-8. *(14)*

1976: Pat Crossman, PROTECTION. Crossman, P., 'Permission and protection'. *TAB, 5,* 19, 1966, 152-4. *(28)*

1977: Taibi Kahler, MINISCRIPT AND FIVE DRIVERS. Kahler, T., 'The miniscript'. *TAJ, 4,* 1, 1974, 26-42. *(15)*

1978: Fanita English, RACKETS AND REAL FEELINGS: THE SUBSTITUTION FACTOR. English, F., 'The substitution factor: rackets and real feelings'. *TAJ, 1,* 4, 1971, 225-30; *and* 'Rackets and real feelings, Part II'. *TAJ, 2,* 1, 1972, 23-5. *(21)*

1979: Stephen Karpman, OPTIONS. Karpman, S., 'Options'. *TAJ, 1,* 1, 1971, 79-87. *(7)*

1980 (joint award): Claude Steiner, THE STROKE ECONOMY. Steiner, C., 'The stroke economy'. *TAJ, 1,* 3, 1971, 9-15. *(8)*

1980 (joint award): Ken Mellor and Eric Sigmund, DISCOUNTING AND REDEFINING. Mellor, K., and Sigmund, E., 'Discounting'. *TAJ, 5,* 3, 1975, 295-302; *and* Mellor, K., and Sigmund, E., 'Redefining'. *TAJ, 5,* 3, 1975, 303-11. *(17, 18, 19)*

1981: Franklin H. Ernst, Jr., THE OK CORRAL. Ernst, F., 'The OK corral: the grid for get-on-with'. *TAJ, 1,* 4, 1971, 231-40. *(12)*

1982: Richard Erskine and Marilyn Zalcman, RACKET SYSTEM AND RACKET ANALYSIS. Erskine, R., and Zalcman, M., 'The racket system: a model for racket analysis'. *TAJ, 9,* 1, 1979, 51-9. *(22)*

1983: Muriel James, SELF-REPARENTING. James, M., 'Self-reparenting: theory and process'. *TAJ, 4,* 3, 1974, 32-9. *(28)*

1984: Pam Levin, DEVELOPMENTAL CYCLES. Levin, P., 'The cycle of development'. *TAJ, 12,* 2, 1982, 129-39. *(2)*

1985, 1986: Not awarded.

1987: Carlo Moiso, EGO STATES AND TRANSFERENCE. Moiso, C., 'Ego states and transference'. *TAJ, 15,* 3, 1985, 194-201. *(–)*

1988 through 1993: Not awarded.

1994 (joint award): Sharon R. Dashiell *(area: Practice Applications).* Dashiell, S., 'The Parent resolution process: reprogramming psychic incorporations in the Parent'. *TAJ, 8,* 4, 1978, 289-94. *(–)*

1994 (joint award): John R. McNeel *(area: Practice Applications).* McNeel, J., 'The Parent Interview'. *TAJ, 6,* 1, 1976, 61-8. *(–)*

1994 (joint award): Vann S. Joines *(area: Integration of TA with Other Theories and Approaches).* Joines, V., 'Using redecision therapy with different personality adaptations'. *TAJ, 16,* 3, 1986, 152-60;

and 'Diagnosis and treatment planning using a transactional analysis framework'. *TAJ, 18,* 3, 1988, 185-90. *(16)*

1995 (joint award): Peg Blackstone *(area: Integration of TA with other Theories and Approaches).* Blackstone, P., 'The dynamic Child: integration of second-order structure, object relations, and self psychology'. *TAJ, 23,* 4, 1993, 216-34. *(–)*

1995 (joint award): Jean Illsley Clarke *(area: Practice Applications).* Applied Transactional Analysis in Parent Education. Illsley Clarke, J., *Self-esteem: a family affair.* San Francisco: Harper, 1978; *Self-esteem: a family affair reader guide.* San Francisco: Harper, 1981. *(–)*

1996: Alan Jacobs *(area: Theory).* Transactional Analysis and Social Applications. Jacobs, A., 'Autocratic power', *TAJ, 17,* 1987, 59-71; 'Nationalism', *TAJ, 20,* 1990, 221-228. *[Two further citations] (-)*

1997: Fanita English *(area: Theory).* Hot Potato Transmission and Episcript. English, F., 'Episcript and the "Hot Potato" game', *TAB, 8,* 32, 1969, 77-82. *(14)*

1998 (joint award): Richard G. Erskine and Rebecca L. Trautmann *(area: Comparison and/or Integration).* 'Ego state analysis: a comparative view', *TAJ, 11,* 1981, 178-185; 'Ego structure, intrapsychic function, and defense mechanisms: a commentary on Eric Berne's original theoretical concepts', *TAJ 18,* 1988, 15-19. *[Seven further citations] (2, 4)*

1998 (joint award): James R. Allen and Barbara Ann Allen *(area: Theory).* Allen, J., and Allen, B., 'Narrative theory, redecision therapy and postmodernism', *TAJ, 25,* 1995, 327-334; 'A New type of transactional analysis and one version of script work with a constructionist sensibility', *TAJ, 27,* 1997, 89-98. *[One further citation] (–)*

1999 through 2001: Not awarded.

2002: Leonard Schlegel *(area: Theory).* Schlegel, L., 'What is transactional analysis?', *TAJ, 28,* 1998, 269-287. *(1)*

2003: Michele Novellino *(area: Theory).* 'Unconscious communication and interpretation in transactional analysis', *TAJ, 20,* 3, 1990, 168-172. *(–)*

2004: Pearl Drego *(area: Permission Ritual Therapy).* 'Changing systems through correlations of injunction inventories,' in Lapworth, P. (ed.), *The Maastricht Papers: Selections from the 20th EATA Conference* (pp. 5-19), Amersfoort: EATA, 2004. Also *Building family unity through permission rituals: permissions and ego state models,* Bombay: Alfreruby Publishers. *(–)*

2005: Graham Barnes: The circularity of theory and psychopathology with specific identification in the construction of schizophrenia, alcoholism, and homosexuality. Chapters 5 and 6 of Graham's doctoral dissertation, *Psychopathology of psychotherapy: a cyber-netic study of theory* (Royal Melbourne Institute of Technology, Melbourne, Victoria, Australia) *and* 'Homosexuality in the first three decades of transactional analysis: a study of theory in the practice of transactional analysis psychotherapy,' *TAJ, 34,* 2004, 126-155. *(–)*

2006: Theodore B. Novey, 'Measuring the effectiveness of transactional analysis: an international study.' *TAJ, 32,* 1, 2002, 8-24. *(–)*

2007 (joint award): Helena Hargaden and Charlotte Sills: New theory of relational domains of transference. Chapters 4 and 5 in Hargaden, H., and Sills, C., *Transactional analysis – a relational perspective*, Hove: Brunner-Routledge, 2002. *(29)*

2007 (joint award): Bernd Schmid: New theory, role concept transac-tional analysis and social roles. In Mohr, G., and Steinert, T. (eds.), *Growth and change for organizations: transactional analysis new developments 1995-2006* (pp. 32-61). Pleasanton, CA: ITAA. (Original work published 1994). *(–)*

2008: Gloria Noriega Gayol: New theory, Mechanisms for transmitting transgenerational scripts. Noriega Gayol, G., 'Codependence: a transgenerational script,' *TAJ 34,* 2004, 312-322; *and* 'Construc-ción y validación del instrumento de codependencia (ICOD) para mujeres mexicanas [Construction and validation of the codepend-ency instrument (ICOD) for mexican women],' April 2002 *Revista Salud Mental. (–)*

2009: Dolores Munari Poda: Practice application, New techniques in the treatment of children and ensuing theory. Munari Poda, D., 'Every child is a group: the girl of the snakes,' *TAJ, 34*, 2004, 52-68. *(–)*

2010: William F. Cornell: The relational and somatic organization of the Child ego state: expanding our understanding of script and script protocol. *(Area: Theory).* Cornell, W.F., 'Life script theory: a criti-cal review from a developmental perspective', *TAJ, 18,* 1988, 270-282; 'Babies, brains, and bodies: somatic foundations of the Child ego state.' In Sills,C., and Hargaden, H.(eds.), *Ego states (key con-cepts in transactional analysis: contemporary views)* (pp. 28-54). London: Worth Publishing, 2003. *[One further citation] (4, 10-13)*

2011: Not awarded.

Details of Eric Berne Memorial Awards after 2011 will be posted peri-odically on:
http://ta-trainingandcertification.net/exam_handbook_pdfs/Section4.pdf.

Appendix D
TA ORGANIZATIONS

As the second edition of this book goes to press (January 2012) there is one TA organization with worldwide coverage: the International Transactional Analysis Association (ITAA). Another organization, the European Association for Transactional Analysis (EATA), covers the continent of Europe. In addition to these two international organizations, there are national or regional TA associations in many countries of the world.

In Chapter 30, we gave a brief sketch of the historical development of ITAA and EATA. Appendix E will describe their activities in TA training and accreditation. In the present Appendix we describe the current structure, membership categories and contact details of these two organizations, as at January 2012. The detail of this information may change before our next edition, so we recommend that you check it on the web sites of the organizations themselves.

The International Transactional Analysis Association

The ITAA is a non-profit educational corporation in the terms of US law. It currently has some 1,200 members in 52 countries. The organization is governed by a Board of Trustees elected directly by the membership.

The ITAA offers five membership categories. *Associate Membership* is a general-interest, non-voting membership that supports the humanistic goals of ITAA. *Student Membership* is a category for full-time college-level students. Unlike Associate Membership, this is a voting category. *Regular Membership* is a support-level, voting membership for professionals who use TA but are certified through another source. This is also the membership for persons working towards competency-based certification from the ITAA BOC (Board of Certification) or EATA COC (Commission of Certification). A 'TA 101' course or exam and signature of a Teaching and/or Supervising Transactional Analyst (TSTA) or Provisional TSTA (PTSTA) are required. *(See Appendix E for details of the P/TSTA qualifications).*

Certified Transactional Analyst Membership is a competency-based membership earned by passing written and oral exams after study under a certified instructor or supervisor *(see Appendix E)*. CTA members may specialize in counselling, psychotherapy, organizational or educational areas.

Certified Teaching and/or Supervising Transactional Analyst Mem-

bers are members who have been previously certified as competent in application of transactional analysis and have subsequently been examined and certified as competent to train and/or supervise others for certification as CTAs or as TSTAs in the educational, organizational, counselling or psychotherapy fields *(see Appendix E)*.

Membership in ITAA is currently extended to individual persons, not to associations (though that is being considered and some national associations have negotiated ITAA membership for their own members). At the time of writing, major changes in the organizational structure of ITAA are under discussion. These are intended principally as a response to the increasingly international scope of ITAA's membership and operations, as well as the ever-increasing importance of regional and national TA associations *(see Chapter 30)*.

Further information may be obtained from: ITAA, 2843 Hopyard Road, Suite 155, Pleasanton, CA 94588, USA. Web site:
www.itaaworld.org
Email via contact form on that web site. Tel / fax: +1 925-600-8112.

The European Association for Transactional Analysis

EATA is a non-profit association within Swiss law. It currently has some 7,550 members, belonging to 34 TA associations in 27 European countries.

EATA is an 'umbrella' organization, in that it is a federation of national and regional TA associations within Europe. Membership in EATA is normally obtained through becoming a member of one of the affiliated national or regional associations. Other than in exceptional circumstances, it is not possible to take out individual membership of EATA.

For this reason, EATA itself has no formal 'membership categories'. Instead, the various different national and regional associations within EATA can develop their own categories of membership. Generally speaking, these are similar to the membership categories already described for ITAA. (Categories of *accreditation* in TA are identical as between EATA and ITAA – see Appendix E).

Governance of EATA is effected by a Council composed of delegates representing the various affiliated national and regional associations.

For further information, contact: EATA Executive Secretary, Silvanerweg 8, 78464 Konstanz, Germany. Tel: +49 7531 95270; fax: +49 7531 95271. Web site: *www.eatanews.org;* email: *EATA@gmx.com.*

Relationship between ITAA and EATA

In legal and functional terms, EATA is completely separate from ITAA, though the latter is still acknowledged as the central TA organization for the whole world. In practice, EATA oversees the conduct and development of TA within the continent of Europe, while outside Europe that function is performed by the ITAA. Though separate, these two international organizations co-operate closely one with another. This close connection is secured by organizational structures that ensure mutual information, coordination and recognition.

National and regional associations

We do not give contact details for the world's numerous national or regional TA associations, because these details change at frequent intervals with changes in the elected officials of the organizations. Also, new associations are continually being formed and existing ones merged or closed.

The current contact details for regional and national organizations are in most cases kept on record by ITAA or EATA. Therefore, if you wish to find the details of a TA organization in any region or country, a good first step is to visit the web sites of these two international associations, as given above. If this fails, we suggest that you enter 'transactional analysis', plus the name of the region or country, in your search engine.

Appendix E
TRAINING AND ACCREDITATION IN TA

As the second edition of this book goes to press (January 2012) there are two organizations offering internationally-recognized training and accreditation in TA. These are the International Transactional Analysis Association (ITAA) and the European Association for Transactional Analysis (EATA).

For ITAA, matters concerning training and accreditation are dealt with by a body known as the Training and Certification Council (T&CC). For reasons of US law, T&CC is a separate organization from ITAA, but works in close liaison with it. The T&CC comprises two committees: the Training Standards Committee (TSC), responsible for training provisions, and the Board of Certification (BOC), which handles arrangements for examination and accreditation of TA professionals. In EATA, these duties are performed by the Professional Training Standards Committee (PTSC) and the Commission of Certification (COC) respectively.

On-going close co-ordination of training and examination procedures as between T&CC and EATA is maintained by a joint committee known as the Transactional Analysis Certification Council (TACC). The effect of this is that all credentials extended by one body are recognized by the other. The training and examination procedures laid down by both bodies are virtually identical, as are their respective Training and Examination Handbooks.

The information given in the remaining sections of this Appendix has been summarized from the editions of the T&CC and the EATA Handbooks that are current at press date (January 2012). You can find complete detail of the information concerned, and track the changes that may be made from time to time in arrangements for training and accreditation, by consulting the T&CC Handbook at:

http://ta-trainingandcertification.net/ta-training-and-exams-handbook.html

or the EATA Handbook at:

www.eatanews.org/handbook.htm

Purposes of training and certification
The purposes of the international training and certification programs are: to ensure there will be competent, ethical practitioners of TA for indi-

viduals and organizations desiring help; to support the development, clarification, simplification, and evaluation of TA theory and methods; to promote competency-based evaluation of TA professionals; and to promote contractual application of TA in all areas of use.

Professional credentials may be obtained for the application of transactional analysis and for teaching and training others in TA in four areas of specialization at the present time: (1) Psychotherapy; (2) Counselling; (3) Organizational; (4) Educational.

Accreditation as a Certified Transactional Analyst (CTA) is available to individuals who have received training and have been certified by certifying boards recognized by ITAA/EATA as competent to practise TA in their area of specialization. Accreditation as a Teaching and/or Supervising Transactional Analyst is available to individuals who have received training and supervision and have been certified as competent to teach TA (Teaching Transactional Analyst, TTA) and/or to supervise others in the application of TA (Supervising Transactional Analyst, STA).

Professionals who are in process of receiving training and supervision for eventual qualification as T/STA are designated as Provisional Teaching and/or Supervising Transactional Analyst (PT/STA) in their field of specialization.

What is involved in TA training and certification?

The steps in the training process for persons who wish to become a Certified Transactional Analyst are:

1. Taking the TA 101 Course or passing the TA 101 Written Examination;

2. Applying for and paying dues for the membership level in ITAA or EATA appropriate to persons training for accreditation as CTA;

3. Signing a Training Contract with a Principal Supervisor who is a TSTA or PTSTA in the area of specialization in which they wish to train;

4. Training and supervision to meet the eligibility requirements for examination by the BOC or COC;

5. Passing the BOC/COC examination for accreditation as a Certified Transactional Analyst (CTA); then

6. Applying for and paying dues for the membership level in ITAA or EATA appropriate to persons qualified as CTA.

For those individuals interested in being certified as a TA trainer and/or supervisor, they may choose to be certified as a Teaching Transactional Analyst, a Supervising Transactional Analyst, or both. The steps in the training process are:

1. Becoming a CTA in the area of specialization in which they wish to train others;

2. Attending an official Training Endorsement Workshop (TEW) and being approved by the TEW staff to initiate training programmes;

3. Applying and paying dues for the membership level in ITAA or EATA appropriate to persons in training for accreditation as T/STA;

4. Signing a Training Contract with a Principal Supervisor who is a TSTA in the area of specialization in which they wish to train (this gives the candidate the designation of PT/STA in their area of specialization);

5. Training and supervision to meet the eligibility requirements for examination by the BOC or COC;

6. Passing the BOC/COC examination for accreditation as a Teaching and/or Supervising Transactional Analyst; then

7. Applying and paying dues for the membership level in ITAA or EATA appropriate to persons qualified as T/STA.

The TA 101

The 'TA 101' is the term Eric Berne introduced to designate an introduction to the basic theory and methods of transactional analysis. The numbers, 101, are typically used in the United States for introductory university courses that provide a broad overview of a topic.

The TA 101 Course is a workshop officially recognized by ITAA/EATA as an introduction to transactional analysis. The purpose of the 101 Course is to provide consistent and accurate information about TA concepts. In order to qualify as an official TA 101 Course, the following requirements must be met:

1. The instructor must be officially recognized to teach a TA 101 Course – i.e. the instructor must be a TSTA (or TTA), a PTSTA (or PTTA), or a TA 101 Instructor.

2. The course must include the content specified in the official TA 101 Outline. *(Authors' note: the 2008 version of the Outline, which is the current version at the date our second edition goes to press, is given in Appendix F.)*

3. The course must be at least 12 hours in length. It may also be presented in various formats over various periods of time which may be longer than 12 hours (e.g. a weekend or several weeks) and include experiential exercises.

The TA 101 Written Examination was introduced as an alternative to taking a course or workshop in order to respond to the growing number of persons around the world who had an adequate knowledge of the basic principles of TA, but were unable to attend an official TA 101 Course. Such students may take the Written Examination and have it graded by a qualified teacher. If they pass, they will be eligible for entry to membership and training as though they had attended a TA 101 Course.

Requirements for accreditation

The following is a brief summary of the requirements for training and supervision laid down for accreditation as CTA and as T/STA, referred to above in the respective lists of 'steps in the training process'.

CTA: the minimum length of the training contract for CTA is one year. However, the emphasis is upon sufficiency of training for the attainment of competence, and most trainees can expect their training to last considerably longer than the minimum. Typically, the total time from the beginning of CTA training until the final examination is between four and six years, depending on the trainee's previous experience. In this period the trainee must fulfil the minimum requirement of 2,000 hours, made up as follows:

- 750 hours of client contact, of which 500 must be in TA;
- 600 hours of professional training, of which 300 must be in TA;
- 150 hours of supervision, of which 75 must be by a PTSTA or TSTA and 40 hours must be with the Principal Supervisor; and
- 500 additional hours of professional development, to be designated by the Principal Supervisor in accordance with national requirements.

Though no minimum hours requirement is laid down by ITAA or EATA for personal therapy, it is expected to be an integral part of training. Some individual countries do lay down a specific hours' requirement for personal therapy, and may also set further additional requirements that vary from one country to another. This is to meet statutory and/or professional norms in each country. The candidate for CTA must demonstrate that they have met any such additional national requirements in order to be eligible for the CTA examination.

Accreditation as CTA entails passing a written and an oral examination. The written examination must be passed before the candidate can go on to the oral examination. The latter is taken before a board of four examiners already qualified as T/STA, PT/STA or CTA, and focuses principally on the examination of audio- or videotaped samples of the candidate's work.

T/STA: for certification as TTA, the candidate must have taught a TA 101 course under the supervision of a TSTA or TTA, and must have completed 300 hours' teaching in the field of specialization, of which at least 45 hours must have been supervised by a TSTA or TTA, and at least 12 hours' presentations at national or international conferences. Certification as STA requires completion of 500 hours' experience supervising in the field of specialization, of which at least 50 hours must have been supervised by a TSTA or STA. In addition all candidates for T/STA must have completed 100 hours' continuing professional education.

The oral examination for accreditation as T/STA is taken before a board of four examiners who are themselves qualified as T/STA. It comprises three parts, covering: Theory, Organization and Ethics; Teaching (for TSTA or TTA candidates); and Supervision (for TSTA or STA candidates). The Theory, Organization and Ethics section of the examination must be passed before the candidate can go on to take either of the other sections.

Appendix F
TA 101 COURSE OUTLINE

Following is the course outline for the TA 101, as issued by the Training and Certification Council. It is the August 2008 revision, the current version as at press date for this second edition of *TA Today*.

Numbers added in brackets and *italic type* indicate the principal chapter or chapters in *TA Today* in which each topic is covered.

Notes:

1. SECTIONS (A, B,) and NUMBERED ITEMS (1,2,a,b,) are essential and mandatory, where BULLETED ITEMS are optional and a guidance to the trainer.

2. The outline below can be taught in any order at trainer's discretion.

3. Items marked * may be communicated to students in written form, rather than by direct teaching.

A. STATEMENT OF THE PURPOSE OF THE TRANSACTIONAL ANALYSIS 101 COURSE *(Appx E)*

B. PROJECTED OUTCOMES

By the end of the 101 participants will be able to:

    1. Describe basic theoretical concepts of transactional analysis
    2. Apply basic transactional analysis concepts to problem solving
    3. Classify a range of interpersonal behaviours and internal processes using basic transactional analysis concepts

C. DEFINITION AND UNDERLYING VALUES OF TRANSACTIONAL ANALYSIS AND ITS AREAS OF APPLICATION

    1. Definition of transactional analysis *(1)*
    2. Value base (philosophical principles) *(1, 27)*
    3. Definitions of autonomy *(27)*
    4. Contractual method *(1, 26)*
    5. Areas of application – differences in process *(28, 29, Appx E)*

- Types of transactions *(7)*
- Rules of communication *(7)*

2. Strokes *(8)*
   - Definition of strokes *(8)*
   - Types of strokes *(8)*
   - Stroke economy *(8)*

3. Social time structuring *(9)*

G. THEORY OF LIFE PATTERNS – SCRIPTS

1. Game analysis *(23)*
   a) Definitions of games *(23)*
   - Reasons for playing games *(24)*
   - Advantages of games *(24)*
   - Examples of games *(23-25)*
   - Degrees of games *(23)*

   b) Ways of describing the process of games *(23)*
   - Drama Triangle *(23)*
   - Formula G *(23)*
   - Transactional game diagram *(23)*

2. Racket analysis *(21)*
   a) Definitions of rackets and their payoffs *(21)*
   - Trading stamps *(21)*
   b) Significance of internal / intrapsychic processes *(21, 22)*
   c) Relationship of rackets to transactions, games and script *(21)*
   - Racket System and racket analysis *(22)*

3. Script analysis *(10-15)*
   a) Life positions *(12)*
   - Definition of life positions, OKness *(12)*
   - Four life positions *(12)*
   - Relationship of life positions to games and script *(12, 24)*
   b) Script *(10-15)*
   1) Definitions of script *(10)*
   2) Origin of script in child's experiences *(10, 13, 14)*
   3) Process of Script development *(10, 13, 14)*
   - Injunctions *(13, 14)*
   - Attributions *(13)*
   - Counter-injunctions *(13)*
   - Early decisions *(10, 14)*
   - Somatic component *(11)*
   - Program *(14)*

- Script change *(27)*
- Script matrix and other script diagrams *(13, 22)*

H. TRANSACTIONAL ANALYSIS METHODOLOGY
- Group and individual method *(28, 29)*

NOTES AND REFERENCES

Chapter 1: WHAT TA IS

1. This definition is on the page headed 'The ITAA' in each issue of the *Transactional Analysis Journal.*
2. On the philosophy and basic concepts of TA, see:

Berne, E., *Principles of group treatment.* New York: Oxford University Press, 1966 (*other editions:* New York: Grove Press, 1966), chapter 10.

James, M. (ed.), *Techniques in transactional analysis for psychotherapists and counselors.* Reading: Addison-Wesley, 1977, chapter 3.

James, M., and Jongeward, D., *Born to win: transactional analysis with gestalt experiments.* Reading: Addison-Wesley, 1971 (*other editions include*: New York: Signet, 1978), chapter 1.

Steiner, C., *Scripts people live: transactional analysis of life scripts.* New York: Grove Press, 1974, introduction.

Stewart, I., *Eric Berne.* London: Sage, 1992, chapters 2 and 3.

Chapter 2: THE EGO-STATE MODEL

1. On the nature and definition of ego-states, see:

Berne, E., *Transactional analysis in psychotherapy.* New York: Grove Press, 1961, 1966, chapter 2.

Berne, E., *Games people play.* New York: Grove Press, 1964 (*other editions include:* Harmondsworth: Penguin, 1968), chapter 1.

Berne, *Principles of group treatment*, chapter 10.

Berne, E., *Sex in human loving.* New York: Simon and Schuster, 1970 (*other editions:* Harmondsworth: Penguin, 1973), chapter 4.

Berne, E., *What do you say after you say hello?* New York: Grove Press, 1972 (*other editions:* London: Corgi, 1975), chapter 2.

James and Jongeward, *Born to win*, chapter 2.

McCormick, P. (ed.), *Intuition and ego states.* New York: Harper and Row, 1977, chapter 6.
2. Berne gave several different definitions of 'ego-state' at various points in his writings. This one is from *Principles of group treatment.* Berne does not use the word 'thinking' in defining ego-states, but the context makes it clear that thinking is to be regarded as part of 'experience'.
3. For a book-length exposition of the empirical study of ego-state clues and many other aspects of TA, see:

Steere, D., *Bodily expressions in psychotherapy.* New York: Brunner/Mazel, 1982.

See also the following journal articles:

Falkowski, W., Ben-Tovim, D., and Bland, J., 'The assessment of the ego-states'. *British Journal of Psychiatry, 137,* 1980, 572-3.

Gilmour, J., 'Psychophysiological evidence for the existence of ego-states'. *TAJ, 11,* 3, 1981, 207-12.

Williams, J., *et al.,* 'Construct validity of transactional analysis ego-states'. *TAJ, 13,* 1, 1983, 43-9.

4. For Berne's explanation of the difference between ego-states and the three Freudian constructs, see the chapters cited above in *Intuition and ego-states, TA in psychotherapy* and *Principles of group treatment.* See also:

Drye, R., 'The best of both worlds: a psychoanalyst looks at TA'. *In:* Barnes, G. (ed.), *Transactional analysis after Eric Berne: teachings and practices of three TA schools.* New York: Harper's College Press, 1977, chapter 20.

Drye, R., 'Psychoanalysis and TA'. *In:* James (ed.), *Techniques in transactional analysis...,* chapter 11.

Stewart, *Eric Berne,* chapter 4, pp.106-10.

5. Berne, *TA in psychotherapy,* chapter 5, p.37. See also Stewart, *Eric Berne,* chapter 2, p.27.

6. For further discussion of how the 'over-simplified model' destroys the structure of TA theory, see Stewart, *Eric Berne,* chapter 4, pp.122-6.

Chapter 3: FUNCTIONAL ANALYSIS OF EGO-STATES

1. On functional analysis, see:

Berne, E., *The structure and dynamics of organizations and groups.* Philadelphia: J.B. Lippincott Co., 1963 (*other editions:* New York: Grove Press, 1966; *and* New York: Ballantine, 1973), chapter 9.

Dusay, J., *Egograms.* New York: Harper and Row, 1977 (*other editions:* New York: Bantam, 1980), chapter 1.

Kahler, T., *Transactional analysis revisited.* Little Rock: Human Development Publications, 1978, chapter 1.

2. On the egogram, see: Dusay, *Egograms,* all chapters. See also: Dusay, J., 'Egograms and the constancy hypothesis'. *TAJ, 2,* 3, 1972, 37-42.

Dusay reserves the term 'egogram' for a bar-chart analysis of a person's functional ego-states which is carried out by someone else. If I do the same analysis on *myself,* then in Dusay's terminology the result would be a 'psychogram'. We have preferred to simplify by using the word 'egogram' for both these concepts.

3. For formulations of the functional model that use a rectangular diagram rather than the three-circles diagram, see:

Stewart, I., 'Ego states and the theory of theory: the strange case of the Little Professor'. *TAJ, 31, 2,* 2001, 133-47.

Temple, S., 'Update on the functional fluency model in education'. *TAJ, 34,* 3, 2004, 197-204.

Chapter 4: THE SECOND-ORDER STRUCTURAL MODEL

1. Basic versions of the second-order structural model are given in most of the references listed at note (1) for Chapter 2. See also:

Berne, *Transactional analysis in psychotherapy*, chapters 16 and 17.

Schiff, J., et al., *The Cathexis reader: transactional analysis treatment of psychosis*. New York: Harper and Row, 1975, chapter 3.

Steiner, *Scripts people live*, chapter 2.

For more advanced treatment, see the following:

Drego, P., 'Ego-state models'. *TASI Darshan, 1,* 4, 1981.

Drego, P., *Towards the illumined child*. Bombay: Grail, 1979.

Erskine, R., 'A structural analysis of ego'. *Keynote speeches delivered at the EATA conference, July 1986*. Geneva: EATA, 1987, speech 2.

Erskine, R., 'Ego structure, intrapsychic function, and defense mechanisms: a commentary on Eric Berne's original theoretical concepts'. *TAJ, 18,* 1, 1988, 15-19.

Hohmuth, A., and Gormly, A., 'Ego-state models and personality structure'. *TAJ, 12,* 2, 1982, 140-3.

Holloway, W., 'Transactional analysis: an integrative view'. *In:* Barnes (ed.), *Transactional analysis after Eric Berne*, chapter 11.

Sills, C., and Hargaden, H. (eds), *Ego States*. London: Worth, 2003.

Summerton, O., 'Advanced ego-state theory'. *TASI Darshan, 2,* 4, 1982.

Trautmann, R., and Erskine, R., 'Ego-state analysis: a comparative view'. *TAJ, 11,* 2, 1981, 178-85.

2. For the 'concentric circles' presentation of the development of the Child ego-state, see:

English, F., 'What shall I do tomorrow? Reconceptualizing transactional analysis'. *In:* Barnes (ed.), *Transactional analysis after Eric Berne,* chapter 15.

English, F., 'How are you? And how am I? Ego states and inner motivators'. *In:* Sills and Hargaden (eds), *Ego States,* chapter 3.

3. For a lead into the general literature on child development, try: Donaldson, M., *Children's minds*. London: Fontana, 1978.

Rather than attempt the daunting task of reading Piaget in the original, you may wish to look at one of the many summarized interpretations of his theories, e.g.: Maier, H., *Three theories of child development*. New York: Harper and Row, 1969.

Erik Erikson's account of the child's emotional development is presented in: Erikson, E., *Childhood and society*. New York: W.W. Norton,

1950.

See also Mahler, M.S., *The psychological birth of the human infant.* New York: Basic Books, 1975.

4. For interpretations of child development within a TA framework, see the article by Fanita English cited at note (2) for this Chapter; see also:

Babcock, D., and Keepers, T., *Raising kids okay: transactional analysis in human growth & development.* New York: Grove Press, 1976.

Levin, P., *Becoming the way we are.* Berkeley: Levin, 1974.

Levin, P., 'The cycle of development'. *TAJ, 12,* 2, 1982, 129-39.

Schiff et al., *Cathexis reader,* chapter 4.

5. Joines, V., 'Differentiating structural and functional'. *TAJ, 6,* 4, 1976, 377-80. See also:

Kahler, *Transactional analysis revisited,* chapter 1.

Chapter 5: RECOGNIZING EGO-STATES

1. For the four ways of ego-state diagnosis, see:

Berne, *Transactional analysis in psychotherapy*, chapter 7.

Berne, *Structure and dynamics of organizations and groups*, chapter 9.

James (ed.), *Techniques in transactional analysis...*, chapter 4. See also the book by David Steere, *Bodily expressions in psychotherapy*, cited at note (3) for Chapter 2.

2. On Berne's energy theory, see: *Transactional analysis in psychotherapy*, chapter 3; and *Principles of group treatment*, chapter 13. See also:

Kahler, *Transactional analysis revisited*, chapter 4.

Schiff et al., *Cathexis reader*, chapter 3.

Chapter 6: STRUCTURAL PATHOLOGY

1. Regarding structural pathology, see:

Berne, *Transactional analysis in psychotherapy*, chapter 4.

Erskine, R., and Zalcman, M., 'The racket system: a model for racket analysis'. *TAJ, 9,* 1, 1979, 51-9.

James, M., and Jongeward, D., *The people book.* Menlo Park: Addison-Wesley, 1975, chapter 8.

James and Jongeward, *Born to win*, chapter 9.

Schiff et al., *Cathexis reader*, chapter 3.

2. For views on the relationship between double contamination and script, see:

Erskine and Zalcman, 'The racket system...', p.53.

Kahler, *Transactional analysis revisited*, chapter 47.

3. Berne, *TA in psychotherapy, chapter 4, pp.29-30.* See also: Kahler, *Transactional analysis revisited*, chapter 2.

Chapter 7: TRANSACTIONS

1. On the analysis of transactions, see:
Berne, *Transactional analysis in psychotherapy*, chapter 9.
Berne, *Games people play*, chapter 2.
Berne, *Principles of group treatment*, chapter 10.
Berne, *What do you say...*, chapter 2.
James and Jongeward, *Born to win*, chapter 2.
Steiner, C., *Games alcoholics play*. New York: Grove Press, 1971, chapter 1.
2. Karpman, S., 'Options'. *TAJ, 1,* 1, 1971, 79-87.

Chapter 8: STROKES

1. On the nature and definition of strokes and hungers, see:
Berne, *Games people play*, Introduction.
Berne, *Sex in human loving*, chapter 6.
Haimowitz, M., and Haimowitz, N., *Suffering is optional*. Evanston: Haimowoods Press, 1976, chapter 2.
James and Jongeward, *Born to win*, chapter 3.
Steiner, *Scripts people live*, chapter 22.
2. Spitz, R., 'Hospitalism: genesis of psychiatric conditions in early childhood'. *Psychoanalytic studies of the child, 1,* 1945, 53-74.
3. Levine, S., 'Stimulation in infancy'. *Scientific American, 202,* 5, 80-6.
4. Steiner, C., 'The stroke economy'. *TAJ, 1, 3, 1971, 9-15.*
5. McKenna, J., 'Stroking profile'. *TAJ, 4,* 4, 1974, 20-4.
6. English, F., 'Strokes in the credit bank for David Kupfer'. *TAJ, 1,* 3, 1971, 27-9.
7. Pollitzer, J., 'Is love dangerous?' Workshop presentation, 1980, unpublished.
8. Kahler, *Transactional analysis revisited*, chapter 16.

Chapter 9: TIME STRUCTURING

1. On the modes of time-structuring, see:
Berne, *Games people play*, chapters 3, 4, 5.
Berne, *Principles of group treatment*, chapter 10.
Berne, *Sex in human loving*, chapter 3 and chapter 4. The latter chapter includes Berne's description of the ego-states involved in intimacy.
Berne, *What do you say...*, chapter 2.
James and Jongeward, *Born to win*, chapter 3.
2. Boyd, L., and Boyd, H., 'Caring and intimacy as a time structure'. *TAJ, 10,* 4, 1980, 281-3.

Chapter 10: THE NATURE AND ORIGINS OF LIFE-SCRIPT

1. Regarding the nature, origins and definition of script, see:

Berne, *Transactional analysis in psychotherapy*, chapter 11.

Berne, *Principles of group treatment*, chapters 10 and 12.

Berne, *What do you say...*, chapters 2, 3-6, 8-10.

English, F., 'What shall I do tomorrow? Reconceptualizing transactional analysis'. *In:* Barnes (ed.), *Transactional analysis after Eric Berne*, chapter 15.

Erskine, R., 'Life scripts: unconscious relational patterns and psychotherapeutic involvement'. *In:* Erskine, R. (ed.), *Life scripts: a transactional analysis of unconscious relational patterns.* London: Karnac, 2010, chapter 1, pp.1-28.

Holloway, W., 'Transactional analysis: an integrative view'. *In:* Barnes (ed.), *Transactional analysis after Eric Berne*, chapter 11.

Goulding, M., and Goulding, R., *Changing lives through redecision therapy*. New York: Brunner/Mazel, 1979, chapter 2.

James and Jongeward, *Born to win*, chapters 2, 4.

Steiner, *Scripts people live*, chapters 3, 4, 5.

Stewart, I., *Transactional analysis counselling in action.* London: Sage (3rd edn), 2007, chapter 3, pp.21-37.

2. Woollams, S., 'From 21 to 43'. *In:* Barnes (ed.), *Transactional analysis after Eric Berne*, chapter 16.

3. For sources on child development, refer to note (4) for Chapter 4. In her work on 'cycles of development', for which she won the Eric Berne Memorial Scientific Award, Pam Levin argues that script development does not come to an end with adolescence. Instead, the developmental stages are re-cycled throughout the individual's life.

Chapter 11: HOW THE SCRIPT IS LIVED OUT

1. On the classification of script content and the way script themes are lived out, see:

Berne, *What do you say...*, chapters 3, 11.

Steiner, *Scripts people live*, chapters 6-12.

2. Woollams, S., 'Cure!?' *TAJ, 10,* 2, 1980, 115-7.

3. Berne, *What do you say...*, chapters 14, 17. For other views on the physiological aspects of script, see also:

Cassius, J., *Body scripts.* Memphis: Cassius, 1975.

Cornell, W., 'Whose body is it? Somatic relations in script and script protocol'. *In:* Erskine (ed.), *Life scripts,* chapter 5, pp.101-25.

Lenhardt, V., 'Bioscripts'. *In:* Stern (ed.), *TA: the state of the art,* chapter 8.

Chapter 12: LIFE POSITIONS

1. On life positions, see:

Berne, *Principles of group treatment*, chapter 12.

Berne, *What do you say...*, chapter 5.

Berne, E., 'Classification of positions'. *Transactional Analysis Bulletin, 1,* 3, 1962, 23.

James and Jongeward, *Born to win*, chapter 2.

Steiner, *Scripts people live*, chapter 5.

2. Ernst, F., 'The OK corral: the grid for get-on-with'. *TAJ, 1,* 4, 1971, 231-40. In agreeing that we use his Corral diagram in this book, Franklin Ernst asked that we give it his revised subtitle 'Grid for What's Happening', as in Figure 12.1.

3. Ernst, F., 'The annual Eric Berne memorial scientific award acceptance speech'. *TAJ, 12,* 1, 1982, 5-8.

Chapter 13: SCRIPT MESSAGES AND THE SCRIPT MATRIX

1. For script messages and how they are communicated, see:

Berne, *What do you say...*, chapter 7.

English, F., 'What shall I do tomorrow? Reconceptualizing transactional analysis'. *In:* Barnes (ed.), *Transactional analysis after Eric Berne,* chapter 15.

Steiner, *Scripts people live*, chapter 6.

Tosi, M., 'The lived and narrated script: an ongoing narrative construction'. *In:* Erskine (ed.), *Life scripts,* chapter 2, pp.29-54.

White, J., and White, T., 'Cultural scripting'. *TAJ, 5,* 1, 1975, 12-23.

Woollams, S., 'From 21 to 43'. *In:* Barnes (ed.), *Transactional analysis after Eric Berne,* chapter 16.

2. Berne, *Transactional analysis in psychotherapy*, chapter 5.

3. Steiner, C., 'Script and counterscript'. *TAB, 5,* 18, 1966, 133-35. For other versions of the script matrix, see:

Berne, *What do you say...*, chapter 15.

English, F., 'Sleepy, spunky and spooky'. *TAJ, 2,* 2, 1972, 64-7.

English, F., reference quoted at note (1) for this Chapter.

Holloway, W., 'Transactional analysis: an integrative view'. *In:* Barnes (ed.), *Transactional analysis after Eric Berne,* chapter 11.

James (ed.), *Techniques in transactional analysis...*, chapter 4.

Woollams, S., reference quoted at note (1) for this Chapter.

Chapter 14: INJUNCTIONS AND DECISIONS

1. Goulding, R., and Goulding, M., 'New directions in transactional analysis'. In Sager and Kaplan (eds.), *Progress in group and family ther-*

apy. New York: Brunner/Mazel, 1972, 105-34. See also:

Goulding, R., and Goulding, M., 'Injunctions, decisions and redecisions'. *TAJ, 6,* 1, 1976, 41-8.

Goulding, R., and Goulding, M., *The power is in the patient.* San Francisco: TA Press, 1978. (Chapters 5 and 16 of this book are reprints of the two articles quoted above).

Gouldings, *Changing lives through redecision therapy*, chapters 2, 9.

Allen, J., and Allen, B., 'Scripts: the role of permission'. *TAJ, 2,* 2, 1972, 72-4.

2. English, F., 'Episcript and the "hot potato" game'. *TAB, 8,* 32, 1969, 77-82.

3. Berne, *What do you say...*, chapter 7.

4. For various versions of the formal script questionnaire, see:

Berne, *What do you say...*, chapter 23.

Holloway, W., *Clinical transactional analysis with use of the life script questionnaire*. Aptos: Holloway, undated.

James (ed.), *Techniques in transactional analysis...*, chapter 4.

McCormick, P., *Guide for use of a life-script questionnaire in transactional analysis*. San Francisco: Transactional Publications, 1971.

McCormick, P., 'Taking Occam's Razor to the life-script interview'. *Keynote speeches delivered at the EATA conference, July 1986.* Geneva: EATA, 1987, speech 5.

For a brief script questionnaire, more typical of those used in current practice, see: Stewart, I., *Developing transactional analysis counselling.* London: Sage, 1996, chapter 6, pp.48-58.

Chapter 15: PROCESS SCRIPTS AND DRIVERS

1. Berne, *Sex in human loving*, chapter 5.

Berne, *What do you say...*, chapter 11.

2. Kahler, *Transactional analysis revisited*, chapters 60-65.

Kahler, T., *The process therapy model,* Little Rock: Taibi Kahler Associates, 2008, pp.103-5, 147-50 and 181-3.

3. Kahler, *Transactional analysis revisited*, chapter 72.

Kahler, T., and Capers, H., 'The miniscript'. *TAJ, 4,* 1, 1974, 26-42. Note that the version given in *Transactional analysis revisited* is a revision of the 1974 *TAJ* article.

Kahler, *The process therapy model,* pp.82-102.

Joines, V., and Stewart, I., *Personality adaptations: a new guide to human understanding in psychotherapy and counselling.* Nottingham and Chapel Hill: Lifespace, 2002, chapter 8, pp.115-126.

4. Kahler, T., 'Drivers: the key to the process of scripts'. *TAJ, 5,* 3, 1975, 280-4.

Kahler, *Transactional analysis revisited*, chapters 60-65 and accompanying Summary.

5. Kahler, *The process therapy model,* reference quoted at note (3) for this Chapter.

Kahler and Capers, 'The miniscript', *op. cit.*

6. Kahler, T., workshop presentation, EATA conference, Villars, 1984, unpublished.

Kahler, *The process therapy model,* pp. 36-9.

Joines and Stewart, *Personality adaptations,* chapter 2, pp.27-33.

7. See for example Lewis, T., Amini, F. and Lannon, R., *A general theory of love.* New York: Vintage, 2000, pp. 387-43.

8. Kahler, *The process therapy model,* pp.101 and182-3.

Chapter 16: PERSONALITY ADAPTATIONS

1. Taibi Kahler, in *The process therapy model,* pp.19-30, gives a historical account of how he developed his model, including the concept of six personality types. In subsequent chapters of his book, he describes in detail his current (2008) thinking on this model and how one can best work with it in therapy.

Paul Ware's work in this field is described in: Ware, P., 'Personality adaptations'. *TAJ, 13,* 1, 1983, 11-19.

2. Joines, V., 'Using redecision therapy with different personality adaptations'. *TAJ, 16,* 3, 1986, 152-60.

Joines, V., 'Diagnosis and treatment planning using a transactional analysis framework'. *TAJ, 18,* 3, 1988, 185-90.

3. Kahler, *op. cit.,* pp.13-29, outlines the history of the research he has carried out in this area. A technical description of his research procedures and results is given in his Appendix D, pp.266-76.

Vann Joines describes his statistical research on personality adaptations in Appendix B of Joines and Stewart, *Personality adaptations,* pp.380-8.

4. Joines, *op. cit.* 1986, p.153; Joines and Stewart, *op. cit.,* pp.5-7.

5. Ware, *op. cit.*

6. Joines, *op. cit.* 1986, p.153.

7. These 'pen-portraits' are abridged from introductory descriptions of the six adaptations in Joines and Stewart, *op. cit.,* pp.13-18. Subsequent chapters expand on the detail of each adaptation. The book includes detailed transcripts of therapeutic work with each adaptation, including explanatory notes.

Chapter 17: DISCOUNTING

1. Schiff *et al., Cathexis reader,* chapter 2. See also:

Mellor, K., and Sigmund, E., 'Discounting'. *TAJ, 5,* 3, 1975, 295-302.

Schiff, A., and Schiff, J., 'Passivity'. *TAJ, 1,* 1, 1971, 71-8.

2. This definition of discounting was suggested by Shea Schiff at a workshop presentation (unpublished). We think it is more graphic than the definition given on page 14 of *Cathexis reader*: 'Discounting is an internal mechanism which involves people minimizing or ignoring some aspect of themselves, others or the reality situation.'

Claude Steiner, in *Scripts people live*, chapter 9, defines the term 'discount' in a different way, as: 'a crossed transaction in which the discountee emits a stimulus from his Adult ego-state to another person's Adult and that person responds from his Parent or Child.' This makes it seem initially as though Steiner is using the word in a much wider sense than the Schiffs. However, his examples indicate that he also has in mind a situation in which one person (the one responding from Parent or Child) 'minimizes or ignores' some aspect of the other person.

Chapter 18: THE DISCOUNT MATRIX

1. Schiff *et al.*, *Cathexis reader*, chapter 2. See also:
Mellor, K., and Sigmund, E., 'Discounting', *TAJ, 5,* 3, 1975, 295-302.
Stewart, *TA counselling in action,* chapter 9, pp.143-62.

Chapter 19: FRAME OF REFERENCE AND REDEFINING

1. Schiff et al., *Cathexis reader*, chapter 5. See also:
Mellor, K., and Sigmund, E., 'Redefining'. *TAJ, 5,* 3, 1975, 303-11.

2. This statement of the meaning of 'redefining' is an interpretation made by the present authors. We think it is clearer than the circular definition given in *Cathexis reader*.

Chapter 20: SYMBIOSIS

1. Schiff *et al.*, *Cathexis reader*, chapter 2. We have altered the Schiffs' definition by one word, substituting 'single person' for their 'whole person'. See also: Schiff, A., and Schiff, J., 'Passivity'. *TAJ, 1,* 1, 1971, 71-8.

The diagram showing symbiosis has evolved through various forms. In their 1971 *TAJ* article, the Schiffs depict it only by using dotted-line and solid boundaries for the ego-state circles. In *Cathexis reader*, they add arrows running between the active ego-states in the two parties. The version of the diagram commonly used in current literature, with an 'envelope' drawn round the active ego-states (as in Figure 20.1), makes its first published appearance in the article by Woollams and Huige, cited in note (2) below.

2. Woollams, S., and Huige, K., 'Normal dependency and symbiosis'.

TAJ, 7, 3, 1977, 217-20.
3. Schiff *et al., Cathexis reader,* chapter 4. See also:
  Schiff, S., 'Personality development and symbiosis'. *TAJ, 7,* 4, 1977, 310-6.

Chapter 21: RACKETS AND STAMPS

1. On the nature and functions of rackets, see:
  Berne, *Principles of group treatment,* chapter 13.
  Berne, *What do you say...,* chapter 8.
  English, F., references given at notes (2) and (4) below.
  Ernst, F., 'Psychological rackets in the OK corral'. *TAJ, 3,* 2, 1973, 19-23.
  Erskine, R., and Zalcman, M., 'The racket system: a model for racket analysis'. *TAJ, 9,* 1, 1979, 51-9.
  Gouldings, *Changing lives through redecision therapy,* chapters 2, 6.
  Joines, V., 'Similarities and differences in rackets and games'. *TAJ, 12,* 4, 1982, 280-3.
  Zalcman, M., 'Game analysis and racket analysis'. *Keynote speeches delivered at the EATA conference, July 1986.* Geneva: EATA, 1987, speech 4.
2. English, F., 'The substitution factor: rackets and real feelings'. *TAJ, 1,* 4, 1971, 225-30.
  English, F., 'Rackets and real feelings, Part II'. *TAJ, 2,* 1, 1972, 23-5.
3. Thomson, G., 'Fear, anger and sadness'. *TAJ, 13,* 1, 1983, 20-4.
4. English, F., 'Racketeering'. *TAJ, 6,* 1, 1976, 78-81.
  English, F., 'Differentiating victims in the Drama Triangle'. *TAJ, 6,* 4, 1976, 384-6.
5. Berne, E., 'Trading stamps'. *TAB, 3,* 10, 127.
  Berne, *What do you say...,* chapter 8.
  James and Jongeward, *Born to win,* chapter 8.

Chapter 22: THE RACKET SYSTEM

1. Erskine, R., and Zalcman, M., 'The racket system: a model for racket analysis'. *TAJ, 9,* 1, 1979, 51-9. See also:
  Stewart, *TA counselling in action,* chapter 6, pp.69-100.
2. The exercises in this chapter were devised originally by M. Zalcman (workshop presentations, unpublished). They are given here in modified versions developed by I. Stewart, A. Lee and K. Brown (workshop presentations, unpublished).

Chapter 23: *GAMES AND GAME ANALYSIS*

1. On the nature of games, see:

Berne, *Intuition and ego-states*, chapter 7.

Berne, *Transactional analysis in psychotherapy*, chapter 10.

Berne, *Games people play*, chapter 5.

Gouldings, *Changing lives through redecision therapy*, chapter 2.

James and Jongeward, *Born to win*, chapters 2, 8.

2. There is no consensus in TA literature on whether a game (in the singular) is to be defined as a sequence of moves engaged in by *one* person, or as a sequence of interlocking moves and counter-moves made by *two* (or more) people. Berne appeared to favour the latter definition by implication, but he was not consistent. In this book we follow the alternative account favoured by the Gouldings, and define a game (singular) as being a sequence played out by *one* person. Thus when two people engage in game-playing, each person is playing his or her own game, and the two games interlock.

This has implications also for the meaning of the Switch. Given that you and I are each playing our own game, you cannot 'pull a Switch on me'. That is to say: it is not possible for you to pull the Switch in *my* game. Instead, you can pull the Switch in *your* game, and expect me to respond to your move by pulling the Switch in my own game.

3. Berne, *Games people play*, chapter 5.

Steiner, *Scripts people live*, chapter 1.

4. Berne, *What do you say...*, chapter 2. The version of Formula G given in this reference is Berne's final revision. See also references in note (9) for this Chapter.

5. Karpman, S., 'Fairy tales and script drama analysis'. *TAB, 7,* 26, 1968, 39-43.

6. Berne, *Transactional analysis in psychotherapy*, chapter 10.

Berne, *Games people play*, chapter 5.

7. Gouldings, *Changing lives through redecision therapy*, chapter 2 and page 79 (for diagram).

8. James, J., 'The game plan'. *TAJ, 3,* 4, 1973, 14-7. The modified version given here was developed by L. Collinson (workshop presentation, unpublished).

9. Regarding the definition of games, see:

Joines, V., 'Similarities and differences in rackets and games'. *TAJ, 12,* 4, 1982, 280-3.

Zalcman, M., 'Game analysis and racket analysis'. *Keynote speeches delivered at the EATA conference, July 1986.* Geneva: EATA, 1987, speech 4.

Chapter 24: WHY PEOPLE PLAY GAMES

1. Berne, *Games people play*, chapter 5.
Berne, *What do you say...*, chapter 8.
James and Jongeward, *Born to win*, chapter 8.
Steiner, *Scripts people live*, chapter 1.
2. Schiff *et al.*, *Cathexis reader*, chapter 2.
3. English, F., 'Racketeering'. *TAJ, 6,* 1, 1976, 78-81.
4. Berne, *Games people play*, chapter 5.
5. James, J., 'Positive payoffs after games'. *TAJ, 6,* 3, 1976, 259-62.

Chapter 25: HOW TO DEAL WITH GAMES

1. Berne, *Games people play*, chapters 6-12 and Index of Games.
2. We do not know of any formally-named games which have a P – R or V – R Switch. As an alternative to classifying games on the basis of their Drama Triangle shifts, they may be classified in terms of the life position they reinforce.
3. Gouldings, *Changing lives through redecision therapy*, chapter 4.
4. James, J., 'Positive payoffs after games'. *TAJ, 6,* 3, 1976, 259-62.
5. Woollams, S., 'When fewer strokes are better'. *TAJ, 6,* 3, 1976, 270-1.

Chapter 26: CONTRACTS FOR CHANGE

1. On the nature and function of contracts, see:
Berne, *Principles of group treatment*, chapter 4 and Glossary.
Gouldings, *Changing lives through redecision therapy*, chapter 4.
James (ed.), *Techniques in transactional analysis...*, chapter 5.
James and Jongeward, *Born to win*, chapter 9.
Lee, A., 'Process contracts'. *In:* Sills, C. (ed.), *Contracts in counselling and psychotherapy.* London: Sage (2nd edn), 2006, chapter 6, pp.74-86.
Steiner, *Scripts people live*, Introduction and chapter 20.
Stewart, *Developing TA counselling,* chapters 9-12, pp.65-108.
Stewart, *TA counselling in action,* chapter 8, pp.119-41.
Stewart, I., 'Outcome-focused contracts'. *In:* Sills, C. (ed.), *op. cit.,* chapter 5, pp.63-73.
Widdowson, M., *Transactional analysis: 100 key points and techniques.* London and New York: Routledge, 2010, part 4, pp.181-203.

2. This 'Contract Checklist' was developed by Ian Stewart for use in workshop presentations (unpublished), but is based on published material cited in the three sources listed in note (1) above for the same author. See also:

James, M., *It's never too late to be happy*. Reading: Addison-Wesley, 1985, chapter 7.

Chapter 27: AIMS OF CHANGE IN TA

1. For views on autonomy, see:
Berne, *Games people play*, chapters 16, 17.
Berne, *Principles of group treatment*, chapter 13.
James and Jongeward, *Born to win*, chapter 10.
Steiner, *Scripts people live*, chapters 26, 27, 28.
2. Berne, *Transactional analysis in psychotherapy*, chapter 16, pp.211-12. See also:
James (ed.), *Techniques in transactional analysis...*, chapter 4.
3. Berne, *Transactional analysis in psychotherapy*, chapter 14.
Berne, *Principles of group treatment*, chapter 12.
Berne, *What do you say...*, chapter 18.
4. TAJ, 10, 2, 1980.
5. Nelson, Portia, 'Autobiography in five short chapters'. *In:* Black, Claudia, *Repeat after me*. Denver: M.A.C. Printing and Publications, 1985.

Chapter 28: TA THERAPYAND COUNSELLING
1. For the Training and Certification Council's description of the psychotherapy and counselling fields of application of TA, see:
http://ta-trainingandcertification.net/ta-what-is-ta-training.html#fields
2. James, M., 'Self-reparenting: theory and process'. *TAJ, 4,* 3, 1974, 32-9. See also:
James, M., *Breaking free: self-reparenting for a new life*. Reading: Addison-Wesley, 1981.
James, M., *It's never too late to be happy*. Reading: Addison-Wesley, 1985.
3. Regarding the three 'traditional schools' of TA, see:
Barnes, G., 'Introduction'. *In:* Barnes (ed.), *Transactional analysis after Eric Berne*, chapter 1.
See also the three papers which follow Barnes's in the same book. They are by leading figures in the classical, Cathexis and redecision schools respectively:
Dusay, J., 'The evolution of transactional analysis'. *In:* Barnes (ed.), *op. cit.*, chapter 2.
Schiff, J., 'One hundred children generate a lot of TA'. *In:* Barnes (ed.), *op. cit.*, chapter 3.
Goulding, R., 'No magic at Mt. Madonna: redecisions in marathon therapy'. *In:* Barnes (ed.), *op. cit.*, chapter 4.

Extended transcripts of redecision therapy, with explanatory notes, can be found in Joines and Stewart, *Personality adaptations,* chapters 19-25, pp.247-348.

4. Crossman, P., 'Permission and protection'. *TAB, 5,* 19, 1966, 152-4.

Steiner, *Scripts People Live,* Chapter 21, pp. 258-67.

5. For detail of the theory, principles and practice of the relational approach, see:

Hargaden, H., and Sills, C., *Transactional analysis – a relational perspective.* London: Routledge, 2002.

Cornell, W., and Hargaden, H. (eds), *From transactions to relations: the emergence of a relational tradition in transactional analysis.* Chadlington: Haddon Press, 2005.

Widdowson, *TA: 100 key points...,* chapters 16-17, pp. 57-62.

In fact Widdowson *(op. cit.,* chapters 2-17, pp.7-62), writing in 2010, recognizes no fewer than eight 'schools and approaches' in current TA. As well as the three 'traditional schools' and the relational approach, he lists radical psychiatry, integrative TA, cognitive-behavioural TA and psychodynamic TA. By contrast, relational writers (e.g. Cornell and Hargaden, *op. cit.)* often view integrative TA and psychodynamic TA, as well as another approach called co-creative TA, as being within the boundaries of the relational approach.

For further information on relational TA, see the web site of the recently-formed International Association of Relational Transactional Analysis (IARTA), at:

www.relationalta.com

Chapter 29: TA IN ORGANIZATIONS AND EDUCATION

1. For further information on developmental TA, see the web site of the recently-formed Institute of Developmental Transactional Analysis (IDTA), at:

www.instdta.com

2. For the Training and Certification Council's descriptions of the organizational and educational fields of application of TA, as quoted in this chapter, see:

http://ta-trainingandcertification.net/ta-what-is-ta-training.html#fields

3. On organizational applications of TA, see:

De Graaf, A., and Kunst, K., *Einstein and the art of sailing: a new perspective on the role of leadership.* Hertford: Sherwood Publishing, 2010.

Hay, J., *Working it out at work: understanding attitudes and building relationships.* Hertford: Sherwood Publishing (2nd edn), 2009.

Hay, J., *Donkey bridges for developmental TA: making transactional analysis accessible and memorable.* Hertford: Sherwood Publishing (2nd edn), 2012.

James, M., *The OK boss.* Reading: Addison-Wesley, 1976.

Jongeward, D., *Everybody wins: TA applied to organizations.* Reading: Addison-Wesley, 1973.

Jongeward, D., and Seyer, P., *Choosing success: transactional analysis on the job.* San Francisco: Wiley, 1978.

Mohr, G., and Steinert, T. (eds), G*rowth and change for organizations.* Bonn: Kulturpolitische Gesellschaft, 2006.

Mountain, A., and Davidson, C., *Working together: organizational transactional analysis and business performance.* Farnham and Burlington: Gower, 2011.

4. Hay, J., personal communication, 2011.

5. Taibi Kahler, originator of the Process Therapy Model (PTM), has also developed the Process Communication Model® (PCM®). The PCM is based on the same theory and research as the PTM, but is in a format that makes it more immediately applicable to non-clinical settings. Kahler has stated that the PCM, not the PTM, should be the model used in non-clinical application. Further information on the PCM, including information on training and certification, can be found at:

www.kahlercommunication.com (in the US), and at

www.processcom.com (in Europe).

6. Regarding educational applications, see:

Barrow, G., Bradshaw, E., and Newton, T. *Improving behaviour and raising self-esteem in the classroom.* Abingdon: David Fulton, 2001.

Ernst, K., *Games students play.* Millbrae: Celestial Arts, 1972.

Hay, J., *Transactional analysis for trainers.* Hertford: Sherwood Publishing (2nd edn), 2009.

James, M., and Jongeward, D., *The people book: transactional analysis for students.* Reading: Addison-Wesley, 1975.

Napper, R., and Newton, T., *Tactics: transactional analysis concepts for trainers, teachers and tutors.* Ipswich: TA Resources, 2000.

7. Newton, T., 'Letter from the guest editor'. *TAJ, 34,* 3, 2004, 194-6.

8. Illsley Clarke, J., and Dawson, C., *Growing up again.* Center City: Hazelden, 1998.

See also the citations listed for the Eric Berne Memorial Award presented to Jean Illsley Clarke in 1995 (Appendix C).

Chapter 30: HOW TA HAS DEVELOPED

1. This outline of Berne's life history has been based principally on:

Cheney, W., 'Eric Berne: biographical sketch'. *TAJ, 1,* 1, 1971, 14-22. Material was also drawn from:

Dusay, J., 'The evolution of transactional analysis'. *In:* Barnes (ed.),

Transactional analysis after Eric Berne, chapter 2.

Hostie, R., 'Eric Berne in search of ego-states'. *In:* Stern (ed.), *TA: the state of the art*, chapter 2.

James, M., 'Eric Berne, the development of TA, and the ITAA'. *In:* James (ed.), *Techniques in transactional analysis...*, chapter 2.

2. Cranmer, R., 'Eric Berne: annotated bibliography.' *TAJ, 1,* 1, 1971, 23-9.

3. Schiff, J., 'One hundred children generate a lot of TA'. *In:* Barnes (ed.), *Transactional analysis after Eric Berne*, chapter 3.

4. This sketch of the early development of ITAA has been traced from the articles by Cheney, Dusay and James, cited at note (1) above.

5. Allaway, J., 'Transactional analysis in Britain: the beginnings'. *Transactions, 1,* 1, 1983, 5-10.

6. Membership numbers for ITAA between 1971 and 1980 have been taken from a graph quoted by McNeel, J., 'Letter from the editor'. *TAJ, 11, 1,* 1981, 4. Numbers from the 1980s until the present have been provided by Ken Fogleman, personal communication, 2011.

7. As regards the restoration of Berne's time-based definitions of the ego-states, see:

Erskine, R., 'Ego structure, intrapsychic function, and defence mechanisms: a commentary on Eric Berne's original theoretical concepts'. *TAJ, 18,* 1, 1988, 15-19.

Hohmuth, A., and Gormly, A., 'Ego-state models and personality structure'. *TAJ, 12,* 2, 1982, 140-3.

Trautmann, R., and Erskine, R., 'Ego-state analysis: a comparative view'. *TAJ, 11,* 2, 1981, 178-85.

8. *The script*, May-June 1987, page 7.

9. The quotation is taken from the Minutes of the ITAA Board of Trustees meeting, Montreal, August 2010.

10. The membership figure for EATA is as reported on *www.eatanews.org*, November 2011.

11. The text of the authors' keynote speech in Montreal is published in: Stewart, I., and Joines, V., 'TA Tomorrow'. *TAJ, 41,* 3, 2011, 221-9.

BIBLIOGRAPHY

Allen, J., and Allen, B., 'Scripts: the role of permission'. *Transactional Analysis Journal, 2,* 2, 1972, 72-4.

Allaway, J., 'Transactional analysis in Britain: the beginnings'. *Transactions, 1,* 1, 1983, 5-10.

Babcock, D., and Keepers, T., *Raising kids okay: transactional analysis in human growth and development.* New York: Grove Press, 1976.

Barnes, G. (ed), *Transactional analysis after Eric Berne: teachings and practices of three TA schools.* New York: Harper's College Press, 1977.

Barnes, G., 'Introduction'. *In:* Barnes (ed.), *Transactional analysis after Eric Berne*, chapter 1.

Barrow, G., Bradshaw, E., and Newton, T. *Improving behaviour and raising self-esteem in the classroom.* Abingdon: David Fulton, 2001.

Berne, E., *A layman's guide to psychiatry and psychoanalysis.* New York: Simon and Schuster, 1957; third edition published 1968. *Other editions:* New York: Grove Press, 1957; *and* Harmondsworth: Penguin, 1971.

Berne, E., *Transactional analysis in psychotherapy.* New York: Grove Press, 1961, 1966.

Berne, E., 'Classification of positions'. *Transactional Analysis Bulletin, 1,* 3, 1962, 23.

Berne, E., *The structure and dynamics of organizations and groups.* Philadelphia: J.B. Lippincott Co., 1963. *Other editions:* New York: Grove Press, 1966; *and* New York: Ballantine, 1973.

Berne, E., 'Trading stamps'. *TAB, 3,* 10, 1964, 127.

Berne, E., *Games people play.* New York: Grove Press, 1964. *Other editions include:* Harmondsworth: Penguin, 1968.

Berne, E., *Principles of group treatment.* New York: Oxford University Press, 1966. *Other editions:* New York: Grove Press, 1966.

Berne, E., *Sex in human loving.* New York: Simon and Schuster, 1970. *Other editions:* Harmondsworth: Penguin, 1973.

Berne, E., *What do you say after you say hello?* New York: Grove Press, 1972. *Other editions:* London: Corgi, 1975.

Boyd, L., and Boyd, H., 'Caring and intimacy as a time structure'. *TAJ, 10,* 4, 1980, 281-3.

Capers, H., and Goodman, L., 'The survival process: clarification of the miniscript'. *TAJ, 13,* 1, 1983, 142-8.

Cassius, J., *Body scripts.* Memphis: Cassius, 1975.

Cheney, W., 'Eric Berne: biographical sketch'. *TAJ, 1,* 1, 1971, 14-22.

Cornell, W., 'Whose body is it? Somatic relations in script and script protocol'. *In:* Erskine (ed.), *Life scripts,* chapter 5, pp.101-25.

Cornell, W., and Hargaden, H. (eds), *From transactions to relations: the emergence of a relational tradition in transactional analysis.* Chadlington: Haddon Press, 2005.

Crossman, P., 'Permission and protection'. *TAB, 5,* 19, 1966, 152-4.

De Graaf, A., and Kunst, K., *Einstein and the art of sailing: a new perspective on the role of leadership.* Hertford: Sherwood Publishing, 2010.

Donaldson, M., *Children's minds.* London: Fontana, 1978.

Drego, P., *Towards the illumined child.* Bombay: Grail, 1979.

Drego, P., 'Ego-state models'. *TASI Darshan, 1,* 4, 1981.

Drye, R., 'Psychoanalysis and TA'. *In:* James (ed.), *Techniques in transactional analysis...,* chapter 11.

Drye, R., 'The best of both worlds: a psychoanalyst looks at TA'. *In:* Barnes (ed.), *Transactional analysis after Eric Berne,* chapter 20.

Dusay, J., 'Egograms and the constancy hypothesis'. *TAJ, 2,* 3, 1972, 37-42.

Dusay, J., *Egograms.* New York: Harper and Row, 1977. *Other editions:* New York: Bantam, 1980.

Dusay, J., 'The evolution of transactional analysis'. *In:* Barnes (ed.), *Transactional analysis after Eric Berne,* chapter 2.

English, F., 'Episcript and the "hot potato" game'. *TAB, 8,* 32, 1969, 77-82.

English, F., 'Strokes in the credit bank for David Kupfer'. *TAJ, 1,* 3, 1971, 27-9.

English, F., 'The substitution factor: rackets and real feelings'. *TAJ, 1,* 4, 1971, 225-30.

English, F., 'Rackets and real feelings, Part II'. *TAJ, 2,* 1, 1972, 23-5.

English, F., 'Sleepy, spunky and spooky'. *TAJ, 2,* 2, 1972, 64-7.

English, F., 'Racketeering'. *TAJ, 6,* 1, 1976, 78-81.

English, F., 'Differentiating victims in the Drama Triangle'. *TAJ, 6,* 4, 1976, 384-6.

English, F., 'What shall I do tomorrow? Reconceptualizing transactional analysis'. *In:* Barnes (ed.), *Transactional analysis after Eric Berne,* chapter 15.

Erikson, E., *Childhood and society.* New York: W.W. Norton, 1950.

Ernst, F., 'The OK corral: the grid for get-on-with'. *TAJ, 1,* 4, 1971, 231-40.

Ernst, F., 'Psychological rackets in the OK corral'. *TAJ, 3,* 2, 1973, 19-23.

Ernst, F., 'The annual Eric Berne memorial scientific award acceptance speech'. *TAJ, 12,* 1, 1982, 5-8.

Ernst, K., *Games students play.* Millbrae: Celestial Arts, 1972.

Erskine, R., 'A structural analysis of ego'. *Keynote speeches delivered at the EATA conference, July 1986.* Geneva: EATA, 1987, speech 2.

Erskine, R., 'Ego structure, intrapsychic function, and defense mechanisms: a commentary on Eric Berne's original theoretical concepts'. *TAJ, 18,* 1, 1988, 15-19.

Erskine, R. (ed.), *Life scripts: a transactional analysis of unconscious relational patterns.* London: Karnac, 2010.

Erskine, R., 'Life scripts: unconscious relational patterns and psychotherapeutic involvement'. *In:* Erskine, R. (ed.), *Life scripts,* chapter 1, pp.1-28.

Erskine, R., and Zalcman, M., 'The racket system: a model for racket analysis'. *TAJ, 9,* 1, 1979, 51-9.

Falkowski, W., Ben-Tovim, D., and Bland, J., 'Assessment of the ego-states'. *British Journal of Psychiatry, 137,* 1980, 572-3.

Gilmour, J., 'Psychophysiological evidence for the existence of ego-states'. *TAJ, 11,* 3, 1981, 207-12.

Goulding, M., and Goulding, R., *Changing lives through redecision therapy.* New York: Brunner/Mazel, 1979.

Goulding, R., 'No magic at Mt. Madonna: redecisions in marathon therapy'. *In:* Barnes (ed.), *Transactional analysis after Eric Berne,* chapter 4.

Goulding, R., and Goulding, M., 'New directions in transactional analysis'. *In* Sager and Kaplan (eds.), *Progress in group and family therapy.* New York: Brunner/Mazel, 1972, 105-34.

Goulding, R., and Goulding, M., 'Injunctions, decisions and redecisions'. *TAJ, 6,* 1, 1976, 41-8.

Goulding, R., and Goulding, M., *The power is in the patient.* San Francisco: TA Press, 1978.

Haimowitz, M., and Haimowitz, N., *Suffering is optional.* Evanston: Haimowoods Press, 1976.

Hargaden, H., and Sills, C., *Transactional analysis – a relational perspective.* London: Routledge, 2002.

Harris, T., *I'm OK, you're OK.* New York: Grove Press, 1967.

Hay, J., *Transactional analysis for trainers.* Hertford: Sherwood Publishing (2nd edn), 2009.

Hay, J., *Working it out at work: understanding attitudes and building relationships.* Hertford: Sherwood Publishing (2nd edn), 2009.

Hay, J., *Donkey bridges for developmental TA: making transactional analysis accessible and memorable.* Hertford: Sherwood Publishing (2nd edn), 2012.

Hohmuth, A., and Gormly, A., 'Ego-state models and personality structure'. *TAJ, 12,* 2, 1982, 140-3.

Holloway, W., 'Transactional analysis: an integrative view'. *In:* Barnes (ed.), *Transactional analysis after Eric Berne,* chapter 11.

Holloway, W., *Clinical transactional analysis with use of the life script questionnaire.* Aptos: Holloway, undated.

Hostie, R., 'Eric Berne in search of ego-states'. *In:* Stern (ed.), *TA: the state of the art,* chapter 2.

Illsley Clarke, J., and Dawson, C., *Growing up again.* Center City: Hazelden, 1998.

James, J., 'The game plan'. *TAJ, 3,* 4, 1973, 14-7.

James, J., 'Positive payoffs after games'. *TAJ, 6,* 3, 1976, 259-62.

James, M., 'Self-reparenting: theory and process'. *TAJ, 4,* 3, 1974, 32-9.

James, M., *The OK boss.* Reading: Addison-Wesley, 1976.

James, M. (ed.), *Techniques in transactional analysis for psychotherapists and counselors.* Reading: Addison-Wesley, 1977.

James, M., 'Eric Berne, the development of TA, and the ITAA'. *In:* James (ed.), *Techniques in transactional analysis...,* chapter 2.

James, M., *Breaking free: self-reparenting for a new life.* Reading: Addison-Wesley, 1981.

James, M., *It's never too late to be happy*. Reading: Addison-Wesley, 1985.

James, M., *Perspectives in transactional analysis*. San Francisco: TA Press, 1998.

James, M., and Jongeward, D., *Born to win: transactional analysis with gestalt experiments*. Reading: Addison-Wesley, 1971. *Other editions include:* New York: Signet, 1978.

James, M., and Jongeward, D., *The people book: transactional analysis for students*. Reading: Addison-Wesley, 1975.

Joines, V., 'Differentiating structural and functional'. *TAJ, 6,*, 4, 1976, 377-80.

Joines, V., 'Similarities and differences in rackets and games'. *TAJ, 12,* 4, 1982, 280-3.

Joines, V., 'Using redecision therapy with different personality adaptations'. *TAJ, 16,* 3, 1986, 152-60.

Joines, V., 'Diagnosis and treatment planning using a transactional analysis framework'. *TAJ, 18,* 3, 1988, 185-90.

Joines, V., *Joines personality adaptation questionnaire administration, scoring and interpretive kit (JPAQ)*. Chapel Hill, NC: Southeast Institute, 2002. (Or on-line at:)
   www.seinstitute.com/books_videos_.html

Joines, V., and Stewart, I., *Personality adaptations: a new guide to human understanding in psychotherapy and counselling*. Nottingham and Chapel Hill: Lifespace, 2002.

Jongeward, D., *Everybody wins: TA applied to organizations*. Reading: Addison-Wesley, 1973.

Jongeward, D., and Seyer, P., *Choosing success: transactional analysis on the job*. San Francisco: Wiley, 1978.

Kahler, T., 'Drivers: the key to the process of scripts'. *TAJ, 5,* 3, 1975, 280-4.

Kahler, T., *Transactional analysis revisited.* Little Rock: Human Development Publications, 1978.

Kahler, T., *The process therapy model.* Little Rock: Taibi Kahler Associates, 2008.

Karpman, S., 'Fairy tales and script drama analysis'. *TAB, 7,* 26, 1968, 39-43.

Karpman, S., 'Options'. *TAJ, 1,* 1, 1971, 79-87.

Lee, A., 'Process contracts'. *In:* Sills, C. (ed.), *Contracts in counselling and psychotherapy,* chapter 6, pp.74-86.

Lenhardt, V., 'Bioscripts'. *In:* Stern (ed.), *TA: the state of the art,* chapter 8.

Levin, P., *Becoming the way we are.* Berkeley: Levin, 1974.

Levin, P., 'The cycle of development'. *TAJ, 12,* 2, 1982, 129-39.

Levine, S., 'Stimulation in infancy'. *Scientific American, 202,* 5, 1960, 80-6.

Lewis, T., Amini, F. and Lannon, R., *A general theory of love.* New York: Vintage, 2000.

Mahler, M.S., *The psychological birth of the human infant.* New York: Basic Books, 1975.

Maier, H., *Three theories of child development.* New York: Harper and Row, 1969.

McCormick, P., *Guide for use of a life-script questionnaire in transactional analysis.* San Francisco: Transactional Publications, 1971.

McCormick, P. (ed.), *Intuition and ego states.* New York: Harper and Row, 1977.

McCormick, P., 'Taking Occam's Razor to the life-script interview'. *Keynote speeches delivered at the EATA conference, July 1986.* Geneva: EATA, 1987, speech 5.

McKenna, J., 'Stroking profile'. *TAJ, 4,* 4, 1974, 20-4.

Mellor, K., and Sigmund, E., 'Discounting'. *TAJ, 5,* 3, 1975, 295-302.

Mellor, K., and Sigmund, E., 'Redefining'. *TAJ, 5,* 3, 1975, 303-11.

Mohr, G., and Steinert, T. (eds), G*rowth and change for organizations.* Bonn: Kulturpolitische Gesellschaft, 2006.

Mountain, A., and Davidson, C., *Working together: organizational trans-actional analysis and business performance.* Farnham and Burlington: Gower, 2011.

Napper, R., and Newton, T., *Tactics: transactional analysis concepts for trainers, teachers and tutors.* Ipswich: TA Resources, 2000.

Newton, T., 'Letter from the guest editor'. *TAJ, 34,* 3, 2004, 194-6.

Nelson, Portia, 'Autobiography in five short chapters'. *In:* Black, Claudia, *Repeat after me.* Denver: M.A.C. Printing and Publications, 1985.

Schiff, A., and Schiff, J., 'Passivity'. *TAJ, 1,* 1, 1971, 71-8.

Schiff, J., 'One hundred children generate a lot of TA'. *In:* Barnes (ed.), *Transactional analysis after Eric Berne*, chapter 3.

Schiff, J., *et al., The Cathexis reader: transactional analysis treatment of psychosis.* New York: Harper and Row, 1975.

Schiff, S., 'Personality development and symbiosis'. *TAJ, 7,* 4, 1977, 310-6.

Sills, C. (ed.), *Contracts in counselling and psychotherapy.* London: Sage (2nd edn), 2006.

Sills, C., and Hargaden, H., *Ego states.* London: Worth, 2003.

Spitz, R., 'Hospitalism: genesis of psychiatric conditions in early child-hood'. *Psychoanalytic studies of the child, 1,* 1945, 53-74.

Steere, D., *Bodily expressions in psychotherapy.* New York: Brunner/Mazel, 1982.

Steiner, C., 'Script and counterscript'. *TAB, 5,* 18, 1966, 133-35.

Steiner, C., 'The stroke economy'. *TAJ, 1,* 3, 1971, 9-15.

Steiner, C., *Games alcoholics play.* New York: Grove Press, 1971.

Steiner, C., *Scripts people live: transactional analysis of life scripts.* New York: Grove Press, 1974.

Steiner, C., and Kerr, C. (eds), *Beyond games and scripts.* New York: Ballantine Books, 1976.

Stern, E. (ed.), *TA: the state of the art.* Dordrecht: Foris Publications, 1984.

Stewart, I., *Eric Berne.* London: Sage, 1992.

Stewart, I., *Developing transactional analysis counselling.* London: Sage, 1996.

Stewart, I., 'Ego states and the theory of theory: the strange case of the Little Professor'. *TAJ, 31, 2,* 2001, 133-47.

Stewart, I., 'Outcome-focused contracts'. *In:* Sills, C. (ed.), *Contracts in counselling and psychotherapy,* chapter 5, pp.63-73.

Stewart, I., *Transactional analysis counselling in action.* London: Sage, 3rd edition, 2007.

Stewart, I., and Joines, V., 'TA Tomorrow'. *TAJ, 41,* 3, 2011, 221-9.

Summerton, O., 'Advanced ego-state theory'. *TASI Darshan, 2, 4,* 1982.

Temple, S., 'Update on the functional fluency model in education'. *TAJ, 34,* 3, 2004, 197-204.

Thomson, G., 'Fear, anger and sadness'. *TAJ, 13,* 1, 1983, 20-4.

Tilney, T., *Dictionary of transactional analysis.* London: Whurr, 1998.

Tosi, M., 'The lived and narrated script: an ongoing narrative construction'. *In:* Erskine (ed.), *Life scripts,* chapter 2, pp.29-54.

Trautmann, R., and Erskine, R., 'Ego-state analysis: a comparative view'. *TAJ, 11, 2,* 1981, 178-85.

Tudor, K. (ed.), *Transactional approaches to brief therapy.* London: Sage, 2001.

Ware, P., 'Personality adaptations'. *TAJ, 13,* 1, 1983, 11-19.

White, J., and White, T., 'Cultural scripting'. *TAJ, 5,* 1, 1975, 12-23.

Widdowson, M., *Transactional analysis: 100 key points and techniques.* London and New York: Routledge, 2010.

Williams, J., *et al.,* 'Construct validity of transactional analysis ego-states'. *TAJ, 13,* 1, 1983, 43-9.

Woollams, S., 'When fewer strokes are better'. *TAJ, 6,* 3, 1976, 270-1.

Woollams, S., 'From 21 to 43'. *In:* Barnes (ed.), *Transactional analysis after Eric Berne,* chapter 16.

Woollams, S., 'Cure!?' *TAJ, 10,* 2, 1980, 115-7.

Woollams, S., and Huige, K., 'Normal dependency and symbiosis'. *TAJ, 7,* 3, 1977, 217-20.

Zalcman, M., 'Game analysis and racket analysis'. *Keynote speeches delivered at the EATA conference, July 1986.* Geneva: EATA, 1987, speech 4.

GLOSSARY

A_0: part of the very early ego-state structure within C_1, representing an instinctual problem-solving mechanism.

A_1: *same as* Adult in the Child.

A_2: *same as* Adult ego-state.

A_3: part of the second-order structure of the Parent, representing Adult content introjected from a parent or parent-figure.

ACTIVITY: mode of time-structuring in which those concerned have the objective of achieving an overtly agreed goal, as opposed to merely talking about it.

ADAPTED CHILD: a behavioural description of the Child in the functional model, indicating how the individual may conform to rules or parental or societal demands.

ADULT EGO-STATE: a set of behaviours, thoughts and feelings that are direct responses to the here-and-now, not copied from parents or parent-figures nor replayed from the individual's own childhood, and based on rational perception.

ADULT IN THE CHILD: part of the second-order structure of the Child, representing the young child's intuitive perception and problem-solving strategies.

AFTER SCRIPT: the process script that reflects the belief: 'If something good happens today, I'll have to pay for it tomorrow.'

AGITATION: the passive behaviour in which the person directs energy into repetitive, distracting activity instead of into problem-solving.

ALMOST SCRIPT: the process script that reflects the belief: 'I almost make it, but not quite.'

ALWAYS SCRIPT: the process script that reflects the belief: 'I must always stay with the same unsatisfactory situation.'

ANGULAR TRANSACTION: an ulterior transaction with a stimulus from one ego state in the first person directed to two different ego states in the second person.

ANTISCRIPT: part of the script that a person has turned around to its opposite, following the opposite instead of the original message.

AREA: (of discounting) whether discounting relates to self, others or the situation.

ATTRIBUTION: a script message that entails the parents telling the child what he is.

AUTHENTIC FEELING: the original, uncensored feeling which the individual in childhood learned to cover with a racket feeling.

AUTONOMY: that quality which is manifested by the release or recovery of three capacities: awareness, spontaneity and intimacy; any behaviour, thinking or feeling that is a response to here-and-now reality, rather than a response to script beliefs.

AWARENESS: the capacity to experience pure sensual impressions in the manner of a new-born infant, without interpretation.

BANAL SCRIPT: *same as* non-winning script.

BASIC POSITION: *same as* life position.

BEHAVIOURAL DIAGNOSIS: judgment of which ego-state an individual is in by observation of that individual's behaviour.

BLOCKING TRANSACTION: a transaction in which the purpose of raising an issue is avoided by disagreeing about the definition of the issue.

C_0: part of the very early ego-state structure within C_1, representing our instinctual drives and hungers.

C_1: *same as* Child in the Child.

C_2: *same as* Child ego-state.

C_3: part of the second-order structure of the Parent, representing Child content introjected from a parent or parent-figure.

CATHEXIS: (in energy theory) theoretical construct representing psychic energy, postulated by Berne to explain shifts between ego-states; (as proper name) name of institute founded by the Schiffs and of the 'school' of TA that uses their approach.

CHILD EGO-STATE: a set of behaviours, thoughts and feelings that are replayed from the individual's own childhood – i.e. an archaic ego-state representing who the person was as a child.

CHILD IN THE CHILD: part of the second-order structure of the Child, representing stored memories of experiences from earlier stages of the child's own development.

COMPLEMENTARY TRANSACTION: a transaction in which the transactional vectors are parallel and the ego-state addressed is the one that responds.

CON: a transactional stimulus that on the psychological level that conveys an invitation into game-playing.

CONDITIONAL STROKE: a stroke relating to what the individual does.

CONSTANCY HYPOTHESIS: (of egograms) the hypothesis that when one ego-state increases in intensity, another or others must decrease in order to compensate, the shift in psychic energy occurring so that the total amount of energy may remain constant.

CONSTANT: (of ego-states) *same as* excluding.

CONTACT DOOR: the first contact area in an individual's Ware Sequence, at which initial contact can most effectively be made.

CONTAMINATION: part of the content of the Child or Parent ego-states that the individual mistakes for Adult content.

CONTENT: (of ego-states) the stored memories and strategies that are classified as belonging in the different ego-states, or subdivisions of ego-states, in the structural model – i.e. *what* is placed in each ego-state; (of script) the set of early decisions, unique to the individual, which specify *what* there is in the individual's script.

CONTRACT: an explicit bilateral commitment to a well-defined course of action; an Adult commitment to oneself and/or someone else to make a change.

CONTROLLING PARENT: a behavioural description of the Parent in the functional model, indicating how the individual may control, direct or criticize.

COUNTERFEIT STROKE: a stroke that superficially appears positive, but which contains a negative 'sting'.

COUNTERINJUNCTIONS: script messages issued from Parent by the parent and stored in Parent by the child.

COUNTERSCRIPT: the set of decisions made by the child in compliance with the counterinjunctions.

CRITICAL PARENT: *same as* Controlling Parent.

CROSSED TRANSACTION: a transaction in which the transactional vectors are not parallel, or in which the ego-state addressed is not the one that responds.

CROSSUP: moment of confusion experienced by a game-player immediately after the Switch.

DECISION: conclusion regarding self, others or the quality of life, adopted during childhood as the best available means of surviving and getting needs met within the constraints of the child's ways of feeling and reality-testing.

DECISIONAL MODEL: philosophical stance which holds that people decide their own destiny, and that these decisions can be changed.

DELUSION: *(used by Berne to mean)* contamination of Adult by Child.

DISCOUNTING: minimizing or ignoring information relevant to the solution of a problem.

DISCOUNT MATRIX: a model that analyses discounting in terms of area, type and level.

DOING NOTHING: the passive behaviour in which the person directs energy into stopping himself or herself from acting, instead of problem-solving.

DRAMA TRIANGLE: diagram that illustrates how persons may adopt and move between any of three scripty roles (Persecutor, Rescuer, Victim).

DRIVER: one of five distinctive behavioural sequences, played out over a time-period between half-a-second and a few seconds, which are the functional manifestations of negative counterscripts.

DUPLEX TRANSACTION: an ulterior transaction involving four ego-states in which the stimuli on the social and psychological levels come from two different ego states in the first person and are directed to two different ego states in the second person.

EARLY DECISION: *same as* decision.

EGOGRAM: a bar-chart diagram showing an intuitive assessment of how much energy is being used in each of the functional ego-states in an individual's personality.

EGO-STATE: a consistent pattern of feeling and experience directly related to a corresponding consistent pattern of behaviour.

EGO-STATE MODEL: a model depicting personality in terms of Parent, Adult and Child ego-states.

ELECTRODE: Berne's label for the Parent in the Child.

EPISCRIPT: a negative script message that a parent passes to a child in the magical hope that by so doing the parent will be released from the impact of that message.

EXCLUDING: (of ego-states) the one ego-state remaining operational when the other two are excluded.

EXCLUSION: the individual blocking out one or more ego-states.

EXECUTIVE: (of ego-states) that ego-state which dictates behaviour, in terms of having control of the muscular apparatus.

EXISTENTIAL POSITION: *same as* life position.

FIRST-DEGREE: (of games or losing scripts) having a payoff that the person is ready to discuss in his or her social circle.

FIRST-ORDER MODEL: an ego-state model in which the three ego-states are not further subdivided.

FIRST RULE OF COMMUNICATION: 'so long as transactions remain complementary, communication can continue indefinitely'.

FORMULA G: Berne's formula for a game showing the six components (Con, Gimmick, Response, Switch, Crossup, Payoff).

FRAME OF REFERENCE: the structure of associated responses that integrates the various ego-states in response to specific stimuli; it provides the individual with an overall perceptual, conceptual, affective and action set, which is used to define the self, other people and the world.

FREE CHILD: a behavioural description of the Child in the functional model, indicating how the individual may express feelings or wants without censoring and without reference to rules or societal demands.

FUNCTION: (of ego-states) how ego-states are expressed in behaviour.

FUNCTIONAL MODEL: an ego-state model that divides the ego-states to show us *how* we express each ego-state in behaviour.

GALLOWS: a communication in which the individual smiles or laughs while making a statement about something painful.

GAME: *(Berne's final definition)* a series of transactions with a Con, a Gimmick, a Switch, and a Crossup, leading to a payoff.

GAME: *(Joines's definition)* the process of doing something with an ulterior motive that (1) is outside of Adult awareness, (2) does not become explicit until the participants switch the way they are behaving, and (3) results in everyone feeling confused, misunderstood, and wanting to blame the other person.

GAME PLAN: series of questions used in analysing the stages in an individual's game.

GIMMICK: a transactional response which on the psychological level conveys that the person has accepted an invitation into game-playing.

GRANDIOSITY: an exaggeration or minimization of some feature of reality.

HAMARTIC SCRIPT: *same as* third-degree losing script.

HISTORICAL DIAGNOSIS: judgment of which ego-state an individual is in by gathering factual information about the individual's parents, parent-figures and own childhood.

INCAPACITATION: the passive behaviour in which the person disables himself or herself in an attempt to force the environment to solve a problem.

INCONGRUITY: mis-match between the overt content of a communication and the behavioural signals shown by the individual who issues the communication.

INFANT: *same as* Somatic Child.

INJUNCTIONS: negative, restrictive script messages communicated from the Child in the parent and housed in the Child of the child.

INTEGRATED: (applied to a person) having an Adult ego-state that incorporates positive qualities of Child and of Parent.

INTERPERSONAL: experienced in terms of communication or relationships between people; shown 'on the outside'.

INTRAPSYCHIC: experienced 'on the inside', or 'in the mind' only.

INTROJECTION: the process by which the young child, during the process of script formation, uncritically copies the behaviour, thoughts and feelings of a parent or parent-figure. (The related verb is 'to introject', and the noun is 'an introject').

INTIMACY: mode of time-structuring in which people express authentic feelings and wants to each other without censoring.

LEVEL: (of discounting) whether discounting relates to existence, significance, change possibilities or personal abilities.

LIFE COURSE: what actually happens in the individual's life (in contrast to life-script, which represents what the person planned to do in early childhood).

LIFE POSITION: a person's basic beliefs about self and others, which are used to justify decisions and behaviour; a fundamental stance that a person takes up about the essential value he or she perceives in self and others.

LIFE-SCRIPT: an unconscious life-plan made in childhood, reinforced by the parents, 'justified' by subsequent events, and culminating in a chosen alternative.

LITTLE PROFESSOR: *same as* Adult in the Child.

LOSER: someone who does not accomplish a declared purpose.

LOSING SCRIPT: a script in which the payoff is painful or destructive, and/or entails failure to accomplish a declared purpose.

MAGICAL PARENT: *same as* Parent in the Child.

MARSHMALLOW-THROWING: giving out insincere positive strokes.

MARTIAN: interpretation of human behaviour and communication that entails observation without preconceptions.

MODE: (of discounting) *same as* level.

NATURAL CHILD: *same as* Free Child.

NEGATIVE STROKE: a stroke that the giver intends to be experienced as unpleasant by the receiver.

NEVER SCRIPT: the process script that reflects the belief: 'I can never get what I most want.'

NON-WINNER: a person who makes neither big wins nor big losses.

NON-WINNING SCRIPT: a script in which the payoff entails neither big wins nor big losses.

NURTURING PARENT: a behavioural description of the Parent in the functional model, indicating how the individual may engage in nurturing, caring or helping.

OGRE (PARENT): *(used by some writers to mean)* Parent in the Child.

OK CORRAL: diagram in which the four life positions are related to specific social operations.

OPEN-ENDED SCRIPT: the process script that reflects the belief: 'After a certain point in time, I won't know what to do.'

OPTIONS: technique of choosing ego-states in transacting so as to break free of familiar, unconstructive 'locked' interchanges with others.

OVERADAPTATION: the passive behaviour in which the person complies with what he or she believes are the wishes of others, without checking and without reference to his or her own wishes.

P_0: part of the very early ego-state structure within C_1, representing the infant's instinctual programs for getting needs met.

P_1: *same as* Parent in the Child.

P_2: *same as* Parent ego-state.

P_3: part of the second-order structure of the Parent, representing Parent content introjected from a parent or parent-figure.

PAC MODEL: *same as* ego-state model.

PARALLEL TRANSACTION: *same as* complementary transaction.

PARENT EGO-STATE: a set of behaviours, thoughts and feelings that have been introjected from parents or parent-figures (often referred to as a borrowed or copied ego-state).

PARENT IN THE CHILD: part of the second-order structure of the Child, representing the young child's fantasized and magical version of messages received from parents.

PASSIVE BEHAVIOUR: one of four modes of behaviour (doing nothing, overadaptation, agitation, incapacitation or violence) that indicate the presence of discounting and are used by the individual as an attempt to manipulate others or the environment into solving his or her problems.

PASSIVITY: how people don't do things, or don't do them effectively, so that someone else will become more uncomfortable with their behaviour than they are and will take over and solve the problem for them.

PASTIME: mode of time-structuring in which people talk about a subject but have no intention of taking action concerning it.

PAYOFF: (of games) the racket feeling experienced by the player at the close of the game; (of script) the closing scene towards which the script is directed.

PERMISSIONS: (in the script) positive, liberating script messages issued from the Child of the parent and stored in the Child of the child.

PERSECUTOR: (in Drama Triangle) person who puts others down or belittles others.

PERSONALITY ADAPTATION: One of six personality styles, identified in research studies, representing six ways in which a person may deal with the world based on what worked best in their family of origin.

PHENOMENOLOGICAL DIAGNOSIS: judgment of which ego-state an individual is in based on how that individual is experiencing the present moment .

PIG PARENT: *(used by some writers to mean)* Parent in the Child.

PLASTIC STROKE: an insincere positive stroke.

POSITIVE STROKE: a stroke that the giver intends to be experienced as pleasant by the receiver.

PREJUDICE: *(used by Berne to mean)* contamination of Adult by Parent.

PRIMARY DRIVER: the driver that an individual shows most frequently, usually also shown first in response to a transactional stimulus.

PROCESS: (of ego-states) the ways in which the individual expresses the ego-states over time – i.e. *how* the ego-states are expressed; (of script) the ways in which the individual lives out the script through time – i.e. *how* the script is lived out.

PROGRAM: the parent's demonstration of how to carry out an injunction or counterinjunction by modelling the behaviour.

PSYCHOLOGICAL-LEVEL MESSAGE: a covert message, usually conveyed by non-verbal clues.

RACKET: a set of scripty behaviours, intended outside awareness as a means of manipulating the environment, and entailing the person's experiencing a racket feeling.

RACKETEERING: mode of transacting in which the individual seeks strokes from others for his or her racket feelings.

RACKET FEELING: a familiar emotion, learned and encouraged in childhood, experienced in many different stress situations, and maladaptive as an adult means of problem-solving.

RACKET SYSTEM: a self-reinforcing, distorted system of feelings, thoughts and actions maintained by script-bound individuals.

REAL SELF: (of ego-states) that ego-state in which the individual experiences himself or herself to be.

REBELLIOUS CHILD: *(used by some writers to mean)* mode of expression of Adapted Child in which the individual rebels against rules instead of following them.

RECOGNITION-HUNGER: the need for recognition by others.

REDECISION: replacement of a self-limiting early decision by a new decision that takes account of the individual's full adult resources.

REDEFINING: distortion of an individual's perception of reality so that it fits his or her script.

REDEFINING TRANSACTION: a tangential or blocking transaction.

RESCUER: (in Drama Triangle) person who offers help to others from a one-up position, in the belief 'they are not adequate to help themselves'.

RESPONSE: (in an individual transaction) the communication that is a reply to the stimulus; (in a game) series of ulterior transactions that follow the Con and Gimmick and repeat their covert messages.

RITUAL: mode of time-structuring in which people exchange familiar pre-programmed strokes.

RUBBERBAND: a point of similarity between a here-and-now stress situation and a painful situation from the person's own childhood, usually not recalled in awareness, in response to which the person is likely to go into script.

SCRIPT: *same as* life-script.

SCRIPT MATRIX: diagram in which the transmission of script messages is analysed in terms of ego-states.

SCRIPT MESSAGE: a verbal or non-verbal message from the parents on the basis of which the child forms conclusions about self, others and the world during the process of script-making.

SCRIPT SIGNAL: a bodily clue which indicates that the individual has gone into script.

SCRIPTY: (of behaviours, feelings etc.) exhibited by the individual when in script.

SECOND-DEGREE: (of games or losing scripts) having a payoff serious enough to be an unacceptable topic for conversation in the individual's social circle.

SECOND-ORDER (STRUCTURAL) MODEL: a structural model in which the ego-states are themselves subdivided to show the ego-state structure of the individual's own Child and of the figures incorporated in the Parent.

SECOND-ORDER SYMBIOSIS: a symbiosis occurring between P_1 and A_1 of one party and C_1 of the other party.

SECOND RULE OF COMMUNICATION: 'when a transaction is crossed, a break in communication results and one or both individuals will need to shift ego-states in order for communication to be re-established'.

SOCIAL DIAGNOSIS: judgment of which ego-state an individual is in by observation of the ego-states used by others in transacting with that individual.

SOCIAL-LEVEL MESSAGE: an overt message, usually conveyed in verbal content.

SOMATIC CHILD: *same as* Child in the Child.

SPONTANEITY: ability to choose freely from a full range of options in feeling, thinking and behaving, including choice of ego-state.

STAMP: a racket feeling that the individual has stored away with the intention of cashing it in later for some negative payoff.

STIMULUS: the initial communication in an individual transaction (to which the response is a reply).

STIMULUS-HUNGER: the need for physical and mental stimulation.

STROKE: a unit of recognition.

STROKE BANK: collected memories of past strokes that the individual can re-use.

STROKE ECONOMY: set of restrictive Parental rules regarding stroking.

STROKE FILTER: an individual's pattern of rejecting and accepting strokes so as to conform with an existing self-image.

STROKE QUOTIENT: an individual's preferred mix of different types of strokes.

STROKING PROFILE: a bar-chart diagram to analyse an individual's preference for giving, taking, asking for and refusing to give strokes.

STRUCTURAL ANALYSIS: analysis of personality in terms of the ego-state model.

STRUCTURAL MODEL: an ego-state model showing *what* is classified as belonging in each ego-state or subdivision of an ego-state (i.e. showing content).

STRUCTURAL PATHOLOGY: contamination and/or exclusion.

STRUCTURE: (in the ego-state model) classification of an individual's behaviour, feeling and experience in terms of ego-states.

SWEATSHIRT: a motto, signalled non-verbally by a person, which acts as a covert invitation into games or racketeering.

SWITCH: point in a game at which the player changes roles in order to collect his or her payoff.

SYMBIOSIS: a relationship in which two or more individuals behave as though between them they form a single person, hence not using their full complement of ego-states.

TANGENTIAL TRANSACTION: a transaction in which the stimulus and the response address different issues, or address the same issue from different perspectives.

TARGET DOOR: the second contact area in an individual's Ware Sequence, at which the bulk of the 'work' is done during counselling, therapy or any other process of effective communication.

THIRD-DEGREE: (of games or losing scripts) having a payoff that entails death, serious injury, illness, or incarceration.

THIRD RULE OF COMMUNICATION: 'the behavioural outcome of an ulterior transaction is determined at the psychological and not at the social level'.

TIME STRUCTURING: how people spend time when in pairs or groups.

TRADING STAMP: *same as* stamp.

TRANSACTION: a transactional stimulus plus a transactional response: the basic unit of social discourse.

TRANSACTIONAL ANALYSIS: *(ITAA definition)* a theory of personality and a systematic psychotherapy for personal growth and personal change.

TRANSACTIONAL ANALYSIS: *(Berne's definition)* (1) a system of psychotherapy based on the analysis of transactions and chains of transactions which occur during treatment sessions; (2) a theory of personality based on the study of specific ego-states; (3) a theory of social action based on the rigorous analysis of transactions into an exhaustive and finite number of classes based on the specific ego-states involved; (4) the analysis of single transactions by means of transactional diagrams (this is transactional analysis proper).

TRAP DOOR: the third contact area in an individual's Ware Sequence, where the most profound change or development takes place but at which the individual may become 'trapped' if the area is approached too soon

during a therapeutic or other relationship.
TYPE: (of discounting) whether discounting relates to stimuli, problems or options.

ULTERIOR TRANSACTION: a transaction in which an overt message and a covert message are conveyed at the same time.
UNCONDITIONAL STROKE: a stroke relating to what the individual is.
UNTIL SCRIPT: the process script that reflects the belief: 'I can't relax, enjoy myself, and have fun until I get all my work done.'

VECTOR: arrow on a transactional diagram connecting the ego-state from which a communication is issued to the ego-state to which it is addressed.
VICTIM: (in Drama Triangle) person who views himself or herself as one-down, deserving to be mistreated or unable to get by without help.
VIOLENCE: the passive behaviour in which the person directs destructive energy outwards in an attempt to force the environment to solve the problem for him.

WARE SEQUENCE: the sequence of three contact areas – thinking, feeling and behaviour – that facilitates maximum rapport during communication. The order of the three areas in the sequence varies among the different personality adaptations.
WINNER: someone who accomplishes a declared purpose.
WINNING SCRIPT: a script in which the payoff is happy or fulfilling, and/or entails success in accomplishing a declared purpose.
WITCH (PARENT): *(used by some writers to mean)* Parent in the Child.
WITHDRAWAL: mode of time-structuring in which the individual does not transact with others.

INDEX

Page numbers in italic type indicate a main entry for the item in question

Options 74
options 74–6, 293, 294, 298, 308, 315, 332
  and games 273–4
organizations, use of TA in 3, 51, 290, 303–6

P₁ see Magical Parent
P₂ see Parent ego-state
P₃ see Parent ego-state, structure of
PAC model see ego-state model
parallel transaction see transactions, complementary
Parent ego-state 4, 11–20, 36, 49–51, 66,
  133–5, 157, 164–9, 196, 207–8, 213–21,
  234–5, 264, 266, 274, 300, 305–8
  structure of 36, 37–8
  see also Controlling Parent; Nurturing
  Parent
passive behaviours 193–6, 218, 300, 309
passivity 173, 191, 290, 306, 308–9, 331
pastimes 92, 94–5, 268, 306
payoff
  of games 254, 255, 259–61, 264, 268–9,
    272, 274–5
  of script 104, 112–13, 117, 135, 145,
    236–7, 263
Perls, Frederick (Fritz) 299, 315
permissions 133, 135–7, 138, 298, 299
Persecutor 255–7, 264, 266, 271, 273, 274,
  283
personality adaptations 152, 171–88, 306
  and diagnostic categories 172
  and driver behaviours 175–6
  personality traits 173–4
  and process scripts 176–7
  and script content 181–2
  surviving v. performing adaptations 175
  and Ware Sequence 178–81
phenomenological diagnosis 45, 51–2, 304
Pig Parent 39
Playful-Resister (Passive-Aggressive) 172,
  173, 175, 177, 179, 185, 188
Poor Me 272–3
potency 298, 299
Power is in the Patient, The 316
prejudice 57
Principles of Group Treatment 104, 260–1,
  290, 314
problem-solving 232–3, 290, 293–302
process scripts see script, process of
program 134, 135–6
protection 295, 298, 304, 332
psychic energy 31, 54
  see also cathexis
psychosis 3, 60, 144

psychotherapy 3, 177, 293–302, 311
  and counselling 293–4

racket feelings 6, 166–7, 227–35, 241, 252,
  259–61, 263, 267, 275
  definition of 227–8, 332
Racket System 239–49, 264, 302, 316, 332
racketeering 234–5, 261, 267–8, 283, 289,
  298, 308
rackets 5–6, 152, 167–8, 225–38
  definition of 227–8
  magic of 229–30
  and personality adaptations 188
  and script 228–9
Rackety Displays 239, 242, 243–4, 245, 246,
  275
Rapo 188, 271–2
reactive environment 300, 309
real Self 52–5
reality-testing 17, 18, 37, 60, 62, 105, 106–7,
  129, 130
Rebellious Child see Adapted Child
recognition-hunger 77, 89
redecision 299, 302, 332
redecision school 297, 299, 326
redefining 5, 206–11, 273–4, 290, 300, 332
  definition of 208
  transactions 209–11
Reinforcing Memories 239, 244–6, 247–9,
  264, 275
relational approach 301–2
reparenting 300
Rescuer 255–7, 267, 272–3, 283
Response 254–5
Responsible-Workaholic (Obsessive-
  Compulsive) 172, 173, 175, 179, 182–3,
  188
risk 92–9
rituals 92, 93–4
rubberbands 115–16, 138–40, 229, 242

San Francisco Social Psychiatry Seminars
  312–13
San Francisco Transactional Analysis Seminar
  313
Schiff, Aaron 315, 331
Schiff, Jacqui Lee 313, 315, 327, 331
Schiff, Shea 301
Schiffian theory 191, 196, 206–8, 212, 216,
  264, 300, 306, 308
Schlegel, Leonard 333
Schmid, Bernd 334
script 3, 5, 41, 103–10, 111–20, 129, 130,
  143, 145–8, 157, 160–3, 191–2, 203, 208,

Ordering information

Lifespace books may be ordered from your bookseller, or directly from Lifespace Publishing at either the UK or US addresses given below. To check current prices, please contact us at our UK or US addresses, or visit: *www.lifespacebooks.com.*

Ordering from UK

Send to: Lifespace Publishing, New Barn, Wycomb, Melton Mowbray, Leics LE14 4QG,England.
Tel./fax 01509 674455; email *uksales@lifespacebooks.com.*

 Please send cheque with your order, payable to "Lifespace Publishing". (Please note, we do not accept card payments for UK orders).

Ordering from US

Send to: Lifespace Publishing, 659 Edwards Ridge, Chapel Hill, NC 27517, USA.
Tel. (919) 929 1171; fax (919) 929 1174;
email *ussales@lifespacebooks.com.*

Please send payment with your order, or charge to Visa/MasterCard. If sending check, please make payable to "Lifespace Publishing". If charging to Visa/MasterCard, please give card number, expiration date and signature; or telephone orders on Visa/MasterCard to the numbers above.

Alternatively you may order direct online: go to
www.seinstitute.com
and follow the link to "Books and Videos".

Trade enquiries

For information on trade terms, please contact our UK office, contact details above.

• Work personally with IAN STEWART...

at The Berne Institute, Kegworth, England.
THE BERNE INSTITUTE aims to promote excellence in the fields of psychotherapy, counselling, training, supervision, and related research. Transactional analysis (TA) is our core model; neuro-linguistic programming (NLP) and other humanistic approaches also play a part in our work. Our Co-Directors, **Ian Stewart PhD** and **Adrienne Lee BA,** and their supporting faculty of Associates, are all UKCP Registered Psychotherapists and EATA-accredited trainers. We offer courses in TA counselling at Foundation and Diploma levels, and a training programme in TA psychotherapy recognised by the United Kingdom Council for Psychotherapy (UKCP) and validated by the University of Middlesex for the degree of MSc. Our other activities include two Advanced Training Groups in TA training and supervision, weekend and midweek workshops, and free monthly seminar sessions. For further details, please contact: The Course Registrar, The Berne Institute, Berne House, 29 Derby Road, Kegworth DE74 2EN, England. Telephone and fax: (0)1509-673649; email via web site, *www.theberne.com.*

• Work personally with VANN JOINES...

at The Southeast Institute, Chapel Hill, North Carolina, USA.
THE SOUTHEAST INSTITUTE FOR GROUP AND FAMILY THERAPY is a non-profit, postgraduate educational institute offering training and supervision in individual, couple, family and group psychotherapy. The primary theoretical approach we teach is an integration of Transactional Analysis and Gestalt Therapy called Redecision Therapy, originally developed by Robert Goulding MD and Mary Goulding MSW. We also offer training in Advanced Integrative Therapy (AIT). We integrate a number of other approaches into our work as well: systems theory, object relations theory, attachment theory, developmental theory, relational theory, body-centered approaches and energy psychology. We offer weekend and week-long workshops, on-going training programs, a postgraduate residential training program, and direct clinical services. We have a faculty of residential and visiting clinicians led by **Vann S. Joines PhD,** and train participants both from the USA and around the world. For more information contact: The Southeast Institute for Group and Family Therapy, 659 Edwards Ridge Road, Chapel Hill, NC 27517, USA. Telephone: (919) 929-1171; fax: (919) 929-1174; email *vjoines@earthlink.net;* web site *www.seinstitute.com.*

By the same authors…

Personality Adaptations
A New Guide to Human Understanding in Psychotherapy and Counselling

Vann Joines and Ian Stewart

This book is a practical guide to understanding personality. It presents a research-based model of six *personality adaptations*. Psychotherapists and counsellors, whether practising or in training, will find this model an invaluable aid to effectiveness in inviting personal change.

The book describes the six adaptations in detail, and provides a framework for understanding how each adaptation develops. It goes on to show how you can assess someone's personality adaptation(s) rapidly and accurately. With this knowledge, you can tap into a vast store of information that will apply to that person. For example, you will gain insight into their preferred area of personal contact (thinking, feeling or behaviour), and learn how you can use these contact areas to maintain rapport and achieve optimal results in therapy or counselling. You will learn the typical "life patterns" that the person is likely to play out over time, and the principal issues that are likely to arise for them in the process of change. The model also shows how you can work most effectively with each personality type to help them achieve personal change that is quick, easy and lasting.

To convey the true "sound" and "feel" of working with this model, the book includes annotated transcripts of actual therapeutic work with each of the personality adaptations.

The model's usefulness is not confined to any one therapeutic or counselling approach. Whatever modality you use, you can apply this model and benefit from this book.

- If you would like to know more about *Personality Adaptations,* you can read the Contents list and Preface on our web site at: *www.lifespacebooks.com*

Lifespace Publishing, Melton Mowbray and Chapel Hill
ISBN 1-870244-01-X   Paperback   Pp. 417